Leo Strauss and His Catholic Readers

Leo Strauss
and His Catholic Readers

EDITED BY GEOFFREY M. VAUGHAN

THE CATHOLIC UNIVERSITY OF AMERICA PRESS
Washington, D.C.

To Jennifer

Copyright © 2020
The Catholic University of America Press
All rights reserved
The paper used in this publication meets the minimum requirements of
American National Standards for Information Science—Permanence of Paper
for Printed Library Materials, ANSI z39.48-1984.
∞

Cataloging-in-Publication data
available from the Library of Congress

ISBN 978-0-8132-3309-3

published with a grant
Figure Foundation
with bedrock intention

CONTENTS

Acknowledgments ix

Introduction 1

Part 1: Encounters with Leo Strauss and Natural Right

1. Reason, Faith, and Law: Catholic Encounters with Leo Strauss
   Robert P. Kraynak 19

2. "Wine with Plato and Hemlock with Socrates": Charles McCoy's Dialogue with Leo Strauss and the Character of Thomistic Political Philosophy
   V. Bradley Lewis 47

3. Wisdom and Folly: Reconsidering Leo Strauss on the Natural Law
   Geoffrey M. Vaughan 77

4. Modernity, Creation, and Catholicism: Leo Strauss and Benedict XVI
   Marc D. Guerra 94

5. Leo Strauss's Critique of Modern Political Philosophy and Ernest Fortin's Critique of Modern "Catholic Social Teaching" Douglas Kries 116

Part 2: Leo Strauss and Catholic Concerns

6. The Mutual Concerns of Leo Strauss and His Catholic Contemporaries: D'Entrèves, McCoy, Simon Gladden J. Pappin 137

7. On the Catholic Audience of Leo Strauss John P. Hittinger 167

8. The Possible Harmony of Reason and Revelation in Politics and Philosophy: A Catholic Reading of Leo Strauss's "Progress or Return?" Carson Holloway   190

9. What Might a Catholic Reader Learn from Strauss about Catholicism? On the Supposed Distinction of Natural Right and Natural Law Gary D. Glenn   217

10. The Influence of Historicism on Catholic Theology J. Brian Benestad   233

Part 3: Leo Strauss on Christianity, Politics, and Philosophy

11. The City and the Whole: Remarks on the Limits and the Seriousness of the Political in Strauss's Thought   Giulio De Ligio   253

12. Aristotelian Metaphysics and Modern Science: Leo Strauss on What Nature Is   James R. Stoner Jr.   277

13. Strauss and Pascal: Is Discussion Possible?   Philippe Bénéton   290

14. Leo Strauss's Profound and Fragile Critique of Christianity Ralph C. Hancock   299

Bibliography   323

Contributors   337

Index   339

ACKNOWLEDGMENTS

In June 2015, a conference was held at Assumption College on the topic of "Leo Strauss and His Catholic Readers." The location was appropriate for being the one-time home of the late Father Ernest Fortin, likely the most famous Catholic priest to be associated with the legacy of Leo Strauss. He was my teacher and known to almost all of the participants. The idea for the conference must be attributed to Marc LePain. However, nothing could have happened without the assistance of my colleague Daniel J. Mahoney, who acted as co-convener and co-host. The two of us remain grateful for the generous assistance of the Fr. Fortin Foundation, the Earhart Foundation, and Assumption College for support that made it possible. I also thank the discussants whose comments were a welcome part of the weekend but the influence of which will be felt unheralded in the pages that follow. These include James W. Ceaser, Daniel P. Maher, and Daniel J. Mahoney.

Unfortunately, what cannot be reproduced in such a volume were the comments from three students of Leo Strauss: Walter Nicgorski, Gary D. Glenn, and my father, Fredrick Vaughan. Whether they first encountered Strauss in his published work, as my father did, or in the classroom, as did the other two, they all agreed that the experience made them better Catholics. While this might surprise many, I would suggest that the essays herein will prove their point.

Chapter 4 has appeared as "Modernity, Creation, and Catholicism: Leo Strauss and Benedict XVI," *Heythrop Journal* (2015). Chapter 10 draws on a review of Charles Curran's work published in *Fellowship of Catholic Scholars Quarterly*, vol. 37 (2014) and of Elizabeth Johnson's *Quest for the Living God* in the same quarterly, vol. 34 (2011).

Leo Strauss and His Catholic Readers

Introduction

GEOFFREY M. VAUGHAN

How should Catholics think about politics? If we wish to go beyond the gloomy pessimism of St. Augustine that law is an unfortunate necessity of our fallen world, there are philosophical resources to do so, including Augustine himself and other saints such as Thomas Aquinas and Cardinal Bellarmine, to name just a few.[1] But this list points to a peculiarity and difficulty for the Catholic—and especially the Catholic—investigation of politics, namely, that these are philosophical resources. By contrast, our Orthodox co-religionists have the historical example of Constantine of whom Eusebius said, "he is the only one to whose elevation no mortal may boast of having contributed."[2] The first Christian emperor holds no such place in the Catholic tradition, as Augustine's paltry notice of him in *The City of God* attests. Even the other great monotheistic faiths have historical examples upon which to call, such as the Davidic Kingdom for Jews and the age of the Rightly-Guided Caliphs for Muslims. The European Middle Ages cannot, for all their glories, offer a politically compelling historical example for Catholics in the twenty-first century.

Rather than history, the Catholic interested in politics must turn to the philosophical tradition, or, in the words of Benedict XVI, "to nature

---

1. On law as necessity, see *The City of God*, XIX.6.
2. Eusebius, *The Life of the Blessed Emperor Constantine* in *Nicene and Post-Nicene Fathers*, Second Series, vol. I, ed. P. Schaff and H. Wace (Grand Rapids, Mich.: Eerdmans, 1955), I.24 (489).

and reason as the true sources of law."³ Even there we have few great figures to call upon from the modern era. The leading authors of modern political thought and the movers of modern politics have been Protestants, atheists, or somewhere in between. Almost to an individual they were hostile to the church. Meanwhile, Catholics from Bellarmine in the seventeenth century to Jacques Maritain in the early twentieth sought to preserve or revive the Thomistic natural law theory developed in the thirteenth. A more recent effort, variously described as the "new natural law theory" or "new classical natural law," was begun by Germain Grisez and found its most political expression in John Finnis's *Natural Law and Natural Rights*.⁴ However, much of the response among Catholics to the project has revolved around the question of whether it is faithful to the work of Thomas Aquinas or no more than a Catholic gloss on modern natural rights.⁵ Whatever the case may be in that regard, it is clear that much of Catholic political thought revolves around the question of following a modern author such as Locke, Kant, or Hegel, or reviving medieval thought. As Leo Strauss asked: progress or return?

Strauss's project was the recovery of classical political philosophy or, more precisely, Platonic political philosophy. The abandonment of classical natural right and its replacement with modern rights as developed by Thomas Hobbes and John Locke led eventually to the historicism of Marx and Hegel, the historicism that has placed almost all modern men and women in a "pit beneath the cave."⁶ Where it was hard enough for the people in Plato's allegory to escape, it is even harder for us. For Strauss, then, a return to classical political philosophy is the first step in recovering a starting point from whence we can begin to see the political world aright. Similarly, Benedict XVI in his "Regensburg Address" lamented the "dehellenization" of Europe that has proceeded in three waves, beginning with the Reformation in the sixteenth century.⁷ He reassured his audience, however, that his "critique of modern reason from with-

---

3. Pope Benedict XVI, "Address to the Bundestag," in his *A Reason Open to God*, ed. J. Steven Brown (Washington, D.C.: The Catholic University of America Press, 2013), 219.
4. John Finnis, *Natural Law and Natural Rights* (Oxford: Clarendon Press, 1980).
5. See, for instance, Russell Hittinger, *A Critique of the New Natural Law Theory* (South Bend, Ind.: University of Notre Dame Press, 1987); Michael Pakaluk, "Is the New Natural Law Thomistic?," *The National Catholic Bioethics Quarterly* 13, no. 1 (2013): 57–67.
6. Leo Strauss, "How to Study Spinoza's *Theologico-Political Treatise*," in *Persecution and the Art of Writing* (Chicago: University of Chicago Press, 1988), 155.
7. Pope Benedict XVI, "Regensburg Address," in *Liberating Logos: Pope Benedict XVI's September Speeches*, ed. Marc Guerra (South Bend, Ind.: St. Augustine's Press, 2014), 32.

in has nothing to do with putting the clock back to the time before the Enlightenment and rejecting the insights of the modern age."[8] For this philosopher-pope, we must have both progress *and* return.

The affinities on the surface of things might in themselves suggest the appropriateness of a study of Strauss and Catholics. Those affinities, however, go to the heart of things. There are two interrelated reasons. First, there is something that James Ceaser has described as "faith-based Straussianism." Indeed, this particular variety of philosophical experience is significant enough to be classified by Michael and Catherine Zuckert as one of the four main responses to Strauss's ambiguous proposition on the theologico-political problem, the problem he identified as the central concern of all his studies.[9] Of the faith-based Straussian community, if there really is one, the preponderant number would be Catholic. This is hard to measure, but informal queries indicate that most would agree. It is certainly the case that students of Leo Strauss can be found at Catholic institutions, from Assumption College to Notre Dame, St. Michael's College at the University of Toronto to the University of Dallas.

The second reason to have a book on Catholic readers of Leo Strauss is that Strauss wrote almost nothing on Catholic authors. Christianity in general, but Catholicism in particular as the most philosophical tradition in Christianity, presented him with a problem. The orthopraxy of Judaism and Islam as religions of law provided him with straightforward foils to the idea of philosophy as a way of life. By contrast, as Strauss noted in his introduction to *Persecution and the Art of Writing*, "in Christianity philosophy became an integral part of the officially recognized and even required training of the student of the sacred doctrine."[10] Orthodoxy, not orthopraxy; theology, not law. This contrast presented Strauss with a problem but his readers, especially his Catholic readers, with an opportunity.

Strauss did not accept the Enlightenment position that the confrontation between reason and revelation can simply be recast as that between reason and unreason. The philosopher cannot disprove the possibility of revelation because any divine act will, by definition, not follow the laws of nature. It would be unreasonable to expect otherwise. Strauss's open-

---

8. Ibid., 36.
9. Michael Zuckert and Catherine Zuckert, *Leo Strauss and the Problem of Political Philosophy* (Chicago: University of Chicago Press, 2014), 314.
10. Strauss, *Persecution and the Art of Writing*, 19.

ness to the possibility of revelation or at least his suspension of judgment is certainly welcoming to the Catholic who would engage with the same subjects as Strauss. It may be this that explains the reciprocal welcoming of Strauss by so many Catholic scholars. But he also presents a significant challenge.

One of Strauss's most consistent positions was his rejection of historicism, the idea that the attempt to replace opinions with knowledge is absurd. Knowledge, to be what it claims to be, would not be different in different periods and would, at least potentially, be accessible at any and every moment in history. Crucially for Strauss, historicism renders political philosophy, and indeed all philosophy, impossible because it asserts that every claim to knowledge is absurd on its face.[11] Historicized knowledge is not absolute. It is conditioned, contextualized, and is the product of irrational forces. "In other words, even the greatest minds cannot liberate themselves from the specific opinions which rule their particular society."[12] This is so in the strong historicism of Hegel and Marx and the weaker versions of Rousseau and modern social science, "as far as it is not Roman Catholic social science."[13] There remained in the Catholic approach to natural right, according to Strauss, an understanding that was not historicist. He could find allies among Catholic scholars or, if not allies, at least fellow travelers. And yet, as the chapters in this volume explain, the Catholic agreement with Strauss can go only so far. Yes, human nature is permanent. Yes, natural right is fixed and not subject to change through history. But history has been entered and altered, according to the Catholic. The incarnation changed the world in ways Plato and Aristotle could not have known. For instance, the Apostle Paul's idea that nature is perfected by grace, not perfect on its own, would be anathema to Aristotle. Strauss's formulation, "graced by nature's grace," does little to resolve the tension.[14]

Strauss is known for describing Western civilization as the product of a dynamic tension between, in a formulation attributed to Tertullian, Athens and Jerusalem.[15] One might suggest that the Catholic would have

---

11. See Strauss, *Natural Right and History* (Chicago: University of Chicago Press, 1965), 30.
12. Leo Strauss, "On a Forgotten Kind of Writing," in *What Is Political Philosophy?* (Chicago: University of Chicago Press, 1988), 227.
13. Strauss, *Natural Right and History*, 2.
14. Leo Strauss, "What Is Political Philosophy?," in *What Is Political Philosophy?*, 41.
15. Leo Strauss, "Progress or Return?," in *The Rebirth of Classical Political Rationalism*, ed. Thomas Pangle (Chicago: University of Chicago Press, 1989), 270. See also Kenneth Hart Green, *Leo*

to add Bethlehem, the place of the incarnation.[16] Father Schall has suggested adding Rome to the mix, the political and religious legacy of which must rival both Athens and Jerusalem.[17] Other points of agreement are, or at least were, much more solid. One might say that Strauss revived a Catholic interpretation of Machiavelli, an interpretation that led Pope Paul IV to put his writings on the Index in 1557. And yet there remain significant differences, many of which are addressed in the chapters of this volume.

Perhaps the most challenging of Strauss's ideas for a Catholic, but not only a Catholic, is his understanding of the philosopher. According to Strauss, the philosopher is the highest of all human types, the only person engaged in what is best for a human to do. "From this point of view the man who is merely just or moral without being a philosopher appears as a mutilated human being."[18] This is a hard thing to reconcile with the fact that Jesus took as his apostles not the wise and learned, but ordinary, perhaps illiterate, fishermen. Moreover, according to St. Paul, Christian doctrine is "unto the Gentiles foolishness" (1 Cor 1:23).[19] Even though the Catholic church is the most philosophically inclined of all Christian communities, it cannot accept that anyone short of the philosopher is a "mutilated human being." Not only were few saints philosophers, the one who was, Thomas Aquinas, is said to have stopped writing upon receiving a vision and declaring all his work "as straw."[20]

Strauss's idea of the philosopher draws the sharpest distinction between himself and his Catholic reader, and yet even that is muddied. According to Strauss, the Platonic philosopher is marked by a longing for knowledge of the whole, something that is most likely unachievable. "In spite of its highness or nobility," he writes, "it could appear Sisyphean or

---

Strauss and the Recovery of Maimonides (Chicago: University of Chicago Press, 2012); David Janssens, *Between Athens and Jerusalem: Philosophy, Prophecy, and Politics in Leo Strauss's Early Thought* (Albany: State University of New York Press, 2008); Steven B. Smith, "Leo Strauss: Between Athens and Jerusalem," *Review of Politics* 53, no. 1 (1991): 75–99; Jeffrey A. Bernstein, *Leo Strauss on the Borders of Judaism, Philosophy, and History* (Albany: State University of New York Press, 2015).

16. James R. Stoner, Jr., has stated (personal communication) that John G. A. Pocock once asked him if the tension for Catholics is not Athens and Bethlehem rather than Athens and Jerusalem. It is to Pocock, therefore, that I attribute this insight.

17. James V. Schall, "A Latitude for Statesmanship? Strauss on St. Thomas," *Review of Politics* 53, no. 1 (1991): 126–47. Pope Benedict XVI would agree; see his "Regensburg Address," 31.

18. Strauss, *Natural Right and History*, 151.

19. This is not unique to the Christian scriptures. See Is 44:25.

20. Strauss was clear that St. Thomas had adopted a very different idea of philosophy and the source of human happiness. See Strauss, *What Is Political Philosophy?*, 285.

ugly, when one contrasts its achievement with its goal. Yet it is accompanied, sustained and elevated by *eros*."[21] *Eros* is central to Strauss's understanding of the philosopher and the activity of philosophy. St. Augustine would recognize the dynamic of the restless heart, even if he would dispute the object of longing. While both the philosopher and the Christian are longing, the Christian is longing for *another*, a person, three persons in one, to be precise. The philosopher's relationship with the object of his longing is of the kind one has with an impersonal object whereas the Christian experience is intensely personal, with the ground of all personhood, modeled upon the relationship among the persons of the Trinity. *Eros* is a longing the Catholic can appreciate but it is not the theological virtue of charity. Charity is a love among persons. Philosophical *eros* involves only the lover. *Eros*, in other words, is not reciprocated. Or, as Father Ernest Fortin put it, "The problem with the philosopher is that he is too proud to acknowledge that his salvation could come from anyone but himself."[22]

The chapters in this volume address many of the issues just mentioned, and highlight both the agreements and disagreements a Catholic might have with Strauss. But the focus of the volume is not to list or even explore a precise number of such points. Rather, the intent is to continue Strauss's engagement with his Catholic contemporaries, reflect upon his insights into issues that are also central to Catholic doctrine or philosophy, and assess what a Catholic might learn from Strauss on any number of topics.

Encounters with Leo Strauss and Natural Right

The first section of the volume encounters Strauss's recovery of classic natural right from a Catholic perspective. As already noted, he began *Natural Right and History* with the observation that Catholic social science alone held out against the modern approach. He suggested that there was some sort of natural affinity. For instance, Robert Kraynak argues that Strauss's enduring contribution to any reader, not only the Catholic, is

---

21. Ibid., 40.
22. Ernest L. Fortin, "Augustine and the Hermeneutics of Love," in his *The Birth of Philosophic Christianity: Studies in Early Christian and Medieval Thought*, ed. J. Brian Benestad (Lanham, Md.: Rowman and Littlefield, 1996), 7.

the opportunity to liberate oneself from historicism. The advantages are twofold, namely, to revive Platonic political philosophy as a real possibility and to reestablish biblical faith as the central alternative to philosophy as a way of life. In Strauss's revival, the lives of both Socrates and Moses—each day conversing with others about virtue (*Apology* 38a) or speaking face to face with the Lord "as a man is wont to speak to his friend" (Ex 33:11)—become the highest possibilities of human life. Strauss chose the life of Socrates, but not without appreciating the alternative.

The question of the reality of that alternative is explored in V. Bradley Lewis's study of Charles McCoy's reflections on Strauss. According to McCoy, the incarnation does not negate philosophy or reason because theology requires the techniques and discipline of philosophy. But philosophy as a way of life in the way Strauss understood it cannot withstand the Gospel message. McCoy traced the problem with Strauss's position back not to the Gospels themselves, however, but to the distinction between Plato's notion of nature as a standard and Aristotle's notion of nature as an authority. It is, at root, a philosophical issue, not a theological one, even though it must become the latter. As Lewis explains McCoy's argument, Strauss had to insist upon the Platonic position that nature is a standard and only a standard because to consider it as an authority would transform philosophy into theology. An authority commands whereas a standard measures. McCoy agreed, of course, but thought Strauss took the wrong stand.

My own contribution to this volume takes the opposite position, namely, that Catholic social teaching as expressed in the natural law would do well to learn from Strauss. Strauss was an appreciative and subtle critic of the natural law in its Thomist and Neo-Thomist versions, but more the latter than the former. According to Strauss, the natural law is an attempt to institutionalize philosophical wisdom in a foolish world, most egregiously by developing laws that would bind irrespective of the regime or form of government. Thomas, and Augustine before him, were far more accommodating of the folly of humanity than Strauss's contemporaries like Jacques Maritain, permitting practices that modern natural lawyers would never allow. This is even more the case with the new natural law as it has developed in the wake of John Finnis's *Natural Law and Natural Rights*. The problem is that natural lawyers ignore the question of the best regime, which was for Strauss the central political question.

More than that, for the natural law considerations of regime are secondary at best, subordinated to laws that ought to be promulgated in any regime. Strauss's recovery of classic natural right forces the Catholic reader to consider, or reconsider, the accommodations that are necessary in any political society this side of the best regime or, thinking eschatologically, this side of Parousia.

Marc D. Guerra compares Strauss's understanding of modernity and creation with that of Pope Benedict XVI, finding remarkable similarities and instructive differences. Guerra's is an effort in what he describes as "thinking the two accounts together." He suggests that Strauss relied much more on cosmology than is often admitted. (James R. Stoner, Jr., explores this at much greater length in a later chapter.) What Guerra does pursue is the distinctively Catholic understanding of creation that Benedict outlines, an account Strauss fails to appreciate fully. Strauss's formulations, he argues, apply to only general notions of revelation, formulations that have more in common with Duns Scotus and voluntarism, where the will is more important than the intellect, than they do with either the official position of the church or with that developed by, perhaps, the greatest intellect to hold the chair of Peter. Nevertheless, Guerra argues that Strauss's keen attention to modernity is a necessary corrective to the church's "accidental" encounter with it.

Douglas Kries addresses the church's encounter with modernity through a study of Ernest Fortin's critique of Catholic social teaching. As Kries notes in his chapter, it was not until the publication of *Rerum Novarum* in 1891 that the church started thinking about modern politics in a systematic way. And yet, as Fortin argued, in doing so it adopted the Lockean, rather than the Thomistic, understanding of property rights. Even with John Paul II's gentle corrective of *Centesimus Annus*, things do not improve. According to Fortin, John Paul II adopted nonteleological personalism, a favorable inclination to modern democracy, and an approval of free markets. Fortin did not object to these positions in themselves so much as to the elision between medieval and modern. What Fortin took from Strauss was a strong appreciation of the break with premodern political philosophy that Machiavelli inaugurated and Hobbes, Locke, and the rest continued. The lesson from Strauss is that the transition from natural law to natural rights is not as straightforward, or uncomplicated, as many Catholics have assumed.

Leo Strauss and Catholic Concerns

The second section of this volume turns to more general concerns that a Catholic reader might share with Leo Strauss or, perhaps, come to share with him. To this end, Gladden J. Pappin looks at three of Strauss's contemporaries, Passerin d'Entrèves, Charles McCoy, and Yves Simon. D'Entrèves and McCoy competed for the position at the University of Chicago that Strauss eventually held for many years and where he was a colleague of Simon. Pappin finds many similar concerns among these thinkers and, as already mentioned, a general agreement regarding the structure of the history of philosophy. They agree with Strauss on the way modernity changed the relationship between philosophy and society. With its modern turn philosophy sought to serve society, not merely protect itself. However, where Strauss was concerned that this change endangered the Platonic political philosophy he sought to revive, his Catholic contemporaries were more concerned with the effects of modern politics on ordinary citizens. How can citizens be obliged to act temperately in the face of unprecedented abundance, or prudently in regards to modern science? These are good questions, questions for all serious citizens and members of the modern world. They are questions that arise from the same perspective as Strauss's but ones that will be prompted only by a charitable interest in others.

According to John Hittinger, one of the advantages Catholics derive from the work of Leo Strauss is the opportunity to see afresh what had become a stale tradition of political philosophy. What Strauss identified as the crisis of our time, the loss of purpose in the West, is fundamentally a crisis of political philosophy, a topic Catholics had largely abandoned since the time of Suarez and Bellarmine. As the earlier flourishing of scholasticism decayed, the church and the wider Catholic community were left unable to address, and in some cases unable to identify, the challenges of positivism and historicism. Hittinger's chapter on the lectures Strauss delivered to the Catholic community of the University of Detroit in 1963 considers both their philosophical and political implications. What was Strauss trying to do in addressing these people in this way? According to Hittinger, he was providing the intellectual resources to respond to a surging tide that would soon wash away at the purpose and deepest convictions of the church.

Carson Holloway's study of Strauss's "Progress and Return" explores the ways in which agreement with Strauss on the crisis of modernity need not lead to a similar conclusion as to the remedy. The Catholic can agree that modern progress, for all the material advantages it has brought us, is ultimately unsatisfying. The modern idea of progress, a perpetual and restless promise of improvement after improvement ending only in death, inverts the promises of Christ. But where would we return? Strauss wanted to revive classical and specifically Platonic political philosophy. It is not so simple for the Catholic. According to Holloway, the Catholic Middle Ages provide the only premodern example of a Christian society because Protestant societies are modern. But the Middle Ages, for all their premodern integrity, are not a standard for either Strauss or the Catholic. According to Strauss, they are the result of an incoherent synthesis of Athens and Jerusalem. For the Catholic, on the other hand, there is no ideal past, no classical age to stand as the apotheosis of history and the highest life humans can achieve. Neither the early church persecuted by the Romans, nor St. Augustine's under siege by the Vandals, nor the fragmented disorder of St. Thomas's thirteenth century hold an appeal beyond nostalgic romanticism. Holloway identifies this as an anthropological advantage of the Catholic perspective and develops it into a challenge to Strauss.

The title of Gary Glenn's chapter gets the question exactly right: "What might a Catholic reader learn from Strauss about Catholicism?" As with other chapters in this volume, Glenn begins with an analysis of Strauss's distinction between natural right and natural law but shifts his attention to why the tradition presented natural law as it has. Glenn argues that accounts of the natural law have always had in mind an audience of ordinary citizens, not philosophers. This is not to say that reading these treatises in the thirteenth, seventeenth, or twenty-first centuries was going to be a popular pursuit. Rather, according to Glenn, the "goal of the natural law teaching is to teach the universally true moral precepts in such a way as to benefit rather than harm the reader." Glenn suggests that there is something exoteric about the natural law, features that make it more palatable and less likely to lead to scandal than a fully exposed study of natural right. He is certainly not suggesting that the natural law is a "noble lie." Instead, and to use Strauss's own words to describe Thomistic natural law, it is a "noble simplicity."[23]

23. Strauss, *Natural Right and History*, 163.

J. Brian Benestad applies Strauss's critique of historicism to the work of two major Catholic theologians, with the intention of showing both how influential historicism is in Catholic theology and how helpful reading Strauss can be for a Catholic. With that in mind, it is instructive to compare his contention that the magisterium said nothing about historicism until John Paul II's publication of *Fides et Ratio* in 1998 to Douglas Kries's observation, noted above, that it did not address modernity until *Rerum Novarum*. Perhaps only a philosopher-pope could write statements that, if unattributed, would seem to come from Leo Strauss. Nevertheless, Benestad's contribution to this volume is a very clear demonstration of the utility of reading Strauss.

Leo Strauss on Christianity, Politics, and Philosophy

Giulio De Ligio opens the final section of this volume with his chapter on "The City and the Whole: Remarks on the Limits and the Seriousness of the Political in Strauss's Thought." His contribution marks a turning point from those contributions that address the specific issue of natural right or concerns that are unique to Catholics, to topics of a broader interest, but ones still rooted in questions of interest to a Catholic readership. Doing so, De Ligio looks to Strauss's warning about both a synthesis and a separation of the two great elements of the human world, namely, philosophy and politics. In his lapidary formulation, "the affirmation of the permanence of the walls of the city—of the political—is accompanied by the rediscovery of the heavens of thought." As De Ligio understands it, this contribution from Strauss is vital for the Catholic intellectual tradition that has not spent a great deal of time on political thought, as well as a tradition of political thought that has neglected larger philosophical questions. The paradox, if it is a paradox, is that to act well one must know the whole, yet to know the whole one must understand the particular. It is Strauss's insight that politics, specifically the difference in regime, is the locus of mediation between the particular and the whole. De Ligio finds in Strauss's account, as well, an instructive mediation between the vocations of politics and philosophy.

James R. Stoner Jr. continues the exploration into questions of the whole that are both on the surface of Strauss's work, and implied. As he writes, "Contrary to appearances, Socrates's turn to the study of human things was based, not upon disregard for the divine or natural things, but upon a new approach to an understanding of all things."[24] In an admittedly provocative argument, Stoner claims that Strauss accepted the tenets of classical metaphysics. There are four parts to his argument. First, Strauss's description of philosophy is not compatible with the modern understanding of the self or the world nor, secondly, is his description of political philosophy compatible with anti-metaphysical modernity. The third part of his argument claims that Strauss's interpretation of the great texts of political philosophy would require him to accept most if not all of the metaphysical claims that they rest upon. As Stoner observes, Strauss regularly drew his reader's attention to the modern breaks with the classical tradition in terms of metaphysics, not only politics. Finally, Stoner suggests that Strauss was circumspect about his interest in classical metaphysics because his critics at the time were more concerned with his revival of classical *philosophy* than any interest in classical politics. But, as Stoner concludes, his case for classical political philosophy and classic natural right both depend on an understanding of the whole that is distinctively, itself, classical.

Philippe Bénéton, in his contribution, draws our attention to the curious contrast between Leo Strauss and Blaise Pascal. On the subject of faith and reason, a subject treated in many chapters in this volume, Bénéton quotes a line of Pascal's that captures, in an important way, Strauss's position: "Two extremes: to exclude reason, to admit only reason."[25] This was not Strauss's rule as it was Pascal's. Instead, it is the starkest way of expressing his contrast between faith, on the one hand, and reason, on the other. Comparing Strauss and Pascal leads Bénéton to several insights. For instance, he argues that Pascal's Christianity opened for him a manner of reading the Bible, a manner going back to the very Gospel writers that was unavailable to Strauss. The Christian position has always been that the Jewish prophets foresaw Jesus Christ in the specifics of his incarnation. But to do so Christians cannot read the Bible, certainly not the Hebrew Bible, literally or only literally. It must also be read, according to the *Catechism of the Catholic Church*, spiritually, that is

---

24. Ibid., 122. Consider also: "All human thought, even all thought human or divine, which is meant to be understood by human beings willy nilly begins with this whole, the permanently given whole which we all know and which men always know." Leo Strauss, "On the Interpretation of Genesis," *L'Homme* 21, no. 1 (1981): 8.

25. Blaise Pascal, *Pensées de Pascal* (Paris: Librairie Garnier frères, 1925), §253.

to say allegorically, morally, and anagogically.[26] As Bénéton writes, "it is Pascal who, following Christian tradition, said that the Bible has a double meaning or that God spoke in an esoteric manner." Only on such a reading can the various Messianic prophecies make sense of the events recorded by the Evangelists. But this also means that there is something un-Straussian about Strauss's reading of religion in general, perhaps, but certainly of Christianity.

The final chapter in the volume is written by Ralph C. Hancock, who presented the second of the two keynote addresses at the conference that inspired this work. As the only non-Catholic contributor, he takes on the large task of assessing Strauss's understanding of Christianity as a whole in the chapter entitled, "Leo Strauss's Profound and Fragile Critique of Christianity." Strauss's main interest in Christianity is its role in the development of modernity. Hancock, therefore, begins his chapter with a brief study of two recent attempts to do the same, namely, those of Larry Siedentop and Alain Badiou. Both of these authors celebrate modernity and are grateful to Christianity for bringing about our understanding of the individual, even if they do not accept the tenets of the faith. This contrast with Strauss, celebrating progress rather than looking to return, allows Hancock to develop his thesis that "the Christian promise of the individual's salvation beyond the *polis* and beyond the law necessarily contains the germ of modern irrational rationalism." It is irrational, he explains, because modernity rests upon an unexamined faith that the purpose of knowledge, its very end, is the mastery of nature. Although Hancock does not point to the comparison, Strauss might himself have written the words, "Man's conquest of nature turns out, in the moment of its consummation, to be nature's conquest of man."[27]

Thinking about Politics

Strauss's legacy is not what one might have predicted at his death in 1973. Within academic circles his work is generally appreciated far more than it was, or at least it is taken seriously enough to be engaged with honestly. Few today would dismiss his arguments as airily as Miles Burnyeat did

---

26. *Catechism of the Catholic Church*, §§115–19. "Anagogical" means to have a spiritual meaning.
27. C. S. Lewis, *The Abolition of Man* (New York: Harper Collins, 2000), 68.

in an essay entitled "Sphynx without a Secret."[28] There is now a sizeable body of books and articles on Strauss, not all of them written by his students or their students. Indeed, some of the more prominent scholars of Strauss never met the man. And yet in the popular mind, insofar as there is any awareness of Strauss, there is a lingering suspicion of his influence on American foreign policy, raised most prominently in the controversy over the Iraq War in 2003.[29] There has also been something of a reversal in his reception among Catholics, who welcomed or appreciated his work during his lifetime but have become more wary of it as time has passed. Uncovering reasons for these shifts in the academic, popular, and Catholic perceptions of Strass would be a project in itself, a project of the sociology of the academy and of public intellectuals as much as a study of Strauss.

Most significant for the question of Strauss's legacy has been the influence he had upon his students. The twentieth century saw many influential academics and many new schools of thought. Deconstruction is attributed to Jacques Derrida, but does not carry his name. John Dunn, Peter Laslett, J. G. A. Pocock, and Quentin Skinner founded what is known as the "Cambridge School" of intellectual history and there is a "Chicago School" of economics. We do find "Lonerganians," "Oakeshottians," and "Voegelinians," but the terms are not fixed in the imagination. As such, the question of whether the authors in this volume are "Straussian" cannot be avoided as it might be when writing on other topics. Unfortunately, the term is used more as a denunciation than as a neutral descriptor of one who follows a particular method or takes a perspective associated with Strauss. Also, being so personal—that is, as a term developed from the man's name rather than an institution, for instance—the term "Straussian" tends to carry with it an accusation of slavish devotion. This is unfair to both Strauss and his students, but is of a piece with his peculiar legacy in this country. Of all the contributors to this volume only one, Gary Glenn, was a student of Strauss's at the University of Chicago. The rest might have studied with Strauss's students or the students of

---

28. M. F. Burnyeat, "Sphynx without a Secret," *New York Review of Books*, May 30, 1985. However, Cambridge University Press considers him significant enough to devote one of the "companion" volumes to Strauss: Steven B. Smith (ed.), *The Cambridge Companion to Leo Strauss* (New York: Cambridge University Press, 2009).

29. For a response to these perceptions by defenders of Strauss, see especially Catherine H. Zuckert and Michael P. Zuckert, *The Truth about Leo Strauss: Political Philosophy and American Democracy* (Chicago: University of Chicago Press, 2006).

Strauss's students. Others have only ever encountered Strauss through his published works. The contributors are some more and some less appreciative of Strauss's arguments, but all have found his work instructive. Therefore, the work here is not that of "Catholic Straussians," if there could be such a thing, but of his Catholic readers.

As the chapters in this volume show, there is much for a Catholic reader to learn from Leo Strauss. Many of his insights are of great assistance to someone trying to understand modernity and its relation to the history of philosophy. Others challenge and remind the Catholic reader of a less than distinguished record on the part of Catholic politics in its theoretical and practical dimensions. A study of Catholic statesmanship of the last two centuries, for instance, would not be an inspiring read. Why? Reading Strauss can alert us to the fact that political philosophy has been superseded within official Catholic channels by *social* teaching. As modernity abandoned the church, the church turned its back on politics. At the same time that we might learn from Strauss, there are many positions in his work that cannot be acceptable to someone whose conscience is in communion with the church. Strauss wanted, for instance, to recover as axiomatic the classical distinction between the wise and the unwise, a separation of the few and the many based on their philosophical insight. This is not a tolerable moral position in Christian reflection, even if it may be a real distinction that can be recognized by those with "eyes to see."[30] However, as Pierre Manent has written in regards to this very contrast, "one might say that the Greeks have eyes, that they have only eyes; the voice of conscience is something one listens to—when one listens."[31] We must have not only eyes to see, but ears to hear.

---

30. See Plato's *Critias* 121b as translated by Eric Voegelin in his *Plato* (Columbia: University of Missouri Press, 2000), 207: "To those who had eyes to see, they appeared ugly for they were losing the most precious of their gifts."

31. Pierre Manent, *Seeing Things Politically: Interviews with Bénédicte Delorme-Montini*, trans. Ralph C. Hancock (South Bend, Ind.: St. Augustine's Press, 2015), 169.

PART 1

Encounters with Leo Strauss and Natural Right

Reason, Faith, and Law

Catholic Encounters with Leo Strauss

ROBERT P. KRAYNAK

The subject of this essay—Catholic encounters with Leo Strauss—may strike the reader as odd, as most Catholics have never heard of the German Jewish scholar Leo Strauss (1899–1973) and most followers of Leo Strauss are not Catholics. Yet there are numerous scholars in the academy today who have spent much of their mature intellectual life thinking about such encounters and sharing their thoughts with others. I am one of them—so much so that I recently described myself to a new colleague by saying: "I am a Catholic, a Straussian, and an American patriot."[1] As it is not always easy to combine these different perspectives, I will try to make sense of my choices by discussing in this essay the intersection of three powerful intellectual currents: Catholic theology, a "Straussian" approach to philosophy, and the principles of American liberal democracy.

The broad thesis that I wish to argue is that Strauss's writings have a complex relation to the Catholic intellectual and political tradition, some aspects of which are positive, some negative, and some so perplexing I may never understand them. Overall, however, Strauss offers a path to

---

1. See also James R. Stoner, "The Catholic Moment in the Political Philosophy of Leo Strauss," July 29, 2014, and reply by David Walsh, August 25, 2014, at http://voegelinview.com/catholic-moment-political-philosophy-leo-strauss/.

a deeper understanding of Catholic faith and politics than one might acquire from inside the Catholic tradition alone because of the bold and uncompromising way that he thought through the entire Western canon of philosophy and theology. In discussing this path, I have divided my essay into four parts: (1) reason and faith; (2) faith and law; (3) Catholic natural law; and (4) the benefits of a Straussian education for Catholics.

The first part shows that Strauss's views on reason and faith provide support for biblical revelation against the modern Enlightenment, while also posing a challenge to Catholic theology by insisting on an exclusive choice between reason and faith. Either one must be a philosopher or a religious believer, but one cannot be both at the same time. Strauss's position seems to run counter to Thomas Aquinas's view that reason and faith can be synthesized into a harmonious whole, and I will try to explain how a thoughtful Thomist might respond.

The second part focuses on Strauss's understanding of revealed religion, with a particular emphasis on his distinction between faith and law. He portrays Judaism and Islam as religions of law, expressed in divinely revealed legal codes rather than in creedal faiths—in jurisprudence rather than theology. He portrays Christianity as all faith and no law, and he implies that it is a weakness of Christianity to defend its creeds using philosophy, as this blurs the exclusive choice between divine law and philosophy. Here, I will take issue with Strauss's sharp dichotomy between religions of faith vs. religions of law and argue that it gives a misleading picture of the three religions, whose real disagreement is about the meaning of monotheism rather than law codes.

In the third part, I will argue that even though Strauss was critical of Christianity for elevating faith over divine law, he supported the *natural* law teachings of Catholicism as an alternative to the relativism and historicism of our times. He took a serious interest in Thomistic natural law thinkers, and wrote respectfully of Heinrich Rommen and Yves Simon, but he treated Maritain's "Neo-Thomism" in a critical fashion. Strauss's positive influence on Catholic thought can be seen in scholars like Father Ernest Fortin and Father James Schall, SJ, who were inspired by Strauss's defense of "the ancients against the moderns" to resist the incorporation of natural rights into Catholic social thought and to offer a tempered view of modern democracy.

In the fourth part, I will offer an assessment of Strauss's views on reason, faith, and law, and will reflect on the ways that Leo Strauss can give Catholic thinkers a deeper understanding of what the pursuit of ultimate truth entails for a philosopher or a theologian. As we shall see, Strauss shows the difficulty of attaining the "fullness of truth" by posing so many exclusive choices. Yet, by making things difficult, he has deepened the minds and souls of many Catholic Straussians.

Strauss on Reason and Faith

The relation between reason and faith is a subject that Leo Strauss wrestled with his entire life and explored in numerous writings. It is the explicit theme of his essays "Jerusalem and Athens" (1967), "The Mutual Influence of Theology and Philosophy" (1979), and "Progress or Return?" (1981), and a less explicit theme in other works, such as *Spinoza's Critique of Religion* (1933) or *Philosophy and Law* (1935), but it is always there in some fashion, even in his last book on Plato's *Laws* (1975).[2] Many scholars claim it was Strauss's central concern, which he discussed under the rubric of the "theologico-political problem," a phrase that can be difficult to pin down but that surely includes the great debates about reason and faith.[3] What can we learn from Strauss on this subject?

Strauss has a distinctive approach to the reason-faith debates that can be summarized in two bold propositions. The first I shall call the "exclusivity thesis"—the claim that reason and faith are exclusive choices. The second I shall call the "irrefutability thesis"—Strauss's view that neither

---

2. Leo Strauss, "Jerusalem and Athens: Some Preliminary Reflections," *The City College Papers*, no. 6 (City College of New York), reprinted in *Studies in Platonic Political Philosophy*, ed. Thomas L. Pangle (Chicago: University of Chicago Press, 1983), 147–73; "The Mutual Influence of Theology and Philosophy," *The Independent Journal of Philosophy* 3 (1979): 111–18; "Progress or Return? The Contemporary Crisis in Western Civilization," *Modern Judaism* 1 (1981): 17–45, reprinted in *Rebirth of Classical Political Rationalism*, ed. Thomas Pangle (Chicago: University of Chicago Press, 1989), 227–70; *Spinoza's Critique of Religion* (New York: Schocken Books, 1965); *Philosophy and Law: Contributions to the Understanding of Maimonides and His Predecessors*, trans. Eve Adler, ed. Kenneth Hart Green (Albany: State University of New York Press, 1995); and *The Argument and Action of Plato's 'Laws'* (Chicago: University of Chicago Press, 1975).

3. For interpretations of the phrase, see Daniel Tanguay, *Leo Strauss: An Intellectual Biography*, trans. Christopher Nadon (New Haven, Conn.: Yale University Press, 2007); Heinrich Meier, "How Strauss Became Strauss," in *Reorientation: Leo Strauss in the 1930s*, ed. Martin D. Yaffe and Richard S. Ruderman (New York: Palgrave Macmillan, 2014); Timothy W. Burns, "Strauss on the Religious and Intellectual Situation of the Present," in *Reorientation: Leo Strauss*; and Leora Batnitzky, "Leo Strauss and the 'Theologico-Political Predicament,'" in *The Cambridge Companion to Leo Strauss*, ed. Steven B. Smith (Cambridge: Cambridge University Press, 2009), 41–62.

philosophy nor revelation can refute each other, so we must live with the tension between the two or choose one without destroying the other side. These propositions are connected in complex ways that take us to the deepest issues of Strauss's thought.

Regarding the exclusivity thesis, we can begin with a bracing passage from "The Mutual Influence of Theology and Philosophy" (1979): "Western civilization has two roots in conflict with each other, the Biblical and the Greek philosophical.... No one can be both a philosopher and a theologian ... or a third which is beyond the conflict between philosophy and theology or a synthesis of both."[4] In another essay, "On the Interpretation of *Genesis*" (1981), Strauss goes further by saying that the Book of Genesis shows

> a deep opposition of the Bible and philosophy ... the first chapter questions the primary theme of philosophy [cosmology] and the second chapter questions the primary intention of philosophy [the quest for independent knowledge]. The Bible confronts us more clearly than any other book with this alternative: life in obedience to revelation ... or life in human freedom, the latter represented by Greek philosophers.... Although many people believe in a "happy synthesis" ... this is impossible.[5]

Why does Strauss make such strong statements against a synthesis of philosophy and divine revelation, requiring an "either/or" choice between reason and faith?

His answer, at first glance, seems to be technical. He says that a "synthesis" in the precise sense combines two elements equally and preserves them both on a new plane. Strauss rejects this notion by arguing that it never happens. Every apparent synthesis is really a subordination of one element to another—for example, the medieval idea that philosophy is the handmaiden of theology is not really a synthesis, but rather a subordination of philosophy to theology. Even so, this purely technical or formal analysis does not go far enough. Strauss points to something deeper: the underlying premises of philosophy and the Bible are incompatible, especially regarding the status of miracles.

On the one side, Strauss argues, if we look at the Bible, its underlying premise is that miracles are possible because the universe is created rath-

---

4. "Mutual Influence," 11.
5. Strauss, "On the Interpretation of Genesis," *L'Homme: Revue Francaise d'Anthropolgie* 21, no. 1 (1981): 15.

er than eternal. The creator is the all-powerful God who exists outside of nature and whose will is mysterious: whose divine name, YHWH, means "I am who I am" or "I will be what I will be," which is mystery itself. The Bible is a book about the actions and revelations of the mysterious or hidden God who is unknowable by reason, who can be believed in only by faith, not understood rationally by philosophy or science. For the omnipotent and mysterious God, nothing is impossible, including miracles that are beyond reason to explain or comprehend.

By contrast, Strauss argues, philosophy and science reject the possibility of miracles because the universe is not a creation: the universe exists eternally, or it originates from laws of nature that are given eternally; hence, the universe's laws are unchangeable and necessary, and miraculous interventions are impossible. Philosophy or science seeks knowledge of nature understood as necessary being governed by necessary laws: a view that is incompatible with the biblical God and its claims of creation and miracles.[6]

Strauss argues in many writings that both philosophers and religious believers often fail to see the underlying incompatibility of these two premises. Most are reluctant to admit the exclusive choice of seeing the universe as created or as eternal, as miraculous or as governed by impersonal necessities. Hence, it is shocking for people to read Strauss's claim that the Hebrew Bible has no word for "nature" because nature in the strict sense means an eternal order that exists on its own power rather than a created order that depends on God.[7]

Even more shocking is Strauss's second major thesis about reason and faith—the irrefutability thesis. Quoting again from "Mutual Influence": "The philosophers have never refuted revelation, and the theologians have never refuted philosophy ... [which may sound] very trivial at first but to show it is not trivial ... [it means] philosophy must admit the possibility of revelation ... [and it means] philosophy itself is possibly not the right way of life ... that philosophy is based on 'faith' ... and cannot give an evident account of its own necessity."[8] This is a very provocative challenge issued by Strauss to both philosophers and theologians, but es-

6. The strongest formulation is: "The Bible teaches divine omnipotence, and the thought of divine omnipotence is absolutely incompatible with Greek philosophy in any form." Strauss, "Progress or Return?," in *The Rebirth of Classical Political Rationalism: An Introduction to the Thought of Leo Strauss*, ed. Thomas L. Pangle (Chicago: The University of Chicago Press, 1989), 252.
7. Leo Strauss, *Natural Right and History* (Chicago: University of Chicago Press, 1953), 81.
8. "Mutual Influence," 117–18.

pecially to philosophers. It puts philosophy and science on the defensive and seems to give aid and comfort to religious believers. It goes back to Strauss's early works on Spinoza and Hobbes, which show that the Enlightenment has never refuted religious faith definitively because science cannot prove false the biblical claim of an omnipotent mysterious God outside of nature who can work miracles. The Enlightenment's case is limited to showing the unknowability of miracles, not the impossibility of miracles, because science limits itself to explanations based on natural causality and assumes fixed laws of nature.[9]

The implication is that modern science and the enlightened intellectuals who think science has refuted religion need to learn a lesson in humility. Without intending it, Strauss delivers a powerful rebuke to modern atheists such as Richard Dawkins and Bill Maher. Strauss exposes their strategy for eliminating religion as unjustified arrogance: it relies mostly on mockery of faith in God and miracles, or discrediting witnesses, rather than providing a rationally conclusive case. Their position boils down to an assertion: it would be a miracle, if there were miracles! But this is a tautology, not an argument or proof. The existence of the omnipotent God of the Bible cannot be disproven by scientific accounts of the Big Bang and Darwinian evolution because they are inherently incomplete and cannot explain where their own laws of nature come from. As a student of mine once said, "Strauss gives religious believers a 'get out of jail for free card'" with this argument that ultimate religious claims of supernatural causality are irrefutable by a science that admits only of natural causes. His books show that the Enlightenment's claim to have refuted biblical religion is based on unjustified pride rather than on reason.

In fact, Strauss insists, the only way to defeat religion theoretically would be to produce a "completed system" of philosophy, a system that would solve all mysteries of the universe and give a clear and distinct account of the whole, showing no need for a mysterious God. In other words, it would require a system explaining the causes of all the great riddles of the cosmos and man, including the origin of the universe, the source of the laws of nature, the origins of life and of man's rational soul, the nature of good and evil, the reasons why we must die, and what happens after death. Strauss suggests that Hegel and Spinoza tried this

---

9. Leo Strauss, *Hobbes's Critique of Religion: A Contribution to Understanding the Enlightenment*, ed. and trans. Gabriel Bartlett and Svetozar Minkov (Chicago: University of Chicago Press, 2011), 85–94.

grand philosophical experiment of attaining absolute wisdom by explaining everything rationally—and they failed, due to arbitrary or hypothetical premises.[10]

Strauss also argues that modern philosophy tried a practical strategy to defeat religion, a "Napoleonic strategy" of conquering nature and replacing the givens of nature with an artificial culture. Modernity has tried a practical strategy of transforming man in a way that would erase all religious longings for eternity or transcendence, replacing religion with secular materialism and creating a completely satisfied consumer-entertainment society of Nietzschean "last men" without higher longings. Here Strauss reminds us that this practical project may have more power and success in advanced industrial societies than the theoretical case against biblical religion, although he also reminds us that the rebellions against secular modernity by romantics (and by extension, the renewed "clash of civilizations") cast doubt on this project. Strauss also contends that modern atheists who claim greater intellectual probity than religious believers by rejecting the comforting myths of religion are dishonest; they have an irrational clinging to religious conscience and an irrational faith in progress.[11] Taken together, Strauss's exclusivity and irrefutability theses give a lot of ammunition to believers in biblical religion against the secular currents of the modern world. He shows the weakness of the Enlightenment's case against religion, and he fearlessly reopens many debates considered closed by modern philosophers and scientists.

Yet Strauss does not make it easy for anyone to rest satisfied, including religious believers. By pressing the other side of the exclusivity and irrefutability arguments, he humbles religious believers as well as secular thinkers. He reminds us that, if philosophy cannot refute religion, neither can religion refute philosophy by using theology or appealing to religious experience. This challenge is harder for us to understand: what would it mean for religion to refute philosophy in some definitive manner? Strauss does not spell out clearly the criteria for religion to defeat philosophy; he is more discrete or esoteric on this point, perhaps because it exposes some weaknesses in religious claims against philosophy. Accordingly, I will have to speculate here and offer interpretations of Strauss that are more conjectural than definitive.

10. Strauss, "On the Interpretation of Genesis," 7; "Mutual Influence," 117.
11. Strauss, *Philosophy and Law*, 32–39, and preface to *Spinoza's Critique of Religion*, 30.

In the first place, Strauss's claim that theology cannot refute philosophy means there are no undisputed miracles or revelations. Even if faith in an omnipotent God cannot be refuted by reason, manifestations of the will of God can never be known with certainty. Some believers might claim that theology could refute philosophy with an unambiguous miraculous sign, such as the second coming of Christ or the last judgment, when all secrets will become manifest. But scenarios like these are sheer speculation about the end of the world.

In the second place, Strauss's claim that theology cannot refute philosophy could refer to the inadequacy of proofs for God's existence or for specific revelations. Such "proofs" would have to be more than plausible or probable—they would have to achieve certitude. Sometimes I think Strauss dismisses these arguments too quickly, without explaining the standard of certainty they need to have. For example, when Strauss makes the case for faith in an omnipotent God underlying creation, he almost implies it is a plausible explanation of where everything comes from as a first cause. It may not be an ironclad proof, but it implies that monotheism is a rationally plausible religious claim, indeed the only plausible religious claim, as polytheism views the gods as acting within nature and not omnipotent. Yet, even if theology can plausibly defend monotheism, it cannot refute philosophy definitively because there are three versions of monotheism. The three versions create disputes over the true revelation, which reason can mediate but cannot resolve with certainty. Hence, Pascal's profound insights on how to read the latter Hebrew prophets in their Messianic claims are partly rational and partly beyond reason, leaving Jewish and Christian interpretations of crucial texts, such as Isaiah's prophecies about the suffering servant in Isaiah 53, as disputed claims.[12]

In sum, Strauss's statement that theology will never refute philosophy could refer to a number of theological arguments that have some plausibility but are never completely convincing or strong enough to refute the alternative claims of philosophy and science. Nevertheless, Strauss does show that biblical faith is a live option in the modern world (and at all times) because it cannot be refuted by philosophy or science, even if it cannot be proven by theologians either. Hence, both sides must admit humility in the contest between reason and faith. Although the stand-

---

12. Blaise Pascal, *Pensees*, trans. A. J. Krailsheimer (London: Penguin, 1995), §483, §487, §495, §502.

off is more humbling for philosophers, the net result is disconcerting for everyone. Strauss seems to leave us with an exclusive choice that is arbitrary: to the religious person, Strauss sounds like Kierkegaard, who saw religion as a leap of faith into the absurd—an irrational faith that philosophy cannot reject but which also allows other irrational claims. To the philosopher, Strauss sounds a bit like a postmodernist, for whom philosophy rests on unevident assumptions that make him less than fully rational. Where do we go from here?

Resolving the Dilemma?

The apparent standoff raises difficult questions. How did Strauss deal with the dilemma that no synthesis of reason and faith is possible, yet neither side can defeat the other with a decisive victory or definitive refutation? Did he flip a coin? Did he leave the choice unresolved? Or did he finally settle the question through complex dialectical steps that are elusive or remain hidden? In seeking answers, one can follow two kinds of leads in Strauss's writings. On the surface of his writings, Strauss counsels people to live with the tension between reason and faith. On a deeper level, Strauss indicates that he resolved the tension by a non-arbitrary decision, choosing philosophy over religion, for reasons that are difficult to pin down.

On the surface, Strauss says repeatedly that the conflict between the two roots of Western civilization may be disturbing at first but it is also the secret source of vitality in the West. As he famously says, every serious person must be either a "philosopher open to the challenge of theology or a theologian open to the challenge of philosophy."[13] The result would be a high civilization that thrives on creative tension and softens the edges of arrogant rationalism and of dogmatic religion by raising the level of debate for everyone.

Probing more deeply, however, one can see that Strauss goes beyond a practical compromise or creative tension; he strove throughout his life to resolve the tension. As scholars such as Daniel Tanguay and Heinrich Meier have shown, Strauss was attracted at different periods of his life to Zionism, to Orthodox Judaism, and even to something he calls "Jew-

---

13. Strauss, "Progress and Return," 270.

ish Thomism." But there is also evidence to indicate that Strauss made a decision in favor of philosophy, siding with Socrates over Moses, and embracing a skeptical version of Socratic rationalism. If this interpretation is correct, then how did Strauss arrive at a settled position in favor of Socratic philosophy?

Here, I would like to offer a few insights to the many profound scholarly interpretations of Strauss by focusing on something that he calls "Jewish Thomism" as a phase of his early career. It is a label that Strauss uses in hindsight to describe the medieval Enlightenment of Maimonides and seems to sympathize with up to his book, *Philosophy and Law* (1935), and then later abandoned for Socratic rationalism. I will try to explain this point by discussing a quotation by Strauss in a letter to Gershom Scholem written in 1952 on the occasion of the death of the Jewish scholar Julius Guttmann. Speaking of himself, Strauss says: "I have moved, so to speak, contrary to Guttmann's moderate rationalism, on the path via a Jewish Thomism to radical 'rationalism' ... [and] I am *now* attempting to reach moderate 'rationalism,' but one that ... would be even less acceptable to Guttmann than my two earlier positions."[14] What does Strauss mean in this statement by "Jewish Thomism," and why did he abandon it for "radical rationalism" and then seek a new kind of "moderate rationalism"?

Strauss seems to equate Jewish Thomism with Maimonides in *Philosophy and Law* where he argues that Jewish philosophers turned to the Bible and divine revelation because they had a keen sense of "the insufficiency of human reason."[15] In this view, medieval Jewish philosophers like Maimonides, in search of ultimate truth, were led by an awareness of the limits of human reason to divine revelation in order to find answers to the ultimate questions, such as the creation of the world. This approach mirrors the teaching of Thomas Aquinas, and it explains why Strauss could refer to his early sympathetic portrayal of Maimonides as "Jewish Thomism."

Thomas, as we know, claimed that reason and faith have a relatively

---

14. Meier, "How Strauss Became Strauss," 29n29.
15. Ibid., 19–20, gives an expanded version of Strauss's reorientation after 1938: "[Strauss] explicitly distances himself from the view that for Maimonides the dependence of the philosophers on revelation is based on the insufficiency of human reason. It is presumably in view of the claim of insufficiency, which plays a prominent role in *Philosophie und Gesetz*, that Strauss says in retrospect that he moved, 'so to speak, contrary to Guttmann's moderate rationalism, on a path via a Jewish Thomism to radical 'rationalism.'"

harmonious relation because reason provides true but incomplete knowledge of the world, and it needs divine revelation to be complete. In other words, reason points to faith as its perfection because reason is aware of the insufficiency of its powers, which implies that faith is beyond reason but not against reason and the two do not contradict each other. Reason can discover some truths about the universe, man, and God; but faith is needed to attain the highest truths of both the natural and supernatural world. For example, reason can "prove" that God exists as the first cause of all contingent being and that God is one and unchanging. But faith in revelation is needed to understand God as personal and benevolent, as expressed in the incarnation and Trinity, because these are mysteries of God beyond reason to prove or comprehend. In this sense, Thomas offers a "synthesis" of reason and faith: they form a harmonious whole because reason is subordinate to faith, not as a tool but as an incomplete forerunner that requires faith for its completion, like steps on the ladder of a hierarchy of perfection.

Although Strauss wrote little about Aquinas, one can find arguments and formulations in his writings that seem to reflect this "Jewish Thomism." Let me cite four examples:

(1) Strauss reminds us that, even though the Bible teaches man about the omnipotent and mysterious God who could create the universe in any random fashion and command any set of laws according to his inscrutable will, the Bible also teaches that God is reasonable, up to a point. God is reasonable in setting up a covenant with man, and in revealing divine laws to the Israelites that God says "will be your wisdom and understanding in the sight of the nations" (Dt 4:6), meaning the Torah will be seen as a set of rational laws to all mankind.[16]

(2) Strauss argues in his essay, "On the Interpretation of *Genesis*," that the six days of creation are supernatural in the sense of occurring by miraculous commands of God. Yet, he also shows that the six days of creation are orderly in following a principle of binary separation and ever greater local motion: from the separation of light and dark on the first day, to the most mobile and free creature on the sixth day, man, made in God's image. Strauss refers to Genesis as a nonmythical account of creation

---

16. "Thus Strauss asserts that 'Jewish orthodoxy based its claim to superiority to other religions from the beginning on its superior rationality (Deuteronomy 4:6).'" Quoted in Tanguay, *Leo Strauss*, 209.

that has an ordering principle for all created beings (separation-motion-freedom), even though the ordering principle is not natural but supernatural.[17] The implication is that the Bible calls upon man to believe in a God who is mysterious but not absurd, as the created universe and the divine law are not random but follow stable patterns that can be seen as rational by mankind.

(3) In discussing the later Hebrew prophets in the "Preface to Spinoza," Strauss criticizes Buber's view that the later prophets were only messengers of shock and awe, sent to make the Israelites feel insecure. Strauss says the latter Hebrew prophets expressed faith in a Messianic era that reflects cosmic justice and the triumph of good over evil. The Hebrew prophets showed that "the Biblical experience is not simply against man's grain: *grace perfects nature, grace does not destroy nature*"—an obvious use of the Thomistic formula of grace perfecting nature as the core of cosmic justice.[18]

(4) Finally, I would cite Strauss's argument in *Philosophy and Law* that the medieval philosophy of Maimonides was not about "religious consciousness," as Julius Guttmann maintained, but about two other subjects: cosmology and law. The first pertains to the doctrine of creation as a truth of divine revelation beyond reason, which Strauss calls the "cosmological orientation" of Judaism in order to emphasize that it is a claim about the world, not merely a representation of consciousness or an existential commitment. The second subject is "the legal foundation of philosophy" in which divine law is examined for permission to philosophize and philosophy takes divine law as its primary theme.[19]

These four arguments reflect a relatively harmonious relation of reason and faith that could explain why Strauss applies the phrase "Jewish Thomism" to his perspective up to 1938 (without abandoning all traces of it in his readings of the Bible afterwards). Nevertheless, Strauss did not stop at the Jewish Thomism of this early period. He even changed his view of Maimonides as he went on to "radical rationalism" and then to "moderate rationalism," which meant choosing philosophy over Judaism. One can only speculate why—the answer is impossible to give with much certainty, even though it is the key to unlocking Strauss. The rea-

---

17. Strauss, "On the Interpretation of Genesis," 9–12.
18. Strauss, *Spinoza's Critique of Religion*, 10 (emphasis added).
19. Strauss, *Philosophy and Law*, 51, 60, 64–66, 91.

sons are deeply buried in Strauss's dialectical approach and esoteric presentations.[20]

However, we know the conclusion: Strauss embraced classical philosophy over biblical faith, not as a system or set of doctrines, but as "a way of life" following the model of Socrates, featuring Socratic ignorance and a searching (*zetetic*) or erotic skepticism. In this view, the philosopher lives happily with merely human wisdom, not because he has refuted divine wisdom, but because he simply does not understand it or experience it: he treats religion like a band of light beyond the visible spectrum and suspends judgment about biblical revelation. The crucial and astonishing claim of Strauss is that the Socratic philosopher can "prove" that his way of life is best because he can live happily without ever possessing a completed cosmology, metaphysics, or theology; and he can live "untragically" without feeling "the misery of man without God" that haunted Pascal. The philosopher's awareness of his ignorance means that he regards wisdom as "the one thing needful," even though the quest for wisdom is inherently incomplete because the whole is only partly intelligible and will always remain mysterious. Hence, dialectical reasoning about the articulated parts of the whole universe, especially the part we know best—the human soul—is the only available approach to knowledge for the Socratic philosopher. As if to offer his personal testimony of the erotic need for this experience, Strauss says in a letter to Voegelin: "Without the giving or being given accounts [*logon dounai te kai dexasthai*], I, at least, cannot live."[21] In other words, Socratic dialectics makes life worth living for Strauss as a philosopher open to the possibility of faith, which he cannot prove or refute and which remains a possibility or temptation, even though he could never embrace it and evidently lived as an unbelieving rationalist.[22]

---

20. See Tanguay, *Leo Strauss*, 52–57, 80–98, for an explanation of Strauss's change in the late 1930s as "the Farabian turn," meaning the adaption of al-Farabi's view of divine revelation as serving the political purpose of providing a law code for the ideal political community (rather than cosmological truths) and of the prophet as a lawgiver modeled on Plato's philosopher-king who as the prophet-philosopher is the best and happiest man.

21. See Strauss, *Faith and Political Philosophy: The Correspondence Between Leo Strauss and Eric Voegelin, 1034–1964*, ed. and trans. Peter Emberly and Barry Cooper (Columbia: University of Missouri Press, 2014), 88, letter of June 4, 1951.

22. See Meier, *Leo Strauss and the Theologico-Political Problem*, trans. Marcus Brainard (Cambridge: Cambridge University Press, 2006), 141–80, for Strauss's lecture notes on "Reason and Revelation" to be delivered at Hartford Theological Seminary on January 8, 1948. The lecture notes are a candid summary of all the great themes of the reason/faith debates under subheadings such as: "2. Revelation must try to prove the absurdity of philosophy," "5. The alternative to philosophy is

In sum, the greatness of Strauss lies in helping to liberate minds imprisoned by modern thought by rejecting the historicist claim that all thought is relative to its historical period. Strauss painstakingly recovers ancient models of wisdom and makes the case for both alternatives, Socrates and Moses, as living claims to truth in our times and all times. While Strauss ultimately sides with Socratic philosophy, he makes orthodox biblical faith the central challenge to philosophy.

The weakness of Strauss (and here is my Thomistic response to his position) is that his apparent resolution of the debate in favor of Socratic philosophy rests ultimately on experiential wisdom, on the personal experience of philosophers who are able to live happily or untragically without a definitive doctrine about the special place of reason in the cosmos that would provide an objective basis for measuring the worth of philosophy or for overcoming despair at cosmic indifference and fear of death. Herein lies the puzzle of Strauss's return to moderate Socratic rationalism: he suspends judgment in skeptical fashion on all doctrines about God or nature and traces the philosopher's happiness solely to the mind's awareness of progress in gaining clarity about the permanent problems, yet he still needs a cosmological doctrine that favors human intelligence in the universe.[23] To argue that philosophy "as a way of life" is justifiable because it makes one happy without supporting doctrines about mind and cosmos is problematic; it even leads some scholars to accuse Strauss of mere "decisionism," making an arbitrary choice based on personal or subjective experience.[24]

---

revelation—philosophy must try to prove that revelation is impossible," "6. Philosophy cannot refute revelation," "8. Revelation cannot refute philosophy and Philosophy cannot explain revelation"—although Strauss offers an attempt in eleven propositions to explain religion by referring to "the need of man for law" (166–67) and concluding with remarks on "The inevitable alternative: philosophy or revelation."

23. Leo Strauss, *What Is Political Philosophy?* (New York: Free Press, 1959), 38–39: "Socrates was so far from being committed to a specific cosmology that his knowledge was knowledge of ignorance ... [or] knowledge of the elusive character of the truth of the whole. Socrates, then, viewed man in the light of the mysterious character of the whole ... in the light of the unchangeable ideas, i.e., of the fundamental and permanent problems.... This understanding of the situation of man which includes, then, the quest for cosmology rather than a solution to the cosmological problem, was the foundation of classical political philosophy."

24. This is the judgment of Tanguay, *Leo Strauss*, 147: "The weak *zetetic* vindication of the philosophic life, so essential to Strauss's thought, reveals its intrinsic limitation ... I do not believe that Strauss succeeded in giving a satisfactory response to the decisionist objection that he himself raised." I think it is implausible to argue that Strauss leaves open the decision, or, as Susan Orr concludes, "if he tips the scales at all, it is toward Jerusalem [over Athens]" in Susan Orr, *Jerusalem and Athens* (Lanham, Md.: Rowman and Littlefield, 1995), 158.

Strauss on Faith and Law

Yet it is hard to believe that Strauss could leave this crucial decision in favor of philosophy to mere personal experience, which suggests that there must be more to consider. Is there something about divine revelation itself that prevents Strauss from moving from the Socratic knowledge of ignorance (the awareness of the mysterious character of the whole) to the next step of "drinking," as it were, from the living water of faith? A clue may be found in Strauss's analysis of revealed religion, which focuses on the distinction between faith and law.

The most striking feature of Strauss's discussion of the three great monotheistic religions—Judaism, Christianity, and Islam—is that he insists on classifying them into two distinct types: religions of law and religions of faith. He portrays Judaism and Islam as religions of law, whose power lies in a divinely revealed legal code for society rather than in a faith expressed in doctrines or creeds; they emphasize jurisprudence over theology. By contrast, Strauss portrays Christianity as a religion of faith, not of law; and he implies that it is a weakness of Christianity to have formulated creeds that require the use of philosophy to explain and defend the dogma of faith. In Strauss's eyes, the doctrines, dogma, or creeds worked out by Christian theologians make Christianity less credible as a claim of revelation than Judaism and Islam, which better preserve the exclusive choice between divine law and philosophy. Christian theology also has the side effect of preserving philosophy in the universities of the West, but only by domesticating philosophy and putting it in the service of Christian apologetics.

This is how Strauss frames the issue in his essay "How to Begin to Study Medieval Philosophy":

> One has to start from the difference between Judaism and Islam on the one hand and Christianity on the other. For the Jew and the Moslem, religion is primarily not ... a faith formulated in dogmas, but a law code of divine origin. Accordingly, the religious science ... is not dogmatic theology, but the science of the law, *halakah* or *fiqh*. The science of the law thus understood has much less in common with philosophy than has dogmatic theology. Hence, the status of philosophy is ... much more precarious in the Islamic-Jewish world than in the Christian world.... This fundamental difference doubtless explains the later collapse of philosophic studies in the Islamic world ... [and it explains] why Thomas asks in the *Summa* whether theology is necessary apart from philosophic disciplines ...

and why Maimonides and Averroes present a discussion [regarding] ... whether the study of philosophy is permitted or forbidden or commanded [by the divine law].[25]

It seems ironic that Strauss apparently thinks Judaism and Islam, which emphasize a revealed law code and denigrate philosophy, are somehow superior as religions to Christianity, which is more receptive to philosophy and more concerned with dogmatic theology than with jurisprudence. Strauss's reasoning is that the power of revelation lies in its claim of being a particular, historical, or contingent event in which the omnipotent God enters the world with the earth-shattering miracle of divine revelation, which must be either accepted or rejected as a divine command. This claim is the maximal challenge to reason, as reason does not appeal to particular, contingent events but has its power as a "universal and human [event]" accessible to anyone, everywhere and always, as knowledge of natural and impersonal necessities. Revelation, by contrast, has its power according to Strauss by being a brute fact, a *factum brutum*, meaning an experience for which there is no evidence. As a brute fact that either happens or does not happen, revelation radically challenges the impersonal necessity of philosophical reasoning which "philosophy as philosophy does not and cannot [accept]."[26] The primary teaching of divine revelation is thus a set of commands to do and to obey, rather than a set of doctrines to believe—a law code, such as the Ten Commandments and the Torah codified into *halakah*, or the *Qur'an* codified into *Shari'a* law. As soon as divine revelation crosses the line from an experience of the omnipotent God that calls one to action by law and becomes "faith" in a proposition through words, letters, or speech that must be believed (e.g., a prophetic utterance), revelation enters the realm of cognitive understanding and becomes a human interpretation of something to be rationally understood and hence, to be proven or disproven. But "faith" in a proposition is philosophy rather than religion. From Strauss's perspective, the only proper response to revelation is loving obedience to the divine law rather than belief in a dogma or teaching—orthopraxy rather

---

25. Strauss, *Rebirth of Classical Political Rationalism*, 221–22. For an insightful account of Strauss's turn to the "primacy of law" in medieval Jewish thought, see Hillel Fradkin, "Philosophy and Law: Leo Strauss as a Student of Medieval Jewish Thought," *Review of Politics* 53, no. 1 (Winter 1991): 40–52.

26. Leo Strauss and Eric Voegelin, *Faith and Political Philosophy: The Correspondence between Leo Strauss and Eric Voegelin, 1934–1964*, ed. and trans. Peter Emberley and Barry Cooper (University Park: Pennsylvania State University Press, 1993), 89; and *Philosophy and Law*, 64.

than orthodoxy. By viewing revelation as a "brute fact" for which there is no evidence or argument, Strauss makes religion a matter of law and not of faith.[27]

Thus, at the heart of Strauss's teaching about philosophy and religion, we find two sets of exclusive choices: (1) reason or faith; and (2) faith or law (a divine legal code). By a kind of logic that resembles the transitive property (where if one asserts that A is opposed to B and B is opposed to C, then it follows that A is opposed to C), Strauss infers that the ultimate choice is between philosophy and divine law, that is, a choice between rational understanding of the world through philosophy vs. unquestioning and loving obedience to the divine law that comes as a brute fact from God's revelation to the prophets and is delivered as such to the people. We can now see why Strauss's references to the "theologico-political problem" in his writings contains an ambiguity that puzzles scholars: it refers to both sets of exclusive choices, interconnected by a radical view of philosophy as the skeptical searching for rational wisdom and a radical view of religion as a divine law revealed without rational understanding that the prophets present as the ideal civil-legal code for the political community.

With these sharp dichotomies in mind, we can now raise the most serious critical questions about Strauss's framework of analysis: is it accurate to view divine revelation as a shattering command received from God as a sheer brute fact without asking for reasoning at all, even by the great figures of the Bible or the *Qur'an*? And, is it fair to characterize Judaism, Christianity, and Islam by classifying them sharply into religions of law vs. religions of faith? In my judgment, Strauss's way of framing the debate in terms of two sets of exclusive choices is misleading and points to the need for a more qualified understanding.

Consider the meaning of "faith" in Judaism and Islam: does revelation refer only to obeying divine law and not also to belief in doctrines or dogma? Let me cite a powerful counter-example to Strauss's interpretation, taken from Islam—the story of Abraham in the *Qur'an* that describes Abraham's embrace of monotheism and rejection of polytheism. The text shows Abraham mixing faith and reason, recognizing that poly-

---

27. See Strauss in "Reason and Revelation," in Meier, *Leo Strauss and the Theologico-Political Problem*, 142: "There cannot be any evidence in favor of revelation but the *fact* of revelation as known through faith. Yet this means that for those who do not have the experience of faith, there is *no shred of evidence* in favor of faith; the unbelieving man has *not the slightest reason* for doubting his unbelief; revelation is nothing but a factum brutum."

theism is rooted in nature worship, in seeing the sun, moon, and stars as divinities because of their power and beauty. He is tempted to believe they are gods, but God seeks to persuade him otherwise:

> Thus did We show Abraham the kingdom of heavens and earth, so he might become a firm believer. When night drew its shadow over him, he saw a star. "That," he said, "is surely my God." But when it faded in the morning light, he said, "I will not worship gods that fade." When he beheld the rising moon, he said, "That is my God." But when it set, he said, "If my Lord does not guide me, I shall surely go astray." Then, when he beheld the sun shining, he said, "That must be my God: it is the largest." But when it set, he said to his people: "I disown your idols. I will turn my face to Him who has created the heavens and earth, and will live a righteous life. I am no idolator."[28]

In other words, Abraham is tempted by nature worship until he sees the stars, moon, and sun fading in and out, until he sees their transience and motion, their lack of permanence; he is led by reasoning to believe in an eternal and invisible God who created nature—to monotheism. Hence, one may infer that Abraham receives monotheism not as a brute fact but as a mixture of reasoning and faith about ultimate reality that is presented in the *Qur'an* itself as a mini-lesson in apologetics—*kalam* or dialectical theology. This brief example casts doubt on Strauss's sharp dichotomy of religions of faith vs. religions of law; it shows that his classification is too rigid. The *Qur'an* is devoted to faith as well as to law, and Islam requires both. Indeed, all three monotheisms emphasize faith and law in varying degrees, not excluding one or the other. It would be more accurate to say that these religions display a continuum of law, faith, and reason rather than a dichotomy or trichotomy.

Similarly, one may say of Judaism that it is clearly more "legalistic" than Christianity: the Torah is mainly a teaching about the divine law (the 613 commands, according to the traditional legal scholars), and the Talmud is a legal commentary on the Torah. Hence, jurisprudence takes precedence over theology in Judaism. But it is also true that the Ten Commandments, which are the core of the Mosaic law, begin with articles of faith. The first and second commandments require belief in God and the rejection of graven images and idols: these two commands are articles of faith and correct belief. They demand orthodoxy not orthopraxis, requiring monotheism rather than polytheism and rejection of belief in

---

28. *Qur'an* 6:75. Taken from *The Koran*, trans. N. J. Dawood (London: Penguin, 1995).

idols. The implication is that no clear separation of faith and law exists in Judaism. Without correct belief about the one true God, there will not be correct action in obeying the other laws. Like Islam, Judaism requires belief in genuine monotheism as the first and primary command of the law and as the prerequisite for the divine legal code.

This is the main point of Maimonides's *Guide of the Perplexed*: most of the first book is spent clarifying the meaning of belief about God as an incorporeal being who is outside of human experience or analogy. And Strauss himself shows in his outline of the *Guide* that the entire work falls into two topics: "Views" and "Actions," with two-thirds of the *Guide* pertaining to views (which are beliefs, more or less rational), while only the last third analyzes actions required by the law. It is a work of theology, at least on the surface, as well as a work on divine law.[29]

Similar observations can be made about the *Qur'an*. As Islam's holy book of revelations, it consists of 114 chapters made up of 6,236 verses. Roughly speaking, six hundred verses (ten percent) contain various commands that make up *Shari'a* law; and, of these, only three hundred verses pertain to civil laws that seem clearly intended to be established as the legal code of the political community—for example, laws pertaining to punishments for crimes, trade and economic contracts, family law and divorce, sanctions for immoral practices, warfare, religious holidays, and tithes for the poor. Other laws that pertain to worship, diet, prayers, fasting, and dress may or may not be intended as civil laws. Most of the 114 chapters of the *Qur'an* deal with matters of dogmatic theology—above all with the nature of monotheism and the central claim that Mohammad is the seal of the prophets because he restored the pure monotheism of Abraham against the corruptions of monotheism by the Christian doctrine of Jesus as the Son of God and the Jewish doctrine of a divinely chosen people. Against Christianity, the *Qur'an* says, "God forbid that He Himself should beget a son" (19:35 and 4:171); it is a violation of monotheism. It also speaks about the corruption of monotheism by Judaism, whose claim of being a chosen people is also a kind of incarnation of God on earth and an insult to pure monotheism. The *Qur'an* has many chapters devoted to eschatology, that is, the doctrines of the last judgment, the afterlife (heaven and hell), and the resurrection of the body after death

---

29. Leo Strauss, "How to Begin to Study *The Guide of the Perplexed*," introduction to Moses Maimonides, *The Guide of the Perplexed*, trans. Shlomo Pines (Chicago: University of Chicago Press, 1963), 1:xi–xiii.

(again roughly speaking, one may say that eschatology makes up thirty percent of the *Quran*, and civil law only ten percent). These doctrines are commanded, not as civil laws requiring actions, but as articles of faith requiring belief.

Conversely, Christianity is not only a religion of faith but also a religion of law. It has developed elaborate creeds over the centuries, such as the Nicene Creed and the Augsburg Confession, which have no analogues in Judaism and Islam. And Christianity requires faith in Jesus Christ as the Son of God, the second person of the Trinity. But Christianity is also a religion of law and legal codes. It differs from Judaism and Islam because the divine law of Jesus in the Gospels is a *moral* law rather than a civil code for a political community. The Christian teaching on divine law is that the myriad of laws in the Mosaic code—the 613 laws of the *Torah*—are reduced to the Ten Commandments, and these in turn are perfected and simplified by reducing them to the two great laws of love or charity. In Matthew's Gospel, the two great commands of love are referred to as either statute or law, *nomos* or *entoleh*: "Master, which is the great commandment [*entoleh megaleh*] in the law [*tou nomou*]? Jesus said to him: you shall love the Lord your God with your all your heart, soul, and mind. This is the first and great commandment. And the second is like to it: you shall love your neighbor as yourself. On these two commandments depend the whole law [*ho nomos*] and the prophets" (22:36–40). Following the example of the Gospels, Catholic theology makes the study of law part of both theology and jurisprudence. In the *Summa Theologiae*, Thomas Aquinas develops his famous typology of laws (eternal, divine, natural, and human law); and he typically frames moral and ethical questions as questions of law: is it lawful to do certain deeds, for example, to use force to defend one's life? And official church law is canon law, which is every bit as Talmudic as Jewish law.

Some of these observations may seem obvious, but it is necessary to keep them in mind in order to challenge Strauss's sharp distinction between religions of faith (Christianity) and religions of law (Judaism and Islam). As a generalization, it does not hold up to scrutiny. All three religions have faith and law, theology and jurisprudence, in varying degrees; they differ only in emphasis. A related problem with Strauss's classification is that, even though he focuses on divine law and on the prophet as the lawgiver of the ideal community, he never analyzes the *content* of legal codes or the type of regime they prescribe. His analysis is formal in the sense of viewing revelation as such as the primary challenge to philosophy; he insists on the brute fact of revelation, regardless of what is revealed, as the essence of religion.[30] The result is that Strauss gives us a misleading impression of the three religions.

From the preceding analysis, I would go a step further and argue that the deepest point of difference among the three monotheistic religions is not their law codes. Rather, it is the meaning of monotheism itself—the meaning of belief in one God who utterly transcends the natural and visible world, who is beyond time and space, yet who also enters time and space to create and to rule the world.

In other words, *the primary disagreement among religions is about the mystery of monotheism: how the infinite God enters the finite world while still remaining infinite and divine.* Hence, the main difference is how they name and define the one true God: Judaism calls the one God YHWH and views his essence as will; Christianity calls the one God a Trinity whose essence is love; and Islam calls the one God Allah (Almighty) whose essence is power. This is a dispute about theology, not jurisprudence. The conclusion I would draw is that Strauss's rigid distinction between reason, faith, and law needs revision; the analysis should recognize a continuum of reason, faith, and law rather than exclusive choices.

Catholic Natural Law and Modern Democracy

Although Strauss was critical of the Christian approach to divine law, he was quite respectful of Catholic natural law for the role it could play in politics. Following his analysis of religions, Strauss recognized that natural law is Christianity's replacement for the divine legal codes in Judaism and Islam. This view flows from the Gospels' division of authority between God's realm and Caesar's realm, with God's realm governed by divine law and Caesar's realm governed by a lesser kind of law, which initially meant the decrees of the emperor or Roman law and eventually meant human law guided by a universal rational standard—natural law. As a consequence, Strauss notes, the Christian tradition is logically more

---

30. See Batnitzky, "Leo Strauss and the 'Theologico-Political Predicament,'" 54–55, who argues that Strauss ultimately cares about the content of religions, but not for religious reasons, only for their historical influence, such as the influence of Christian Scholasticism on the origins of modernity.

open to Aristotle's *Politics* than to Plato's *Republic* because Aristotle's naturalistic approach to politics, his prudent application of natural right, is best suited for Caesar's realm. The Christian distinction of two powers, spiritual and temporal, explains why the Catholic natural law teaching developed by Thomas Aquinas acquired such significance: natural law fills in the blanks for organizing Caesar's realm left open by the Gospels, whose moral law of love or charity is not a civil-legal code and says very little about concrete political questions, such as the best form of government, the best economic system, diplomacy, warfare, and international law.

Given the importance of natural law for Christianity, Strauss took a serious interest in Thomistic natural law because he saw it as an antidote to the moral relativism of modern times and as a bridge back to classical natural right. At the same time, Strauss sought to make Thomistic thinkers more open to classical prudence and to a less ideologically rigid approach to politics; he encouraged Catholic thinkers to recover some of the latitude of classical statesmanship and to separate natural law from religious influences (which is somewhat ironic, given his praise of divine legal codes in Judaism and Islam). These two aims—resisting relativism and encouraging prudent flexibility—produced somewhat opposing tendencies in Strauss's five or six writings touching on Catholic natural law, namely, his discussion of Aquinas in *Natural Right and History*, an essay entitled "On Natural Law," two book review essays on Heinrich Rommen and Yves Simon, and scattered remarks on Neo-Thomism in his correspondence with Eric Voegelin. Following Strauss's objectives of opposing relativism while encouraging Catholic natural law thinkers to be more prudent and flexible, I would argue that he arrives at a comparative ranking of contemporary Thomists as follows: Heinrich Rommen is the most impressive, Yves Simon is "sober and manly," and Neo-Thomists such as Jacques Maritain and perhaps Mortimer Adler are less reliable. Let me explain the reasons for Strauss's comparative ranking.

At the beginning of every discussion of natural right, Strauss tips his hat to Catholic and non-Catholic followers of Aquinas: they are the only serious scholars today opposing moral relativism in its various forms, positivism and historicism. Their hearts and minds are in the right place, even if they underestimate the challenges posed by modern natural science to the natural teleology of Aristotle that underlay traditional natural law.³¹ Nevertheless, Strauss's comments on Thomas Aquinas in *Natural Right and History* and in his essay, "On Natural Law," are respectful but critical: he argues that original Thomistic natural law is unduly influenced by religious notions (revealed theology and biblical revelation) and hence it is not purely rational or natural. The Christian influence made Catholic natural law less flexible than Aristotle's approach on such issues as the indissolubility of marriage and opposition to birth control and even on the role of particular circumstances in choosing the best form of government. Strauss encourages Catholic natural law thinkers to be more aware of "recovering for statesmanship a latitude considerably constricted by the Thomistic teaching." He reminds readers that "Montesquieu's *Spirit of the Laws* is misunderstood if one disregards the fact that it is directed against the Thomistic view of natural right … and is nearer to the spirit of the classics than to Thomas," implying that statesmen should heed Montesquieu's lessons about the role of material circumstances, such as geography, climate, population, and history, in determining what laws and institutions are best for their nations.³²

The opposing tendencies of resisting relativism while encouraging prudent flexibility help to explain Strauss's judgments on the Catholic thinkers of his generation. Strauss refers positively to Neo-Thomism (whose leading spokesman was Jacques Maritain) when it stands as the only serious rival to moral relativism; and he recognizes the attraction of Neo-Thomism even for non-Catholics (such as the Chicago professor Mortimer Adler, a secular Jew who converted to Episcopalianism and Catholicism under the influence of Aristotle and Aquinas). In a letter to Voegelin, Strauss refers to Neo-Thomism in commenting on the reception of his Walgreen lectures in 1950: "the reaction of the public [seemed] … favorable, especially among the younger ones, who at first see only an alternative between positivism-relativism-pragmatism and Neo-Thomism, and can scarcely imagine that one can draw the consequence from one's ignorance that one must strive after knowledge."³³ Here we see Strauss acknowledging the weakness of relativism and the initial attraction of Neo-Thomism even for non-Catholics as an alternative to relativism; he

---

31. Strauss, "On Natural Law," in *International Encyclopedia of the Social Sciences*, ed. David L. Sills (New York: Collier and Macmillan, 1968), 2:80–90, reprinted in *Studies in Platonic Political Science*, 137: "Natural law, which was for many centuries the basis of the predominant Western political thought, is rejected in our time by almost all students of society who are not Roman Catholics."
32. Strauss, *Natural Right and History*, 164.
33. Strauss, *Faith and Political Philosophy*, 74.

then recommends his own path of Socratic ignorance leading to the philosophical quest for knowledge independently of theology, metaphysics, or cosmology.

At the same time, Strauss harshly criticizes the Neo-Thomists for their weak and ineffectual efforts to oppose modern thinking with a revival of Aristotle or the recovery of original Thomism. I take this to be a reference to Maritain, whose book *Man and the State* would have been known to Strauss (as a University of Chicago Press book of 1951). In a letter to Voegelin, Strauss refers to numerous attempts that have been tried since the Enlightenment at "the restoration of the Platonic-Aristotelian philosophy," and he mentions Neo-Thomism as another failed attempt: "Neo-Thomism is *in its intent* more radical [than other restorations]—in its implementation, of course, it is of a low level, and not worth considering."[34] I take this to mean that Neo-Thomism claims to be a bold effort to restore classical and medieval philosophy against the Enlightenment, making it radically antimodern in its intention. But Neo-Thomism fails in its execution, meaning it does not really restore Plato, Aristotle, or Thomas Aquinas. I also take this to mean that Strauss is criticizing Maritain for using Thomistic language about natural law while actually incorporating modern ideas, such as the French Revolution's "rights of man," into Catholic natural law. In other words, Strauss is saying that Neo-Thomism is more "Neo" than "Thomist" and fails to counter the modern Enlightenment with a genuine recovery of premodern thought.

Strauss displays more respect for Yves Simon in reviewing his book, *Philosophy of Democratic Government* (1951). He notes that Simon's "philosophy is based on Thomistic principles" and it "attempts to combine the Thomistic principles with the democratic spirit," with more or less success. On the positive side, Simon acknowledges that Thomas is not in principle in favor of democracy and views democracy as only one of the legitimate forms of government under certain circumstances. Simon tries to find a principled connection with democracy in the "transmission theory" of government, which has roots in Thomas but is really developed by the sixteenth century Neo-Scholastics Cajetan, Bellarmine, and Suarez. Simon is honest enough to admit that "neither of these thinkers meant to recommend democracy"; rather, they viewed it as only one of the legitimate regimes that the multitude could transmit to the rulers. But Simon

34. Ibid., 18.

pushes the case by referring to the "equalitarian dynamics of human nature ... and of modern societies." On the negative side, Strauss is critical of Simon's argument that the alleged progress in man's "conscience" and the technological progress of the modern world make democracy "natural" in ways that Thomas or Suarez did not realize. Yet, after accusing Simon of wishful thinking about the naturalness of democracy, Strauss notes Simon's advice about virtuous restraints on popular rule and praises Simon for "this sober and manly conclusion." I infer that Strauss prefers Simon to Maritain because Simon is more of an Aristotelian than Maritain: Simon is guided by sober Aristotelian prudence and classical virtue rather than by enthusiasm for the French Revolution's rights of man.[35]

In similar fashion, Strauss writes about Heinrich Rommen's book, *The State in Catholic Thought: A Treatise in Political Philosophy* (1945). Strauss might also have been familiar with Rommen's treatise, *The Natural Law: A Study in Legal, Social History, and Philosophy* (1936). Strauss treats Rommen as a genuine political philosopher who goes to first principles and makes a Catholic case for democracy on prudential grounds, breaking with the Catholic monarchist tradition in the name of a prudent adaption to modern times. Strauss praises Rommen in saying "it is something of a surprise to come across a book on political fundamentals which is more than an open or thinly disguised apology for democracy." Nevertheless, he criticizes Rommen for his chapter on natural law "in which he deals almost exclusively with natural rights as distinguished from duties." Strauss is also critical of Rommen for claiming his principles are "based on reason and not on revelation" and then declaring that "respect for theology, faith, and revelation" is the essence of political philosophy and that "no state can live without the beneficent force of divine religion." Strauss seems to think that the problem with Rommen is inconsistency, not the fact that a state might wish to establish a religious basis for civil law, as Judaism and Islam propose in their views of divine law.[36]

Regarding Strauss's influence on Catholic political thought, one can see it best in Catholic scholars Ernest Fortin and James Schall, SJ. Fortin's impressive collection of writings show that he has learned from Strauss the superiority of the "ancients against the moderns" because

---

35. Strauss, *What Is Political Philosophy?*, 306–11.
36. Ibid., 281–84.

they gave priority to virtue and duty over freedom, rights, and material well-being. Fortin uses this insight to critically review much of Catholic social thought, from Leo XIII up through John Paul II and the "new natural law theory" of John Finnis. Fortin criticizes the incorporation of modern natural rights into Catholic social thought and seeks to recover a genuine Aristotelian or Augustinian Thomism which includes virtue as well as rights in the idea of the common good.[37] He also takes to heart Strauss's praise for classical prudence in recognizing a variety of legitimate regimes and developing a tempered view of democratic societies which always need reminders to cultivate the moral, intellectual, and spiritual perfection of man. In *Reason, Revelation, and the Foundations of Political Philosophy*, Schall shows a distinctive Straussian awareness of the need for recovering a classical perspective on the common good that is free of the bias of modern Catholic social teaching in favor of rights over duties and of equating justice with the entitlements of the welfare state. Schall even recognizes the need to transcend the plane of rights, as in the expression "the right to life," which does not capture the virtue of gratitude in having children and is best expressed as receiving the "gift of life."[38] Very few Catholic thinkers have been able to free their minds from the historical bias in favor of liberal modernity and its equation of social justice with modern versions of human rights. It is likely that Fortin and Schall were emboldened by studying Strauss beyond the traditional Catholic resources, enabling them to take steps toward a genuine recovery of Thomistic natural law.

Conclusion: The Benefits of a Straussian Education for Catholics

I began by arguing that the greatness of Leo Strauss is found in the bold and uncompromising way that he thought through the entire Western

---

37. See the third volume of Ernest Fortin, *Human Rights, Virtue, and the Common Good*, ed. J. Brian Benestad (Lanham, Md.: Rowman and Littlefield, 1996).

38. Schall, "Aquinas and the Proper Life of Man," in James V. Schall, *Reason, Revelation, and the Foundations of Political Philosophy* (Baton Rouge: Louisiana State University Press, 1978), 93–128; Schall, "On the 'Right' to be Born," in *Political Philosophy and Revelation: A Catholic Reading* (Washington, D.C.: The Catholic University of America Press, 2013), 217–26; and Schall, *Jacques Maritain: The Philosopher in Society* (Lanham, Md.: Rowman and Littlefield, 1998), 82–97, criticizing Maritain's misuse of natural rights.

canon of philosophy and theology without any preconceived assumptions about the superiority of modern thought. He sought to answer the question of what is ultimate truth in an age when the very idea of "truth" had lost its meaning. His distinctive way of answering that question was to sketch out a complex path of dialectical reasoning that resulted in a series of exclusive choices, some of which we have explored here: reason vs. faith (or philosophy vs. theology), faith vs. law, and ancients vs. moderns. When a Catholic thinker first encounters Strauss, there is a tendency to be disoriented by the challenge of facing exclusive choices that most Catholic theologians blur over by assuming that all good things can be reconciled into a harmonious whole. For many, the exclusive choices almost seem like an affront to belief in a providential God who has ordered the universe in such a way that all good things are possible to combine in a unified and consistent way. Strauss shatters that dream with powerful textual studies that involve relentless scrutiny of the difficult choices.

When scholars take these studies seriously as guides to wisdom, they are humbled and empowered: their dogmatism and intolerance are tempered by learning how difficult it is to attain the fullness of truth, but they are uplifted by the seriousness of the quest for truth. Strauss's chosen path to wisdom is one of the most difficult, as he settles on a lean version of Socratic ignorance which leads us on a never-ending quest for knowledge in the face of the mysterious character of the whole universe, focusing on the human soul in its erotic longings for permanent things without ever attaining them and leaving us forever in suspense. In this critical spirit, I have applied Socratic questioning to Strauss himself and challenged his thinking by offering balanced assessments of his teachings on the major choices.

On the subject of reason and faith, Strauss emphasizes the tensions between philosophy and revelation that we might overlook, although I argued that his case for choosing Socratic philosophy over faith seems inadequate because it is based primarily on the philosopher's own experience of happiness without a supporting cosmology for justifying the perfection of human reason as a way of life. On faith and law, Strauss overstates the oppositions between faith, law, and reason. He seems to denigrate unfairly the role that theology plays in Islam and Judaism and the role that law plays in Christianity. As a result, he avoids studying the content of revelation and shies away from the ultimate mysteries of monotheistic theology. This means Strauss never addresses the issue that he identifies as crucial: "the all-important question which is coeval with philosophy, although the philosophers do not frequently pronounce it—the question of *quid sit deus*," or what is God?[39] On Catholic natural law, Strauss offers advice that is useful and true, namely, that Catholic natural law could use more classical prudence and less doctrinarism in defending modern liberal democracy and human rights, while restoring genuine Thomistic ideas of the temporal common good. [40]

Overall, Strauss makes us aware of the immense difficulties in the quest for ultimate truth about the best way of life. Even when we depart from his guidance and seek to overcome his exclusive choices in some areas, he gives us a deeper and richer sense of Catholic thought than is commonly available in the established theological schools. By wrestling with his uncompromising demands every day, I can say that I have found a rich intellectual and spiritual life as a Catholic or "faith-based" Straussian.

---

39. Leo Strauss, *The City and Man* (Chicago: Rand McNally, 1964), 241.
40. See James V. Schall, "A Latitude for Statesmanship? Strauss on St. Thomas," *Review of Politics* 53, no. 1 (Winter 1991): 126–45.

2

"Wine with Plato and Hemlock with Socrates"

Charles McCoy's Dialogue with Leo Strauss and the Character of Thomistic Political Philosophy

V. BRADLEY LEWIS

Leo Strauss has had many Catholic readers. There are also many kinds of Catholics, and many kinds of Catholic political thinkers presently on the scene (compare, for example, John Finnis, Pierre Manent, and Charles Taylor). Charles N. R. McCoy (1911–84) represents one quite specific type, the Thomist. Of course, there are also many kinds of Thomists: there are existential Thomists, Aristotelian Thomists, and transcendental Thomists; there are the Thomists associated with certain geographical centers like Toronto, Laval, River Forest, and Toulouse. There are primarily historical Thomists and now the analytical Thomists. McCoy was an Aristotelian Thomist associated with the Laval school, about which I will say more presently, but mainly that made him a highly systematic Thomist for whom the ultimate and formative concern of philosophy as such was metaphysics. Moreover, once one has studied metaphysics thoroughly there is no return to the sublunary world of human affairs that is not newly refracted by the perspective of *prima philosophia*. That is not to say that political philosophy is reduced simply or rigidly to applied metaphysics, but the political world looks different from this vantage point. What distinguished McCoy from other Thomists interested in political philosophy, however, is what also made him a serious and, at once, both critical and admiring reader of Leo Strauss, that is, his interest in the history of political philosophy.

McCoy's most important work was his 1963 book, *The Structure of Political Thought*.[1] That book is, so far as I can tell, the only history of political philosophy written from an explicitly Thomistic perspective. The book makes an argument about the history of Western political thought that is closely connected to McCoy's substantive views about political philosophy. It is a history written from within the standpoint of a philosophical tradition and in that respect can be compared to Sidgwick's history of ethics. Like Sidgwick's history it aims less for comprehensiveness than for a kind of illustration; it is an interpretive history centered on an account of the decisive differences between the true political philosophy and subsequent deviations from it. McCoy's narrative bears some important resemblance to Strauss's own understanding of the history of political philosophy. In some cases—for example, Hobbes, Locke, and Rousseau—McCoy explicitly endorses Strauss's own interpretations. In one case, that of Machiavelli, McCoy seems to have arrived independently at a view very close to that of Strauss. There are two other intersections of McCoy's work and that of Strauss. First, McCoy contributed the chapters on Augustine and Aquinas to the first edition of the *History of Political Philosophy* edited by Strauss and Joseph Cropsey.[2] Those chapters were dropped and replaced by new chapters written by Father Ernest Fortin in the second edition. Second, McCoy wrote a substantial critical essay on Strauss's thought published in the *Review of Politics* in 1973.[3] It is dense and bears the marks of long familiarity with Strauss's writings.

McCoy was not, as I said above, Strauss's only Catholic reader, even

---

1. Charles N. R. McCoy, *The Structure of Political Thought: A Study in the History of Political Ideas* (New York: McGraw-Hill, 1963). Most of McCoy's other substantial writings are collected in *On the Intelligibility of Political Philosophy: Essays of Charles N.R. McCoy*, ed. James V. Schall and John J. Schrems (Washington, D.C.: The Catholic University of America Press, 1989). For a complete bibliography of McCoy's writings see John J. Schrems, "A New Annotated Bibliography of Charles N.R. McCoy," *Catholic Social Science Review* 11 (2006): 275–92.

2. "St. Augustine" and "St. Thomas Aquinas," in *History of Political Philosophy*, ed. Leo Strauss and Joseph Cropsey (Chicago: Rand McNally, 1963), 151–59, 201–26.

3. "On the Revival of Classical Political Philosophy," *Review of Politics* 35 (1963): 161–79, reprinted in *On the Intelligibility*, 131–49 (citations below follow the latter).

putting aside those Catholic readers who can be considered in some sense Straussians, like Father Fortin. What McCoy's dialogue with Strauss illustrates is a dialogue between a certain kind of humanistic approach to political things and one that develops out of a highly systematic tradition of philosophical inquiry.[4] In what follows I first give a somewhat fuller introduction to McCoy and his Thomism. Then, I discuss the three main intersections between McCoy and Strauss: McCoy's chapters in the Strauss-Cropsey history, *The Structure of Political Thought*, and his 1973 essay on Strauss. Finally I make some suggestions about the most important differences between Strauss and McCoy and their implications for the enterprise of Thomistic political philosophy. Here a major locus of disagreement concerned their respective understandings of differences not simply between ancient political philosophy and Aquinas, but about ancient philosophy itself, specifically about Aristotle. This is at the center of a major difference about the character of natural right, which, I argue, is ultimately bound up with a deeper and more significant disagreement about the character of the common good.

Charles N. R. McCoy

Charles Nicholas Reiten McCoy was born in Brooklyn in 1911 and earned his bachelor's degree at Dartmouth College in 1932.[5] He earned two doctorates: the first in political science and the second in philosophy. His political science dissertation was written under Jerome Kerwin at the University of Chicago on the riveting topic of "The Law Relating to Public Inland Waters" and completed in 1938. More important than the topic of the thesis was the fact that it was written under Kerwin, who was a serious and theoretically minded Catholic.[6] During this time McCoy

   4. I understand the notion of a tradition of philosophical inquiry pretty much in the way described by Alasdair MacIntyre in especially *Whose Justice? Which Rationality?* (Notre Dame, Ind.: University of Notre Dame Press, 1988), chap. 18; and *Three Rival Versions of Moral Enquiry: Encyclopaedia, Genealogy, and Tradition* (Notre Dame, Ind.: University of Notre Dame Press, 1990), chaps. 3 and 6.
   5. For the biographical information reported here see the memorial notice by Charles Dechert published in *Laval théologique et philosophique* 41 (1985): 109; A. J. Beitzinger's review of *On the Intelligibility* in *Review of Politics* 53 (1991): 416–18; and James V. Schall, SJ, "Transcendent Man in the Limited City: The Political Philosophy of Charles N.R. McCoy," *The Thomist* 57 (1993): 66–67.
   6. It has been plausibly suggested that McCoy wrote on public law under Kerwin in part to avoid working under the main political theorist at Chicago at that time, Charles Merriam. See the introduction to *On the Intelligibility*, 7.

also came under the influence of Richard McKeon, whose Aristotelianism probably influenced McCoy's increasing interest in political philosophy and perhaps his decision to earn a second doctorate. His philosophy dissertation was completed at Laval University in Quebec under the legendary Charles De Koninck in 1951 and concerned Feuerbach's thought and its role in the development of Marxism. McCoy was ordained a priest for the Archdiocese of St. Paul, Minnesota, in 1941 and taught at what was then called the College of St. Thomas from 1941–47, after which he taught at the St. Louis University for six years. In 1953 he moved to the Catholic University of America, where he served for most of that time as chair of the politics department, leaving in 1963. From 1963 to 1976 he taught at the University of Santa Clara; he also established a relationship with Stanford University that allowed him to lecture there for a number of years. He died in Santa Clara in 1984.

It is necessary to say a few words about McCoy's philosophical doctor father, Charles De Koninck, with whom he remained close and whose thought was a decisive influence on McCoy's approach to political philosophy.[7] De Koninck was born in Belgium, but his family emigrated to the U.S. and settled in Detroit when he was a boy. He returned to Belgium to complete his education, culminating in his doctorate completed at Louvain in 1934. He then began teaching at Laval University in Quebec, where in 1939–56 he served as dean of the philosophy faculty. De Koninck died in Rome in February 1965 while serving as a *peritus* to then-Archbishop (of Quebec, and later Cardinal) Maurice Roy during the Second Vatican Council. His most sustained scholarly work was in the philosophy of nature and the philosophy of science.[8] His philosophical method was a strict and highly systematic Thomism, which included what he took to be developments beyond the letter of Thomas's texts by his great commentators, especially Cajetan and John of St. Thomas. He was careful to distinguish philosophy as an enterprise founded on principles accessible to natural reason from theology grounded in revelation and emphasized the importance of logic and the philosophy of nature as necessary prelude to metaphysics and natural theology.

7. Ralph McInerny, "Charles De Koninck: A Philosopher of Order," *New Scholasticism* 39 (1965): 491–516 is a good overview of De Koninck's life and work. It is worth noting here that Father Ernest Fortin also studied briefly with De Koninck and later spoke of him with great respect: see "Why I Am Not a Thomist," in his *Ever Ancient, Ever New: Ruminations on the City, the Soul, and the Church*, ed. Michael P. Foley (Lanham, Md.: Rowman and Littlefield, 2007), 176–77.

8. Most of his writings are collected in *Œvres de Charles De Koninck*, 5 vols. to date (Québec: Les Presses de l'Université Laval, 2009–).

While De Koninck's most important work was in these subjects he maintained an interest in political philosophy. The character of this interest was in some respects more negative than positive. De Koninck was a serious student of Marxism and its philosophical roots, which he took to be grounded in metaphysical errors. Indeed, De Koninck took the most serious political challenges in the modern period to be rooted in bad metaphysics. This led to his involvement in a famous intra-Thomistic controversy about the nature and primacy of the common good in the mid-1940s. De Koninck witnessed with some dismay the increasing prominence of the movement called philosophical personalism among Catholic intellectuals, worrying that it was grounded in dangerously mistaken notions about both the person and the common good that, far from protecting against totalitarian politics as personalist authors argued, would eventually lead to totalitarian results by setting the good of the person against a reified political community liberated from its natural subordination to the most common good, which is God. While he did not name the personalists he opposed, most readers took him to be attacking the thought of Jacques Maritain, the most well-known Catholic thinker alive at the time. One of Maritain's friends, Father Ignatius Eschmann, a German Dominican who taught at the Pontifical Institute for Medieval Studies at the University of Toronto, wrote a harsh critique of De Koninck's book entitled "In Defense of Jacques Maritain," which provoked De Koninck's thermonuclear reply, an essay entitled "In Defense of St. Thomas" that ran to some 103 pages in small type.[9] This controversy took place during the period when McCoy was writing his doctoral dissertation and the letters he exchanged with his dissertation director included discussion of the controversy, which was naturally of interest to McCoy, who had already earned a doctorate in political science.[10]

De Koninck's account of the common good was somewhat abstract—his main concerns were metaphysical. He was most concerned to defend the primacy of the common good, most fully God, as always already built

---

9. De Koninck's book and reply as well as Eschmann's article are available in *The Writings of Charles De Koninck*, vol. 2, ed. and trans. Ralph McInerny (Notre Dame, Ind.: University of Notre Dame Press, 2009) as well as in *Œvres de Charles De Koninck*, vol. 2, part 2.

10. The letters are available in the Charles De Koninck Papers, Jacques Maritain Center, University of Notre Dame, Box 15, File 22. I have discussed this controversy in "Personalism and Common Good: Thomistic Political Philosophy and the Turn to Subjectivity," in *Subjectivity Ancient and Modern*, ed. R. J. Snell and Steven F. McGuire (Lanham, Md.: Lexington Books, 2016), 175–96. See also for more detailed historical information Florian Michel, *La pensée catholique en Amérique du Nord* (Paris: Desclée de Brouwer, 2010), 228–47.

into the proper good of the individual person. This entailed an account of other types of nested common goods, most importantly the order of the universe and the political community. Beyond maintaining that the dignity of the person was best protected by the subordination of the political common good to that of the universe and God himself (no trivial thing), De Koninck provided relatively little specific in the way of political judgments. However, he was later involved in some other more properly political controversies that reveal something of his views. In discussions in Quebec about religious freedom in the schools De Koninck defended religious freedom on grounds of the state's subordination to the transcendent common good and the citizen's prior ordination to religious truth. In the early 1950s De Koninck served as an expert advisor to a panel appointed by the provincial government to study the relationship between the Canadian federal government and the governments of the confederated provinces. De Koninck wrote a lengthy paper defending the integrity of the provinces and their autonomy relative to the national government based on his understanding of Aristotle and Aquinas.[11] Both positions make De Koninck sound similar to many political conservatives in the U.S. and one can see this in McCoy's thought as well, particularly in his understanding of constitutionalism. McCoy, however, was far more steeped in the history of political philosophy than De Koninck, who, apart from his interest in Marxism, concentrated his efforts in understanding and expounding Thomism. McCoy was no less a Thomist, but he did devote his energies to the whole history of political philosophy, eventually (as noted above) writing the only history of the subject written from an explicitly Thomist perspective. That perspective is most clearly set out in McCoy's chapter on Aquinas in the first edition of the Strauss-Cropsey history.

McCoy's Aquinas

It has often been observed that Strauss's substantive philosophical views are difficult to determine, closely interwoven as they are with his interpretations of the works of the great texts in the history of political philos-

---

11. See "La Confédération, rempart contre le Grand État" (1956), in *Œuvres de Charles De Koninck*, 3:65–97.

ophy. This was not the case with McCoy. Much of McCoy's admiration for Strauss was for Strauss's readings of modern philosophers especially, who McCoy himself also endeavored to read carefully and to understand on their own terms. Nevertheless, McCoy's formative concerns were philosophical in a systematic way quite distinct from those of Strauss. This is not unexpected in a thinker self-consciously identified with a philosophical tradition like Thomism, and accordingly one sees it most clearly in McCoy's understanding of Aquinas's own thought. There are two crucial points to be made here. First, McCoy considered Aquinas's views to be simply correct; Aquinas established a perspective from which political things could best be understood both normatively and empirically. Second, Aquinas did this on the basis of Aristotle, that is, by extending and, in some cases, correcting Aristotle's own political philosophy in a way that was compatible with Aristotle's own principles. One can perhaps see the sense in which McCoy considered Aquinas's political thought to be the simple truth of the matter by comparing the 1963 chapter on Aquinas that he contributed to the first edition of the Strauss-Cropsey *History of Political Philosophy* to the 1967 article on "political philosophy" as such that he contributed to the *New Catholic Encyclopedia*.[12]

The chapter on Aquinas begins with a lengthy (it takes up about a third of the chapter) discussion of the question of church and state, the main point of which is that Aquinas's views about this were a development out of Aristotle's argument for the superiority of the contemplative to the practical life. Politics is architectonic in its supervision of all aspects of life in their practice, but not over the content of speculative science. It is this that, from an Aristotelian perspective, establishes the independence and transcendence of the church and is thus the ultimate locus of human freedom. McCoy follows this with a discussion, broken up into several distinct parts, of constitutional government, where, again, starting with Aristotelian principles, Aquinas is said to develop an account of self-government and of the constitutional mixed monarchy more clearly than did Aristotle. It concludes with a statement of the limitations inherent in even the best political regime relative to the imperfections of human life that establishes on Thomistic grounds a kind of moderate political realism. This is all supported by eighty-three notes with detailed references to both Aristotle and Aquinas. The encyclopedia article on po-

---

12. The entry is reprinted in *On the Intelligibility*, 275–90.

litical philosophy begins with an account of the human good that emphasizes the distinction between the speculative and the practical and the architectonic character of politics as a practical science. It then presents an exposition of constitutionalism, of the best form of government, and of the limitations of law. The substantive content is nearly identical to what is in the Aquinas chapter as is the order of its presentation. The only real differences are that the article contains only six footnotes (all to Aristotle, Aquinas, and St. Robert Bellarmine) and concludes with a discussion of the idea of an international community of states. McCoy wrote a companion article for the encyclopedia on the history of political philosophy that is essentially a summary of *The Structure of Political Thought*. The content of the main points of normative political philosophy itself, however, is essentially the same as the exposition of the thought of St. Thomas.

It is well to dwell a bit more on the chapter on Aquinas from the first edition of the Strauss-Cropsey *History* in light of the fact that the chapter was dropped from the second edition, along with McCoy's chapter on Augustine, and replaced with chapters by Ernest Fortin. It would seem that the reasons for the replacement of McCoy's contributions with chapters by Fortin could plausibly be inferred by noting interpretive and contextual differences between them, and, such inference can perhaps be supported by noticing some differences between McCoy's account and that given by Strauss himself in some of his writings. I will limit myself here to pointing out some key differences in the two chapters on Aquinas.

First, there is an important difference in what may be called methodological perspective. McCoy's systematic interests are evident in his somewhat greater attention to subsequent Thomistic thinkers at points in his essay, especially Bellarmine and Suarez. Fortin's concern is more with Thomas's predecessors and contemporaries among writers of the patristic period and the political thinkers of the Jewish and Islamic traditions. This shows McCoy's concern to expound what was for him a living tradition, that is, a doctrine that developed in the face of changing political phenomena and its own internal disputes. Fortin was more concerned to situate Aquinas within the world of alternative answers to philosophical problems connected to the relationship of the various religious thinkers to either Plato or Aristotle and about the relationship of reason and revelation. He was also relatively unconcerned with the Thomistic tradition as such, aiming to understand just what he took to be the substance of Thomas's thought. It is noteworthy that neither McCoy nor Fortin were much concerned with the sorts of issues that often concern medievalists in the more technical sense—for example, the relationship of Aquinas's views to, say, contemporary masters at the University of Paris or Naples or of Aquinas's traditional or innovative posing of questions relative to the antecedent and contemporary framing of the various *quaestiones disputatae*. Both treat Aquinas as a thinker to be understood rather than, as it were, explained.

Second, there is an important substantive difference related to Aquinas's Aristotelianism, an issue which comes to the fore at the very beginning of each chapter. McCoy writes that Thomas "substantially adopts the political doctrine of Aristotle," qualifying the statement only to the extent of saying that with respect to two questions "Thomas's thought extends beyond Aristotle's treatment."[13] In an earlier essay McCoy wrote that "the work of St. Thomas was to remove from Aristotle's achievement certain ambiguities and latent errors."[14] McCoy took Aristotle to have essentially soundly established political philosophy and Aquinas in his commentaries and in his own expositions to have offered authoritative interpretation, development, and, in some case, correction. This is very much in keeping with the Laval approach.[15] Fortin, by contrast, begins his own chapter by characterizing Aquinas's political philosophy as "a modification of Aristotle's political philosophy in the light of Christian revelation or more precisely as an attempt to integrate Aristotle with an earlier tradition of Western political thought represented by the Church fathers and their medieval followers and compounded for the most part of elements taken from the Bible, Platonic-Stoic philosophy, and Roman law."[16] Fortin subsequently writes of Aquinas's use of Aristotle as "reinterpret[ation],"

---

13. McCoy, "St. Thomas Aquinas," 201.

14. "St. Thomas and Political Science," in *On the Intelligibility*, 25 (the essay was originally published in 1947).

15. A window on that approach is provided by a 1946 letter from Charles De Koninck to Father Jules Baisnée, a professor at the Catholic University of America, written just after the publication of Eschmann's critique of De Koninck's book on the common good. De Koninck recounts his previous relationship with Eschmann, including the time Eschmann spent teaching at Laval just after his exile from Germany began. De Koninck writes, "We had received him and, I must say, spoiled him as a poor victim of the Nazis. Only once had there been a slight altercation between him and myself, when I insisted that he use as the basis of his lectures in our Faculty the very text of Aristotle's Politics and the commentary of St. Thomas and Peter of Auvergne. But I thought this might be settled later when he had become better acquainted with our method." The letter, dated March 3, 1946, is in the Charles De Koninck Papers, Box 14, File 3.

16. Fortin, "St. Thomas Aquinas," 248.

as "transforming it in both content and in spirit," and as having "modified [it] ... profoundly."[17] So Fortin and McCoy disagree about the extent of Thomas's Aristotelianism. How so?

A third contrast illustrates best the difference over Aquinas's relationship to Aristotle. I noted above that McCoy held Aquinas to go beyond Aristotle in two respects. We now need to note that these were, first, Aquinas's view of the proper relationship of church and state (the former nonexistent in Aristotle's time), and, second, his views about the nature of constitutional government and the best regime. The first of these questions occupies about a third of McCoy's chapter. As noted above, McCoy held that Thomas's view was a development of Aristotle's account of the superiority of the speculative to the practical and its implications for the limitations he defended of the state's architectonic authority over human affairs. By contrast, Fortin's chapter scarcely discusses the church-state question. The longest section in Fortin's chapter is devoted to what was in his view Aquinas's most consequential deviation from Aristotle, his account of the natural law. It occupies nine pages of his twenty-three-page essay. McCoy's discussion of natural law is contained in his section on constitutional government. This seems initially a bit odd, though perhaps less so on reflection: McCoy begins with Aristotle's thesis that nature acts for an end and Aquinas's gloss on this to the effect that "reason is put into things by the divine art so that they be moved to a determinate end."[18] This is precisely God's government of the universe; it is a government in which human beings, unlike other beings, are not merely subjects, but participants through their knowledge of ends and consequent mastery of their own actions. This knowledge of ends and self-direction is the natural law and so the natural law is the basis of human self-government both individually and politically. Human self-government is a participation in the divine government as natural law is a participation in eternal law. McCoy's development of this point is very matter-of-fact as is his seemingly insouciant acknowledgement of its theological character.

For Fortin, Aquinas's natural law indicates his distance from Aristotle insofar as the natural law as a "more doctrinal or more strictly deductive" approach to human affairs largely supplants Aristotle's concern with what was for the classical philosophers generally the central topic of

---

17. Ibid., 248, 253, 257; see also 270.
18. McCoy, "St. Thomas Aquinas," 208 (quoting Aquinas, *In Physics* VIII, lectio 14, no. 8).

political philosophy, the question of the best regime.[19] This goes along with Aquinas's reworking of Aristotle's classification of the moral virtues, and, more importantly, the role of *conscientia* and *synderesis* in Thomas's moral theory, notions that have no precise equivalents in Aristotle (one must note, however, that, while *synderesis* is a name not used by Aristotle, it refers to the immediate grasp of practical first principles on analogy to Aristotle's virtue of *nous* by which speculative *archai* are immediately grasped). In his own characterization of Thomas's account of natural law Fortin presses three points. First, natural law "not only recommends or discourages certain actions as intrinsically noble or base, it commands or forbids them under pain of retribution if not in this life at least in the next," thus presupposing the existence of God and the immortality of the soul.[20] Second, "the natural law supplies only the most general standards of human behavior or the unshakable foundations on which man's knowledge of the moral order rests."[21] Third, Fortin emphasizes the absolute character of principles of the natural law even in the face of the "most extreme situations" such as to preclude "the very possibility that the common good or the preservation of society should at times compel one to act in a manner contrary to these principles."[22] Thus, he concludes:

> Between the requirements of justice and those of civil society there is a fundamental and necessary harmony. The perfect social order exists or is capable of existing in deed and not only in speech. Justice in the absolute sense is not only approximated by civil justice, it actually coincides with it. By the same token man's perfection as an individual turns out to be identical with his perfection as a citizen.[23]

There is more to be said about these three points, but first it is worth noticing that Fortin is here following closely Leo Strauss's own understanding of Aquinas.

Strauss makes the same point about the non-Aristotelian provenance of the ideas of *conscientia* and *synderesis* and the larger point that the notion of immutable rules is alien to Aristotle's notion of what is *phusei dikaion*.[24] He suggests his own interpretation of Aristotle's famously

---

19. Fortin, "St. Thomas Aquinas," 259.
20. Ibid., 265.
21. Ibid.
22. Ibid., 266–67.
23. Ibid., 267.
24. Leo Strauss, *Natural Right and History* (Chicago: University of Chicago Press, 1953), 157–59.

mysterious statement in *Nicomachean Ethics* V.7 that while there is a difference between natural and conventional right "all of it is changeable" as referring to concrete decisions founded upon more general principles. This is offered as an alternative to Aquinas's interpretation, grounded not in decisions but in rules. McCoy's view—although it is not stated in precisely this way, nor as an answer to Strauss—does not seem to me to be so very different from that of Strauss. For example, he notes toward the end of his discussion of natural law in the Strauss-Cropsey chapter that "there is indeed a difference in degree of imperiousness even in the things that are known naturally, a degree of difference that constitutes one of the ways in which the distinction between primary and secondary precepts of natural law is made."[25] Strauss himself emphasizes the first principles; Fortin goes so far initially as simply to identify the natural law with them. Thomas, however, never said this, but said that only the first principles were *per se nota*. The secondary principles required more in the way of judgment and consequently allow for more variability and error. Final judgments or decisions are still further from the first principles and in many cases require more than average wisdom to get right. That is the very point of the famous example about borrowed weapons.[26] But this is not the end of the matter.

For Aquinas the natural law is law, indeed, law in the fullest sense.[27] It therefore fully possesses the character of law as Aquinas defines it in his famous formulation, a formulation that follows Aristotle's four forms of causality and assigns as law's final cause the common good. This is the nub of the problem, as Strauss suggests that Thomas's notion of natural law is to an important degree in tension with the common good. Strauss understood the common good to consist in what is demanded by commutative and distributive justice, but more basically, in "the mere existence, the mere survival, the mere independence, of the political community, of the political community in question."[28] "In extreme situations," Strauss writes, "there may be conflicts between what the self-preservation of society requires, and the requirements of commutative and distributive justice."[29] Such extreme situations involve war and also internal threats to

---

25. McCoy, "St. Thomas Aquinas," 210.
26. *Summa Theologiae*, I-II, q. 94, a. 4, co.
27. *Summa Theologiae*, I-II, q. 90, a. 4: "Lex enim naturalis maxime habet rationem legis."
28. Strauss, *Natural Right and History*, 160.
29. Ibid.

peace and Strauss says that what may be demanded in such situations to protect the society cannot be anticipated in advance because it is to some degree determined by what the enemy may do, "possibly an absolutely unscrupulous and savage enemy." The ordinary rules are justly changed in such circumstances. He goes on, "One could say that in all cases the common good must be preferred to the private good and that this rule suffers no exception." In extreme cases the common good may justify acts that are not justifiable according to the ordinary rules of justice, but what defines an extreme situation is not formulable in terms of rules.[30]

Aquinas's understanding of the natural law does not seem to allow for such exceptions. It is striking that while Strauss explicitly takes up Aquinas in the immediate sequel to the passages just discussed, he does not state this precise point, but rather intimates it by focusing on the extent to which Thomas's account seems to rely on not only natural theology, but biblical revelation. He concludes that Montesquieu's position on these matters is closer to that of the classics in that he tried "to recover for statesmanship a latitude which had been considerably restricted by the Thomistic teaching."[31] This discussion is generally in terms of the natural law simply and it is certainly crucial for understanding Strauss's view; however, I think the real issue here is a bit deeper than that: it is Strauss's understanding of the common good. This is the nerve of his disagreement with McCoy. For Strauss the common good is the common good of particular societies; for McCoy, however, the common good is a complex analogical idea, but one can say that the common good in the fullest sense is God, and secondarily the order of the universe. The temporal or political common good comes third, and even here, it is not simply restricted to closed political societies, but exists even at the international level in the relationship of human beings to one another simply as such. But to see this more clearly we need to look at McCoy's most elaborate

---

30. Ibid., 160–61.
31. Ibid., 164. Strauss does not give examples here of what he means beyond a general suggestion about the need for espionage. Espionage, however, can mean many things. I think John Finnis was correct in surmising that Strauss had in mind some of the tactics used by the allies in World War II as well as the possible use of nuclear weapons against the Soviet Union and the general policy of deterrence. See "Moral Absolutes in Aristotle and Aquinas," in Finnis, *Reason in Action, Collected Essays: Volume 1* (Oxford: Oxford University Press, 2011), 187–89; and "Limited Government," in Finnis, *Human Rights & Common Good, Collected Essays, Volume 3* (Oxford: Oxford University Press, 2011), 86–87. Elizabeth Anscombe famously argued against the allied policy and subsequent deterrence strategy on natural law grounds in "War and Murder" (1961) and "Mr Truman's Degree" (1957), reprinted in *Collected Philosophical Papers of G. E. M. Anscombe, Volume III: Ethics, Religion and Politics* (Oxford: Blackwell, 1981), 51–71.

statement of his own view of the history of political philosophy in his only book, *The Structure of Political Thought*.

The Structure of Political Thought

The Structure of Political Thought is an interpretive history of political philosophy, that is, it aims at constructing and illustrating a narrative, not at anything like an exhaustive academic history even in the sense attempted by Sabine. Moreover, it is driven by a substantive normative account of political philosophy. Indeed, the very title of the book refers not, as one might initially think, to the structure of the history of political thought, but to the structure of political thought itself.[32] It is a kind of Thomistic "Critique of Political Reason" written as a history rather than as an expository treatise. Alternately one might better compare it to the history of philosophy in Aristotle's *Metaphysics*. For our purposes the most important aspects of the book are, first, McCoy's actual characterization of the "structure" of political thought, and second, how the history he recounts is related to this structure. Aspects of the history are quite similar to Strauss's understanding of the history of political philosophy, but others are not. At the center of both of these issues is McCoy's understanding of the common good.

By the "structure of political thought" McCoy meant the "subordination of practical science to theoretic science and, within the sphere of practical science, on the subordination of art to prudence."[33] This was essentially the achievement of Aristotle, although it was perfected by Aquinas. At the root of these distinctions are Aristotle's logic and theory of knowledge, which are deployed to establish the character of political knowledge as first practical and second a prudence as distinct from an art. Man's intellect is measured by its objects in theoretical science, but in practical science it does the measuring; however, as there are already ends proper to human beings given by nature, this measuring is constrained. It also depends on the right disposition of the will and can be

---

32. On this see the discussion in James V. Schall, SJ, "'Man for Himself': On the Ironic Unities of Political Philosophy," *Political Science Reviewer* 15 (1985): 72–73.
33. McCoy, *Structure of Political Thought*, 157. This is the clearest statement of the idea in the book and I merely note—the reader may make of it what he will—that it occurs on page 157 of a total of 314, that is, at the precise center of the text.

opposed by the sense appetites. This means that rule always meets with opposition, but must proceed as the reason does relative to the passions in an individual, politically, that is, over subjects who are themselves free. The artist, by contrast, is the master of his materials, materials that cannot resist. Political rule's prudential character means that it must in some respects be cooperative, but also that it must be concerned with the habits and mores of citizens. It must also contend with the variability and obscurity endemic to contingent particulars.

This concern for the distinction between prudence and art already indicates something about the nature of freedom, as Aristotle's conception of prudence and political rule recognize that the root of political self-government is personal self-government. The character of freedom is further explained by McCoy's treatment of the relationship between the practical-political and the contemplative. For McCoy's Aristotle the very integrity of political life depends on the primacy of the contemplative because "the rule of the appetite by the rational principle (which produces the political virtues) presupposes theoretic rectitude concerning man's nature and end."[34] "Without the primacy of speculative truth," he continues, "all practical regulation dissolves: Man, human good, and society become simply and wholly what we want them to be." This would be the transformation of prudence into art and its end result is "universal despotism."[35] This primacy of the theoretical is also politically important insofar as it presupposes a particular understanding of the common good. How so?

McCoy repeatedly returned to Aristotle's statement in the *Nicomachean Ethics* that if man were the best thing in the cosmos then political science and prudence would be the most perfect knowledge, but man is not the highest thing.[36] Turning then to the *Metaphysics*, he notes that for Aristotle the universe contains the highest good both in the order of its parts and separately, as an army does in its internal order but also in its leader on whom it depends. In the case of the universe this leader is/are the gods whose whole life is one of exemplary contemplative activity. So too man's highest activity is the possession of this highest object of thought.[37] It is noteworthy that McCoy appends to a statement of Aristo-

34. Ibid., 47.
35. Ibid.
36. Ibid., 48 (quoting Aristotle, *Nicomachean Ethics* 1141a20).
37. Ibid., 48–49 (quoting Aristotle, *Metaphysics* 1075a12 and 1072b14).

tle's injunction to pursue this most godlike life in the sixth book of the *Nicomachean Ethics* a footnote in which he quotes Strauss's essay, "On Classical Political Philosophy," on the transcendence of the philosophical life over the political.[38] I suspect that at this time McCoy took Strauss's view to be rather closer to his own than he later did, but this is a point to which we shall return in the next section. It is in the immediate sequel that McCoy connects all this more clearly to his understanding of the common good. The highest objects of thought are the first causes of the order of the universe, which is its intrinsic good and the fullest imitation of the highest beings themselves (McCoy always uses the singular although this is not necessarily the case in Aristotle). Both these extrinsic and intrinsic common goods are more divine than the proper goods of beings, and the human common good is more divine than the private goods of any individuals just insofar as it is a good that is communicable to many.[39] The nobility of the political life then derives from its analogical relationship to the common good in the highest sense, which is both the final cause of everything in the universe and the object of the highest powers of man.

McCoy goes on to emphasize three aspects of the common good. First, it cannot be conceived of as opposed to the proper goods of the individuals who make up society because its order is not that of a logical whole; it extends to the many members of society in their diversity not through the indetermination of commonality by mere predication, but as a common final cause. Second, neither can it simply be identified with the proper good of individuals; rather it is good precisely in its communicability to many individuals and not as including the totality of their singular goods. Third, the common good as final cause of human societies is different from the common goods of organic wholes or mere collectivities. In neither of these is there any action of the parts that is not principally an action of the whole. This is obviously true in the case of organic wholes; in the case of collectivities (e.g., a society of ants or bees) it is true because the individual parts do not engage in self-direction. A society of human beings by contrast is a unity of order wherein the whole exercises genuine agency, but so can the parts, whose direction to their common good must include an element of freedom. It is this that distinguishes Aristotle's view from any kind of organicism or totalitarianism.[40]

38. Ibid., 49n2.
39. Ibid., 50.
40. Ibid., 51–53.

Three things about this account deserve our attention. It is, first of all, reported as the view or doctrine of Aristotle, which is to say again that the basic structure of political thought was the achievement of Aristotle. Second, however, while the account is reported as that of Aristotle and in a chapter on Aristotle, its exposition is often done in terms that are not readily recognizable in Aristotle, but are Thomistic. In the first twenty-four pages of the Aristotle chapter there are thirteen citations of texts of Aquinas to twenty-four citations of Aristotle himself. Indeed, it is difficult to determine where Aristotle ends and Aquinas begins. Moreover, and third, it is worth noting again how indebted McCoy's account is to that of De Koninck (who is cited twice in those pages). McCoy's actual treatment of Aquinas is unevenly divided between two chapters and this division tracks the principal division of his Strauss-Cropsey chapter on Aquinas: the first is part of a chapter on church and state and the second is part of a chapter on constitutional government. The section of the church-state chapter is brief and largely devoted to Aquinas's understanding of the independence of the church and the relationship of ecclesiastical and temporal authority, although that chapter begins by restating McCoy's interpretation of Aristotle on the transcendence of the common good as guarantee of the integrity of political life. The form of that transcendence in the medieval period is bound up with the church-state question. The chapter on constitutional government is entirely about Aquinas, and its second paragraph states, "all that I have said on Aristotle's political doctrine is not only substantially adopted by St. Thomas Aquinas, but indeed, that doctrine is greatly in debt to the extraordinarily profound and thorough explication made of it by St. Thomas."[41] The rest of the chapter is in its order and content very similar to the Strauss-Cropsey chapter.

The last quotation is important also as underscoring the idea that animates McCoy's book: note the treatment of "that doctrine" as the subject of the second clause. Aristotle's achievement was to have given expression to the fundamental truth about political things, the structure of political thought, and the doctrine is in Aquinas's debt for extensions and improvements.[42] There could be no more clear affirmation of the notion

---

41. Ibid., 133.

42. Here, I think, we see another aspect of McCoy's understanding Thomistic-Aristotelianism as a kind of MacIntyrean tradition *avant la lettre*, an understanding that sometimes strains at the book's historical character. William P. Haggerty, "Beyond the Letter of his Master's Thought: C. N. R. McCoy on Medieval Political Theory," *Laval théologique et philosophique* 64 (2008): 467–83, rightly notes the structural oddness of the chapters that discuss Aquinas and points out the curiosity of McCoy's

of a *philosophia politica perennis*. That is the story of the first half of the book; the second half of the book describes the progressive repudiation of that structure by modern thinkers culminating in Marxism, which is its precise opposite.

McCoy stands with Strauss in seeing in Machiavelli a fundamental break with the classical-Christian tradition—however, they diverge a bit after Machiavelli. Where Strauss famously saw three waves of modernity, McCoy saw two. The modern theory of politics began with a reversal of the order of art and prudence: Machiavelli represented the politician as artist, free to exercise his creative ambitions on the material of his community. McCoy made much of what was then the innovation of reading Machiavelli's *The Prince* in light of the *Discourses* to achieve a unitary account of the great Florentine's thought. Where many of these interpreters saw a more benign thinker, a humanist and Italian patriot motivated by his conceptions of virtue and the common good, Strauss famously saw a "teacher of evil" and so did McCoy. He anticipates later interpreters like Roger Masters, who saw in Machiavelli also the influence of the new physics. For McCoy Machiavelli was a reductionist who deployed terms like virtue and common good, but emptied them of their previous content. He was indeed motivated by patriotism, but a patriotism freed from the limits of the transcendent common good and the natural law. For him the statesman was a creative genius who would use all his guile to awaken a corrupt citizenry to the attractions of essentially pagan Roman greatness. McCoy does not cite Strauss in his Machiavelli chapter, which seems initially odd since *Thoughts on Machiavelli* had appeared in 1958, five years before *The Structure of Political Thought*. However, McCoy's Machiavelli chapter was essentially a reprinting of an article he had published in the *American Political Science Review* in 1943, years before Strauss's first publications on Machiavelli.[43] McCoy arrived at his view simply by comparing the picture that emerged from the recent scholarship and his own reading of Machiavelli to his account of the "structure" erected by Aristotle and Aquinas. There is one other interesting aspect of McCoy's view: he did not reject the idea that Machiavelli should be read as a Renaissance

---

criticism of Marsilius of Padua's church-state theory, one that is predicated on a strict defense of the letter of Aristotle's teaching, and defense of Aquinas's account as fundamentally more in line with Aristotle's deepest principles but against the strict letter.

43. McCoy, "The Place of Machiavelli in the History of Political Thought," *American Political Science Review* 37 (1943): 626–41.

humanist; he instead pointed to the limitations of humanism as an intellectual movement. "The revival of learning in the fifteenth century," he wrote, "differed from its predecessors in that it was an artistic rather than a philosophical movement."[44] This artistic perspective linked Machiavelli's politics to the new science. McCoy's fundamental attitude was that of the schoolmen, not the humanists, and this too indicates something about his relationship to Strauss.

The second phase of modernity completes the repudiation of the Thomistic-Aristotelian view: it "seeks a new moral basis for society and does so by reversing the order between theoretic science and practical science (in which art already has the ascendency)."[45] It will seek, McCoy wrote, the liberty proper to divine art "and it will define the good in terms not of the end which man seeks but rather in terms of the very *being* of man which becomes the principle from which all things are made—all things humanly significant, which becomes the totality of significance."[46] He traces this process first through the transformation of the idea of natural law beginning with Bodin's theory of sovereignty and Grotius's explicit secularization, thence through Hobbes, Locke, and Rousseau. In his treatment of the last three McCoy is indebted to Strauss, as acknowledged in numerous references to articles of Strauss and to *Natural Right and History*. The fundamental nature of the process, however, is characterized by McCoy in a way that is not so close to Strauss: he describes it as the rejection of the Aristotelian notion of a prime intellect (explicitly theologized by Aquinas) and the assimilation of the human to the nonhuman in a reductionist account of nature that is confined to material and efficient causality. The unfolding of the tale, however, does seem close especially to *Natural Right and History*, including McCoy's critical treatment of Burke. However, the last two chapters are a distinctive study of Marxism as the final culmination of the modern project in the development first in Feuerbach and later in Marx of a humanism that, with its goal of the achievement by man of "species being," finally makes the entire universe subject to human domination, although a thoroughly pyrrhic victory for the individual who is swallowed whole by society conceived according to a view of the common good that is at once reduced to

---

44. McCoy, *Structure of Political Thought*, 159.
45. Ibid., 158.
46. Ibid.

the human and imminent and also completely alienating. Here again the influence of De Koninck is powerful.⁴⁷

The "structure" then is achieved in the Thomistic-Aristotelian account of the priority of contemplation to politics and of prudence to art in the political realm, and then gradually rejected until reaching its complete antithesis in activist Marxism. But that description is a bit too simple because the formative Aristotle chapter is preceded by a chapter on Plato and followed by a chapter on the political thought of late antiquity. Both of these evince substantial differences of perspective with Strauss. The discussion of Plato is surprisingly brief. McCoy took Platonic philosophy to have emerged from Heraclitus's speculations about being and becoming and Socrates's discovery of inductive thought. Plato essentially grafted the one onto the other, but in so doing he committed a philosophical error that led to a dangerously erroneous political philosophy. According to McCoy Plato identified the "real existence of things with their existence in the mind," the real order with the logical order.⁴⁸ This confusion gave birth to the theory of ideas, leading directly to the misguided political doctrines of Plato's *Republic*, which envisions an idealized political order in which the real parts of political society are absorbed into the whole.⁴⁹ Suffice it to say that this is a very different reading indeed from that of Strauss.⁵⁰ It is, however, very close in spirit to the reading of the *Republic* and the attendant criticisms found in the second book of Aristotle's *Politics* and endorsed in the fragment we have of Thomas's commentary.

McCoy's discussion of the political thought of late antiquity is quite abstract and flies very high above any actual texts from the period, relying rather on secondary works by contemporary scholars and observations of McCoy's own constructed out of comparisons to Aristotle and Aquinas. McCoy emphasizes what he takes to be the paradox that the larger size of political units achieved in the world of the Persian and Roman empires, far from giving rise to a loftier conception of the common good, yield-

---

47. Feuerbach was the subject of McCoy's doctorate under De Koninck. One can see the influence by comparing *Structure of Political Thought*, chaps. 9 and 10, to De Koninck, *De la primauté du bien commun contre les personalistes*, part 2, in *Œvres de Charles De Koninck*, 2:2:159–68, 185–92.

48. McCoy, *Structure of Political Thought*, 18.

49. Ibid., 22.

50. The first to criticize McCoy's reading of Plato was, interestingly, another student of Charles De Koninck, Ralph McInerny in his review of *Structure of Political Thought* in *New Scholasticism* 39 (1965): 405–7. See also Schall, "Man for Himself," 77.

ed philosophies that "emphasized opposition between the common good and individual good."⁵¹ The ideal of citizenship was replaced by a kind of alienation and a withdrawal of philosophy from the political world. They privileged private self-sufficiency over the political common good and reduced the scope of the contemplative life to the affairs of the individual. McCoy admits an exception here for late Stoicism, which does value the political virtues, but in a way that elevates them over the speculative. This led to a kind of proto-humanism according to which, contrary to Aristotle's view, man was really the best thing in the universe. The one positive contribution of this era came from the Stoic understanding of natural law combined with the substance of Roman civil law, but the full development of these ideas had to await their recontextualization by a Christian political theology that had also reappropriated Aristotle. As in the case of Plato, McCoy's views here are very different from those of Strauss, at least with respect to the one Hellenistic movement of thought about which Strauss wrote, Lucretius's Epicureanism. But this raises again the question of the nature and primacy of speculative thought, which is to say of philosophy and its relationship to the common good, and on this question, at any rate, we have a very direct engagement by McCoy with Strauss's views in his 1973 article on Strauss, to which I now turn.

McCoy's Strauss

While McCoy's essay on Strauss evinces great admiration, its purpose is critical, and the center of criticism concerns Strauss's views about the relationship between Plato and Aristotle.⁵² Both see an important difference between the two, but take opposite sides in the ancient dispute. McCoy begins by crediting Strauss with the revival of classical political philosophy, but agrees with some of Strauss's critics that the revival has been effected in a series of writings characterized by a studied obscurity. McCoy's intention is to penetrate the obscurity concerning Strauss's views about classical natural right. It is clear that Strauss sees the fullest articulation of the classical view in Plato, but the very terms in which

---

51. McCoy, *Structure of Political Thought*, 76.
52. Even the essay's critical purpose, however, testifies to McCoy's respect for Strauss as a thinker; he devoted no comparable critical study to any other contemporary. Beitzinger, moreover, called the essay "arguably the best paper [McCoy] ever wrote."

Strauss defended this view seem to have provoked McCoy: the "divine madness" and "intemperance of thought" Strauss associates with Plato seem to offer little attraction beside the moderation and sobriety of Aristotle, who is also understood by Strauss to offer a natural right already occluded or compromised. Put another way, McCoy attributes to Strauss the view that in Aristotle there is already the sort of "lowering of the goals" that he famously attributed to modern political philosophy. In *Natural Right and History* Strauss had suggested (a suggestion repeated by Fortin in his replacement chapter on Aquinas) that the classical account of natural right was significantly modified by Aquinas in light of biblical revelation, but McCoy sees the key modification to have been already effected by Aristotle. How so?

Platonic natural right is for Strauss grounded in an ascent to *the* good; all beings are referred to this and it is in light of this that the philosopher evaluates everything. Aristotle, however, takes beings on their own terms, opening the way for the development of separate sciences of the distinct kinds of beings, including political science, grounded in the prudence of the statesman, who is also the good citizen. Prudence is an extension of the perspective of the good citizen, not simply the distracted glance of the philosopher. For Aristotle the speculative mind is measured by its objects and, while practical reasoning itself measures, it is bounded by the ends that already exist in things. For Plato there is a very real sense in which man is the measure—at any rate, the man who is the philosopher. This is encapsulated by Strauss's formulation that for Platonic natural right nature is a "standard," while for McCoy's Aristotelianism it is an "authority." Philosophy can see and judge by standards, but it recognizes no authorities.[53] For both Plato and Aristotle the political life is inferior to the life of philosophy, but for Aristotle this inferiority mirrors the subordination of the practical to the speculative, categories not yet defined in Plato. Most importantly, for Aristotle the special sciences are themselves subordinate to the science of being as being, metaphysics, which is also divine science or natural theology.

McCoy illustrated the way in which these rival accounts related to the question of natural right by comparing Plato and Aristotle on two questions, that of private property and of what McCoy called the principle of indigenousness. In the former case, Strauss holds that perfect

---

53. McCoy, "Revival," 135, 138 (quoting Strauss, *Natural Right and History*, 87, 92).

justice gives to each what is for his own good: the wise man takes the large coat from the small boy and gives it to the bigger boy and gives that boy's smaller coat to the small boy. In the latter case Strauss implies that perfect justice would necessarily be extended globally, thus evincing an indifference to particular societies.[54] Aristotle, by contrast, rejects common possession as unreasonable and at odds with the facts of human nature. Similarly he rejects anything like the world state in his observations about the limitations on the size of political communities. Aristotle held that a world state—even a very large state—implies an attempt to put order into the unlimited.[55] Both of these cases show the difference between taking one's stand on the basis of the logical order as if it really existed and allowing prudence to meet the world as it is.

Withal, McCoy argues, Strauss did understand the tensions between the ideal and the real, the "recalcitrance" that society shows toward the standard, and was prepared to accept Aristotle's views as a kind of second best accommodation. But why, under the circumstances, prefer Plato's overall understanding of natural right? McCoy thinks the answer is to be found in the difference between understanding nature as a "standard," as Strauss held, and understanding nature as an "authority," as Strauss thought Aristotle wrongly did. Taking nature as an authority accepts the deflection of the mind from its ascent to the good itself, halting at the various levels of being where that good is occluded. It also seems to accept as authoritative all of the irrationalities of the world rather than delimiting the truly just and unjust, good and bad. Here McCoy defends Aristotle's view, again, as interpreted in key part by Aquinas and De Koninck. Nature does, on Aristotle's view, operate as a kind of "'reason' put into things so that they may act for determinate ends (*Physics* II)," but "the ultimate reasons of things are not subjectified in the things themselves of the world."[56] Nature does not intend particular contingent outcomes; it does not intend this man or that man, but its intentions cannot be realized but *in* this man or that man. The contingencies of the world as such have their *per se* cause only in God.

To take nature as the "authority" according to Strauss would be to transform philosophy into theology. On this point he and McCoy agree. They disagree, however, about the implications of this outcome. For

---

54. Ibid., 136 (quoting Strauss, *Natural Right and History*, 147–48, 148–49).
55. Ibid., 136–37.
56. Ibid., 139.

McCoy it is simply a necessity. Strauss's view settles on the claim that the most just life is that of the philosopher who instructs us on what is right by nature through the construction of the city in speech, which is "the perfect moral order, the good itself." But McCoy sides with Aristotle in holding that "the good itself" is a logical universal that exists only in predication; it exists only in speech and has no "authority" in nature. Moreover, if one considers the "good" itself as an ontological principle that might exist really, then one has left political science and entered into metaphysics and natural theology. Knowledge of the good as such is not of much use to politics as such. Both points are indebted to Aristotle's criticism of Plato in *Nicomachean Ethics* I.6. But McCoy goes beyond this.

In nature as a "standard" Strauss hoped to find a transcendent guide in the world, but a generic nature cannot provide such a thing. Society resists it, as Strauss acknowledged. This is the tension between philosophy and politics, between Socrates and the city, and McCoy did not think Strauss was ever able to explain the reason for it. The reason is in the notion of the good itself, which, as a logical universal in the order of predication, is not a universal cause; it "does not belong, as a universal, to the real world, to nature as 'authority.'"[57] Strauss's Platonic philosopher-ruler guided by the good itself constitutes the disappearance of the statesman into the philosopher and of the real world into the logical order. At this point, McCoy's own exposition becomes a bit murky due to his splitting what seem to me crucial parts of his argument between his text and his notes. In a footnote to the passage just discussed about the good being a logical universal, but not a universal cause, McCoy notes that one should remain attentive to the causal order itself. Ultimately, the notion of nature as "authority" does depend on a universal cause in the order of reality, the common good in the full sense discussed above in connection with McCoy's exposition of Aristotle in *The Structure of Political Thought*. The common good is a good that diffuses itself to many particular individuals, to the parts of the whole in—not against—their diversity. It is one good, but it does not make society a unitary substance; it is common because it is also in the proper good of the members and so is in no sense an alien good. The political community is also such a common good for its members by analogy as is the good of a family for its members.[58] The

---

57. Ibid., 140.
58. Ibid., 141n45.

common good in the fullest sense is the separate common good of the universe of *Metaphysics* XI, but the notion illuminates the analogically common goods.

Strauss's real mistake here, although I do not think McCoy made his view as clear as he might have, was a mistake about the common good. He took it to be a generic universal good in the order of predication rather than the causally common good in the order of reality. McCoy is clear about why he thinks Strauss thought what he did: it was an attempt to avoid the theological implications in Aristotle's view, implications only fully developed by Aquinas.[59] It is this aspect of Aristotle's account that underwrites nature's status as "authority." McCoy goes on to argue that a consequence of Strauss's preference for nature as "standard," a means of avoiding the theological conclusions, was actually Strauss's own practical lowering of goals.[60] According to Strauss the early modern philosophers reverted to nature as standard, but rejected the classical view as too closely connected to the theology developed out of it by the medieval theologians. Their standard was a modern idea of nature shorn of final causality and thus reduced to efficient and material causes. There is certainly no possibility here for nature as "authority." Whatever ends left in nature are internal to nature itself via the "substitute intelligence" left over after the divine art, that of the first mover, has been purged: essence is reduced to existence. "Law" on this view describes not an orientation to goods, but merely the immanent properties of things.[61] This approach was oddly more similar to Plato's own because Plato's understanding of teleology was different from Aristotle's.[62] The similarity of the moderns to Plato's view was a formal one that took the form of a precise reversal of Plato. Where he, one might say, reduced the real to the rational, they reduced the rational to the real, first by lowering the ends of the city to the ends of the species in the early moderns and then flatly identifying the real with the character of the human species in Marx. Where the opposition between philosophy and reality is resolved in favor of the former for Plato, it is resolved in favor of the latter by Marx.[63] The two-thousand-year history of political philosophy

---

59. Ibid., 142.
60. I think Schall is quite correct in thinking that "McCoy classified Strauss, in spite of Strauss's own efforts to disassociate himself from this school, to be a modern natural rights thinker because of the manner in which Strauss understood Aristotle's notion of natural right." "Man for Himself," 98.
61. McCoy, "Revival," 144.
62. Ibid., 145 (quoting Strauss, *The City and Man*, 21).
63. Ibid., 146.

begins with a regime of armed philosophers and ends with a regime of armed workers. Rather than politics passing into philosophy, philosophy passes into practice. But this practice is not politics; there is neither deliberation nor liberty and so nothing like self-government, but only a blind natural process by which individuals become identified with their species being and so cease to be individuals at all.

Totalitarianism, McCoy thought, was the inevitable outcome of the "Platonic" approach to philosophy understood as ignoring the various levels of being in favor of "the good itself," which is a logical universal. At the end of modern political philosophy the immoderation of thought characteristic of Plato reversed his absorption of politics by philosophy into an absorption of philosophy by politics, which issues in totalitarianism.[64] This McCoy thought was a consequence of Strauss's fear of philosophy's absorption by theology. His preference for Plato's idealism yielded to an acceptance of Aristotle's inferior political order as a compromise with what was really unreason. It is this compromise and its implications that McCoy has in mind in the quotation from which I have taken this chapter's title. Strauss's Platonism is loyal to a standard that is in some sense at odds with nature as it is; he maintains a loyalty to it while accepting a compromise, making the loyalty itself really a kind of faith, a point that Strauss himself perhaps acknowledged. The last line of McCoy's essay is this: "This is a touching, even admirable faith; it is also, I believe, a quite desperate one: Strauss drinks wine with Plato and hemlock with Socrates."[65]

We must assume that when a man like McCoy uses the word "faith" he does so in earnest. Strauss's Platonism is a matter of faith because its object is hoped for but unseen. It is touching and admirable because it really is sincere faith, a deep and serious dedication to something great enough to transcend one's own narrow interests and so deeply human; it calls forth an effort that Strauss himself acknowledged could look "Sisyphean." But it is, in McCoy's judgment, "desperate." It is the only path open for a truly serious man who lacks religious faith, but who wishes to avoid triviality and self-absorption on the one hand, and the complete absorption of human life by political activism on the other. But it opts for

---

64. McCoy also described this line of thought without reference to Strauss in "The Logical and the Real in Political Theory: Plato, Aristotle, and Marx," *American Political Science Review* 48 (1954): 1058–66.

65. McCoy, "Revival," 149.

loyalty to a country it will never see, a promised land it will never enter. It is divine madness forced into a straitjacket of terrestrial sobriety and necessarily manifest in a carefully circumspect irony.

Conclusion

Leo Strauss famously wrote that "the problem inherent in the surface of things, and only in the surface of things, is the heart of things."[66] On the surface Charles McCoy's reading of Strauss was the reading of a nonreligious Platonist by a Roman Catholic Thomist and this is at the heart of things. This fundamental difference plays itself out in a number of different ways. At a basic methodological level, McCoy could keenly appreciate Strauss's acuity as an interpreter of the great texts in the history of political philosophy, especially the moderns. He cited Strauss as an authority in his discussions of Hobbes, Locke, and Rousseau. He seems to have arrived on his own at critical evaluations of Machiavelli and Burke that were similar in spirit to Strauss's views. But I think that even here there is a more fundamental difference in approach. Strauss's methods are those of a great humanist scholar. He was far more than an intellectual historian in the usual sense because he took so seriously the claims of the thinkers he studied to be the truth and put those claims through their paces in a way that few scholars have ever done. However, his methods were always akin to Socrates's turn to *logoi*; his philosophical quest was always a search for the truth of things in, as his students like to say, old books. McCoy's interest in the history of political philosophy was rather different. Philosophy for McCoy was a systematic enterprise aimed at stating with increasing precision the truths of things. His history of political philosophy is not aimed at discovering the permanent horizon of fundamental problems, but at stating how the structure of political thought was discovered and explicated only to be progressively repudiated with the direst practical consequences.[67] That repudiation turns out to

---

66. Leo Strauss, *Thoughts on Machiavelli* (Chicago: University of Chicago Press, 1958), 13.

67. The "permanent horizon of fundamental problems" is a well-known formulation of Strauss: see, e.g., *Natural Right and History*, 32, and *What Is Political Philosophy?* (Chicago: University of Chicago Press, 1988), 228–29, as well as the illuminating discussion in Daniel Tanguay, *Leo Strauss: An Intellectual Biography*, trans. Christopher Nadon (New Haven, Conn.: Yale University Press, 2007), 89–94, 123–43, 177–89.

have been a kind of reversal of the situation in political philosophy before the decisive work of Aristotle that McCoy associated with Plato's identification of the order of reality with the logical order, and this is the heart of things with respect to his disagreement with Strauss.

McCoy's understanding of Plato is, to my mind at any rate, the most questionable part of his history. The best defense that can be made of it would point to precedents for it in Aristotle and Aquinas. It has always seemed to me that the best reading of Aristotle's criticism of Plato is one that takes Aristotle as not necessarily thinking Plato meant the things attributed to him in the second book of the *Politics*, but as evidence that there were many who did read Plato this way and that it was a more urgent matter to set them right about the things themselves than about Plato's own views. Be that as it may, there are other aspects of Plato that Aristotle rejected that were more important for later Aristotelians, for example the questions about the logical and ontological status of the good. These may be less amenable to the sort of hypothesis I just made about the political questions. McCoy too may have been on more solid ground here, and Strauss himself sided with Plato against Aristotle on some of these matters. For McCoy they came to a head in the question about natural law that occupied center stage in his essay on Strauss. Here I think McCoy's view is essentially that Strauss defended what he took to be the classical view (nature as "standard') mainly against Thomas's view (nature as "authority") on the grounds that Thomas's view was both overly rigid and grounded in theology.

As to the theological background to Thomas's view I do not see how McCoy did or could have disagreed. Nature as "authority" is grounded in God's having given things their natures and thus their natural inclinations as a part of the creation of the world. Natural law is a participation in eternal law. McCoy's view, however, was that this view was much closer to that of Aristotle than Strauss probably would have allowed. Certainly there is no doctrine of creation in Aristotle, but McCoy placed great emphasis on Aristotle's understanding of the prime intellect and took biblical revelation and the theological speculation that emerged from it to be essentially an extension and completion of that line of thought. He seems to me to have paid short shrift to the Neo-Platonic aspects of Thomas's view, but that is another matter. However, I think that when we look at the other issue, the rigidity of the natural law, we confront something more basic.⁶⁸ Here what is crucial is not so much the natural law precepts themselves (although they certainly matter) but their end: the common good. It is important that McCoy's exposition of the idea of the common good was always carried out in terms of Aristotle's discussion in the *Metaphysics*, with its distinction between the intrinsic and extrinsic common goods. McCoy already saw Aristotle's account as pointing to God as the extrinsic common good of the universe and everything in it and Aquinas's account as the logical completion of this. That the completion may have been impossible without the perspective afforded by revelation may be true, but to McCoy that was no argument against it.

The central issue here was what McCoy took to be the Platonic understanding of the common good (Plato did not call it this) as a logical universal true only in the order of predication. For Aristotle and Aquinas the common good was rather a universal cause, the cause of the natures of things and all their motions in the natural world. What revelation added to this was first a kind of confirmation, and second, a companion account, not available to philosophy, of the role of the common good as the cause of contingent particulars through providence. This is related to the issue regarding the rigidity of the natural law because Strauss's Platonic view seemed to separate the logical universal, the "good itself," from the temporal common good of particular societies. That gulf creates the problem of situations in which the common good seems to require acts that would otherwise be precluded as wrong in their objects. But McCoy's Thomistic-Aristotelian account of the common good is analogical, understood as a nested series of common goods all related to the extrinsic common good of the universe, God. The primacy of this common good is the most important limit on the power of the state and the most important root of the dignity of the human person because, while persons are ordered to the temporal common good, their ordination to the universal common good transcends this. Acts that are intrinsically wrong, wrong in their objects as distinct from their intentions, are acts that are always at odds with this ordination to the common good of the universe.

One final point: to the argument that McCoy's account amounts to the transformation of philosophy into theology, I think McCoy's response

---

68. Nevertheless it is worth noting that the "rigidity" of Thomistic natural law should not be overstated: the number of act-types that Thomas considered wrong in their objects as distinct from their intentions was certainly small. This is why he generally identified the moral species of acts with intention.

would first be to defend Aquinas's interpretation and extension of Aristotle as either the most plausible reading of Aristotle, or, at least as plausible as any other. But beyond this, I think it would be—it must be—to acknowledge that in at least one sense the charge is true. If one is a Christian, one cannot be a philosopher in the sense that Plato and Aristotle were philosophers. Philosophy does not disappear; reason does not lose its efficacy. Indeed, there would be no theology without philosophy. Nevertheless, if the Gospel is true, the world is different, and one cannot act as if it is not. Philosophy is preserved as a kind of method; the canons of sound reasoning remain valuable, not least to the science of sacred doctrine, but it is no longer the way of life that it was before Christianity. Strauss's writings are, among other things, a salutary provocation to Christians not to forget this.[69]

---

69. I am grateful to Daniel Mahoney, James V. Schall, Robert Sokolowski, and especially John C. McCarthy for helpful comments on earlier drafts of this paper.

3

Wisdom and Folly

Reconsidering Leo Strauss on the Natural Law

GEOFFREY M. VAUGHAN

Leo Strauss's project has been characterized as the recovery of classical political philosophy, more specifically, of Platonic political wisdom. For Strauss, this meant a recovery of classic natural right, most famously and extensively developed in the 1949 Walgreen Lectures that became *Natural Right and History*. A curious feature of that argument is the ambiguous treatment of the natural law tradition. Sometimes it is categorized as within the tradition of classic natural right, sometimes outside of it. Why the ambiguity? I believe the answer is to be found not in any difference in the content of natural right—hence the natural law can be considered classic natural right—but in the degree to which natural lawyers think there is no need to accommodate folly.

According to Strauss, classic natural right is concerned not with particular laws or policies, but with the regime, the overall arrangement and distribution of offices and honors. The best regime is that ruled by a philosopher, by someone with wisdom. It is not a tyranny, however. This means that the philosopher must rule not only for the good of the ruled, but must also not force them to obey. In the best regime the wise rule with the consent of those without wisdom. Garnering their consent, it turns out, is at least as difficult as anything else about the best regime. The result is that all political arrangements short of the best, yet still good regimes, are the result of an accommodation that wisdom makes with folly, an accommodation necessary to acquire the consent of those who are not wise. I shall argue that Strauss considered natural law to be a version of classic natural right because it retained the ancient perspective that all politics is an accommodation that wisdom must make with folly. However, he also thought it an unwise ambition to codify wisdom as statute or institutionalize it as an office. This ambition either made it impossible to accept political necessity or to appear hypocritical when it did. This is what rendered the natural law especially vulnerable to the modern challenge and makes it especially difficult to revive as a governing political philosophy today.

Classic or Catholic Natural Right?

Leo Strauss was interested in what he called in *Natural Right and History* and elsewhere "classic natural right." In an encyclopedia entry from 1968 on natural law, Strauss reveals this interest by dwelling on classic natural right and its modern revision rather than natural law. Surprisingly, he shortchanged what one would expect to be the entry's focus, the moral theories developed by St. Thomas Aquinas.[1] We should have no doubt that Strauss was well-aware of his misdirection. His redirection reveals that he both knew what was expected and that he had no intention to deliver the goods. In short, he changed the very subject of the entry: "The primary question concerns less natural law than natural right, *i.e.* what is by nature right or just: is all right conventional (of human origin) or is there some right which is natural (*physei dikaion*)?"[2] In positioning philosophy above law, he deprecated the term "natural law" as a contradic-

---

1. Leo Strauss, "On Natural Law," in *Studies in Platonic Political Philosophy*, ed. Thomas L. Pangle (Chicago: University of Chicago Press, 1985), 137. The history of natural law theories from the Stoics to today is a complicated and contentious one. For the purposes of this essay I will take Strauss's position that the Thomistic account is central. See *Leo Strauss on Plato's Symposium*, ed. Seth Benardete (Chicago: University of Chicago Press, 2003), 3. A very useful history of the natural law up to Aquinas is Anton-Hermann Chroust, "The Philosophy of Law of St. Thomas Aquinas: His Fundamental Ideas and Some of His Precursors," *American Journal of Jurisprudence* 19 (1973): 1–38.

2. Strauss, "On Natural Law," 138. See also Fortin, "Augustine, Thomas Aquinas, and the Problem of Natural Law," in *Classical Christianity and the Political Order*, ed. J. Brian Benestad (Lanham, Md.: Rowman and Littlefield, 1996).

tion in terms. His rationale for doing so was that Greek philosophy began by distinguishing nature from law.

Plato's idea of natural right, Strauss explained, was not a natural law teaching. Plato certainly objected to the conventionalist or positivist position that whatever the law of the city decreed to be just is just. But he did not put in the place of civic law other laws, immutable laws. The problem is not so much that there is no natural right or justice as that searching for a *law* is misguided. According to Strauss's reading of Plato, "law can never be more than an approximation to the verdicts of wisdom."[3] Natural right is to be found in wisdom, not law. Law is always a compromise, an approximation. As Strauss wrote in *On Tyranny*, "Law and legitimacy are problematic from the highest point of view, namely, from that of wisdom."[4] For example, a speed limit is not *really* the right speed for a given road: some people would be quite capable of driving much faster, and others should not be driving anywhere near the posted limit. Likewise, different vehicles will respond differently to the conditions of the road. Yet no one could suggest that each and every driver be assigned a specific speed limit for each road, a limit which corresponded also to the type of vehicle and each possible road condition. Law redresses the impracticality of rendering a wise decision in each instance. But this means that law, however just, can never be right, that is, directly and totally applicable to the case at hand. "Political society requires the dilution of the perfect and exact right, of natural right proper: of the right in accordance with which the wise would assign to everyone what he deserves according to his virtue and therefore would assign unequal things to unequal people."[5] In other words, law is either too specific to be naturally right (as in the case of speed limits), or too imprecise to be implemented effectively.[6]

To some extent any doctrine of natural law must expect that its application will reconcile the tension between legal justice and equity, or positive right and natural right. By contrast, Strauss (taking his cues from Plato and Aristotle) held that only a very rare political arrangement, the

---

3. Strauss, *Studies in Platonic Political Philosophy*, 139. Cf. *Statesman* 294a–295e.
4. Leo Strauss, *On Tyranny: Revised and Expanded Edition*, ed. Victor Gourevitch and Michael S. Roth (New York: Free Press, 1991), 99.
5. Strauss, *Studies in Platonic Political Philosophy*, 139.
6. Constitutional lawyers use the term "void for vagueness." For cases establishing and reaffirming this doctrine see Connally v. General Construction Co., 269 U.S. 385 (1926), Cantwell v. Connecticut, 310 U.S. 296 (1940), Musser v. Utah, 333 U.S. 95 (1948), United States v. Harris, 347 U.S. 612 (1954), Grayned v. City of Rockford, 408 U.S. 104 (1972), Village of Hoffman Estates v. The Flipside, 455 U.S. 489 (1982), and Dowling v. United States, 473 U.S. 207 (1985).

best regime, could achieve this reconciliation. In his summation of the doctrine of classic natural right, Strauss explained what he took to be the proper relation between law and regime: "The classic natural right doctrine in its original form, if fully developed, is identical with the doctrine of the best regime. For the question as to what is by nature right or as to what is justice finds its complete answer only through the construction, in speech, of the best regime."[7] As he explained, the best regime is a practical or really possible regime but so unlikely as to be utopian. Thus, "under more or less unfavorable conditions, only more or less imperfect regimes are possible and therefore legitimate."[8] These imperfect regimes are legitimate, but they are more than that. Given imperfect conditions, attempting to impose a more perfect regime would be unjust. In the name of justice it would be indistinguishable from tyranny. The best regime is the one ruled by the wise where the unwise willingly submit to their guidance.[9] Imperfect yet legitimate regimes would then be ones in which the wise ruled to the greatest extent possible, limited by the need to win the acquiescence of the unwise.[10] The negotiations required to produce this acquiescence are the accommodations wisdom must make with folly. The negotiations are necessarily fraught, for as Strauss wrote, "Because the city as a whole is characterized by a specific recalcitrance to reason, it requires for its well-being a rhetoric different from forensic and deliberative rhetoric as a servant to the political art."[11] The natural law understood as "law" (or any rule existing prior to this political negotiation) cannot make these accommodations without conceding an obvious breach of the natural law, thereby undermining the authority of the human law.[12]

---

7. Strauss, *Natural Right and History* (Chicago: University of Chicago Press, 1965), 144.

8. Ibid., 139. See also Jaffa, *Thomism and Aristotelianism* (Chicago: University of Chicago Press, 1952), 182.

9. Strauss, *Natural Right and History*, 147. This easy arrangement is not so simple. As Catherine and Michael Zuckert put it, "Those who claim a right to rule in the name of wisdom prove by the very fact of raising that claim that they are not among the wise, and therefore they cannot raise a claim to rule on that basis." *The Truth about Leo Strauss* (Chicago: University of Chicago Press, 2006), 165. See also Tanguay, *Leo Strauss: An Intellectual Biography*, trans. Christopher Nadon (New Haven, Conn.: Yale University Press, 2011), 127.

10. In dividing the people between wise and unwise, Strauss told us that classic natural right maintained two positions that applied to both groups: (1) man is a political animal, and (2) human nature has a *telos*, even if not all are equally capable of fulfilling it. See Strauss, *Natural Right and History*, 129, 133, 145–56. For Thomas Aquinas on the different abilities for moral and intellectual virtue, see *Summa Theologiae* I-II, q. 96, a. 2.

11. Leo Strauss, *The City and Man* (Chicago: University of Chicago Press, 1964), 22.

12. A recent example demonstrates this point. Pope Benedict XVI made comments in a recent

Natural law institutionalizes, or believes it can institutionalize, what would be for Plato the decisions of the wise. Strauss explained that the Stoics were the first to assert that there was a natural law because they were also the first to teach that there was a divine lawgiver who could mete out rewards and punishments for obeying or disobeying the law.[13] As we can see from his analysis of Plato, however, the divine origin of the natural law is not merely important at the level of *enforcement*. Rather, only a divinity could conceive of a law that would apply in all cases, under all conditions, to all people and adhere to justice each and every time. Such an achievement is certainly beyond the powers of the human mind, because it would combine the universality of legal justice and the specificity of equity. According to Strauss, echoing Aristotle, "Whereas a good ruler is necessarily beneficent, laws are not necessarily beneficent."[14] Nevertheless, and related to this, the Stoics expected much more from most people than Plato or Aristotle did: "One is tempted to say that the Stoics treat the study of philosophy as if it were a moral virtue, *i.e.* as something which could be demanded from most men."[15] The natural law of Thomas Aquinas goes even further than this, according to Strauss, not quite demanding that everyone study philosophy, but insisting that rationality is the path to morality. This, at least in principle, is a path open to all. He explained, "Differently stated, as a *rational being* man is by nature inclined toward acting according to reason; acting according to reason is acting virtuously; natural law prescribes therefore the acts of virtue."[16]

If the natural law were merely rules handed down to the people from some lawgiver, that would be one thing. But it is more than this. Aquinas, and perhaps even the Stoics, had to claim that the wisdom of Plato's philosopher-king was somehow or in principle within reach of every-

---

publication on the permissibility of using condoms under certain circumstances. While many Catholic scholars were at pains to explain that this was not a break with *Humanae Vitae* (1968), it was widely taken as such and either praised or blamed accordingly. Again, birth control arises as central to the modern break with the Thomistic natural law.

13. Strauss, *Studies in Platonic Political Philosophy*, 141.

14. Strauss, *On Tyranny*, 74.

15. Strauss, *Studies in Platonic Political Philosophy*, 141. See also Clark A. Merrill, "Leo Strauss's Indictment of Christian Philosophy," *Review of Politics* 62, no. 1 (2000): 85.

16. Strauss, *Studies in Platonic Political Philosophy*, 142 (emphasis added). We find John Locke making a similar argument in his *Reasonableness of Christianity*: "The writers and wranglers in religion fill it with niceties, and dress it up with notions, which they make necessary and fundamental parts of it; as if there were no way into the church, but through the academy or lyceum." See John Locke, *The Reasonableness of Christianity*, vol. 6 of *The Works of John Locke in Nine Volumes*, 12th ed. (London: Rivington, [1695] 1824), 157.

one because man is defined for them as a *rational being*. In other words, life according to reason is not the singular achievement of a few but the inherent capacity of all, if not now, then at some point in the future.[17] Making this claim also entails supposing that politics need not be a compromise that wisdom must make with folly; rather, it can be understood rationally and proceed according to a rational plan.[18] Put another way, if all citizens are capable of acting rationally in all their affairs (or are morally expected to do so), political society is no longer a dilution of natural right that would have to be managed with prudence.[19]

On a number of points, according to Strauss, classic natural right and Thomistic natural law do have commonalities. Where do they diverge? According to Strauss, the distinguishing mark of natural law is its depoliticization of right which leads it to position law over and above the regime. Accordingly, "The notion of God as lawgiver takes on a certainty and definiteness which it never possessed in classical philosophy. Therefore natural right or, rather, natural law becomes independent of the best regime and takes precedence over it."[20] These natural laws are directed to the wise and foolish equally and do so without regard to political arrangements. Strauss still called this classic natural right, but in a "profoundly modified form." Now Strauss's objections to natural law become clear. So too does his strange habit of sometimes placing Thomistic natural law in the tradition of classic natural right and sometimes outside of it.

There are two tendencies in the natural law to which Strauss objected. The first is to take the fundamental premises of classic natural right and formalize or institutionalize them; that is, to codify the characteristics of the best regime as laws that apply regardless of the favorable or unfavorable conditions in which they are to be applied. The second is to see any accommodations as merely provisional, and even pedagogical. From Strauss's perspective a life lived according to the dictates of practical rea-

---

17. See Aquinas, *Summa Theologiae* I-II, q. 1, a. 1; II-II, q. 57, a. 1; *Disputed Questions on the Cardinal Virtues*, q. 1, a. 11. See also Ralph McInerney, *Ethica Thomistica: The Moral Philosophy of Thomas Aquinas* (Washington, D.C.: The Catholic University of America Press, 1982), 46. See also Anton-Hermann Chroust, "The Philosophy of Law of St. Thomas Aquinas," *American Journal of Jurisprudence* 19 (1973): 14.

18. See Fortin, "The Political Thought of St. Thomas Aquinas," in *Classical Christianity and the Political Order*, ed. J. Brian Benestad (Lanham, Md.: Rowman and Littlefield, 1996), 169.

19. See Fortin, "Rational Theologians and Irrational Philosophers: A Straussian Perspective," in *Classical Christianity and the Political Order*, ed. J. Brian Benestad (Lanham, Md.: Rowman and Littlefield, 1996), 169–70, and "Augustine, Thomas Aquinas, and the Problem of Natural Law," 211.

20. Strauss, *Natural Right and History*, 144. See also Strauss, "The Mutual Influence of Theology and Philosophy," *Independent Journal of Philosophy* 3 (1978): 112.

son is indistinguishable from a life of wisdom. The mistake made by advocates of the natural law is to turn a way of life into statutes: "Philosophy was certainly in the Christian Middle Ages deprived of its character as a way of life and became just a very important compartment."[21] The inflexibility of natural law that the moderns saw as its characteristic problem and the reason it had to be rejected is, according to Strauss, only a symptom of a deeper and much more important mistake. Inflexibility is the unfortunate but obvious result of not realizing that all politics requires that wisdom make an accommodation with folly. In an illuminating passage on the possibility of natural law he writes: "a law solving justly a problem which exists in a given country at a given time only, is not less rational, it is in a sense more rational, than a law valid in all countries at all times."[22]

According to Strauss, modern natural right's objection to natural law has two distinct components. One is the philosophical question regarding the theological origins of the laws. The other is the practical question of legislative latitude or flexibility in response to the needs of the state.[23] Modern natural right rejects the notion of external laws, finding their proper source inside the individual rather than in nature. The result was what Strauss called "natural public law."[24] The problem with flexibility is similar. Echoing his earlier comments about the reaction against Thomism, Strauss wrote, "The historical thought of the nineteenth century tried to recover for statesmanship that latitude which natural public law had so severely restricted."[25] The objections of classic natural right, which we might identify with Strauss, can be collapsed into one: how could one system of universal laws apply in all the variety of cases where reason must accommodate folly? And note: the variety arises because folly varies so much, not because reason does.

The position of classic natural right—that the best regime is inappli-

---

21. Strauss, "Mutual Influence," 113.
22. Leo Strauss, *Persecution and the Art of Writing* (Chicago: University of Chicago Press, 1988), 133. Consider also the following comment: "The philosophers would not call the governmental part [the natural law] of the Law of Reason rational (cf. p. 133 above), but the rules of which that part consists, are rational laws according to the mutakallimûn." Ibid., 138n136.
23. On this point I am very much indebted to James V. Schall, "A Latitude for Statesmanship? Strauss on St. Thomas," *Review of Politics* 53, no. 1 (1991): 126–45. Where I depart from Schall, as should be clear below, is that the exercise of latitude is self-defeating because the natural law is presented as just that, a law, rather than a decree of prudence.
24. Strauss, *Natural Right and History*, 190.
25. Ibid., 192.

cable in all but the most rare conditions—allows it to retain an objective standard of justice (the best regime) without being forced to institute it in all times and places.[26] The balance between objective right and flexible practice is a more difficult problem for the natural law. If the laws cannot adapt or be adapted they are not applicable; if they can adapt or be adapted they are not, properly speaking, universal laws. Yet they are presented as laws, not decrees of prudence. This was the matter on which Strauss caught Aquinas trying to save Aristotle. As Strauss read them, Aristotle argued that natural right is changeable and Aquinas added the distinction that does not exist in Aristotle, specifically that "the axioms from which the more specific rules of natural right are derived, are universally valid and immutable; what are mutable are only the more specific rules (e.g., the rule to return deposits)."[27] The dispute between classic natural right and Thomistic natural law turns on the extent to which Aquinas's innovation leaves room for accommodating folly when forming a regime. Aquinas's advocacy of a mixed regime suggests he was in accord with the classics to a large extent.[28] However, his focus on the natural law pushed him away from an accommodating regime to a perfecting natural law. Accordingly, he wrote, "the purpose of human law is to bring people to virtue, not suddenly but gradually."[29] Strauss's ambiguous identification of Thomistic natural law with classic natural right matches the ambiguity within the doctrine itself: Aquinas could accommodate folly but only in such a way that would eventually ameliorate that same folly and even educate it out of existence.[30]

26. See Strauss, "Restatement," in *On Tyranny*, 187.
27. Strauss, *Natural Right and History*, 157. But see John Finnis, "Aristotle, Aquinas, and Moral Absolutes," *Catholica: International Quarterly Selection* 12 (1990): 7. This is perhaps why Strauss saw a tension between Athens and Jerusalem rather than a triumph of one over the other. For Strauss, according to my argument, questions about the existence of God are secondary to questions about how he might legislate. This counterintuitive order arises because of his insistence that we must begin with political opinions. See Strauss, *Natural Right and History*, 125. See also Douglas Kries, "Strauss's Understanding of the Natural Law Theory of Thomas Aquinas," *The Thomist* 57, no. 2 (1993): 217, and Susan Orr, *Jerusalem and Athens* (Lanham, Md.: Rowman and Littlefield, 1995), 149.
28. See *Summa Theologiae* I-II, q. 105, a. 1. See also Fortin, "Thomas Aquinas as a Political Thinker"; James M. Blythe, "The Mixed Constitution and the Distinction between Regal and Political Power in the Work of Thomas Aquinas," *Journal of the History of Ideas* 47, no. 4 (1986): 547–65; and Douglas Kries, "Thomas Aquinas and the Politics of Moses," *Review of Politics* 52, no. 1 (1990): 84–104.
29. *Summa Theologiae* I-II, q. 96, a. 3, ad 2.
30. However, according to Aristotle, "the intention of the lawgiver is to lead men to virtue" (*Nicomachean Ethics* II.1). This is cited by Aquinas, *Summa Theologiae* I-II, q. 90, a. 3, obj. 2. Strauss would suggest that Aquinas and the natural law tradition was far more convinced than Aristotle that this would be possible. This is a textual and empirical question I cannot address here.

Right without Regimes?

One of the clearest statements we have from Strauss on contemporary natural lawyers comes in a letter he wrote to Alexandre Kojève. In the letter Strauss thanked his correspondent for recognizing the genuine problems that existentialists deny and both Marxists and Thomists trivialize.[31] The comment came in response to a pre-publication copy of Kojéve's review of Strauss's commentary on Xenophon's *Hiero*, the central concern of which is the relationship between political power (the tyrant Hiero) and wisdom (the philosopher Simonides).[32] Strauss seems to have been saying that both Marxism and Thomism have a tendency toward a trivialization of the form of government or the regime. Marxists distinguish between a base and superstructure, where the superstructure or form of government is a mere epiphenomenon resulting from material forms of production at the base. Thomists measure human law by how closely it resembles natural law, not by how it is made or who makes it.[33] Human law is merely a more or less effective means of putting the natural law in practice, the rightness of the natural law always being the legitimating principle. So long as they instantiate the natural law, what is the difference? But this is exactly what Strauss denied. He explained, "Every political society derives its character from a specific public or political morality, from what it regards as publicly defensible, and this means from what the preponderant part of society (not necessarily the majority) regards as just."[34] The regime shapes the public or political morality that the citizens hold, be it a monarchic, aristocratic, or democratic conception. Laws do not simply more or less approximate the natural law. The regime sets the terms by which people think about justice itself.

Strauss wrote a generally favorable review of his colleague Yves Simon's *Philosophy of Democratic Government* and, it seems, was influential in encouraging the lectures that became Simon's *The Tradition of the Nat-*

---

31. Strauss to Kojève, September 4, 1949, in *On Tyranny*, 244. The letter is photographically reproduced on page 214 and shows the arrows Strauss used to identify the word "trivialize" with Marxism and Thomism.

32. Confirmation that this is Strauss's preoccupation can be found throughout his initial commentary and his "Restatement." For confirmation that Kojève agreed, see Alexandre Kojève, "Tyranny and Wisdom," in *On Tyranny*, 135, 152.

33. See Fortin, "New Natural Rights Theory," in *Classical Christianity and the Political Order*, ed. J. Brian Benestad (Lanham, Md.: Rowman and Littlefield, 1996), 273, and Merrill, "Leo Strauss's Indictment," 92, 98.

34. Strauss, *The City and Man*, 48.

ural Law.[35] Nevertheless, in that review Strauss took issue with Simon's tendency to take the current political and social arrangement as "the normal condition." According to Strauss, "Simon can trace the equalitarian dynamics of modern societies to an equalitarian dynamics of human nature because he regards the modern situation (let us say the situation that exists or is emerging since the middle of the nineteenth century) as the normal situation."[36] From Strauss's perspective, Simon did not see that modern liberal democracy is a particular regime with a particular—egalitarian—conception of justice. He continued, "This amounts to saying that the conditions required for democracy are the normal conditions, the conditions required by human nature." They manifestly have not been the normal conditions for the vast majority of people, or for the vast majority even in the twentieth century. But if one ignores the role a regime plays for establishing the context of all discussions of justice, as Strauss thought natural law was prone to do, this truth is more difficult to see.[37]

We have one other direct exchange on the natural law between Strauss and a contemporary. In his response to Fuller's offprints of the Hart-Fuller Debate in 1958, Strauss wrote, "The two essays together constitute an excellent commentary on Aristotle's analysis in the *Nicomachean Ethics* of equity and bring out the wisdom of that analysis."[38] He was most likely referring to the second half of the fifth book of the *Ethics*. Chapter 7 of that book begins Aristotle's examination of the question of what is just by nature and what is just by convention. In chapter 10 Aristotle distinguishes between what is legally just and what is equitable (*epieikeia*). The equitable corrects or improves upon legal justice because legal justice (as positive law) must apply itself equally to all cases, whereas equity can correct for this blunt instrument. The Hart-Fuller Debate had Hart arguing on behalf of legal positivism, that the justice of laws is based upon

---

35. See the address given by Simon's son, Anthony O. Simon, in 2004 at http://www.thomasinternational.org/conferences/20040718palermo/simon_paper.htm.

36. Strauss, *What Is Political Philosophy?*, 310.

37. Jacques Maritain famously wrote that "democracy is the only way of bringing about a moral rationalization of politics." Maritain, *Man and the State* (Washington, D.C.: The Catholic University of America Press, 1998), 59. For similar comments see Yves Simon, *Philosophy of Democratic Government* (Chicago: University of Chicago Press, 1961), 94; Hadley Arkes, *First Things: An Inquiry into the First Principles of Morals and Justice* (Princeton, N.J.: Princeton University Press, 1986), 47; Christopher Wolfe, *Natural Law Liberalism* (New York: Cambridge University Press, 2009), 176, 249–51.

38. Strauss to Fuller, March 19, 1958. The debate itself appears in H. L. A. Hart, "Positivism and the Separation of Law and Morals," *Harvard Law Review* 71, no. 4 (1958): 593–629, and Lon L. Fuller, "*Positivism and Fidelity to Law—A Reply to Professor Hart*," *Harvard Law Review* 71, no. 4 (1958): 630–72.

"fundamental accepted rules specifying the essential lawmaking procedures."[39] Fuller argued, instead, that there is a "morality of law itself" which no positive law can override.[40] While not exactly Thomistic natural law, Fuller's stance, when set against Hart's argument, nicely focuses the debate between positivism and natural law.

Strauss's comments to Fuller on the debate are illuminating. Strauss concurred with Fuller that there can be no rule of law without a distinction between a legislative and a judicial function, and that a judge cannot fulfill his function or be loyal to the law without recourse to the *ratio legis*. According to Strauss, Fuller's "clear and forceful analysis of the German situation under the Nazis follows from these premises with evident necessity." But then he proceeded to the most interesting part of the letter: "You wisely limit your argument to the immediate implications of law as law. These implications include extra-legal or pre-legal beliefs regarding the just and decent. But as your way of expression shows you are aware of the facts [sic] that these beliefs themselves require examination and that this examination need not lead to the assumption of a higher 'law.'"[41] Strauss then finished his comments with his reference to Aristotle's *Ethics*. When Strauss wrote the words "higher law," the word "law" alone was in quotation marks. When Fuller used the words they were both in quotation marks.[42] This may seem like an insignificant difference, but I would suggest that it is consistent with Strauss's argument that there can be a higher principle—natural right—without this implying that there is a higher "law."

A few years after Strauss's correspondence with Fuller, Germain Grisez published what would be the beginning of what is now called the "new natural law" theory.[43] A key characteristic of the school is its rejection of any theological or metaphysical origins for the natural law.[44] Indeed, the main proponent, John Finnis, chastised Strauss for his "prominent but vague assertion" that the natural law was connected to a teleological view

39. Hart, "Positivism," 603.
40. Fuller, "Positivism and Fidelity to Law," 644. See also Lon L. Fuller, *The Morality of Law* (New Haven, Conn.: Yale University Press, 1964).
41. Strauss to Fuller.
42. See, for example, Fuller, "Positivism," 656.
43. Germain Grisez, "The First Principle of Practical Reason: A Commentary on the *Summa Theologiae*, 1–2 Question 94, Article 2," *Natural Law Forum* 10 (1965): 168–201.
44. See, for example, Grisez's comment: the "moral obligation to obey divine commands, although rightly accepted by believers, is not self-evident." In Germain Grisez, *Way of the Lord Jesus, Vol. 1: Christian Moral Principles* (Quincy, Ill.: Franciscan Press, 1983), 115.

of the universe.[45] As such, one could imagine that the new natural law was designed to meet the objection that it is based upon a theological position.[46] As for the second early modern objection that Strauss identified, that the natural law is too inflexible, the new natural law does little to settle Strauss's concerns.

Strauss did not need to see the publication of a book that argued for the radical redeployment of the Western nations' nuclear weapons in the face of Soviet threats (because, the authors argue, to continue the policy of deterrence is "to choose to do evil that good may come of it") for him to worry about the prudence of natural lawyers.[47] He was, more or less, committed well in advance to the Roman maxim that the laws are silent in war. Consider the following passage: "A decent society will not go to war except for a just cause. But what it will do during a war will depend to a certain extent on what the enemy—possibly an absolutely unscrupulous and savage enemy—forces it to do. There are no limits which can be defined in advance, there are no assignable limits to what might become just reprisals."[48] Extreme actions may be necessary to save the polity and, not knowing all the possible attacks an enemy might make, it would be imprudent to limit beforehand the possible responses. This seems not to be an unreasonable position, nor is it excessively Machiavellian.

---

45. Finnis, *Natural Law and Natural Rights*, 52. But more generally see, among others, Henry B. Veatch, *For an Ontology of Morals* (Chicago: Northwestern University Press, 1971), 123; Ralph McInerny, *Aquinas on Human Action* (Washington, D.C.: The Catholic University of America Press, 1992), 162–77; Anthony J. Lisska, *Aquinas's Theory of Natural Law* (New York: Oxford University Press, 1996), chap. 5; and Henrik Syse, *Natural Law, Religion and Right* (South Bend, Ind.: St. Augustine Press, 2004), chap. 2.

46. Strauss announced early in *Natural Right and History* that twentieth-century followers of Thomas Aquinas had been forced to abandon a comprehensive view of teleology in the face of modern science. Teleology became reserved for the science of man while abandoned for natural science. He described this as typically modern (Strauss, *Natural Right and History*, 8). As for the question of its teleological foundations, this is still disputed among proponents of the natural law. A number of scholars have raised objections to the new natural law for precisely these reasons. See, as only a brief list, Ralph McInerny, *Ethica Thomistica*, and "The Principles of Natural Law," *American Journal of Jurisprudence* 25 (1980): 1–15; Henry Veatch and Joseph Rautenberg, "Does the Grisez-Finnis-Boyle Moral Philosophy Rest on a Mistake?," *Review of Metaphysics* 44, no. 4 (1991): 807–30; Veatch, *Swimming Against the Current in Contemporary Philosophy* (Washington, D.C.: The Catholic University of America Press, 1981); Russell Hittinger, *A Critique of the New Natural Law Theory* (Notre Dame, Ind.: University of Notre Dame Press, 1987); Paul E. Sigmund, "Law and Politics" in *The Cambridge Companion to Aquinas*, ed. Norman Kretzmann and Eleonore Stump (New York: Cambridge University Press, 1993).

47. Finnis, Joseph M. Boyle, Jr., and Germain Grisez, *Nuclear Deterrence, Morality and Realism* (Oxford: Clarendon Press, 1987), 327; Finnis, *Natural Law and Natural Rights* (Oxford: Clarendon, 1980), 224–26.

48. Strauss, *Natural Right and History*, 160. See also Catherine and Michael Zuckert, *The Truth about Leo Strauss*, 183–84. But see a similar passage from Aquinas, *Summa Theologiae* I-II, q. 97, a. 6: "necessitas non subditur legi" (necessity is not subject to the law).

The point must be made that these extreme cases, while important, were not central to Strauss's argument about natural right. Yes, he argued that the rules sometimes had to change: "It suffices to repeat that in extreme situations the normally valid rules of natural right are justly changed, or changed in accordance with natural right; the exceptions are as just as the rules."[49] But Strauss made clear that these extreme situations must not guide our thoughts, however much they must be faced when they do arise. It was Machiavelli, he argued, who made the mistake of being so guided and it was for this reason that he denied natural right: "Machiavelli denies natural right, because he takes his bearings by the extreme situations in which the demands of justice are reduced to the requirements of necessity, and not by the normal situations in which the demands of justice in the strict sense are the highest law."[50] Where Finnis, Boyle, and Grisez argued that the normal standards of justice must be applied to the unique historical moment when two superpowers faced each other with nuclear weapons, and where Machiavelli argued that even quotidian political considerations must be guided by that very extreme type of danger, Strauss tried to steer a middle course. Extreme measures can be used in extreme situations, but those are always the special cases and they cannot be used to define natural right for normal conditions any more than the normal conditions of natural right can be expected to speak to the extreme cases. In other words, while amputation may sometimes be necessary and therefore can never be proscribed even by the injunction to do no harm, neither should it be the first procedure to come to a doctor's mind when faced with a skinned knee. Our laws cannot all be drafted in anticipation of extreme situations, even if we must remain aware that such hard cases can arise. Aquinas would probably agree.

According to Strauss, the proximate cause for Montesquieu's rejection of Thomistic natural law was its inflexibility regarding birth control and divorce. The new natural law is no more flexible.[51] From Grisez's 1964 book *Contraception and the Natural Law* to contemporary efforts on issues such as marriage, abortion, and embryonic stem-cell research, the new natural law movement has become one of the most consistent and un-

---

49. Strauss, *Natural Right and History*, 160.
50. Ibid., 162. See also Aristotle, *Politics* 1254a36–38. Strauss made the same claim about Hobbes in *Natural Right and History*, 196.
51. Strauss, *Natural Right and History*, 164. Compare here Christ's admonition in Mt 19:9 and Mk 10:5, in both cases blaming the prior hardness of hearts for the permissive Mosaic divorce laws.

wavering voices in American politics.[52] But here, too, they might be able to respond to Strauss. If, as Strauss claimed, he wanted to avoid the Charybdis of "relativism," he could hardly object if the new natural law has chosen to follow the advice of Circe and steer closer to Scylla and "absolutism."[53] At the same time, and to take the one issue that has become far more prominent than in Strauss's day, some of the new natural lawyers have developed a flexible and politically viable policy regarding abortion. The Born Alive Infant Protection Act (2002) seeks to protect children who have survived an abortion, not to criminalize all (or any) abortions themselves. While it might be a first step in the direction of further restrictions on abortion, it recalls Strauss's comments on the maintenance of inflexible principles "by means of a most flexible policy."[54]

When it comes to the question of the best regime and its relation to justice, so central to Strauss's concerns, the new natural law has only a few passing similarities with classic natural right. Finnis opens *Natural Law and Natural Rights* with a statement affirming the role of political society: "There are human goods that can be secured only through the institutions of human law, and requirements of practical reasonableness that only those institutions can satisfy."[55] Much later in the same work he endorses the classic view that the regime must accommodate the unique characteristics of the people: "As the classics said, the ruler may be one, few, or many ('the multitude,' 'the masses'). There are social circumstances where the rule of one will be best, and other circumstances where the rule of a very narrow, or a very wide, class will be best."[56] But Finnis's views on politics are not entirely in accord with the classics. For instance, he sees politics as a mere instrument for the good of the family and thereby takes his bearings from a pre-civil perspective. It may not be the same pre-civil perspective as Hobbes, Locke, and the subsequent liberal tradition through Rawls, but it is a pre-civil perspective nonetheless. This is in accord with the natural law tradition's inattention to the regime, seeing politics as nothing more than a means of coordinating individuals and families.

52. For a critical voice see Stephen Macedo, "Against the Old Sexual Morality of the New Natural Law," in *Natural Law, Liberalism, and Morality*, ed. Robert P. George (Oxford: Clarendon Press, 1996).
53. Strauss, *Natural Right and History*, 162.
54. Strauss, *What Is Political Philosophy?*, 281.
55. Finnis, *Natural Law and Natural Rights*, 3.
56. Ibid., 252. It is not as if Finnis is unaware of the problem of wisdom. He writes, "there are many moral questions which can only be rightly answered by someone who is wise, and who considers them searchingly." Finnis, *Natural Law and Natural Rights*, 30; see also 15, 102.

The "salient coordinator" theory of politics has developed in the natural law tradition precisely because of its utilitarian view of politics. Thomas Aquinas famously argued that law and some sort of political authority would have been required had Adam and Eve remained in the state of innocence. According to Aquinas, the law is necessary to direct people toward the common good even if before the Fall there would have been no need to punish criminals.[57] It is not surprising, then, that Finnis endorses John Stuart Mill's conception of politics as stated in *On Liberty*.[58] As such, politics based upon the natural law (or the new natural law) punishes external actions only, not internal dispositions.[59] Moreover, and fully in line with Mill, Finnis claims that "the modern grammar of rights provides a way of expressing virtually all the requirements of practical reasonableness."[60] In response we can recall Strauss's comments on Yves Simon to the effect that this can be true only if liberal democracy is the fulfillment of human nature, that is, it is the best regime. For Strauss this would be the case only if liberal democracy was rule by wisdom without the need to accommodate folly. And yet, if James Madison is to be believed, the accommodations in liberal democracy are not ones that wisdom makes with folly but, rather, accommodations that less-than-angelic people make with each other. The problem of factions and his remedy of enlarging the republic are both attributable to the fact that neither are we angels nor are we ruled by them. As he argued, "It is in vain to say, that

---

57. Thomas Aquinas, *Summa Theologica* I, q. 96, a. 3. See also Finnis, *Aquinas*, 248n148 and 265n66; Robert P. George, "Kelsen and Aquinas on the Natural Law Doctrine," in *Thomas Aquinas and the Natural Law Tradition: Contemporary Essays*, ed. John Goyette, Mark S. Latkovic, and Richard S. Myers (Washington, D.C.: The Catholic University of America Press, 2004), 250.

58. See Finnis, *Aquinas*, 266. For this section I rely on Christopher Tollefsen, "Pure Perfectionism and the Limits of Paternalism," in *Reason, Morality, and the Law: The Jurisprudence of John Finnis*, ed. John Keown and Robert P. George (New York: Oxford University Press, 2012). For criticisms of Finnis's position from natural lawyers, see Michael Pakaluk, "Is the Common Good of Political Society Limited and Instrumental?," *Review of Metaphysics* 55, no. 1 (September 2001): 57–94; and Mark C. Murphy, "The Common Good," *Review of Metaphysics* 59, no. 1 (September 2005): 133–64.

59. See John Finnis, "Hart as a Political Philosopher," in *Philosophy of Law: Collected Essays* (New York: Oxford University Press, 2011), 269; and "Law and What I Truly Should Decide," *American Journal of Jurisprudence* 48 (2003): 115.

60. Finnis, *Natural Law and Natural Rights*, 198. But see Mary Ann Glendon, *Rights Talk: The Impoverishment of Political Discourse* (New York: Free Press, 1970). He has also read this back into Aquinas, arguing that while there is no term in his work commensurate with human rights, "Aquinas clearly has the concept." John Finnis, *Aquinas: Moral, Political, and Legal Theory* (New York: Oxford University Press, 1998), 136. See also Lloyd L. Weinreb, "Natural Law and Rights," in *Natural Law Theory*, ed. Robert P. George (New York: Oxford University Press, 1992); John P. Hittinger, "Jacques Maritain and Yves Simon's Use of Thomas Aquinas in Their Defense of Liberal Democracy," in *Thomas Aquinas and His Legacy*, ed. David M. Gallagher (Washington, D.C.: The Catholic University of America Press, 1994).

enlightened statesmen will be able to adjust these clashing interests, and render them all subservient to the public good. Enlightened statesmen will not always be at the helm" (Federalist 10). By establishing a constitutional order rather than a set of laws, Madison was more in line with Strauss's idea of natural right as a regime than with the natural law.

Optimism in the Political Order

Natural law theory presented Strauss with a particular problem. Thomistic natural law was, as he stated several times, part of classic natural right, even "one of the three different manners in which the classics understood natural right," namely, "the Socratic-Platonic, the Aristotelian, and the Thomistic."[61] Yet in his recovery of classic natural right he did not encourage the revival of natural law, even though it would seem to have been in line with his project. Yes, according to Strauss's historical account Thomistic natural law was the proximate cause for the turn to modernity and the development of modern natural right. It is certainly plausible that because of the historical reaction against natural law, its theological origins, or its inflexibility made it an inappropriate way to revive classic natural right. All these could be true. I have argued that, however much he was concerned about these issues, there was a deeper concern. Natural law theories tend toward an inadequate understanding of politics because they lose sight of the accommodations that wisdom must always make with folly in anything short of the best regime.

Although Strauss was mildly critical of Aquinas, he was much more critical of his contemporary Neo-Thomists. Jacques Maritain's work with the United Nations must certainly have worried Strauss about natural lawyers and the "universal and homogeneous state."[62] Together with the

---

61. Strauss, *Natural Right and History*, 146. But see, by contrast, where he includes the entire medieval period within his definition of "modernity." Leo Strauss, "The Three Waves of Modernity," in *An Introduction to Political Philosophy: Ten Essays by Leo Strauss*, ed. Hilail Gildin (Detroit: Wayne State University Press, 1989), 93.

62. Strauss, "Restatement," in *On Tyranny*, 192. The precariousness of the Universal Declaration of Human Rights was revealed in Maritain's report of a comment that "we agree about the rights *but on condition that no one asks us why.*" Maritain, introduction to *Human Rights: Comments and Interpretations: A Symposium*, ed. UNESCO (New York: Allan Wingate, 1949), 9. This is further confirmed by John Humphrey, first director of the United Nations Division of Human Rights, who commented in his diary that the world needed "something like the Christian morality without all the tommyrot." *On the Edge of Greatness: The Diaries of John Humphrey, First Director of the United Nations Division of Human Rights*, ed. Allan John Hobbins (Kingston: McGill-Queens University Press, 2000), 1:39.

embrace of international political institutions in the twentieth century went an embrace of liberal democracy by natural law advocates, including the encyclical of Pope John XXIII *Pacem in Terris* (1963) and much of the work of John Paul II. Is liberal democracy the best regime *simpliciter* or merely the best under current conditions, conditions that may or may not hold long into the future? If not, where must the accommodations be made? What must give? What price is the natural law willing to pay so that the world is not consumed in lust, or greed, or some other vice?[63] Some price must be paid in accommodating folly.

In practice, natural law advocates have found ways to make accommodations but these were always understood as temporary. As far as Strauss was concerned, the accommodations are in tension with both the presentation and purpose of the natural law. Insofar as the natural law is presented as an absolute standard of right and not a decree of prudence, the temporary repeal of any of its rulings undermines its authority. As for its purpose, educating to virtue, the natural law would seem to be far more optimistic than the rest of the classical tradition of natural right. But optimism is not merely a mood. Optimism in this sense looks to the improvement of the political order *through* the political order. The best regime may even be possible by means of the laws of a less than best regime. This would mean that one regime could transform itself into another, and do so both peacefully and based upon its own principles.[64] Strauss's concerns about the natural law are well founded. At its most classical—the accommodation of folly—it is also at its most modern or progressive. Anyone wishing to recover a Catholic political philosophy would need to understand this and address it.

63. On this matter Aquinas quoted St. Augustine: "If you do away with harlots, the world will be convulsed with lust." See *Summa Theologiae* II-II, q. 10, a. 11 (Blackfriars translation).
64. On the question of whether Rome was able to achieve something like this, see Pierre Manent, *The Metamorphoses of the City*, trans. Marc LePain (Cambridge, Mass.: Harvard University Press, 2013).

 4

Modernity, Creation, and Catholicism

Leo Strauss and Benedict XVI

MARC D. GUERRA

Leo Strauss and Pope Benedict XVI are not names usually uttered in the same sentence—and for good reason. One is most popularly known as a twentieth-century historian of political philosophy. The other is best known today for holding the curious title of pope *emeritus* of the Catholic church. Strauss is recognized in academic circles as a political philosopher who authored a wide range of unconventional, penetrating, and controversial interpretations of classic works in ancient, medieval, and modern political philosophy. Benedict is recognized in academic circles as a theologian who has authored a series of magisterial reflections on virtually all areas (systematic, scriptural, sacramental, liturgical, moral, and fundamental) of Catholic theology. Strauss takes the philosopher Plato as the model for human thought; Benedict presents Augustine as the archetype of a thinker whose reason remains open to God. Strauss ultimately argues that Socratic or *zetetic* philosophy, which is necessarily the preserve of only a few, embodies the highest form of human life; Benedict consistently argues that communion with the incarnate *Logos*, Jesus Christ, is the one thing needful for all human beings. This last disagreement, more than anything else, of course, explains why Strauss and Benedict are two thinkers whose thought is very seldom thought together.

Despite the profound differences that separate these two thinkers, Strauss and Benedict, however, do share a basic common interest: each thinker goes out his way to unearth the nature of the West and to identify the concrete roots of the West's remarkable intellectual, spiritual, and political vitality. What is more, both men are led to do this, at least in part, because they take the contemporary West to be in "crisis."[1] Further still, both men argue that the modern West is imperiled from within. Each says that the uniquely Western phenomenon that is modernity has gradually brought about the crisis of the West. Given all this, it is not surprising that Strauss and Benedict both claim that grasping the true nature of modernity is a timely imperative for modern human beings.

Strauss on Modernity

"Modern man was originally guided by a positive project."[2] As Strauss presents it, this positive project was not the creation of nature or God, but of the "great minds" of the early modern period. Seeking to create something new, the intellectual architects of modernity understood their project to require a profound break with the premodern thought of classical philosophy and the Bible. "Only in light of the quarrel between the ancients and the moderns can modernity be understood."[3] Modernity was "understood from the beginning in contradistinction to antiquity; modernity could therefore include the medieval world."[4] For Strauss, the modern project threatened the existence of the historic West from the start. For it sought to separate the modern world from two rival claims whose irreducible tension had given birth to the West: the claims of the Bible and those of classical philosophy, of Jerusalem and Athens.

---

1. See, for example, Pope Benedict XVI, "Europe's Crisis of Culture," in *The Essential Pope Benedict XVI: His Central Writings & Speeches*, ed. John F. Thornton and Susan B. Varenne (New York: HarperOne, 2007), 325–35, and Leo Strauss, "The Crisis of Our Time," in *The Predicament of Modern Politics*, ed. Harold J. Spaeth (Detroit: University of Detroit Press, 1964), 41–54.
2. Leo Strauss, "The Three Waves of Modernity," in his *An Introduction to Political Philosophy: Ten Essays by Leo Strauss*, ed. Hilail Gildin (Detroit: Wayne State University Press, 1989), 83.
3. Leo Strauss, "On the Basis of Hobbes's Political Philosophy," in his *What Is Political Philosophy?: And Other Studies* (Chicago: University of Chicago Press, 1988), 172.
4. Strauss, "The Three Waves of Modernity," 93.

The thinker to spearhead this break was Machiavelli. "Machiavelli rejects the whole philosophic and theological tradition."[5] Opposing the allegedly utopian teachings of classical philosophy and the Bible, Machiavelli advanced a new teaching that looked at things not as men have fancied them, but as they purportedly really are. In contrast to thinkers like Plato and Augustine, Machiavelli claimed to base his thought not on imaginary ends that purportedly perfected man's given potentialities, but on a realistic appreciation of who men really are and how they really live. Moreover, he claimed that it was an error to view human life as subject to the exterior movements of quixotic chance or inscrutable divine providence. *Fortuna* could—and ought to—be controlled by man's use of force. Neither final causes nor chance nor divine governance stood in the way of solving the problem of human living. In breaking with premodern thought in this way, for Machiavelli "the political problem becomes a technical problem."[6]

Strauss identified two movements in modern thought that quickly followed on Machiavelli's heels and furthered the project he initiated. The first came in natural science. Taking its bearing from Machiavelli's rejection of final causes, modern natural science ushered in both a new understanding of nature and a new understanding of science. Knowledge would no longer be seen as something man received by contemplating nature—rather it was now conceived as something man made. According to the new science, this approach would at last make us masters and possessors of nature. But the success of this new approach came at a price: "however much man may succeed in his conquest of nature, he will never be able to understand nature ... there is no natural harmony between the human mind and the universe ... man can guarantee the actualization of wisdom, since wisdom is identical with free construction."[7] The second movement reestablished a connection between politics and natural right, a connection that Machiavelli's initial argument had severed. For Strauss, this was Hobbes's—and in a derivative way Locke's—great accomplishment. Hobbes replaced nature with man and replaced law with rights. He forged a tie between justice and politics (built on man's newly discovered fundamental right to self-preservation) that was, in Strauss's view, in keeping with Machiavelli's innovative spirit.

5. Ibid., 86.
6. Ibid., 87.
7. Leo Strauss, *Natural Right and History* (Chicago: University of Chicago Press, 1953), 174–75.

Modernity would receive its first full-throated challenge, according to Strauss, from Rousseau—a challenge that for Strauss marked the first internal crisis of modernity. Protesting the reduction of man to an economic and comfort-seeking being, Rousseau sought to restore a classical sense of nobility to man as a political being. Yet Rousseau ultimately did this on modern grounds. His "return to antiquity was, at the same time, an advance of modernity."[8] According to Rousseau, Hobbes got primitive man wrong. He failed to go back far enough. Believing he spoke of man as he had originally existed, Hobbes actually spoke of how present-day man would have lived in man's primitive state. Human life in the state of nature, Rousseau mused, was marked by the isolated individual's enjoyment of the sweet sentiment of his own existence and by the premoral sense of compassion that he felt for sentient beings like himself. It was only through the accidents of history—through man's ability to adapt to unforeseen changes in his environment—that we became the type of being we are and live the type of lives we now do. "In post-Rousseauian language, man's humanity is due not to nature but to history, to the historical process, a singular unique process which is not teleological."[9] For Strauss, Rousseau brought to the surface an essential feature of modernity: the replacement of nature with history as the defining principle of human beings and human life.

Rousseau's "passionate and forceful attack on modernity in the name of what was at the same time classical antiquity and a more advanced modernity, was repeated, with no less passion and force, by Nietzsche, who thus ushered in the second crisis of modernity—the crisis of our time."[10] Rousseau's alleged discovery of history would be taken up and reworked by thinkers such as Kant, Hegel, and Marx. Despite their substantive differences, each of these thinkers nonetheless maintained that history had an end, that history was teleological and that it thus revealed an intelligible order to human life. Nietzsche accepted the category of history, but rejected these thinkers' claims about its *telos* and intelligibility. What history really showed was that man cannot look to nature or to God or to history itself for any normative guidance, to any nonhistorical standard that would prevent things from ultimately existing in a state of flux. "The truth is not attractive, lovable, life-giving, but deadly, as is shown by the

8. Ibid., 252.
9. Ibid., 90.
10. Ibid., 252–53.

true doctrines of the sovereignty of Becoming ... the world is itself, the 'thing-in-itself,' 'nature' (aph. 9) is wholly chaotic and meaningless ... all meaning, all order originates in man, in man's creative acts, in his will to power."[11] Modernity's original emancipation of the human will from natural and divine restraints terminated not, as is so often claimed, in nihilism, but in the vindication of irrationality and the elevation of the creative human will. "For the oblivion of eternity, or, in other words, estrangement from man's deepest desire and therewith from the primary issues, is the price modern man had to pay, from the very beginning, for attempting to be absolutely sovereign, to become the master and owner of nature, to conquer chance."[12]

It is in light of this understanding of modernity that Strauss makes his case for the true happiness of the Socratic philosopher's way of life.[13] It is in light of this understanding of modernity that Strauss seeks to recover an appreciation "of classical philosophy, which is nonhistoricist thought in its pure form."[14] And it is in light of this understanding of modernity that Strauss points to our current need to cultivate "a nonhistoricist understanding of nonhistoricist philosophy ... [and] an understanding of the genesis of historicism that does not take for granted the soundness of historicism."[15] Such an understanding would allow us to rediscover "the conflict between the Biblical and the philosophic notions of the good life," which Strauss says is the "core, the nerve, of Western intellectual history, Western spiritual history."[16] On a political level, this rediscovery could show late modern human beings why there is no intrinsic reason for the West—even the modern West—to give up on itself. On the level of the individual, this rediscovery, Strauss asserts with a rhetorical flourish, could explain why "every one of us" ought to be either a "philosopher open to the challenge of theology" or a "theologian open to the challenge of philosophy."[17]

Strauss typically draws attention to the fact that the "great minds"

11. Leo Strauss, "Note on the Plan of Nietzsche's *Beyond Good and Evil*," in his *Studies in Platonic Political Philosophy* (Chicago: University of Chicago Press, 1983), 177.
12. Strauss, "What Is Political Philosophy?," in *What Is Political Philosophy?*, 55.
13. See, for example, Leo Strauss, "Progress or Return?," in his *The Rebirth of Classical Political Rationalism: An Introduction to the Thought of Leo Strauss*, ed. Thomas L. Pangle (Chicago: University of Chicago Press, 1989), 259.
14. Strauss, *Natural Right and History*, 33.
15. Ibid.
16. Strauss, "Progress or Return?," 270.
17. Strauss, "Relativism," in *The Rebirth of Classical Political Rationalism*, 27.

behind the modern project openly announced their intention to break with premodern thought and premodern action. But there is more to his account of the coming into being of modernity than this reading of Strauss permits. Speaking on behalf of modern thought, Hobbes famously boasted that we understand only what we make. Though he rejected the ultimate truth of Hobbes's claim, Strauss understood modernity to be something that was made, not created *ex nihilo*. The founders of modernity necessarily relied on what came before modernity to articulate what modernity is—and what it is not—and to construct the world they envisioned. Strauss suggests as much in his observation that modernity, strictly speaking, could actually include medieval elements. More directly, Strauss occasionally suggests that the modern project "could not have been conceived without the help of surviving ingredients of Biblical faith."[18] And for the most part, with the important exception of Maimonides's claim that creation has a beginning but no end (a claim that Strauss suggests foreshadows the modern idea of progress), he tends to describe these ingredients as being of Christian origin. As he states with uncharacteristic candor in a 1936 essay, "it is not the Bible and the Koran, but perhaps the New Testament, and certainly the Reformation and modern philosophy, which brought about the break with ancient thought."[19]

Strauss alludes to a number of these ingredients in his writings. To mention only a few, he suggests a relationship between Christianity and certain strands of modern thought such as (1) the belief that philosophy ought to be practical; (2) that the end that all men pursue and are capable of attaining is essentially the same; (3) that the world as we know it is in

---

18. Strauss, *Introduction to Political Philosophy*, 83.
19. Leo Strauss, "Some Remarks on the Political Science of Maimonides and Farabi," *Interpretation* 18, no. 1 (1990): 4–5. Strauss immediately prefaces this statement with the remark that "there is a profound agreement between Jewish and Muslim thought on the one hand and ancient thought on the other." And he immediately follows this statement with the remark that the "guiding idea upon which the Greeks and the Jews agree is precisely the idea of the divine law as a single and total law which is at the same time religious law, civil law and moral law." Two things are worthy of note. First, Strauss here lumps Judaism and Islam together. Rather than looking at what either religion in particular positively says, he treats them as two members of the same species, the species of religion as all-encompassing divine law. Second, Strauss states that modern philosophy, the Reformation, and perhaps the New Testament broke with ancient, Jewish, and Muslim thought on the notion of a total divine law. Strauss does not address the reason why each of these things broke with the notion of a total divine law—modern thought on the basis of the individual, the Reformation on the basis of each man's private and unmediated relation with God, and the New Testament on the claim that all men, individually and collectively, are ordered to an end that transcends the limits of a temporal law, even a total, but still temporal, divine law. Rather, he treats the claims of modern thought, the Reformation, and perhaps the New Testament as collective instances of the same kind of thing—they are all presented as instances of a group that rejects the notion of a divine and total law.

some sense deficient and that man's given estate needs to be relieved; (4) that all men's lives, not just those of a naturally selected few, transcend the rule of a single and total divine code; (5) and that *pathos*, not laughter or resigned serenity, is man's proper response to the human limitations he encounters in this world. Tracing the paths of all of Strauss's suggestions on this front lies well beyond the scope of this paper and, more importantly, beyond the capabilities of this writer. Still, for the time being, it suffices to draw attention to two of these suggestions—both of which are made with an eye to Machiavelli and both of which suggest that for Strauss modernity is, at least in part, a reaction to, rejection of, and mutation of Christian themes and categories.

Strauss periodically notes that Machiavelli embarked on his project spurred on by "anti-theological ire."[20] Machiavelli's project involved the theological and the political: "He seems to have diagnosed the great evils of religious persecution as a necessary consequence of the Christian principle."[21] The Christian principle affected a change not just in political practice, but in political and transpolitical thought as well. Strauss points out that by Machiavelli's time the classical tradition had undergone a series of profound changes. Significantly, one of these was that the "contemplative life had found its home in monasteries."[22]

The migration of the contemplative life into the monastery was itself predicated on a profound earlier change in the classical understanding of the best way of life and the nature of philosophy. Catholic Christianity embraced philosophy. But it did not embrace philosophy as the self-sufficient, best way of life. On the contrary, it embraced philosophy as an elevated form of reason that could help elucidate the divine truths of sacred doctrine. In short, Catholicism embraced philosophy, but only as the domesticated *ancilla* of theology.[23]

Machiavelli would do something similar, according to Strauss. Fueled by "antitheological passion," he would "take the extreme step."[24] He would promulgate the notion that philosophy finally did not transcend the limited life of the city. Machiavellian modernity would press philosophy not into the service of a divine science that reflected on the divine

---

20. Strauss, "What Is Political Philosophy?," 44.
21. Ibid.
22. Ibid., 43.
23. Leo Strauss, *Persecution and the Art of Writing* (Chicago: University of Chicago Press, 1952), 21.
24. Leo Strauss, "Marsilius of Padua," in his *Liberalism Ancient and Modern* (Ithaca, N.Y.: Cornell University Press, 1989), 201.

end of all men, but into the service of the people and the problem of human living. Henceforth, philosophy would be seen as something useful, a tool that could be used to satiate all, or at least the majority, of men's felt needs and desires. "Modern philosophy comes into being when the end of philosophy is identified with the end which is capable of being actually pursed by all men."[25]

Strauss also argues that while Machiavelli was a vehement critic of Christianity, he borrowed one crucial thing from Christianity and applied it to his own ends. "The only element of Christianity which Machiavelli took over was the idea of propaganda."[26] Like the Jesus he describes, Machiavelli too is an unarmed prophet. He too seeks to rule not by armed force, but by publicly disseminating his own revolutionary teaching. Strauss's Machiavelli knew that his victory, like Jesus's, would have to be posthumous. His victory could only be secured after the new modes and orders he set in motion had had time to take hold of men's minds and change the way in which men viewed, and acted in, this world. Seeking to fight fire with fire, Machiavelli "attempted to destroy Christianity by the same means by which Christianity was originally established."[27] His calculated reaction to Christianity turned Christianity's tactic of spreading the good news of the Gospel on its head, brazenly disseminating the belief that the modern teachers of universal enlightenment, not God, were the true saviors of mankind.

Benedict on Modernity

On the surface, Pope Benedict XVI's account of modernity seems to bear a striking resemblance to that of Strauss, particularly if one focuses predominantly on his 2006 lecture "Faith, Reason, and the University: Memories and Reflections."[28] As one commentator on this lecture has remarked, while Benedict emphasizes different stages in modernity's development, he does not contradict "Strauss' schema" as he, like Strauss,

---

25. Strauss, "Liberal Education and Responsibility," in *Liberalism Ancient and Modern*, 19.
26. Strauss, "What Is Political Philosophy?," 45.
27. Ibid.
28. Citations from Pope Benedict XVI, "Faith, Reason and the University: Memories and Reflections," are taken from the copy of the address reprinted in *Liberating Logos: Pope Benedict XVI's September Speeches*, ed. Marc D. Guerra (South Bend, Ind.: St. Augustine's Press, 2014).

traces modernity back to "an original philosophic break with the premodern tradition."[29]

But when Benedict's account of modernity is viewed in a larger context, and particularly when his Regensburg Lecture is read in light of his *In the Beginning ... A Catholic Understanding of the Story of Creation and the Fall*, one starts to see profound and substantive differences between his understanding of modernity and that of Strauss.[30] Whereas Strauss presents modernity chiefly as a project to make something new, Benedict views modernity largely as the product of three misguided attempts to *return* to the past. More deeply, whereas Strauss subtly implicates Catholic Christianity in the founding of modernity, Benedict depicts modernity as a falling away from Catholicism's unique mediation of the classical Greek, Roman, and biblical elements in the West. This falling away, in Benedict's presentation, gradually gives birth to what is, in effect, a break from the past: most palpably, a break from Catholicism's appropriated—and transformed—understanding of the Greek conception of *logos* and the religion's distinctive understanding of creation. Inasmuch as Catholic Christianity provides a way of mediating "the encounter of Jerusalem, Athens, and Rome," it is able to articulate an alternative to (not a progenerating cause of) modernity's characteristic theoretical and practical conundrums.[31]

Benedict takes the obscuring of Catholicism's teaching on creation as being "closely connected" with "the spirit of modernity."[32] Indeed, for him, obfuscating what he calls "faith in creation" is a "fundamental part of what constitutes modernity."[33] Failing to appreciate that Catholicism's understanding of creation simultaneously reflects and demands the religion's embrace of a "critically purified Greek" understanding of reason, such obfuscation alters man's understanding of reason as well as his understanding of faith. It falsifies modern man's understanding of the nature of theoretical and practical reason, and distorts Christians' understanding of their own faith.

---

29. Nathan Schlueter, "Leo Strauss and Benedict XVI on the Crisis of the West," *Modern Age* 55, nos. 1–2 (Spring 2013): 5.

30. Joseph Cardinal Ratzinger, *In the Beginning ... A Catholic Understanding of the Story of Creation and the Fall*, trans. Boniface Ramsey, OP (Grand Rapids, Mich.: Eerdmans, 1995).

31. Pope Benedict XVI, "Address at the Reichstag Building, Berlin," on September 22, 2011, as found in *Liberating Logos*, 47.

32. Ratzinger, *In the Beginning*, 82.

33. Ibid.

As Benedict frequently notes, the claim that the world was created through God's *Logos* is a truth affirmed in the opening verses of the Gospel of John as well as a truth Christians profess in their creeds. To say that Christians have faith in creation is not simply to say that they believe in creation. The truths articulated in the church's profession of faith reflect a distinctive kind of knowledge, one in which man's reason is "quickened" and "elevated" by grace. While the central claims of Christian faith (most fundamentally that God is three divine persons in one divine nature) cannot be demonstrably proven, the "act of faith is an event that expands the limits of individual reason ... [and] brings the isolated and fragmented individual intellect into the realm of Him who is logos, the reason, and the reasonable ground of all being, all things, and all mankind."[34] In faith "God no longer appears as Supreme Being in the process of becoming, or as Being per se, but as a Person ... [who] touches the ground of my own being, without which I would not be ... without which nothing is."[35] The Christian faith thus articulates truths that "[signify] a reality which Scripture makes known but which is not itself simply identical with Scripture. Revelation, therefore, is more than Scripture to the extent that reality exceeds information about it."[36] This partly explains the "fundamental decisions of the early councils" to turn to Greek philosophy in formulating the Christian creeds.[37] Giving verbal expression to the unchanging "elements of the biblical faith," these councils assured "the rational nature of biblical faith, which in fact goes beyond reason itself and any possible 'experiences' it may have yet nonetheless appeals to the reason."[38] For Benedict, such claims give man access to the very heart of reality. Benedict even speculates that there may have been something providential, not accidental, about "the encounter of the faith of the Bible and Greek philosophy."[39] To say therefore that Christians have faith in creation is to say that they have faith in the act of the triune God who reveals himself as creating, redeeming, and sanctifying man.

34. Joseph Cardinal Ratzinger, "The Church and Scientific Theology," *Communio: International Catholic Review* 7, no. 4 (1980): 339.
35. Joseph Cardinal Ratzinger, *Principles of Catholic Theology: Building Stones for a Fundamental Theology*, trans. Sister Mary Frances McCarthy, SND (San Francisco: Ignatius Press, 1987), 73–74.
36. Karl Rahner and Joseph Ratzinger, *Revelation and Tradition*, trans. W. J. O'Hara (New York: Herder and Herder, 1966), 7.
37. Joseph Cardinal Ratzinger, *Truth and Tolerance: Christian Belief and World Religions*, trans. Henry Taylor (San Francisco: Ignatius Press, 2004), 92.
38. Ratzinger, *Truth and Tolerance*, 93; Pope Benedict XVI, *Deus Caritas Est*, par. 12.
39. Ratzinger, *Truth and Tolerance*, 95.

The modern suppression of faith in creation began, for Benedict, with the sixteenth-century Dominican, Giordano Bruno. Bruno advocated a return to the idea of a divine cosmos. Renaissance, for Bruno, meant "relinquishing the Christian so that the Greek can be restored in all its pagan purity."[40] Bruno posited a cosmos that reflected a divine fullness that was at peace with itself. Benedict consequently detects in Bruno's thought "the aesthetic prelude to an increasingly prominent idea in the modern mind: the dependence implied by faith in creation is unacceptable ... [because it is taken to be] the real barrier to human freedom."[41]

Galileo engendered the second modern obfuscation of creation. He advocated not a return to the idea of a divine cosmos, but an exaggerated "reversion to the mathematical side of platonic thought."[42] Knowledge of God is now identified with knowledge of the mathematical structures of nature—the concept of mathematical nature taking the place of an intelligible order created by a personal God who eternally stands outside of his creation. God "is no longer God but a scientific hypothesis ... [just as] a God who has nothing to do with the rational creation, but is effectively only in the inner world of piety, is also no longer God."[43] For Benedict, only when "creation and covenant come together can either creation or covenant be realistically discussed—the one presupposes the other."[44]

While Bruno and Galileo sought to return to a form of purified Greek thought, the third obfuscation was driven by a desire to return to what was seen as a primitive and pure form of Christianity. Catholic Christianity's rapprochement with Greek philosophy, in Luther's eyes, corrupted Christian truth. This corruption, he insisted, could be seen in medieval theology's preoccupation with "the question of being, and therefore in the area of the doctrine of creation."[45] Luther understood being to stand for everything that is proper to human beings. Redemption therefore takes place only when man "is liberated from the chains of the past, from the shackles of being"; it takes place only when man is set "free from the curse of existing creation."[46] Christ, for Luther, offers man an escape from his sinful past and from his sinful existence. Where Galileo saw geometry in nature, Luther saw evil in history.

40. Ratzinger, *In the Beginning*, 83.
41. Ibid., 84.
42. Ibid.
43. Ibid., 85.
44. Ibid.
45. Ibid., 87.
46. Ibid.

As a result of these early modern obfuscations, the notion of creation now stands at the "crossroads ... of intellectual history."⁴⁷ Each of these obfuscations eschews an understanding of reason that would allow one to think about creation in a theoretical way. Each rejects an understanding of reason that is genuinely metaphysical in scope for something else: either a poetic interpretation of the world or a mathematical conception of the world or a biblical fundamentalist view of the world. Benedict notes that presently this crossroads is concealed by modern science's mechanistic conception of nature and by a resentment of technology—which Benedicts detects in Rousseau—that issues in the view that modern man is the true enemy of all that is natural. But this concealment has a theological component as well. Increasingly, we see nature undermined, if not brushed aside, in the name of asserting the radical primacy of the realm of grace.

Benedict clearly thinks that such a theological concealment is a mistake. To him, it is yet another instance of the "Gnostic disenchantment with creation."⁴⁸ Citing 1 Corinthians 15:46 ("It is not the spiritual which is first but the physical, and then the spiritual"), he warns that "we must never try to take the second step before the first ... if we skip this sequence, creation is denied, and grace is deprived of its foundation."⁴⁹ For this reason, he states that today we must "develop a Christian pedagogy that accepts creation and gives concrete expression to the two poles of the one faith."⁵⁰ Such a pedagogy would make clear that human beings "are dependent—that is the primary truth about them"; moreover, it could help give expression to Christianity's claim that "only love can redeem [men], for only love transforms dependence into freedom."⁵¹

Benedict elaborated on the intellectual, moral, and spiritual implications of an understanding of reason that is, in principle, incapable of thinking about creation in his well-known 2006 lecture at the University of Regensburg. Benedict there addressed the effects that nominalism and voluntarism have on modern thought in both its secular and religious forms. He speaks of the political problem that nominalism and voluntarism pose in radical Islam and emphasizes the ways these doctrines inform Western ideas about the sovereignty of the individual. Most of

---

47. Ibid., 92.
48. Ibid., 95.
49. Ibid., 94.
50. Ibid.
51. Ibid., 98–99.

all, however, his lecture aims to explain "three stages in the programme of dehellinization" that have altered Christians' understanding of their faith.[52]

Benedict locates the first stage of dehellenization in the Reformation. As we have already seen, Luther—and by extension Calvin—objected to what was seen as the near-total absorption of the Christian faith into an alien Aristotelian framework. Thus, the Reformers turned to the principle of *sola scriptura* in the hope of reclaiming the true content of the way of life proclaimed by the Christ of the Gospels. Formalizing a theoretically unbridgeable gap between faith and reason, they paved the way for holding the truths held by Christian faith apart from those grasped by human reason—a position Benedict notes was anticipated by the late medieval nominalism and voluntarism of Duns Scotus. The Reformers framed the question of faith and reason in such a way that the content of Christian faith conceptually had no substantive intellectual connection to what human reason grasps about "reality as a whole."[53] As a consequence, Christian piety would gradually supplant Christian faith, Christianity would less and less be seen as a faith formulated in doctrines that are proposed to man's intelligence and more and more as a religion in which one piously and sincerely believes.

The second stage of dehellenization aimed to forge a new alliance between faith and reason. Taking Adolf von Harnack as the representative of this position, Benedict claims that this approach preserved the Reformers' basic prejudice against Catholic Christianity's understandings of the nature and scope of reason. The proponents of this stage sought to make faith more rational and scientific. Accepting modern science's self-imposed "limitation of reason," liberal nineteenth- and twentieth-century theologians proposed a historically critical and hence allegedly scientific study of the Christian faith.[54] Christianity, it was alleged, only gained scientific legitimacy when shorn of everything that could not be documented by a critical study of the historical record. This reinterpretation of Christian faith revealed a Christ who was merely "the father of a humanitarian moral message."[55] Methodologically denying Christ's divinity and the reality of man's transcendent destiny, this historically critical study of Christian

---

52. Pope Benedict XVI, "Faith, Reason and the University," 31.
53. Ibid., 32.
54. Ibid., 33.
55. Ibid.

faith affirmed a Christ who "put an end to worship in favor of morality."[56] Insisting that practical and empirical reason should be privileged over theoretical reason, this stage of dehellenization came to conclusions that at least formally resembled Hobbes's bold denial of any *summum bonum* or Kant's defense of the radical autonomy of practical reason.

Contemporary Christians currently live in the third stage of dehellenization, according to Benedict. Appealing to the modern experience of cultural pluralism, it is now claimed that Christianity's traditional understanding of the relationship between faith and reason is itself culturally conditioned. Christianity does not reveal something fundamentally true about the nature of faith or reason—let alone their relation to each other. We are now told that that relationship is accidental, a byproduct of Christianity gaining its initial cultural foothold in a particular place at a particular time. The third stage of dehellenization accordingly represents a genuine flight from reason. It requires faith and reason to be subsumed into the allegedly broader and more fundamental category of culture. Drawing the logical conclusion from the first stage's rejection of reason and metaphysics, the third stage of the dehellenization asserts that because what men believe has no discernible correlation to what reason grasps about reality, all theoretical and practical claims (including Christianity's theoretical and practical claims), must be built on a construction.

As we have seen, Benedict notes the conflict that Bruno posits between creation and human freedom. He also suggests that Rousseau anticipated contemporary claims about man's hostility to nature. And he observes that late modern thought reduces all of human life to a construction. It is therefore no exaggeration to say that Benedict deeply believes that the eclipse of creation in modernity has had discernible and powerful social and political effects. However, unlike Strauss, he sees these effects as being largely accidental, the derivative practical consequences of the theoretical movements of modern reason. Social and political modernity, for Benedict, was not so much born out of a deliberate desire to solve the problem of human living, as it embodies the practical results of modern reason's new theoretical way of conceiving nature.

This new abstract and mathematicized way of conceiving nature necessarily looks upon the human person as a problem: "The fact of human

56. Ibid.

beings is an obstacle and irritation for [modern] 'science,' because they are not something science can exactly 'objectify.'"[57] As Benedict insightfully points out, the very practitioner of the science that dogmatically seeks to map everything out on a field of space and extension ironically cannot make scientific sense of his own personal existence and his own personal actions. Further still, the being who cannot be objectified is also a free being. He is a person who can and does act (sometimes well, sometimes badly) in the world and in social and political life. For "the modern age the dualism becomes typically one between 'divine' geometry, on the one hand, and a world of intrinsic corruption, on the other. Without the mystery of redemptive love, which is also creative love, the world inevitably becomes dualistic: by nature, it is geometry; as history, it is the drama of evil."[58]

The thinker who sought to overcome this particularly modern form of dualism, according to Benedict, was Hegel. Eschewing Christianity's claim that the God who is love and *Logos* is the God who creates and redeems, Hegel presented a God that exists in the historical "process of reasoning, which can come into being only in the other and in exchange with it."[59] Hegel interpreted the whole universe, the whole of history, as the unfolding, historical process of reason. For Hegel, individual moments in this process found their meaning only as parts of history viewed as a whole. "Evil is necessarily bound up with finitude, and so, from the standpoint of the Infinity, is unreal."[60] Hegel's attempt to solve the problem of modern dualism, as Benedict presents it, was, however, largely theoretical. Marx was the thinker who pressed Hegel's theoretical position into a call to radical action. Abolishing the free human person in the name of the whole, Marx claimed that only the species counts: "All that matters is the logic of the system and the future, a future in which humans are redeemed by ... self-creation, which is accomplished through work."[61] The "decisive option underlying all the thought of Karl Marx is ultimately a protest against the dependence that creation signifies: *the hatred of life as we encounter it.*"[62] Protesting man's dependency on creation is, then, a practical imperative of modern thought. It is, Benedict sug-

---

57. Ratzinger, *In the Beginning*, 86.
58. Ibid., 88–89.
59. Ibid., 89.
60. Ibid.
61. Ibid., 90–91.
62. Ibid., 91; emphasis added.

gests, the unintended, but unavoidable, consequence of modernity's loss of faith in creation.

Strauss and Benedict on Modernity

Strauss and Benedict thus each offer us a rich account of the nature and origins of modernity. But they are two distinct and different accounts. Benedict is undoubtedly right to note that modernity's flight from a theoretical understanding (and appreciation) of creation is, in the end, crucial for modern thought. And he is also right to observe that this flight engenders a "crisis of modern consciousness."[63] Within this crisis of consciousness, reason is reduced to a form of methodological empiricism that cannot wrestle with the fundamental question of being or, for that matter, pressing elemental questions of moral truth. Moreover, this crisis reduces Christian faith, at best, to the level of a mystical insight. The loss of faith in creation, Benedict convincingly demonstrates, transforms modern man into a myopic giant. Indeed, it allows modern man to be a being who is methodologically incapable of knowing anything substantively true about himself, the world, or the God who created both himself and the world.

At the same time, while Strauss, as we shall see, does not advance an account of creation that can, in fact, explain the human person's basic dependence on God's creation, he is nonetheless right to draw attention to the fact that the modern world presents itself as a conscious, sustained social and political project to an amazing degree. Strauss reminds us that early modern thinkers like Machiavelli, Hobbes, Descartes, Spinoza, and Locke knowingly set out to introduce new modes and orders. The intellectual architects of modernity aspired to create a new technological, social, and political world that solved the problem of human living once and for all. Strauss, then, allows us to see something that Benedict, taken on his own, does not: the social and political revolution that began in the early modern period is not accidental to modernity, but is essential to it.

Fleshing out the dialectic between Strauss's and Benedict's respective understandings of modernity—their substantive points of agreement and disagreement—could prove quite promising. Among other things, it

63. Ibid., 83.

could help us avoid the kind of one-sided and overly simplified accounts of modernity that we sometimes encounter today, in both Catholic and non-Catholic quarters. These academically fashionable accounts are apt to describe modernity (and the challenges and promises of modernity) in arrestingly dualistic tones: modernity is either said to represent one triumph after another or it is said to represent one mistake after another. Such dualistic accounts undoubtedly have their Catholic analogues. For example, today it is not uncommon to hear social and political modernity described either as the fruit of the Gospel's message about the free and dignified human person or as the wholesale rejection of that rich message.

At the very least, thinking Strauss's and Benedict's accounts of modernity together could help us better understand why Catholicism and Catholic thought finally cannot be categorized as either simply ancient or simply modern. Thinking the two accounts together, in other words, could help us understand why Catholicism's essential claims about human dependence, human reason, human freedom, human equality, and human dignity ultimately transcend the binary nature of a simple and formulaic ancient/modern distinction.

Strauss and Benedict on Creation

It remains the case, however, that Benedict's argument about how faith in creation allows for a proper understanding of human reason and its theoretical and practical operations (including its political judgments and proposals) finds no exact parallel in Strauss's thought. Strauss appears to make the exact opposite claim. Strauss identifies the profoundly different ways in which the Bible and Greek philosophy understand creation as *the* basic ground of the conflict between the Bible and Greek philosophy. What allows for the proper understanding of the intrinsic problem with modern thought for Benedict, that is, faith in creation, for Strauss affirms a teaching that attempts to unstring the bow that energizes Western civilization. More deeply, what one thinks about creation ultimately makes, for both Benedict and Strauss, all the difference in the world.

At times Strauss seems to depreciate the importance of the question of creation. For instance, he movingly remarks that by "becoming aware of the dignity of the mind, we realize the true dignity of man and therewith the goodness of the world, whether we understand it as created or as uncreated, which is the home of man because it is the home of the human mind."[64] Yet at other times he emphasizes that the question of creation stood at the epicenter of the medieval conflict between philosophy and theology. Strauss goes on to note that if one enlarges medieval debates about the eternity of the visible universe to include debates about "any cosmos or chaos which might ever exist" it becomes clear that "Greek philosophy teaches the eternity of cosmos or chaos."[65] By contrast, "the Bible teaches creation ... the Bible teaches divine omnipotence."[66] And the notion of divine omnipotence, Strauss argues, is "incompatible with Greek philosophy in any form": "In all Greek thought, we find in one form or the other an impersonal necessity higher than any personal being."[67] Strauss remarks that where the Bible takes religious experience as genuine experience, Greek philosophy views such an experience as questionable at best.

The question of creation finally comes down to the question of whether a cosmos is marked by intelligible necessity or arbitrary and unfathomable divine will. Put somewhat differently, Strauss asserts that "Greek philosophy is based on this premise: that there is such a thing as nature or natures—a notion which has no equivalent in Biblical thought." Strauss here explicitly speaks of Hebraic biblical thought; he does not mention Christian biblical thought. But in some respects, this would seem, for Strauss, to be a distinction without a difference. The question of nature or natures, for him, rests on the difference between eternal impersonal necessity and omnipotent and unfathomable divine will. Contrary to what a certain kind of Catholic thinker is prone to dismissively claim about Strauss, metaphysics and metaphysical concerns do loom large in his thought—they are just not placed in the forefront of his thought, that is, in a certain understanding of the "first" in the "first philosophy." Indeed, for Strauss, the very possibility of the philosopher's way of life—and thus the kind of happiness that the Socratic philosopher acquires from getting "the highest possible degree of clarity which he can acquire"—hinges on a question of cosmology.[68]

64. Strauss, "What Is Liberal Education," in *Liberalism Ancient and Modern*, 8.
65. Strauss, "Progress or Return?," 252.
66. Ibid.
67. Ibid.
68. Ibid., 259.

As one would expect, Benedict does not understand Christianity's teaching on creation along the lines Strauss draws. Indeed, his reflection shows that Strauss's either/or formulation is not the *only* viable way that reason can think about creation—in fact, it suggests that Strauss's formulation may not be the best or most reasonable way to formulate the question of creation. As he presents it, there is something pinched and misleading about such formulations. Notably, such a binary schema misses the mark when it comes to Christianity: it fails to take the Catholic faith's distinctive claim—not simply some general notion of revealed religion's claim—about creation seriously. Benedict would, however, recognize that Strauss's way of framing this question bears some resemblance to the way that the followers of the thirteenth-century Franciscan, Duns Scotus, came to frame this question. Scotus's thought gave rise to the view that we can only know God's *voluntas ordinate*. As a result, human beings, it was said, could only know an infinite array of possibilities (not potentialities), an ever-expanding collection of concepts that, in truth, had no real connection to what the mind could know about reality.

However, as Benedict points out, this is not the understanding of either God or creation that the Catholic faith proposes. Catholicism sets forth a particular claim directed to man's reason: the "faith of the Church has always insisted that between God and us, between his eternal Creator Spirit and our created reason there exists a real analogy, in which ... unlikeness remains infinitely greater than likeness, yet not to the point of abolishing analogy and its language."[69] That claim does not see God as either divine will or divine reason, or sees God as more divine will than divine reason. Rather, it argues that God's essence is his existence (*ipsum esse subsistens*) and that for this reason there cannot be the kind of rival juxtaposition between divine reason and divine will that voluntarism posits. While it is true that created things depend upon a cause both "to become" and "to be," God exists in another order, an uncreated, eternal order that we know by way of analogy. God alone, Catholicism maintains, is the kind of being in which he is his own existence. Benedict adamantly rejects the notion that God becomes "more divine when we push him away from us in sheer, impenetrable voluntarism."[70]

This is the understanding of God that informs Catholic Christianity's

---

69. Pope Benedict XVI, "Faith, Reason, and the University," 30.
70. Ibid.

teaching on creation. The God whose essence is his existence, the God who wills his own goodness necessarily, stands outside of his creation. The created order is dependent on him for its existence and perfection; he is in no way either dependent on creation or made more perfect by creation. By freely willing to create and sustain the universe, God activates and sustains "in act all those secondary causes whose activity contribute to the unfolding of the natural order which he intends to produce."[71]

Benedict's reflections on the gratuitousness of creation reveal that to ask, along with the *Euthyphro*, whether God is omnipotent or dependent on an order outside of himself misses the mark when it comes to grappling with Catholicism's claim. By claiming that the world was created through God's eternal *Logos* who became flesh, the Catholic faith proposes something new, something unknown—and unknowable—prior to the incarnation. It thus rejects claims like Strauss's that assert that man's understanding of the "permanent problems" (and thus the potential answers to these problems) has stayed, and will forever stay, the same. In the incarnation, God "brought to pass something new," "but this new thing had been prepared for, and history, for all its confusion and errors, had been leading up to it."[72] "The real novelty of the New Testament lies not so much in new ideas as in the figure of Christ himself, who gives flesh and blood ... an unprecedented realism."[73] Christian revelation sets in motion a way of thinking about God's omnipotence and his freedom that suggest that some things simply cannot be done because of the nature of reality itself—a reality that finds its complete expression in God. Thus, God's creation of the world does not render human reason impotent or make the life of reason impossible, according to Benedict. Quite the contrary, it is the very act that allows man's created reason to participate in (and come to know something about) the created and uncreated intelligible orders.

The God of *Logos* and Freedom

The importance of creation being the free act of God cannot be overestimated for Benedict. He insists that the proper model for thinking about

---

71. International Theological Commission, "Communion and Stewardship: Human Persons Created in the Image of God," 2000–2002 Plenary Session, no. 63.
72. Ratzinger, *Truth and Tolerance*, 95–96.
73. Pope Benedict XVI, *Deus Caritas Est*, par. 16.

creation is not the craftsman, who fashions something along some predetermined pattern, but the "creative mind." Christian belief in creation is first and foremost a belief in the primacy of the *Logos*. But it is also a belief "that the original thought, whose being-thought is represented by the world, is not an anonymous, neutral consciousness, but rather freedom, creative love, a person."[74] "Christian faith gave a completely new significance to this God ... removing him from the purely academic realm and thus profoundly transforming him."[75] Divinity is no longer understood simply as the highest being, whose perfection demands it remains fixed and unchanged knowing only itself. The "highest possibility of Being" is revealed to be a divine person who "includes the element of relationship."[76] And the world that this God creates is understood to reflect this fact: it is a world populated with persons with unique and irreducible identities—not simply instances of basic human types such as the believer or the citizen or the philosopher. To be a human person is necessarily to live a life that is tied—in obligations and in friendship and in love—to other persons, including the Trinitarian God who is a person in the most proper sense of the term. The life of the person made in God's image shares very little in common, then, with the reported life of modernity's autonomous rights-bearing individual or Strauss's largely solitary Socratic philosopher. "Existing in [his] own right," the human person "comes home to [himself], and this act is an answer in freedom to God's love ... the being of the other is not absorbed or abolished, but rather, in giving itself ... becomes fully itself."[77]

To believe in the primacy of *Logos*, Benedict explains, is to believe in "the primacy of the particular" rather than the universal.[78] Yet it is also to believe in "the primacy of freedom as against the primacy of cosmic necessity."[79] Catholicism argues that we live in a world that is created, sustained, and governed by a God who both stands outside of the world and enters into the world he created. Such a God reveals himself both as "I am" and "the God of Abraham, Isaac, and Jacob"; and he freely acts out

---

74. Joseph Cardinal Ratzinger, *Introduction to Christianity*, trans. J. R. Foster and Michael J. Miller (San Francisco: Ignatius Press, 2004), 158.
75. Ibid., 143.
76. Ibid., 147–48.
77. Joseph Cardinal Ratzinger, *The Spirit of the Liturgy*, trans. John Saward (San Francisco: Ignatius Press, 2000), 32–33.
78. Ratzinger, *Introduction to Christianity*, 158.
79. Ibid.

of love on behalf of his creation: "for God so loved the world that he gave his only begotten Son"(Jn 3:16). A world created by such a God is the antithesis to the mathematicised world of modern natural science; it is the antithesis to a world in which God is said to do geometry. At the same time, it is a world that comes with "the somber mystery of the demonic."[80] It is a world that "accepts the mystery of darkness for the sake of the greater light constituted by freedom and love."[81]

Such freedom does not vindicate modernity's claims about the emancipation of the human will and unbound powers of human sovereignty. "Humans are dependent—that is the primary truth about them."[82] The recovery of what is meant by Christian faith in creation, allows us to see the true nature and dignity of man, because it roots this nature and dignity in the creative act of the uncreated personal God. As such, it also allows us to see the dehumanizing and false view of human beings and the human sovereignty that lies at the heart of so much—but not all—of modern thought and modern action.

However, Catholic Christianity's teachings on God, man, and creation only shed light on the problem of modernity accidently. While these teachings may point to a way of mediating the competing claims of Jerusalem, Athens, and Rome, their essential concern, as Benedict reminds us, lies elsewhere. They are directed toward announcing the good news of the Gospel. This news transcends the concerns of identifying the permanent problems or defending the importance of the philosophical way of life or describing the resigned serenity of the Socratic philosopher—however important these concerns may be. For it involves showing that the human person does not have to remain estranged from the object, to use Strauss's words, of "[his] deepest desire." Most deeply, it consists, as Benedict's thought points out again and again, in making clear that "the triune God intended not only to make a place for human beings in the universe but also, and ultimately, to make room for them in his own Trinitarian life."[83]

---

80. Ibid., 160.
81. Ibid.
82. Ratzinger, *In the Beginning*, 98.
83. International Theological Commission, "Communion and Stewardship," no. 63.

 5

Leo Strauss's Critique of Modern Political Philosophy and Ernest Fortin's Critique of Modern "Catholic Social Teaching"

DOUGLAS KRIES

Ernest L. Fortin, AA, began his reading of Leo Strauss in the early 1950s; in recalling his initial encounter with Strauss's work well over forty years later, he says that he read *Persecution and the Art of Writing* first, followed soon by *Natural Right and History*. "They were very powerful books," he stated, "and the more you got into them, the more you were persuaded by their argument."[1] Indeed, so persuaded was Fortin that by the time the end of his career was approaching, he was described as "the world's only, or at least most visible and vocal, Straussian theologian."[2]

Fortin's "Straussian theology" was wide-ranging and covered many topics. Nevertheless, Harvey C. Mansfield—a friend of Fortin and fellow student of Strauss—has suggested recently that Fortin's most notewor-

1. Michael P. Foley, "An Interview with Ernest L. Fortin, A.A., and Photographs of His Life," in *Gladly to Learn and Gladly to Teach: Essays on Religion and Political Philosophy in Honor of Ernest L. Fortin, A.A.*, ed. Michael P. Foley and Douglas Kries (Lanham, Md.: Lexington Books, 2002), 292.
2. Daniel J. Mahoney, foreword to *Ernest L. Fortin: Collected Essays*, ed. J. Brian Benestad (Lanham, Md.: Rowman and Littlefield, 1996), 2:ix.

thy efforts are his studies of Dante and of patristic authors.³ These two foci of Fortin's writings each have their roots, it would seem, in *Persecution and the Art of Writing*. The current essay, however, will treat a third focus of Fortin's work, namely Fortin's criticism of modern Catholic social thought—a topic which has its roots in the second of Strauss's books that Fortin read, *Natural Right and History*.

All of Fortin's work runs contrary to contemporary prejudices, but this third topic seems always in particular danger of falling into neglect; nevertheless, this is precisely where Fortin's work is most capable of profiting the Catholic church in our time. The present essay will therefore begin by explaining how Leo Strauss came to identify modern natural rights teaching with Thomas Hobbes. It will then show how Fortin attempted to use Strauss's interpretation of modern natural rights thinking in order to engage what he perceived to be a failure on the part of leading scholars to distinguish carefully between natural rights and natural law. Finally, the essay will argue that Fortin's signal accomplishment on behalf of the Catholic church occurred in May 1991, in an address at the Lateran University in Rome criticizing modern Catholic social thought extending forward from *Rerum Novarum*—even as John Paul II was asserting something quite different about Catholic social teaching with the publication of *Centesimus Annus* in another part of Rome.

The Genesis and Development of Leo Strauss's Teaching on Natural Rights

The orbit of Leo Strauss's early intellectual life seems to have been defined by two poles that he came to realize were in tension with each other.⁴ On

---

3. Mansfield makes these remarks in an interview conducted with William Kristol and posted to the website of *The Weekly Standard* on May 11, 2015. Fortin's work on Dante is available especially in four essays in *Collected Essays* (1:251–305) and in the monograph *Dissent and Philosophy in the Middle Ages: Dante and His Precursors*, trans. Marc LePain (Lanham, Md.: Rowman and Littlefield, 2002). His work on patristic authors, especially Augustine, is found in all of the volumes of the *Collected Essays*. On Augustine and *Persecution and the Art of Writing*, see Douglas Kries, "Augustine as Defender and Critic of Leo Strauss's Esotericism Thesis," *Proceedings of the American Catholic Philosophical Association* 83 (2010): 241–52.

4. This section of the essay is heavily reliant upon Timothy Burns, "Strauss, Leo," in *Encyclopedia of Modern Political Thought*, ed. Gregory Claeys (Thousand Oaks, Calif.: SAGE Publications, 2013), 779–84, and Martin D. Yaffe and Richard S. Ruderman, eds., *Reorientation: Leo Strauss in the 1930s* (New York: Palgrave Macmillan, 2014).

the one hand, the young Strauss was thoroughly surrounded by the German Enlightenment project. He had begun his studies in the Marburg school of Neo-Kantianism and he finished his doctorate at Hamburg under Ernest Cassirer—himself a student of one of the founders of Marburg Neo-Kantianism, Hermann Cohen. On the other hand, the young Strauss was Jewish and realized early on that Weimar Germany was a difficult place wherein to be Jewish, even though Weimar Germany was supposed to be the German regime built on the Enlightenment project. Strauss never describes himself as pious, let alone orthodox, but he did openly affiliate himself with Zionist groups. He was well-aware of Jewish thinkers who had allied themselves with the German Enlightenment, for he was editing the works of Mendelssohn, studying Wellhausen, and corresponding with Guttmann. His growing dissatisfaction with the German Enlightenment, however, caused him to become increasingly dissatisfied with Jewish Enlightenment thinkers. He knew, though, that he could not simply reject the idea of a *rapprochement* between modern Enlightenment and Judaism unless he was able to determine that Spinoza, the advocate of such a *rapprochement*, was decisively wrong.

His first book, then, published in Germany in 1930, was *Spinoza's Critique of Religion*, the thesis of which was that indeed Spinoza had been unable to disprove orthodox faith; his thought represented instead a sort of arbitrary rejection of the possibility of revelation that was not based on actual sound argumentation.[5] The work was divided into two parts, with the first being devoted to "The Tradition of the Critique of Religion" and the second to Spinoza's particular critique. The treatment of the tradition of the critique of religion concluded with a substantial discussion of Thomas Hobbes. In 1933–34, Strauss worked on a manuscript he had titled after his Spinoza book: *Hobbes's Critique of Religion*.[6] He abandoned that work, but turned to another book on Hobbes with a different and broader title: *The Political Philosophy of Hobbes: Its Basis and Its Genesis*. This book was completed, but written in German; it was first published in English translation in 1936, the year after Strauss left Germany for England.

---

5. But the qualifying remarks of Christopher Bruell on Strauss's conclusions in *Spinoza's Critique of Religion* must also be considered. See Bruell's "A Return to Classical Political Philosophy and the Understanding of the American Founding," in *Leo Strauss: Political Philosopher and Jewish Thinker*, ed. Kenneth L. Deutsch and Walter Nicgorski (Lanham, Md.: Rowman and Littlefield, 1994), 335–38.

6. The unfinished manuscript has now been published in *Hobbes's Critique of Religion and Related Writings*, ed. and trans. Gabriel Bartlett and Svetozar Minkov (Chicago: University of Chicago Press, 2011).

Strauss announces at the beginning of *The Political Philosophy of Hobbes* that in fact Hobbes was the founder of the Enlightenment political project. Spinoza's work was apparently not as uniquely crucial as it once seemed in Strauss's eyes, for surely the Enlightenment project has to be considered in the form provided by its founder. Strauss now sees that Hobbes is the founder of modern political philosophy because he was the originator of "modern natural law," which was, in fact, actually a doctrine about natural rights. It is because of this novel theory of rights that Hobbes is a founder of a new project:

> Traditional natural law is primarily and mainly an objective "rule and measure," a binding order prior to, and independent of, the human will, while modern natural law is, or tends to be, primarily and mainly a series of "rights," of subjective claims, originating in the human will. I have tried to establish this view in the present study by comparing the political doctrine of Hobbes, as the founder of modern political philosophy, with that of Plato and Aristotle, as the founders of traditional political philosophy.... Hobbes obviously starts, not, as the great tradition did, from natural "law," i.e. from an objective order, but from natural "right," i.e. from an absolutely justified subjective claim which, far from being dependent on any previous law, order, or obligation, is itself the origin of all law, order, or obligation. It is by this conception of "right" as the principle of morals and politics that the originality of Hobbes's political philosophy (which includes his moral philosophy) is least ambiguously evinced.[7]

When *The Political Philosophy of Hobbes* was first published in America in 1952, Strauss added a second preface to it. He now says that the book is "in need of considerable revision," but the only revision he mentions is that whereas he had claimed in 1936 that Hobbes was "the originator of modern political philosophy," he now recognizes that in fact Machiavelli was that originator.[8]

The very next year, in 1953, Strauss published *Natural Right and History*. The fifth chapter of this book is devoted to "Modern Natural Right," and in that chapter thirty-six pages are devoted to Hobbes. This first subsection of chapter 5 is basically a reprint of an essay titled "On the Spirit of Hobbes' Political Philosophy" that was published in 1950.[9] Strauss ex-

---

7. Leo Strauss, preface to *The Political Philosophy of Hobbes: Its Basis and Its Genesis*, trans. Elsa M. Sinclair (Chicago: University of Chicago Press, 1952), vii–viii.
8. Strauss, "Preface to the American Edition," in *The Political Philosophy of Hobbes*, xv.
9. "On the Spirit of Hobbes' Political Philosophy" first appeared in the *Revue Internationale de Philosophie* 4, no. 14 (October 1950): 405–31. The information for Strauss's publications used through-

plains in his Hobbes pages in *Natural Right and History* that Hobbes was extending the project of Machiavelli, who was the Columbus "who had discovered the continent on which Hobbes could erect his structure."[10] Strauss fits Hobbes into the Machiavellian scheme without, however, substantively changing his earlier understanding of Hobbes. Timothy Burns has argued recently that the drift of the unfinished argument of *Hobbes's Critique of Religion* has found its proper conclusion in *Natural Right and History*, and most importantly for our purposes, Strauss repeats in *Natural Right and History* his claim from *The Political Philosophy of Hobbes* that Hobbes had changed traditional natural law into modern natural rights.[11] Absent from *Natural Right and History*, of course, is the old claim of *The Political Philosophy of Hobbes* that Hobbes was the founder of modern political philosophy; it is replaced with the claim that Hobbes was the founder of liberalism: "If we may call liberalism that political doctrine which regards as the fundamental political fact the rights, as distinguished from the duties, of man and which identifies the function of the state with the protection or the safeguarding of those rights, we must say that the founder of liberalism was Hobbes."[12]

Chapter 5 of *Natural Right and History* also includes a lengthy discussion of Locke that follows the lengthy discussion of Hobbes.[13] The principal thesis of these pages of *Natural Right and History* is that Locke essentially follows the lead of Hobbes, and that Locke's teaching on natural rights, including the right of property, is profoundly Hobbesian in substance.[14] Locke's teaching on natural rights, Strauss says, is in effect a development of the basic impulses of Hobbes rather than a development of any premodern natural law position:

Locke's teaching on property, and therewith his whole political philosophy, are revolutionary not only with regard to the biblical tradition but with regard to the philosophic tradition as well. Through the shift of emphasis from natural duties

---

out this essay is taken from the bibliography compiled by Thomas L. Pangle in Strauss, *Studies in Platonic Political Philosophy* (Chicago: University of Chicago Press, 1983), 249–58.

10. *Natural Right and History* (Chicago: University of Chicago Press, 1953), 177.

11. Strauss, *Natural Right and History*, esp. 179–86. See Timothy W. Burns, "Leo Strauss on the Origins of Hobbes's Natural Science and Its Relation to the Challenge of Divine Revelation," in *Reorientation: Leo Strauss in the 1930s*, ed. Martin D. Yaffe and Richard S. Ruderman (New York: Palgrave Macmillan, 2014), 131–47.

12. Strauss, *Natural Right and History*, 181–82.

13. The pages on Locke are essentially a reprinting of a substantial article that was published a year previous to *Natural Right and History* as "On Locke's Doctrine of Natural Right," *Philosophical Review* 61, no. 4 (1952): 475–502.

14. Strauss, *Natural Right and History*, esp. 227–36.

or obligations to natural rights, the individual, the ego, had become the center and origin of the moral world, since man—as distinguished from man's end—had become that center or origin. Locke's doctrine of property is a still more "advanced" expression of this radical change than was the political philosophy of Hobbes.[15]

If Strauss's position on Hobbes and the significance of his thought for modern political philosophy underwent some development prior to 1953 and the publication of *Natural Right and History*, we have to ask ourselves whether there were further developments in Strauss's interpretation after 1953. In 1970, Strauss wrote a new preface for the seventh impression of *Natural Right and History*. He says at the beginning of this new one-page preface that he has "deepened" his understanding especially of "modern natural right" in the years between 1953 and 1970.[16] He implies that his reading of Vico has prompted this deepening of his understanding, but he also says that he has not written on Vico so interested readers could consult his articles on Hobbes and on Locke that were published in 1954 and 1958, respectively, and then republished in 1959 in *What Is Political Philosophy?* Strauss especially refers his readers to what he wrote on the "nerve" of Hobbes's argument in a footnote to the Hobbes essay in *What Is Political Philosophy?* If we study the Hobbes and Locke essays in *What Is Political Philosophy?*, however, we notice that the former is a review essay on a book written in French by Polin, and the latter is a review essay of von Leyden's edition of Locke's early *Essays on the Law of Nature*. The footnote to which Strauss draws our attention in the 1970 preface is devoted to Hobbes's teaching on the nature of "science" and the relationship of that teaching to "power" and to "pride."[17]

Thus, if we study the essays of *What Is Political Philosophy?*, we can perhaps see why Strauss says that he has deepened his thought on Hobbes and Locke in some ways since 1952, but the two essays do not seem to be radically discontinuous with what was said in *Natural Right and History* concerning the question of natural rights. We therefore seem justified in attempting to offer a distillation of the key pages on Hobbes from chap-

---

15. Ibid., 248.
16. Strauss, "Preface to the Seventh Impression," in *Natural Right and History*, vii.
17. Strauss also published, in German, a new preface to *The Political Philosophy of Hobbes* upon the publication of the original German manuscript of the work in 1965. See *Hobbes Politische Wissenschaft* (Berlin: Hermann Luchterhand Verlag, 1965). An English translation by Donald J. Maletz was published in *Interpretation* 8 (1979–80): 1–3, and was republished in *Jewish Philosophy and the Crisis of Modernity*, ed. Kenneth Hart Green (Albany: State University of New York Press, 1997).

ter 5 of *Natural Right and History* that will serve as a summary of the basics of Strauss's teaching as it would influence the work of Ernest Fortin. The elements of the distillation must include at least the following:

1. *Rejection of Teleology*. Hobbes accepted Machiavelli's rejection of teleology as the standard for human affairs. This means that in the Hobbesian view natural law must be deduced from how human beings actually live rather than from some statement of allegedly-wise people about how human beings should live.

2. *Replacement of Reason with Passion*. How human beings actually live will reflect what is most powerful in human affairs, but what is most powerful in human affairs is not reason but passion. The most powerful of passions is fear of death at the hands of others; this teaching on fear has a correlative teaching on desire, namely, that the most powerful of desires is the desire for self-preservation.

3. *The Assertion of Right*. Because the most powerful of desires is the desire for self-preservation, the primary moral principle is a right to self-preservation, not a duty to a teleologically-conceived common good.

4. *The State*. The state will therefore be based not on a duty to the common good but on the protection of a right. Thus, the premodern position of deriving legal rights from antecedent moral duties will be altered to the modern position of deriving duties from antecedent rights.

5. *Education*. Because the word "right" only names what each human being most desires anyway, the sort of education that is needed is not moral formation but enlightenment that permits and encourages people to pursue their own desires.

6. *Primacy of Individual Judgment or Consent*. Because right belongs in the first instance to an individual, the individual is the proper judge of the means required for self-preservation. This means that consent is more important than wisdom and that consent is the origin of all moral obligations.

7. *The State of Nature*. Because rights belong in the first instance to an individual who by right judges the proper means required for his self-preservation, there exists a pre-political state of nature containing perfect rights but no perfect duties.

8. *The Social Contract*. Consent or individual judgment will be ineffective without a compact, and thus a social contract is required to protect natural rights.

9. *Consent within the Contract.* If consent is the source of the authority of the social contract, then even within the social contract, the most important moral consideration is the keeping of contracts that have their basis in consent.

10. *Virtue.* Because consent is crucial to the social contract establishing the sovereign authority and to all other contracts, peaceableness is the supreme virtue and something like vanity or *amour propre* is the supreme vice because it yields warlike characteristics.

11. *Legitimate Regimes.* The only possible legitimate regime is the one established by means of a contract in order to protect rights.

12. *Political Hedonism.* Along with the desire for self-preservation, a second powerful human passion is the desire for pleasure. This desire was recognized to an extent by Hobbes but certainly and unambiguously recognized by Locke as the source of further natural rights, and therefore political hedonism was born.[18] Political hedonism means that the sovereign must guarantee pleasure to those who adhere to the social contract.

Given these twelve points, we can paint with broad strokes the development of Leo Strauss's encounter with modern political philosophy in the following way: pursuing philosophical studies within the universities of Weimar Germany, Strauss found himself working within the horizon of the German philosophical Enlightenment project. But precisely because of the precarious situation faced by Jews in Weimar Germany, he began to question radically the Enlightenment project. This predicament suggested that an intellectual encounter with Spinoza, the first champion of Jewish Enlightenment, was what was needed most. But in studying Spinoza, he realized that the author he needed to study even more in order to grapple with the Enlightenment was Hobbes. Although he eventually learned that Machiavelli rather than Hobbes was the founder of modern political philosophy, Strauss was still able to assert that Hobbes was the founder of modern liberalism because Hobbes was the founder of the modern notion of natural rights. Strauss's thoughts on Hobbes received their lengthiest articulation in *The Political Philosophy of Hobbes*, from 1936; they receive a more mature, albeit shorter explication in the Hobbes essay from 1950 that found its way into *Natural Right and History* in 1953. These mature thoughts on Hobbes received not some alter-

---

18. See Fredrick Vaughan, *The Tradition of Political Hedonism: From Hobbes to J. S. Mill* (New York: Fordham University Press, 1982).

ations but some "deepening" in 1954 in the review essay that would find its way into *What Is Political Philosophy?* At least by 1950, Strauss had discovered the significance of Machiavelli for grappling with modern political philosophy, and his writing turns with greater frequency toward the Florentine, culminating in *Thoughts on Machiavelli* in 1958. Strauss never retracts or fundamentally alters, however, what he had determined regarding Hobbes as the founder of modern liberalism, which he understood to be the view that the fundamental political fact is natural rights.

Ernest Fortin's Encounter with Leo Strauss

How did it happen that Ernest Fortin, an Augustine scholar who was a member of the Augustinians of the Assumption, came into contact with the thought of Leo Strauss? Fortin stated on more than one occasion that he was first introduced to Strauss through Allan Bloom. As the story goes, in 1950 Fortin had been sent by his religious order from Rome to Paris to write a dissertation at the Sorbonne with Marrou. A few years later, Bloom was also studying in Paris as an exchange student through the University of Chicago. The two met because they were the only Americans who happened to be attending a seminar on Plato's *Laws* by the Dominican classicist Festugière. In looking back at these events in Paris after the death of Bloom in 1992, Fortin relates:

> For the twenty-three year old Bloom, learning political theory meant reading Leo Strauss, some of whose books and unpublished articles he had brought with him from America. I still have some of them, which he sold to me when, as not infrequently happened, he was broke. Here all of a sudden were possible answers to many of the questions that kept coming up in my work. Strauss knew something that neither I nor my Sorbonne professors, world-famous scholars all of them, knew. A new world had opened up with which it would take me a long time to become familiar. The rewiring had barely begun.[19]

In a talk to Assumption College students in 1969, a much younger Fortin described his encounter with reading Strauss in this way:

> Through Bloom I was led to Bloom's teacher, Leo Strauss.... Strauss is not only a great thinker, he is a man of tremendously impressive scholarship, one of the very few men in our time who has achieved a grasp of the Western tradition as

---

19. *Collected Essays*, 3:317.

a whole. For years I had felt that I was being cheated out of something important. Strauss revealed to me that missing dimension, the other side.... From that moment on, my own thinking acquired a new orientation. I read everything by Strauss that I could get my hands on.[20]

In speaking of Bloom and the encounter with Strauss's work on yet a third occasion, an interview conducted in 1999, two years after Fortin had suffered a major stroke, Fortin mentions by title the books of Strauss that he was reading in Paris:

The first book of his that I read was *Persecution and the Art of Writing*.... In fact, Bloom gave me his copy, which I still have. At about the same time I was also reading Strauss's *Natural Right and History*, but I had a very difficult time understanding it. I developed a good deal of resistance to that book, as did many other students. I was very often tempted to put it down. The book was trying to open the minds of students, to help them to overcome their prejudices.... They were very powerful books, and the more you got into them, the more you were persuaded by their argument.[21]

After completing his dissertation and returning to the United States in 1955, Fortin was able to study with Strauss himself for about a year, beginning in 1962. He describes Strauss's classroom as follows: "[Strauss was] very soft-spoken: you could barely hear him beyond the third row. But what he was saying was so powerful.... The atmosphere was absolutely electrifying. You had to get there early to get a seat, and if you didn't, you lined the walls either standing or sitting on a heater."[22]

As impressed as Fortin was with Strauss's *Natural Right and History*, Fortin did not himself begin to write extensively on the problem of modern natural rights until 1982. While he treats the topic in a number of his writings, it would seem that at least ten essays and reviews must be emphasized in a collection of his writings on the subject.[23] The first point

---

20. Ibid., 4:324.
21. Michael P. Foley, "An Interview with Ernest L. Fortin," 292. The last line of this passage was also quoted in the introductory paragraph of this essay.
22. Foley, "An Interview with Ernest L. Fortin," 294.
23. Fortin's writings on the topic are as follows:

1. "The New Rights Theory and the Natural Law," *Review of Politics* 44 (1982): 590–612 (*Collected Essays*, 2:265–86).
2. "Book review of Felicien Rousseau, *La croissance solidaire des droits de l'homme*," *Review of Metaphysics* 38 (1984): 683–86 (*Collected Essays*, 2:362–65).
3. "Natural Law and Social Justice," *American Journal of Jurisprudence* 30 (1985): 1–20 (*Collected Essays*, 2:223–41).
4. "Making Ends Meet: The Dilemma of Catholic Thought," *Free Inquiry* 8, no. 1 (1987):

to mention about these ten writings is that, while Fortin frequently cites Hobbes by name in these essays, and often even quotes him, he does not usually mention by name either Strauss or his interpretation of Hobbes in *Natural Right and History*. Fortin instead returns to Hobbes's texts themselves, even though his interpretation of those texts surely echoes the Straussian interpretation. In the very first essay in the sequence isolated in note 23 above, from 1982, he writes, "The real 'watershed' in the history of the rights doctrine is not to be located somewhere between Thomas and Suarez; it occurs with Hobbes, who set the stage for all subsequent discussions of this matter by denying that human beings are political by nature ... and by proclaiming the absolute priority of rights to duties."[24] Fortin then quotes a substantial passage from *De cive* in an accompanying footnote. Fortin cites Hobbes most extensively, however, in the last of the ten essays, quoting him again, although this time from *Leviathan*. As he had done in the first essay, he emphasizes in this final essay the novelty of Hobbes's rights doctrine: "The likeliest supposition is the one according to which there exists a specifically modern notion of rights that comes to the fore with Hobbes in the seventeenth century and distinguishes itself from all previous notions, not so much by its definition

---

36–39; revised version published as "The Trouble with Catholic Social Thought" in *Boston College Magazine* (*Collected Essays*, 3:303–13).

5. "Book review of Russell Hittinger, *A Critique of the New Natural Law Theory*," *Review of Metaphysics* 43 (1989): 838–41 (*Collected Essays*, 2:360–62).

6. "Book review of David Hollenbach, *Justice Peace, and Human Rights*," *Crisis* 7, no. 2 (1989): 48–51 (*Collected Essays*, 4:303–7).

7. "From *Rerum Novarum* to *Centesimus Annus*: Continuity or Discontinuity?," *Faith and Reason* 17, no. 4 (1991): 399–412 (*Collected Essays*, 3:223–29).

8. "Sacred and Inviolable: *Rerum Novarum* and Natural Rights," *Theological Studies* 53 (1992): 203–33 (*Collected Essays*, 3:191–222).

9. "Human Rights and the Common Good," *Catholic Commission on Intellectual and Cultural Affairs (CCICA) Annual* 13 (1994): 1–16; slightly revised versions published as "Recovery Movement" in *Boston College Magazine*, as "The Natural Wrong in Natural Rights" in *Crisis*, and as "Menschenrechte und Allgemeinwohl" in *Communio* (*Collected Essays*, 3:19–28).

10. "On the Presumed Medieval Origin of Individual Rights," in *Final Causality in Nature and Human Affairs*, ed. Richard Hassing (Washington, D.C.: The Catholic University of America Press, 1997), 86–106; later published in *Communio* (*Collected Essays*, 2:243–64).

Most of Ernest Fortin's essays were collected and published in three volumes in 1996 as *Ernest L. Fortin: Collected Essays*, ed. J. Brian Benestad (Lanham, Md.: Rowman and Littlefield, 1996). A fourth volume of *Collected Essays*, edited by Michael P. Foley, was added in 2007. The information for Fortin's publications used throughout this essay is taken from the bibliography in *Collected Essays*, 4:329–42; that bibliography is updated from the one compiled by Foley and Kries in *Gladly to Learn and Gladly to Teach*, 303–16.

24. *Collected Essays*, 2:273.

of right as a power, as by its proclamation of rights rather than duties as the primary moral counter."[25] This theme is repeated a few pages later: "If Hobbes is to be taken at his word, the modern rights theory was no mere attempt to erect a new structure on the old foundation of classical and Christian ethics. Its ambition was to lay down an entirely new foundation, to wit, a selfish passion—the desire for self-preservation—and go on from there to devise a political scheme that would be in accord with it from the start."[26]

Passages such as the preceding could be multiplied, but one from a third essay will suffice; it is chosen not only because in it Fortin recognizes Hobbes as the originator of the natural rights view, but also because Fortin stresses in it the key point of a distinction between the ancient or medieval teleological view of human nature and the modern nonteleological view:

> To the best of my knowledge, the true originator of the rights doctrine is Hobbes, from whom it was taken over by virtually all of the great early modern thinkers, Spinoza, Locke, and Rousseau foremost among them. That doctrine emerged by way of a reaction against premodern thought and signals a radical departure from it. Its underlying premise is that, contrary to what had been previously assumed, human beings are not intrinsically ordered to a natural end, in the attainment of which they find their happiness or perfection.[27]

Although Fortin surely embraces the interpretation of Hobbes he absorbed from *Natural Right and History*, and although he often cites passages from the works of Hobbes to support that view, he does not devote himself extensively to establishing or proving the Straussian interpretation. He presumably had concluded that such a task had already been adequately completed by Strauss himself. Fortin's concern was rather to engage a number of medievalist scholars, especially Catholic ones, who were arguing and had been arguing for some decades that the transition from the natural law of Thomas Aquinas and his follows to modern natural rights or human rights was one of continuity rather than discontinuity. These scholars, according to Fortin, had run together premodern thinking with modern thought, teleological thinking with nonteleological thinking, natural law with natural rights. The result, in Fortin's view at least, was an unfortunate confusion that had established itself within

25. Ibid., 2:249.
26. Ibid., 2:256.
27. Ibid., 3:305.

Catholic thinking about morality and about politics. That was "the trouble with Catholic social thought," to borrow one of Fortin's titles.

Fortin knew that the critique of Catholic political thought for which he was arguing ran counter to the prevailing winds of Catholic scholarship. He knew that the confused view held by the previous generation of Catholic scholars included the predominant figures of Jacques Maritain and John Courtney Murray. He did not seek to engage defenders of Maritain and Murray, however, but turned to more contemporaneous scholars arguing for similar positions.[28] He began his attempt to overturn the established view by engaging the prominent and learned John Finnis, who, especially with Germain Grisez, had articulated something called "the new natural law theory." Fortin published in the *Review of Politics*, then probably the most visible Catholic journal of political thought (at least in America), an extensive review essay of Finnis's latest book, *Natural Law and Natural Rights*, whose very title compares to Maritain's *The Rights of Man and Natural Law*.[29] Two years later, Fortin published a review of Felicien Rousseau's *La croissance solidaire des droits de l'homme*, whose title, he notes, oddly translates as *The Solidary Growth of the Rights of Man*.[30] The review of Felicien Rousseau was much shorter than that of Finnis, and published in the *Review of Metaphysics*. Fortin says that Rousseau's volume is a tale of two books; that is, his treatment of Thomas Aquinas and the natural law theory is quite well done, but he then makes the mistake of failing to distinguish it from natural rights or the rights of man.

Fortin's attempt to engage Finnis seemed to go nowhere. In a review of Russell Hittinger's *A Critique of the New Natural Law Theory*, another book critical of Finnis as well as of Grisez, Fortin complains of the unwillingness of Finnis and his associates to engage their critics constructively.[31] Fortin continued to say complimentary things about Felicien Rousseau, however, or at least to say complimentary things about the half of Rousseau's book that he considered accurate and well done.[32] He at least seemed to think that Rousseau was someone worth continuing to engage on the question.

In the last of the essays in the sequence listed in note 23 above, "On

28. Ibid., 2:266; cf. 306.
29. This is the first item on the list in note 23 above.
30. The review is the second item in the list above. Fortin's comments on the title of Rousseau's book are found in the third item (235).
31. This review is fifth on the list in note 23 above.
32. See, e.g., *Collected Essays*, 3:219n40, 312n11.

the Presumed Medieval Origin of Individual Rights," Fortin attempted to engage three well-respected medievalist scholars, Michel Villey, a French legal scholar; Richard Tuck, who had published an important book on the origin of natural rights theory in 1979; and a medieval historian from Cornell, Brian Tierney. All of these scholars had, in one form or another, run together medieval theories of natural law with modern theories of natural rights. It is clear from Fortin's essay that he thinks that the most formidable of these authors is Tierney. He notes that Tierney had been able to demonstrate impressively that some legal scholars from the late Middle Ages had indeed used the word "right" in the subjective sense of something one possesses. Fortin was convinced, however, that the rights in question are actually derivative from antecedent laws and duties and hence not rights in the distinctively modern sense of the term. Fortin suffered a stroke not long after the publication of this essay; Tierney generously continued to respond to the arguments of Fortin and other Strauss scholars in the *Review of Politics* in 2002.[33] Tierney makes clear, however, that he does not grasp or perhaps appreciate what Straussians claim about "modernity" and about Hobbes, and so it is not clear that the conversation was or is really headed anywhere except, one might hope, perhaps back to the texts of Hobbes himself.[34]

Fortin's various attempts to enter into conversation and argumentation about the distinction between the modern and the premodern with Catholic or medieval scholars is surely important, but of much greater importance, it would seem, was the conversation he attempted in May 1991. That month marked the centennial anniversary of the release of *Rerum Novarum*, the encyclical of Pope Leo XIII addressing the social question. Whatever one thinks about it, it is difficult to deny but that contemporary Catholic thinking about politics in the modern age dates from the promulgation of that letter, and thus various commemorations of its centennial were held throughout the Catholic world. Fortin himself attended an academic conference marking the occasion that was held at the

---

33. Brian Tierney, "Natural Law and Natural Rights: Old Problems and Recent Approaches," *Review of Politics* 64, no. 3 (2002): 389–406. Tierney's essay was responded to by John Finnis, Douglas Kries, and Michael P. Zuckert; Tierney responded to these responses in the same issue.

34. Brian Tierney, "Author's Rejoinder," *Review of Politics* 64, no. 3 (2002): 419–20. In addition to his attempts to bring Strauss's *Natural Right and History* into dialogue with some of the most famous scholars of his day, Fortin also was willing to express his views on the radical novelty of modern natural rights thinking to a more popular audience, or at least to an audience of non-specialists. See, in particular, items four and nine on the list in note 23 above.

Lateran University in Rome on May 6–9; Pope John Paul II had released *Centesimus Annus* on May 1. With the collapse of the Berlin Wall and the apparent termination of the Cold War, there was something about the moment that seemed practically to call for a whole reconsideration of the church and her place in the political order.

Fortin delivered a paper at the Lateran conference called "*Rerum novarum* and Modern Political Thought," which was published in the conference proceedings in 1992. Fortin revised and enlarged his paper and published it as "Sacred and Inviolable: *Rerum Novarum* and Natural Rights" in *Theological Studies*. "Sacred and Inviolable" would also not appear until 1992, but Fortin published a much shorter essay, without annotations, before the end of 1991 in *Crisis*. This latter essay was titled "From *Rerum Novarum* to *Centesimus Annus*: Continuity or Discontinuity?" Although it appeared in print prior to "Sacred and Inviolable," "Continuity or Discontinuity?" actually serves more as an extension of or appendix to the former.[35] In the view of this interpreter, "Sacred and Inviolable" is probably the most important of Fortin's many essays, at least from the standpoint of the church, for if taken seriously it would force the church to reconsider in a radical way her whole posture toward modernity and her entire way of thinking about modern times.

The overall goal of "Sacred and Inviolable" is to bring *Natural Right and History* to bear on the thought behind *Rerum Novarum*. Fortin is uncharacteristically blunt in the introduction to the essay and states his thesis directly:

> My thesis is twofold. I shall claim that the encyclical represents an attempt to synthesize or fuse into a single whole elements derived from two independent and largely antithetical traditions, one rooted in a teleological and the other in a non-teleological view of nature. The first of these, represented preeminently in the Christian West by Aristotle and his medieval disciples, I shall refer to as the "premodern" tradition. The other, which originated with Machiavelli in the sixteenth century and achieved its most popular form in the political philosophy of John Locke a century and a half later, I shall refer to as the "modern" tradition. Secondly, I shall claim that the two components of the proposed synthesis coexist only in an uneasy tension with each other.[36]

One cannot help but wonder why the encyclical was attempting to synthesize these two disparate elements to begin with. On Fortin's tell-

---

35. These two essays are items seven and eight on the list in note 23 above.
36. *Collected Essays*, 3:192.

ing, part of the problem had to do with historical accident; the rest had to do with intellectual confusion on the part of the scholars helping to write the document. The confused scholars, in his narrative, are Taparelli d'Azeglio and Matteo Liberatore who, lacking familiarity with medieval theories of property, unwittingly adopted the position of John Locke. Echoing chapter 5 of *The Second Treatise of Government*, they even founded the new, sacred and inviolable right of property on the concept of labor.[37]

The theme of confused thinkers trying to synthesize two incompatible positions, the modern and the premodern, is a theme by now familiar to us from Fortin's writings on natural law and natural rights. What is especially striking about "Sacred and Inviolable," however, is Fortin's open use of *Natural Right and History* to emphasize the difference between the two traditions in a document addressed to Catholic scholars and ecclesiastics. Because the authors of the encyclical had relied, according to Fortin, upon Locke, he mentions Locke in his thesis statement. In the essay itself, however, he turns back to Hobbes. One of his annotations references the very pages from *Natural Right and History* that are at the heart of Strauss's interpretation of Hobbes and from which the brief distillation of Strauss's view in the first part of this paper were derived.[38] Indeed, Fortin quotes the very line from Burke that Strauss quotes in his Hobbes pages: "The little catechism of the rights of men is soon learned; and the inferences are in the passions."[39] Fortin again quotes chapter 14 of *Leviathan* and argues, "What distinguishes the new notion from the old is not the understanding of rights as powers but the concentration on rights rather than duties or law as the absolute moral phenomenon."[40] He continues, "I do not wish to imply that Hobbes's revolutionary view of morality is the one that *Rerum novarum* was trying to pass off as authentic Christian doctrine," but it certainly seems as if that is exactly what Fortin is doing.[41]

In explaining what he politely termed the "tensions" in *Rerum Novarum*, Fortin had noted that the concern with the right of private property was perhaps understandable especially in light of the concern with so-

---

37. Ibid., 3:196–99; Fortin had written at greater length on Taparelli d'Azeglio in "Natural Law and Social Justice" (2:233–34).
38. Ibid., 3:221n58.
39. Strauss, *Natural Right and History*, 183; Fortin, *Collected Essays*, 3:208.
40. *Collected Essays*, 3:205.
41. Ibid.

cialism that was already present in Leo's day. In taking up, briefly, John Paul II's *Centesimus Annus*, Fortin comments that, with communism apparently collapsing, John Paul gently resolved the excesses of *Rerum Novarum*, at least with respect to a sacred and inviolable right to property. Moreover, Fortin speculates that perhaps Leo would have been open to such corrections himself had he been able to see beyond the immediate circumstances that surrounded him. If nothing else, his conclusion that John Paul interprets Leo in a very benevolent manner is a generous one.

The problem, though, is that in some other ways there are even more "tensions" within *Centesimus Annus* than within *Rerum Novarum*: "If *Centesimus annus* takes a less extreme view of private property than *Rerum novarum*, in other respects it shows itself far more open to modern modes of thought."[42] John Paul's encyclical, Fortin suggests, turns out to be very favorably inclined toward liberal democracy and free markets. While these modern political institutions have their advantages, it seems unwise in Fortin's view for the church to be too closely identified with such seemingly amoral enterprises: "The fact of the matter," he quips, "is that modern liberalism has always been better at taking care of our bodies than of our souls."[43] But the basic problem with *Centesimus Annus*, in Fortin's interpretation, is that the 1991 encyclical abandons Thomism or any other form of teleological thought in favor of a nonteleological personalism. John Paul winds up with something like Kantian human rights. The suggestion is that just as Leo's letter seems unwittingly to follow the times rather than address them from a higher standpoint, so does John Paul's. Why, one is led by Fortin to wonder, cannot the church herself get clear on where her allegiances lie?

Conclusion

The narrative this essay traces began with a young Jewish scholar's attempt to come to grips with modern politics and theistic faith and ends with a mature Christian scholar's attempt to get the Catholic church herself to do a better job of coming to grips with modern politics and theistic faith. One wonders what Strauss would have thought if he had lived to see his writings on Hobbes used in Rome to critique the words of popes.

42. Ibid., 3:224.
43. Ibid., 3:226.

Both Strauss and Fortin struggled to understand modern enlightenment and its relationship to premodern enlightenment. They thought they had acquired some insight into this intellectual problem, and they expressed these insights by drawing contrasts. While commenting on yet another book written by an author who could not seem to distinguish clearly between the modern and the premodern, Fortin states the contrast he thought he had acquired with the aid of Strauss in direct terms:

> Indeed, the rights doctrine as we now understand it is a typically Western product that dates only from the seventeenth century and that plays no role whatever in Catholic social thought until the end of the nineteenth or beginning of the twentieth century. Prior to that time, the only rights spoken of in the Church's official or semi-official teaching were legal rights, not natural or universal human rights. Duty was the fundamental moral phenomenon. One was instructed first and foremost in one's obligations, i.e., in what one owed to others, not in what one could claim from them.[44]

Fortin was concerned that the church, in unwittingly bringing into her teaching foreign elements, would wind up failing to preach an alternative to the modern perspective. To be sure, the church in every age has to live in the temporal flow of the present and to speak to the world as it currently exists. Fortin feared that if she neglected to articulate the premodern moral and political wisdom gained at such a great cost in earlier times, the church would have nothing unique or worthwhile to say to the modern world.

---

44. Ibid., 4:306. This is item six on the list of Fortin's essays given in note 23 above. One novel feature of this review is that within it Fortin recommends a published lecture by Josef Pieper as providing a possible way for the church to talk about rights correctly even in modern times; see Pieper, "The Rights of Others," in his *Problems of Modern Faith: Essays and Addresses*, trans. Jan van Heurck (Chicago: Franciscan Herald Press, 1985), 218.

PART 2

Leo Strauss and Catholic Concerns

6

The Mutual Concerns of Leo Strauss and His Catholic Contemporaries

D'Entrèves, McCoy, Simon

GLADDEN J. PAPPIN

Leo Strauss was concerned to understand the relationship of the philosopher to political life, and he pursued that understanding through studies of how different philosophers understood their relationship to politics. Strauss's practice of reading philosophers esoterically fulfilled this intention by suggesting the points at which each philosopher needed to or chose to conceal a deeper thought, whether for reason of protection or pedagogy. In Strauss's view, modern science presents itself as immediately beneficial to society, indeed the guarantee of society's progress.[1] This shift in science's relation to society began and took root in the attempt to refound politics on scientific ground. Scientific terms entered common discourse through this route and through the spread of scientific education. The popularization of science through useful inventions created a new situation in which the language of science was not the preserve of philosophical speculation, but part of the ordinary understanding of and analysis of political phenomena. Or rather, the scientific account of those

---

1. See further notes 68–70, 72, 92–94, and 96–99 below.

phenomena *replaced* the ordinary understanding. Because philosophy in the classical sense sought to move from ordinary, partisan political opinion to knowledge, the replacement of ordinary opinion with views stated in scientific terms obstructs the normal origin of philosophical thinking. From Strauss's standpoint as a defender of philosophy and its true conditions, this "pit beneath the cave" makes the ascent to philosophical understanding more difficult.[2] It is bad for the would-be philosopher. But is it also bad for the ordinary citizen, the nonphilosopher? This aspect makes the question also one of not merely parochial interest, as it highlights a crucial tension within Strauss's interpretation of modernity. The "popularization" of philosophy distorts the philosopher, but it also distorts the ordinary citizen, providing him a preformed scientific view (accurate or not) of the correct politics and distancing him from his customary partisanship.

In what follows I illustrate the ways that several scholars working prior to and contemporaneously with Strauss began to approach the same question concerning the changed relationship of philosophy and society in modern science, but diverged from him due to an interest in the character of ordinary citizens more than that of the philosopher. Alexandre Passerin d'Entrèves (1902–85), Charles N. R. McCoy (1911–84), and Yves Simon (1903–61) each worked variously on the history of political thought and the philosophical character of contemporary circumstances. (I treat them in this order, that of historian-philosopher, political philosopher, and philosophical student of contemporary affairs.) The researches of d'Entrèves were chiefly historical and never explicitly placed within a Catholic framework. But he did direct his research toward understanding the tradition of natural law historically, in ways that differentiate him both from Strauss, Thomistic philosophy, and other historians. McCoy, a priest and professor at The Catholic University of America and Santa Clara University, with doctorates in political science and philosophy, openly situated his work with respect to what he called "the heart of modern man's religious crisis."[3] That crisis, he said, "is the astounding and

---

2. Leo Strauss, *Persecution and the Art of Writing* (Glencoe, Ill.: Free Press, 1952), 155. For additional points at which Strauss deploys this metaphor, see Laurence Lampert, *The Enduring Importance of Leo Strauss* (Chicago: University of Chicago Press, 2013), 198n18.

3. Charles N. R. McCoy, "Contemplation Passes into Practice: Religion and Reality," *Catholic Social Science Review* 11 (2006): 307. For portraits of McCoy's life, see the chronology in *On the Intelligibility of Political Philosophy: Essays of Charles N. R. McCoy*, ed. James V. Schall and John J. Schrems (Washington, D.C.: The Catholic University of America Press, 1989), ix; Charles R. Dechert, "*In me-*

frightening loss of touch with the authentic sources of the Western classical and Judaeo-Christian tradition"—a fact for which "the blame lies everywhere."[4] Yves Simon, a Catholic and student of Jacques Maritain, wrote in the Aristotelian tradition particularly on the matter of prudence; in the words of Vukan Kuic, he was interested in "not 'texts' but actual problems."[5] What brings these three scholars together and establishes a fruitful dialogue with Strauss is their analysis of and critical response to the political situation caused by the advent of modern science, to which they respond in different ways. My chief contention is that McCoy and Simon, and to a lesser extent even d'Entrèves, begin from the standpoint (shared with Strauss) that modernity inaugurates a new relationship between philosophy and science, but investigate the consequences of that new relationship for ordinary moral life rather than for the figure of the philosopher. Their analysis of contemporary politics thus departs from that of Strauss in an important way. What is more, I suggest that McCoy and Simon's concern for what happens to prudence and moral virtue in modernity is justifiable even within the analytical framework outlined by Strauss.

According to Strauss, the philosopher who began the new relationship between philosophy and the city was Niccolò Machiavelli. Strauss sets the stage for *Thoughts on Machiavelli* by objecting to scholarly portraits of Machiavelli as a patriot or as a scientist, both of which Strauss considers "misleading" but not altogether false.[6] This position against existing scholarship is hardly the only element of Strauss's contribution: among other things, he uncovers the "anti-theological ire" motivating Machiavelli's work, and the project Machiavelli intended to begin and perpetuate through his works. The sharp point Strauss placed on the theological import of Machiavelli's work made it of immediate concern to those who considered some version of the "theologico-political problem" an important

---

moriam Charles N. R. McCoy (1911–1984)," *Laval théologique et philosophique* 41, no. 1 (1985): 109; A. J. Beitzinger, "Retrospect on Charles N. R. McCoy," *Review of Politics* 53, no. 2 (Spring 1991): 416–18. For generous appreciations of McCoy's thought, see William P. Haggerty, "Beyond the Letter of His Master's Thought: C.N.R. McCoy on Medieval Political Theory," *Laval théologique et philosophique* 64, no. 2 (2008): 467–83; James V. Schall, SJ, "'Man for Himself': On the Ironic Unities of Political Philosophy," a book review of McCoy, *The Structure of Political Thought*, in *Political Science Reviewer* 15 (1985): 67–107; and James V. Schall, SJ, "Transcendent Man in the Limited City: The Political Philosophy of Charles N. R. McCoy," in *Reason, Revelation, and Human Affairs: Selected Writings of James V. Schall*, ed. Marc D. Guerra (Lanham, Md.: Lexington Books, 2001), 143–61.

4. McCoy, "Contemplation Passes into Practice," 307.
5. Vukan Kuic, *Yves Simon: Real Democracy* (Lanham, Md.: Rowman and Littlefield, 1999), 12.
6. Leo Strauss, *Thoughts on Machiavelli* (Glencoe, Ill.: Free Press, 1958), 10–11.

area of study. But the force of Strauss's analysis has caused his most eminent student in the study of Machiavelli to write that "All scholarly studies on Machiavelli can now be divided into those written before Strauss and those written after him, and the latter between those that take account of him in some fashion and those that willfully, or blithely, ignore him."[7] Today's readers of Machiavelli can, at least superficially, take both sides of the 1958 divide, by reading scholarship on Machiavelli before and after Strauss. Catholic readers of Strauss have a particular reason to do so, however: Strauss's discovery appealed to a view of Machiavelli that prevailed in Catholic circles long before the advent of modern positivistic scholarship of the "patriot" and "scientist" readings. It was, after all, Pope Paul IV who placed Machiavelli's *opere* on the *Index librorum prohibitorum* in 1557.[8] For Catholics reading Strauss four hundred years later, what were the existing reasons to study Machiavelli's influence, and how did Strauss modify or supplant them?

The question is not one of idle interest. Even in the era before Strauss, Catholic scholarship did not necessarily fall into the initial categories (identifying Machiavelli as a patriot or scientist) that Strauss picked as his targets. To be sure, there were Catholics whose reading of Machiavelli suffered deservedly at Straussian hands. The Jesuit scholar Leslie J. Walker, dean of Campion Hall, Oxford, famously compiled a list of historical inaccuracies Machiavelli made in his *Discourses on Livy*, and Strauss rightly called attention to Machiavelli's own hints that his "errors" were always for the sake of another purpose.[9] For Catholics coming to an interest in Strauss in his heyday, Strauss offered a clear contrast with the positivist and historical schools that narrowed Machiavelli's ambitions, excused him or flattered themselves by finding in him the progenitor of their value-free science. But scholarship before Strauss that, like him, was motivated to understand the character of modern politics stands in a different position from that of the positivists. To identify that motivation as Strauss's only interest would be, as he says of the historians he

---

7. Harvey C. Mansfield, "Strauss on *The Prince*," *Review of Politics* 75 (2013): 641.
8. Allessandra Petrina, *Machiavelli in the British Isles: Two Early Modern Translations of "The Prince"* (Farnham: Ashgate, 2009), 5. For the early history of Catholic opposition to Machiavelli, see Robert Bireley, *The Counter-Reformation Prince: Anti-Machiavellianism or Catholic Statecraft in Early Modern Europe* (Chapel Hill: University of North Carolina Press, 1990).
9. Leslie J. Walker, SJ, *The Discourses of Niccolò Machiavelli* (London: Routledge and Kegan Paul, 1950), 2:311–12. Strauss, *Thoughts*, 35–37, 106. See the criticism of Harvey C. Mansfield, *Machiavelli's New Modes and Orders: A Study of the "Discourses on Livy"* (Chicago: University of Chicago Press, 1979), 436n37.

critiques, "misleading." D'Entrèves, McCoy, and Simon indicate how an approach to the same question of the relationship of modernity and philosophy would look, but in light of different interests—and, as we will see, philosophically no less valid ones.

State and Obligation in Alexandre Passerin d'Entrèves

What was it that enabled or propelled Simon and McCoy to examine directly the aspect of ordinary, nonphilosophical life that Strauss typically downplayed? For a first answer to that question, let us turn to Alexandre Passerin d'Entrèves, the Italian-born Oxford historian of political thought who did not, as McCoy and Simon did, make common cause with Christianity or Catholicism a significant aspect of his scholarship.[10] (As is well known, d'Entrèves was in the running for the chair at the University of Chicago that Strauss took.)[11] Nevertheless, d'Entrèves speaks occasionally of "our Christian civilization" and the "Christian inheritance [of which] the Western nations may well be proud."[12] D'Entrèves's scholarship sweeps widely across the history of medieval political thought, the development of the notion of the state, and the history of the natural law. While commonly known as an historian of political thought, d'Entrèves presents the 1967 English edition of his *The Notion of the State* (first published as *La dottrina della stato* in 1962) in order "to defend a certain type of approach to political theory."[13] Though taking the word "state" as his guidepost apparently separates d'Entrèves from the philological exacti-

---

10. For a biographical and intellectual overview, see Cary J. Nederman, introduction to A. P. d'Entrèves, *Natural Law: An Introduction to Legal Philosophy* (New Brunswick, N.J.: Transaction, 1994). For an overview of d'Entrèves's major contributions, with an eye toward differentiating d'Entrèves from the Cambridge School as well as from accounts which emphasize the modernity of Marsilius of Padua and Machiavelli, see Cary J. Nederman, "A Middle Path: Alexander Passerin d'Entrèves," chap. 4 in *Lineages of European Political Thought: Explorations along the Medieval/Modern Divide from John of Salisbury to Hegel* (Washington, D.C.: The Catholic University of America Press, 2009).

11. Edward Shils, "Robert Maynard Hutchins, 1899–1977," in *Remembering the University of Chicago: Teachers, Scientists, and Scholars*, ed. Edward Shils (Chicago: University of Chicago Press, 1991), 192. See the further commentary of Steven B. Smith, "Leo Strauss: The Outlines of a Life," in *The Cambridge Companion to Leo Strauss*, ed. Steven B. Smith (Cambridge: Cambridge University Press, 2009), 31.

12. A. P. d'Entrèves, "The Case for Natural Law Re-Examined," *Natural Law Forum* 1, no. 5 (1956): 49; and *The Medieval Contribution to Political Thought: Thomas Aquinas, Marsilius of Padua, Richard Hooker* (New York: Humanities Press, 1959), 87.

13. A. P. d'Entrèves, *The Notion of the State: An Introduction to Political Theory* (Oxford: Clarendon, 1967), vi.

tude which inclined Strauss to speak instead of city, country, and church, d'Entrèves simply begins from the available political phenomenon and works toward its constituent elements.[14]

D'Entrèves's use of "state" is not as inflexible as the title might indicate, however: he distinguishes three separate notions—might, power, authority—corresponding (roughly) to Machiavellian, positivist, and premodern accounts of the state. Even if Strauss's inquiry into classical political philosophy yields (as I think it does) approaches useful to correcting aspects of contemporary tendencies, the existence of the state excuses d'Entrèves's choice to treat classical political accounts as, for example, an "authority" conception *of the state*. Authority is also the touchstone of Yves Simon's broad attempt to rethink the consequences of Aristotelian political science in a contemporary context.[15] D'Entrèves's distaste for the foundation of the state in power is evident in his reference to Hobbes's creation of a "myth," "the myth of Leviathan," which contained a "menace" in the form of its denial of intrinsically legitimate power to anything other than the duly authorized state.[16] (D'Entrèves favorably cites Strauss's identification of Hobbes as the founder of modern liberalism.)[17] For d'Entrèves the foundation of modern law in the state is "the direct consequence of the imperative conception of law." His own preferred acceptance of a "real plurality of legal systems" depends on rejecting that conception, and indeed d'Entrèves's work often takes the form of jurisprudence.[18]

While beginning from Hobbes the modern political philosophers interpret politics in terms of power, d'Entrèves says that ordinary speech continues to fall back on the term "order" (implying a right order), which the moderns abandoned.[19] The horrific wars of the twentieth century suggest that an account of political right in terms of power alone is no longer sufficient, and d'Entrèves even turns, like Strauss, toward the con-

---

14. Leo Strauss, *The City and Man* (Chicago: Rand McNally, 1964), 30. See further, Harvey C. Mansfield, "Machiavelli's *Stato* and the Impersonal Modern State," chap. 12 in *Machiavelli's Virtue* (Chicago: University of Chicago Press, 1996). On the distinction of state and society as the fundamental aspect of liberalism, see Pierre Manent, *An Intellectual History of Liberalism*, trans. Rebecca Balinski (Princeton, N.J.: Princeton University Press, 1994), 65–66.

15. Yves Simon, *Nature and Functions of Authority* (Milwaukee, Wis.: Marquette University Press, 1940), and *A General Theory of Authority* (Notre Dame, Ind.: University of Notre Dame Press, 1962).

16. D'Entrèves, *Notion*, 102–3.

17. Ibid., 203n1.

18. Ibid., 125.

19. Ibid., 159.

cepts of "country" and "nation" to explain additional reasons (beyond the rationale supplied by Hobbes and modern positivists) that the state is invested with authority.[20] The Christian account of divine right, he adds, was not generally an account of the content or origin of political power but of its form or character. Consent and equality now constitute the origins of justifiable political power in the modern world, and d'Entrèves's concern lies with "the exercise of power" more than with its origin.[21] D'Entrèves inclines toward a liberal view of the proper scope of the modern state, and he attempts to emphasize both the modern state's foundation in "negative liberty" as well as the opportunity it affords for the real development of "positive liberty"—while registering the codicil that "positive liberty" can run amok, particularly when its role in Rousseau is misunderstood.

D'Entrèves wants to color the modern state with an image of the common good, which is "not the exclusive preserve of the Aristotelian and Thomistic traditions."[22] Borrowing from what he calls the "whole spirit of Christianity," d'Entrèves suggests that a proper understanding of the common good need not be inimical to certain lessons learned by modern liberalism, which in this respect can be said "to uphold the purest Christian tradition."[23] Perhaps most important, d'Entrèves recommends that the common good not be identified with any specific content to be implemented, because in the modern context such implementation would likely be through the figure of the expert. Instead the common good "implies adding a special qualification ... to a state of affairs [which] is dependent on, and conditioned by, our preferences."[24] The simplest way to the nexus between our preferences and the common good is through the approval of the "good citizen," whose real love of his political community could provide the proper measure of the state's observance of the common good. In this way d'Entrèves seeks to join "the liberty of the ancients with that of the moderns." The enduring aspects of the liberty of the ancients "may be," he says, "far removed from what the realists call 'the effectual truth,'" but he suggests that a full account of politics must include them. In a remarkable closing line for an otherwise restrained analysis of mod-

20. Ibid., 167–68.
21. Ibid., 189–90, 199.
22. Ibid., 223.
23. Ibid., 226.
24. Ibid., 228.

ern political theory, d'Entrèves hints that "the 'heavenly city of the philosophers' has," in fact, "proved to be far more effectual in shaping man's political destiny than the mere possession of force."[25]

As may be evident from the elements gathered thus far, d'Entrèves's work has numerous resonances with that of Strauss. Though the structure of his study reflects the themes of Oxford political theory scholarship in his day, he adopted contemporary themes and terms intentionally: "I have tried as far as possible," he says, "to use the language of my own time."[26] In point of fact, d'Entrèves's emphasis on the state was déclassé even in his own day from the point of view of the value-neutral scholars seeking more scientific terms.[27] Machiavelli is a crucial figure for d'Entrèves, and he highlights the occasions of Machiavelli's use of *stato* which he judges anticipate the modern sense of state. For all that, he thinks that Machiavelli is a "product of his age" as well as its "supreme interpreter," not because historical context determines thought but because—in a way that could be amenable to Strauss's interpretation—Machiavelli took advantage of an existing situation to inaugurate the new political emphasis on "effectiveness."[28] Though the approach Machiavelli begins is "political art" and "not political science," "in his method ... he did indeed anticipate" modern science—so much so that d'Entrèves implies modern political scientists hold views possibly even more shocking than those of Machiavelli.[29] Like Strauss but without reference to Strauss, d'Entrèves suggests that Machiavelli's "method of 'effectual truth,'" described in chapter 15 of *The Prince*, "is in complete control" of his thought.[30] D'Entrèves identifies elements of Machiavelli's influence in Hegel, Marx, and more recent thinkers such as Pareto.

With these sympathies established, I turn to d'Entrèves's account of natural law, and for a particular reason: d'Entrèves's interest in natural law was an expression of his wish to find a rationale for obedience to the law on behalf of the ordinary citizen. In 1954, d'Entrèves was invited to the University of Notre Dame Law School to deliver lectures on natural

25. Ibid., 230.
26. Ibid., 229.
27. See d'Entrèves's observation that contemporary writers have shied away from the term *sovereignty*, while their substitute description of the legal order as *complete* or *exclusive* merely communicates the same thing. A. P. d'Entrèves, *Natural Law: An Introduction to Legal Philosophy*, rev. ed. (London: Hutchinson, 1970).
28. D'Entrèves, *Notion*, 35.
29. Ibid., 39, 42.
30. Ibid., 40.

law to coincide with the founding of the *Natural Law Forum*, a journal dedicated to reviving the study of the natural law in a legal context.³¹ D'Entrèves did not exactly fit the bill of Notre Dame's midcentury goals. Although d'Entrèves thought that elements of the natural law were an abiding and essential part of the understanding of modern law, he would never plump for contemporary Catholic accounts of the natural law and instead integrated his understanding into a broader account of liberalism.³² Though Strauss made no direct published references to d'Entrèves of which I am aware, he did remark favorably on Eric Voegelin's criticism of the "Oxford philosophers," which included d'Entrèves, in correspondence with Voegelin.³³ But d'Entrèves's approach, while situated within the Oxford context (by himself!) and not identifiably "Catholic" still less "Straussian," was roundly critical of what he saw as the reigning positivism in legal philosophy.³⁴ Indeed d'Entrèves's downplaying of his Catholic inspiration was a deliberate strategy. While encouraging interest in the natural law tradition, d'Entrèves also lightly warned his Notre Dame audience against a prideful tendency to write off modernity as though it had contributed nothing. "It is no use," he said, "inscribing such principles [i.e., of the Catholic faith] on our banners unless we are prepared to undertake also the modest everyday work which is required in order to make them living and guiding."³⁵ Instead d'Entrèves generously stated the case of his interlocutors who advanced alternative explanations of the meaning of law—whether ascribing its content to will, filling out its content from an arbitrary presupposition, or likening its character to the rules of a game.

Because contemporary legal philosophers view the rationale for obeying the law as a problem, d'Entrèves suggested that the "natural law" was

---

31. D'Entrèves, "Case for Natural Law." The essay is reprinted in his *Natural Law*, 119–72. See the useful contemporary history of the return of natural law thinking by Leo R. Ward, "The 'Natural Law' Rebound," *Review of Politics* 21, no. 1 (January 1959): 114–30.

32. Compare, for example, Heinrich A. Rommen, *The Natural Law: A Study in Legal and Social History and Philosophy* (Indianapolis, Ind.: Liberty Fund, 1998).

33. Strauss to Voegelin, May 22, 1953, in *Faith and Political Philosophy: The Correspondence between Leo Strauss and Eric Voegelin, 1934–1964*, ed. and trans. Peter Emberley and Barry Cooper (University Park: Pennsylvania State University Press, 1993), 98. Voegelin's essay is "The Oxford Political Philosophers," *Philosophical Quarterly* 3, no. 11 (April 1953): 97–114. Voegelin's critique of d'Entrèves is chiefly aimed at defending Thomas Aquinas against d'Entrèves's charge that Aquinas endorsed a sort of totalitarianism in politics by his rejection of religious liberty (102–5). Notably Strauss refers to "the Oxford philosophers" rather than political philosophers.

34. D'Entrèves, "Case for Natural Law," 6.

35. Ibid., 51.

simply what earlier philosophers used to describe the sense that something other than force or fear compelled obedience to the law. He rejected however the path of insisting, as Heinrich Rommen did (d'Entrèves's example), on an account of law that depends on "ontological" premises no longer widely shared. Once again, though, he emphasized that he was "arguing on the assumption that we are here to find a common ground for our case"—in other words, not or not only because of his rejection of the Thomist account.[36] And indeed, as a defense against "the objection of historical relativism" d'Entrèves advanced Strauss's *Natural Right and History*.[37] D'Entrèves's interest in turning to the natural law in order to explain obedience to the law was not merely a move in the parlor discussions of his Oxford colleagues. It was rather an attempt to find a justifiable answer to the question posed in the *Crito*, among other places: why should I obey the law? This interest gave a different character to d'Entrèves's investigations, but they were investigations well worthwhile for any student of the actual effects of modern politics on the life of ordinary citizens—for the student of, so to speak, "Really Existing Modernity." Like Strauss though in a different manner, d'Entrèves sought to recover and maintain the perspective of the ordinary citizen faced with the question why he should obey the law.

Machiavelli, the Political Art, and Virtue: Charles N. R. McCoy

D'Entrèves, McCoy, and Simon share in different ways the view that modern science and politics have fundamentally altered the human world in ways that must be acknowledged even when met with various forms of criticism. Strauss highlights above all the changed conditions of science or philosophy. Classical philosophy had sought to move from opinion to knowledge, and in so doing it potentially undermined the opinions that had the political enforcement of the city; philosophy did not address the people as a whole directly, but rather educated potential philosophers among them. Strauss implies that Machiavelli borrowed or learned from Christianity the possibility that philosophy would address the people

36. Ibid., 35.
37. Ibid., 47.

directly. Indeed, in his treatise *De vera religione* (written in 390) Augustine makes much the same point. By and large, he says, the philosophers "were not fit to change the minds of their fellow-citizens, and convert them from idolatrous superstition and worldly vanity to the true worship of the true God."[38] In addressing the people as a whole and seeking to benefit them, modern science both responds to the conditions changed by Christian preaching (the openness of the many to philosophical terms, e.g., *consubstantialis* as a part of the Nicene Creed) and encourages popular openness to natural science.

Interest in Machiavelli as the founder of modernity was, of course, not new with Strauss's *Thoughts on Machiavelli*. But while Strauss positions himself against the "patriotic" and "scientific" interpretations of Machiavelli, certain earlier scholars had also arrived at a rejection of these interpretations—though without having made the other discoveries that Strauss asserts.[39] While Jacques Maritain's 1941 lecture "The End of Machiavellianism" is not a close analysis of Machiavelli's texts, he offers a suggestion made contemporaneously by Charles N. R. McCoy and again later by d'Entrèves (unaware of the connection), that "nowhere is it possible to find a more purely artistical conception of politics."[40] In Maritain's reading, Machiavelli assumes that the "political artist" follows Machiavelli's teaching while "all others" retain the traditional moral teachings, making them putty in the hands of a conniving prince.[41] My intention is not to dwell on Maritain's interpretation of Machiavelli, but instead to move toward a point that the three Catholic students of political philosophy I focus on (d'Entrèves, McCoy, Simon) identify in common with Strauss while interpreting in a dramatically different manner. To do so I will borrow only one further line from Maritain, the lead article from the first number of the *Review of Politics* in January 1939: "modern civilization," writes Maritain, "seems as if it were pushed by the very contra-

---

38. Augustine, *Of True Religion*, in *Augustine: Earlier Writings*, ed. and trans. J. H. S. Burleigh (Philadelphia: Westminster, 1953), II.2.

39. See, for example, Paul Janet, *Histoire de la science politique dans ses rapports avec la morale* (Paris: Ancienne Libraire Germer Ballière et C[ompagn]ie, 1887), vol. 1, bk. 3, chap. 1.

40. Jacques Maritain, "The End of Machiavellianism," *Review of Politics* 4, no. 1 (January 1942): 7. For a commentary on Maritain's account, see Raymond Aron, "Sur le machiavélisme. Dialogue avec Jacques Maritain (1982)," *Commentaire* 8, nos. 28–29 (Winter 1985): 511–16; and his "French Thought in Exile: Jacques Maritain and the Quarrel over Machiavellianism," trans. Paul Seaton and Daniel J. Mahoney, in *In Defense of Political Reason: Essays*, ed. Daniel J. Mahoney (Lanham, Md.: Rowman and Littlefield, 1994), 53–63.

41. Maritain, "End of Machiavellianism," 9.

dictions and fatalities suffered by it, toward contrasting forms of misery and intensified materialism."[42] The impulse to master nature does not stay limited to the modern scientists, even though it begins from them. Maritain accordingly calls for a "humanism" that, "far from being limited to the élite, ... would care for the masses."[43] Here, too, my intention is not to endorse Maritain's integral humanism or even to outline its characteristics, but instead to suggest that the Catholics approaching the analysis of modern politics offer an account of its foundation similar to that of Strauss, but sharing Maritain's concern with the "misery" that may come alongside modern benefits. By attempting to be philanthropic modern science raises the question of whether it in fact is, and the basis on which one would adjudicate that claim.

This sequence of thoughts comes to the fore most clearly in the work of Charles N. R. McCoy. His essay "Machiavelli and the New Politics: The Primacy of Art," printed eleven years before Strauss delivered the Walgreen lectures on Machiavelli, begins as follows: "The structure of political thought in the Greek-medieval tradition was built on the subordination of practical science to theoretic science and, within the sphere of practical science, on the subordination of art to prudence."[44] McCoy defines art as the correspondence of intention and production: every art intends to produce a certain end. In the classical tradition, prudence directs action toward a certain end. McCoy attempts to link Machiavelli's shift toward an art with modern natural science by grouping both modern politics and modern science under the heading of "art." Experimental natural science begins to proceed by the formulation of hypotheses composed by human reason. To the extent that nature follows these hypotheses or that the hypotheses describe natural motions accurately, art as it were makes the laws of nature. Aristotle's distinction between natural and experimental philosophy offers a different path: the philosophy of nature (for example, in the knowledge of motion or the knowledge of universals) reveals

---

42. Jacques Maritain, "Integral Humanism and the Crisis of Modern Times," *Review of Politics* 1, no. 1 (January 1939): 16.

43. Maritain, "Integral Humanism," 15.

44. Charles N. R. McCoy, *The Structure of Political Thought: A Study in the History of Political Ideas* (New York: McGraw-Hill, 1963); reprinted with an introduction by Thomas M. Neumayr and Richard J. Dougherty (New Brunswick, N.J.: Transaction, 2016), 157. Citations refer to the McGraw-Hill edition. An earlier version of McCoy's Machiavelli chapter was published as "The Place of Machiavelli in the History of Political Thought," *American Political Science Review* 37, no. 4 (August 1943): 626–41. For the most recent bibliography of McCoy's work, see John J. Schrems, "A New Annotated Bibliography of Charles N.R. McCoy," *Catholic Social Science Review* 11 (2006): 275–92.

necessary relationships, whereas experiment and dialectical knowledge yield hypotheses that are either good or bad. In this way McCoy likens the relationship between the universal principles and natural science to the relationship between the principles of human life and practical science. (Notably, he does so with a reference to the *Physics* for the former, and a reference to Thomas Aquinas for the latter.)[45]

On this basis, McCoy blames Machiavelli for "removing from the experimental part of the science the common experience of first principles."[46] Machiavelli proceeds as though the first principles of practical reason—for example, to do good and avoid evil—were not actually available to the ordinary person. McCoy accordingly indicts Machiavelli for a "failure" to distinguish theoretical and practical science, for "ignoring the first principles of the science [of politics]," and for "failing to perceive that man is substantially [a] *rational animal*."[47] The combined consequence of these three judgments is that Machiavelli redefines virtue to depart from the habitual choice of the classical virtues toward the free selection of (classical) virtues or vices according to necessity. McCoy judges this move to be an imposition of the character of theoretical science on political life. Theoretical inquiry considers things as they necessarily are or considers what is, and so Machiavelli "is interested only in the disposition of things and not at all in the disposition and habits that form character."[48] Like Strauss will be in subsequent years, McCoy is already critical of the interpretations that whitewash Machiavelli by crediting his use of terms such as the common good, virtue, and liberty, instead of realizing that he retained them in order to subvert them.[49] McCoy, too, comes to the conclusion that "*The Prince* is not only at bottom consistent with the views expressed in the *Discourses*, but indeed ... *The Prince* is at the bottom of the views expressed in the *Discourses*."[50]

In one sense, Machiavelli's project would not appear to require that ordinary people adopt the new primacy of art that McCoy identifies. Machiavelli's advice is given to princes, at least in its acute sense, and Machiavelli distinguishes between princely and popular humors. McCoy instead

---

45. McCoy, *Structure*, 164n14.
46. Ibid., 165.
47. Ibid., 166, 170, 171. Strauss would explain Machiavelli's choices, but not blame him for "failure."
48. Ibid., 174.
49. Ibid., 176.
50. Ibid., 178.

speaks of the prince as the "exemplar" of the new virtue, and says that the people in a republican regime must acquire virtue lest they become corrupt.[51] McCoy is surely right that the prince is "an artist whose work it is to bring the people out of their lethargic state." But his statement that the "virtues of the prince are the *virtù* which Machiavelli conceives as the desirable thing in a whole people" raises an important difficulty.[52] McCoy's concern that the new understanding of virtue transforms it into an art modeled on theoretical science is analogous, in this limited respect, to Strauss's concern that modern science imposes a philosophical viewpoint on ordinary political opinion and in so doing distorts ordinary opinion as well as the path toward philosophy. Both identify a danger in making political reasoning operate in the manner of philosophy.

In McCoy's account, politics shifts toward being an art which, through successive attempts at describing human nature according to natural science, founds itself in "laws ... increasingly understood" by human beings.[53] For ordinary people to practice the new virtue on this view, they must actually practice the art of choosing virtue and vice according to necessity. Strauss takes a different view of the relationship between the prince's virtue and the popular humor. The distinguishing characteristic of the people is according to Machiavelli goodness, *bontà*. To the extent that the new prince's virtue is, on Strauss's reading as well as McCoy's, a distortion of philosophy, Strauss is more concerned with the distortion caused to philosophy by its use in the calculation of, rather than the habituation to, virtue.

As an interpreter of Machiavelli McCoy attempts less than Strauss, but reading McCoy discloses a set of concerns different from Strauss's which are, however, useful in understanding the character of modernity. In a difficult set of remarks toward the end of his book, McCoy opposes the classical understanding of the human intellect "as separable of itself" from the modern account of nature which "reduces the material and mental spheres to a common denominator."[54] When modern physical science abandons the view that nature consists of substances or natures in favor of the view that nature consists of ever-smaller building blocks that operate according to general laws, no parts of nature can be

51. Ibid., 175–76.
52. Ibid., 177.
53. Ibid., 180.
54. Ibid., 258.

held to have purposes legitimately shaping or directing activity. In the final versions of the new view, which McCoy locates in Marxism, the arrangement of human life into families, cities under law, morality, and the like are no more natural than any other arrangement, and hence must be abolished in order to pave the way for human liberty.

The prior view by contrast highlights "the capacity [of men] to share in the Divine activity by way of proportion in the political life and by way of union and informing in the life of science and wisdom."[55] In other words, the elementary structures of political life reflect human nature and can be understood as a proportional participation in a higher good. The Marxist culmination of modernity "bring[s] to full perfection the notion of political 'art' by transposing into practice—into unassailable 'facts'—the whole order of things that Aristotle, by reserving to the speculative intellect, had made the bastion of human freedom."[56] The objects of the speculative intellect were the "bastion of human freedom" because the exemplars of the virtues existed in God and could be understood by the human intellect. Those exemplars secured the possibility of achieving liberty through their practice.

The elements of what McCoy considers political art (a term he often, as here, places in quotation marks) are three: (1) political art applies as a criterion of correct political conduct the artistic standard of efficaciousness; (2) political art transposes into the realm of ethical and political conduct the theoretical intellect's concern with necessity, and its lack of concern with the good; (3) political art further transposes into and then identifies in practice the activities of the theoretical intellect that were previously a separate location of human liberty. The objects of the speculative intellect are no longer substances and their operation but the laws of nature that enable human beings to bend nature to their own will. In that way the "order of things" previously studied by the speculative intellect becomes immediate—a set of "unassailable 'facts.'"

McCoy draws attention to Marx's remark in *Capital* that "Labour is, in the first place, a process in which both men and Nature participate, and in which man of his own accord starts, regulates, and controls the material re-actions between himself and Nature."[57] The classical-Christian and modern theories of politics produce two models of participation: in the

55. Ibid.
56. Ibid., 259.
57. Ibid., 293, quoting Marx, *Capital*, part 3, chap. 7 (New York: Modern Library, 1936), 197.

classical-Christian account the divine exemplars of virtue establish the grounds for human participation in the good; in the modern account the participation of both man and nature in labor or production places (in a phrase McCoy borrows from Cassirer) "the material and mental spheres" on the same plane.[58] The intellect is a part of the natural world operating according to the same laws, and lacks a specific end just as much as the rest of nature. As McCoy puts it:

> The self-liberation envisaged by liberalism is precisely that man may experience very tangibly the material infinity experienced theoretically by the modern physicist, and free himself from the world of common experience.... If modern physics were taken to mean, indeed, that the human intellect by becoming aware of its own infinity through measuring its powers by the infinite universe, reaches things as they really are in nature so that nature be considered "operable" in itself, modern social science means that in the world produced by human effort, man is freed from the imaginary boundaries of "indefectible principles" and "natural associations" so that he may experience practically and not merely theoretically the generic nature of his being: a shadow world of facts that have about them indeed the quality of myth and magic.[59]

McCoy's invocation of myth and magic interprets Cassirer's famous assertion about their persistence in modern times.[60] Whereas previously myth and magic performed a social function in explaining to men what was special or significant in their activities, their own technological efforts are the obvious locus of what is special. Because those efforts presume the dispensing of specific ends or purposes of human nature, their significance is unclear. For that reason, the science which produces material things according to the operability of the laws of nature needs a narrative of its significance and trajectory. (McCoy's remark also calls to mind Arthur C. Clarke's Third Law: "Any sufficiently advanced technology is indistinguishable from magic.")[61]

To appreciate the delicate way in which McCoy presents an alternative to Strauss, let us turn briefly to McCoy's essay "On the Revival of Classical Political Philosophy," which first appeared in the *Review of Politics* in 1973.[62] The heart of McCoy's criticism of Strauss concerns the

---

58. McCoy, *Structure*, 191; and "The Dilemma of Liberalism," 75.
59. McCoy, *Structure*, 255.
60. See McCoy's essay on Cassirer, "Man's Lost Intellectual Center," chap. 9 in *Intelligibility*.
61. Arthur C. Clarke, "Clarke's Third Law on UFO's," *Science* 159, no. 3812 (January 19, 1968): 255.
62. McCoy, "On the Revival of Classical Political Philosophy," chap. 10 in *Intelligibility*. Originally published in *Review of Politics* 35, no. 2 (April 1973): 161–79.

favor Strauss gives to the Platonic account of nature as a "standard" of the good rather than its Aristotelian account as an "authority" informing the particular goods of each substance within nature. The Aristotelian view identifies natural right as a part of political right, which though not dissolving the tension Strauss identifies between politics and philosophy ceases to equate the just life with the philosophical life simply. (McCoy does not consider Strauss's suggestion that Aristotle's "obfuscation," as Strauss calls it indirectly, might have been a deliberate strategy rather than a defective form of philosophy.) "Aristotle's position," McCoy says, "is that nature indeed is a kind of 'reason' put into things so that they may act for determinate ends (*Physics* II), but that the ultimate reasons of things are not subjectified in the things themselves of the world."[63] Plato also accepts the second half of this statement: in the account of the good as a standard, the class explains why one can predicate its name of many different things (e.g., the class of artisan which contains weavers, carpenters, and so forth), but the class is not the cause of those things. "Strauss," McCoy complains, "would have it that as weaver and carpenter disappear into 'artisan,' so statesman should disappear into philosopher, the political into the philosophical."[64]

McCoy draws attention to a possible discordance in Strauss's thought concerning the role of nature in classical and modern philosophy. While Strauss says that nature is "abandoned" in modern philosophy (eventually for history), McCoy also appears to accept Charles Beard's statement (quoted by Strauss but attributed to Strauss by McCoy) that the modern revolutionaries have "resorted to nature," which in Strauss's words "is true, *mutatis mutandis*, of all philosophers *qua* philosophers."[65] While modern science involves a departure from Aristotle's understanding of the law, "the new sense of nature," says McCoy, "retains the idea of 'law' as Plato had understood it."[66] In the new view, "the good becomes simply convertible with being and law describes the 'properties' of each nature," just as the good in Plato's account was convertible with being.[67] The character of law describing each nature undergoes a profound change (from a description of excellence to a description of mechanics), but its

63. McCoy, "Revival," 139.
64. Ibid., 142.
65. Ibid., 143.
66. Ibid., 144.
67. Ibid.

relationship to being does not. In both classical Platonism and modern politics, "the quest for the best regime" and "the study of the cosmos" go together, as Hobbes's account of man stands in relation to the new scientific account of man.[68] The character of the good sought by Plato, the transcendent foundation of the universal categories and the foundation of the philosopher's claim to rule, cannot produce laws with an immediate political effect. The "good" identified by modern science with the laws undergirding all phenomena provides useful knowledge to the scientist who knows the laws, because they describe the motion of all things (including the human intellect) in terms sufficiently simple to allow human manipulation. The individual producer or worker, however, does not necessarily have to understand the laws of nature beyond an elementary level; he simply has to work according to them, through operating devices (smartphones, for example) whose operation depends on others' knowledge of aspects of the laws of nature.

Let us remind ourselves of Strauss's characterization of the change that philosophy undergoes in the new political science proposed by Machiavelli:

> Instead of saying that the status of philosophy becomes obscured in Machiavelli's thought, it is perhaps better to say that in his thought the meaning of philosophy is undergoing a change.... Philosophy transcends the city [in the classical regime], and the worth of the city depends ultimately on its openness, or deference, to philosophy.... Machiavelli's philosophizing on the other hand remains on the whole within the limits set by the city qua closed to philosophy. Accepting the ends of the *demos* as beyond appeal, he seeks for the best means conducive to those ends. Through his effort philosophy becomes salutary in the sense in which the *demos* understands, or may understand, the salutary. He achieves the decisive turn toward that notion of philosophy according to which its purpose is to relieve man's estate or to increase man's power or to guide man toward the rational society, the bond and the end of which is enlightened self-interest or the comfortable self-preservation of each of its members.... By supplying all men with the goods which they desire, by being the obvious benefactress of all men, philosophy (or science) ceases to be suspect or alien.[69]

Strauss's statement that Machiavelli accepts "the ends of the *demos* as beyond appeal" implies that Machiavelli's philosophy gives the people what they want: security, liberty, and "the goods which they desire." This

---

68. Ibid., 147.
69. Strauss, *Thoughts*, 295–96.

suggestion highlights a potentially illuminating discordance in Strauss's thought, a discordance that marks the entry point for McCoy's different set of considerations.

Some pages before the conclusion of his *Thoughts on Machiavelli*, Strauss suggests the following as a way of understanding Machiavelli's position: in Machiavelli's view, "Aristotle did not see that the relation of the founder to his human matter is not fundamentally different from the relation of a smith to his iron or his inanimate matter: Aristotle did not realize to what extent man is malleable, and in particular malleable by man. Still, that malleability is limited and therefore it remains true that the highest achievement depends on chance."[70] In his statement contrasting Machiavelli and Aristotle, Strauss suggests that the people's "malleability" is a core element of Machiavelli's view, while in the later statement he illustrates the new relationship of philosophy to the city by way of a static depiction of popular desire. The subsequent development of modern science and technology, particularly in the division of labor, began to satisfy popular desire also by employing people in the making of products that would satisfy them. The shift from agriculture toward industrial production raises the question of how far the manipulability of human nature goes. Human beings involved in processes of scientific production—for example, the manufacturing of pharmaceuticals or of electronic devices—cannot be the rude or poor members of the *demos* who simply want liberty and basic material possessions.

In his essay "What Is Political Philosophy?," Strauss implies that modern technology, even if it has not directly changed the popular character, has opened up a potential which was previously not present. "The difference between the classics and us with regard to democracy," he comments, "consists exclusively in a different estimate of the virtues of technology."[71] The "virtues" of technology lie in its elimination of grave want and the hitherto unknown possibility of universal education. Only this latter possibility makes democracy desirable or defensible from an elevated standpoint, because democracy becomes in this way enlightened. Strauss's interpretation of Machiavelli as the founder of modernity has always been clouded by Strauss's only oblique references to the relationship between Machiavelli's politics and the subsequent development of

---

70. Ibid., 253.
71. Leo Strauss, *What Is Political Philosophy?* (Glencoe, Ill.: Free Press, 1959), 37.

natural science. "The artistic aspect of the prince's imitation of virtue," McCoy writes, "is seen in his ability to practice now one extreme and now the other lying outside the intermediate.... It is by art that he extends the limits of human nature."[72] If the virtuous prince "extends" human nature through art, *a fortiori* may he attempt to extend nonhuman nature through Machiavelli's new account of art (i.e., his technology). As Strauss puts it, "The brain which can transform the political matter soon learns to think of the transformation of every matter or of the conquest of nature."[73] But is the political matter transformed only in its external arrangement, or is it really transformed in such a way that the classical account of philosophy and the city is disrupted even on the level of theory? To answer that question, I turn in the final section to Yves Simon's reflections on the changed condition of moral virtue, and especially the virtue of prudence, in the era of modern science.

Prudence and Modern Science according to Yves R. Simon

In his Walgreen Foundation Lectures delivered at the University of Chicago in 1948 (one year prior to Strauss's *Natural Right and History* lectures), Yves Simon dedicated his last lecture to the topic "Democracy and Technology." Simon began from two points exactly opposed to those of Strauss: first, the Jeffersonian point that democracy depends on mores cultivated by farm life and is thus incompatible with technology; second, that the evaluation of technology depends on its comparison with agricultural civilization in terms of their effects on man's happiness, autonomy, and community-centeredness.[74] The spread of technology affects democracy in numerous profound ways. By making human labor more quickly effective, technology alters men's relationship to the works of preceding generations. In this respect, the natural conservatism of the people begins to be hobbled, not through a conscious spirit of innovation but through the experience of depending chiefly on inventions of one's own generation. As men invent more things, they thereby begin

---

72. McCoy, *Structure*, 173.
73. Strauss, *Thoughts*, 297.
74. Yves R. Simon, *Philosophy of Democratic Government* (Chicago: University of Chicago Press, 1951), 261–62.

to see more of their own doings in daily life (a point that was for Marx the beginning of alienation). Even the presence of biological life recedes as more elements of the human environment are constructed artificially, from dwelling places to foods. The increasingly reliable success of technical products (such as airplanes) also heightens the contrast between the smooth world of technology and the frustrating recalcitrance of the human world. Though access to education is higher overall, that education is in ever higher proportion technical rather than humanistic education. Last, the character of technological rationalism inculcates a tendency to expect leadership to take the form of scientific expertise.[75]

In light of Strauss's skill at uncovering the intentions of the great philosophers, the accomplishments of contemporary students of politics may be less impressive to the reader wishing to understand the meaning of the great texts. On the other hand, Strauss's own interest in the great texts was, it should go without saying, directed in part by his concern that historicism as well as modern science had obscured the character and proper activity of the philosopher. Strauss's works and the works of his Catholic contemporaries may instead be seen as alternative ways of grappling with the commonly noticed issue of the relationship between technology, or applied modern science, and ordinary life. I do not intend this suggestion to be a comprehensive account either of Strauss's intentions in recovering political philosophy, or of his Catholic contemporaries' intentions whose efforts began from different points and with different goals in mind. But on this point there is a remarkable commonality in identifying a topic of crucial philosophical importance, and a striking difference in the way that topic's significance was conceived. Viewed from the philosopher's standpoint in relation to the city, Strauss's account of Machiavelli's new science looks accurate: Machiavelli reconceives philosophy or science as the city's benefactress. If as Strauss suggests the *demos*'s desires are static, however, then what accounts for the growth of popular dissatisfaction? Marx articulated the dissatisfaction of labor with its own conditions; he did not singly create that dissatisfaction.

Simon begins by addressing the situation of democracy's relationship to technology, and his account of the training of free men in technological democracy is particularly interesting on this point. The assembly-line worker, Simon suggests, might indeed otherwise have the capacity to per-

---

75. Ibid., 274–80.

fect his intellectual understanding of some science or art. Strauss's statement regarding the technological rationale for defending modern democracy suggests something similar: limitation on the growth of human intellectual faculties depended in a significant way on material want. In the absence of those limitations, more people will use or develop their intellectual faculties. That development does not necessarily imply an increase in the proportion of philosophers as Strauss imagines them. But in Simon's view it does mean a revision to Aristotle's tendency to equate real intellectual activity only with those overseeing the architectonic arts (such as architecture itself). Skilled labor has a potential similar to that of those practicing the architectonic arts.[76] Even leaving aside skilled labor, Simon observes the vast increase of engineers involved in planning (a form of architectonic art), who are just as separated from the material execution of their designs as the aristocrats of the classical world.[77] Technological methods of production increase the number of those whose work involves the use of higher faculties while also limiting their time to use those faculties in education or recreation other than work.

Simon's fears for the effects of technology on education are particularly poignant, as he predicts the continued decline of humanistic education amid the overall increase of technical instruction. Even liberal education, though, is insufficient in his view to correct the tendencies brought on by the proliferation of technology, whatever those tendencies may be. "The proper use of techniques, in so far as it can be taught, remains abstract and devoid of necessary influence upon action," he writes. Simon elaborates his thought in the following way: "The fully determinate and unmistakably effective knowledge of the right use is not science, but prudence.... Moreover, the knowledge of the right use, even in so far as it is scientific and teachable, involves difficulties which render unlikely its uninterrupted maintenance and continuous progress. In this respect the science of the proper use of techniques—one function of ethics—resembles metaphysics rather than positive science."[78]

Simon's meaning is not entirely clear, but I believe he suggests the following. In Aristotle's account, the "knowledge" guiding correct action is not science but the virtue of prudence, which knows how to select the appropriate means for a given good end. Modern scientific techniques

---

76. Ibid., 298.
77. Ibid., 299.
78. Ibid., 282–83.

bear a certain similarity of cast to prudence insofar as they, too, provide the means necessary for a given end, but in leaving aside the goodness of that end they follow the model of the arts rather than prudence. The same science that invents modern technique (whether in the natural sciences, engineering, or the like) is, however, also the science that establishes a new ethics, or set of standards by which to orient modern technique. Modern technique is not and cannot be simply guided by the classical, nonscientific account of virtue, for that account did not require or even envision the advent of technology. The modern knowledge of the "proper use of techniques" is itself technical, scientific, and thus teachable as a part of technical education. In the context of business ethics, for example, hiring and firing are techniques for the optimization of profit; they are not chiefly vicious or virtuous actions, but necessary ones. The scientific account of the "proper use of techniques" is not ordered toward Aristotle's account of virtue, but rather is coeval with the abandonment of that account in favor of one based on self-preservation and the relief of man's estate. As a consequence, however, the new account of the "proper use of techniques" is scientific rather than connatural with virtue, and so does not guide action in the manner of prudence as a habit. Accounts of the proper use of techniques are fragile achievements, as fragile as the science of metaphysics itself, and have no efficacy when not buttressed by the practice of virtue. Like McCoy, Simon identifies elements of Platonism in the new arrangement. Our reliance on knowledge rather than habit, he writes, "is merely a modernized version of the Socratic error."[79]

Simon indicates an aspect of philosophy's transformation in modernity that is less apparent in Strauss's account. In bringing the benefits of and use of science to the whole people, modern science has also required that moral virtue be supplanted with a new science of ethics—which, however, is no less difficult to discover and to maintain than the old science of metaphysics. Modern science's benefits to mankind require a knowledge of their proper use which may be as difficult or ineffectual as classical philosophy. Simon's suggestion is not a reiteration of Rousseau's complaint about the incompatibility of science and virtue; it is a complaint regarding the consequences for upright choice brought on by the spread of scientifically or technologically enabled action.[80] As Simon

---

79. Ibid., 282.
80. For Simon on Rousseau, see Yves R. Simon, *The Definition of Moral Virtue*, ed. Vukan Kuic (New York: Fordham University Press, 1986), 2–8.

indicates in a letter to Maritain in 1961 (the year of Simon's death), Simon had grown over time to view moral philosophy as existing "primarily for the sake of explaining the things of morality" rather than for directing human action, as he had once thought.[81] In an unpublished lecture on "Freedom of Choice and the Ethics of Liberty" at the University of Chicago (likely delivered in 1948), Simon writes that "When natural evidence does not suffice [to establish a proper course of action], we turn to moral science. From Socrates to the most up to date positivist productions: a desperate effort to construct a science which should let us know what we should do."[82] While Simon here exaggerates the similarity between Socratic and modern attempts to construct a science of ethics, in a 1953 essay "From the Science of Nature to the Science of Society" he draws a sharp contrast—similar to that drawn by Strauss—between the "contemplative" aims of Greek philosophy and the "demiurgical" efforts of modern science.[83]

Rather than positing a conflict of philosophy and the city that modern science attempts to resolve, Simon posits a "harmony of common sense as philosophy (on the one hand) and science (on the other hand)" that is disrupted "insofar as science follows a nonontological line." These suggestions, from an unpublished lecture "Common Sense and Science" that Simon likely delivered at Mount Saint Agnes College (since 1971 part of Loyola University Maryland), unfold in the following way.[84] Because modern science analyzes concepts "into definite possibilities of observation and measurement rather than into ways of being," it departs permanently from common sense and seeks "to achieve self-sufficiency on the level of scientifically elaborated thought." Modern science's extraordinary contributions to the material betterment of mankind thus create a situa-

---

81. Simon to Maritain, February 15, 1961, in Yves R. Simon, *Practical Knowledge*, ed. Robert J. Mulvaney (New York: Fordham University Press, 1991), 106–7. As Simon elaborates in his further reply to Maritain's objections, the ability of prudence to obtain certainty regarding a course of action does not constitute the same sort of certainty as the sciences proper. Such disciplines "belong to the habitus of the practical intellect." *Practical Knowledge*, 110–11.

82. Yves R. Simon archives, Jacques Maritain Center, University of Notre Dame, Box YS 10/08. I am grateful to John O'Callaghan, director of the Jacques Maritain Center, for facilitating access to the Simon archives as well as to the Center's library.

83. Yves R. Simon, "From the Science of Nature to the Science of Society," in *Practical Knowledge*, 116. Simon, however, grants that this portrayal involves "oversimplification" (133n3).

84. "Common Sense and Science," Yves R. Simon archives, Box YS 28/25. A handwritten note on the first page of a draft with corrections by hand reads "to Sis M. Cleophas and the lecture Committee." The reference is likely to Sister Mary Cleophas Costello, RSM, sometime president of Mount Saint Agnes College. Portions of the lecture were reworked and included in *Freedom of Choice*, ed. Peter Wolff (New York: Fordham University Press, 1969), 83–94.

tion in which his ordinary activity involves applied science, but in which the old accounts of ethics (presuming the arts but not technology) render uncertain judgments regarding his proper actions in the contemporary situation. While on the basis of Strauss's discoveries concerning Machiavelli and Hobbes one might object to Simon's assumption that the new natural science preceded the new social science, Simon is at least correct that the rise and progress of natural science furthered the efforts to offer a scientific account of ethics (e.g., Spinoza). If Strauss is correct that popular habits differ fundamentally and permanently from the open-ended character of philosophical inquiry, then modern science puts ordinary people in the impossible situation of needing to implement a science of proper use which, in the absence of virtue, is inaccessible to them as a whole.[85] Simon does not attempt to identify Machiavelli as the originator of modern science, though he did receive a personally inscribed copy of McCoy's article on Machiavelli in the *American Political Science Review*.[86] He does, however, emphasize the character of modern philosophy in a way reminiscent of Machiavelli, noting that modern natural science "is steadily communicable, not only in terms of essential possibility ... but also in a factual sense."[87] Because modern science is "demiurgical," it delivers proof of its understanding in the form of material goods. What is more, says Simon, "experience shows that men able to master it [i.e., the modern science of nature], or some parts of it, are not exceedingly few in the educated section of society."[88]

As Walter Nicgorski notes in his elegant treatment of Simon's emphasis on the continuing importance of prudence, Strauss "deeply admired his work" and "strongly praised Simon's analysis of modern democracy"—facts also evident from Strauss's review of Simon's *Philosophy of Democratic Government*.[89] While this review understands Simon to take

---

85. Note also Simon's comments in *Philosophy of Democratic Government*: "The mental habits generated by the technological relation of man to nature are characterized by strict discipline and remarkable clarity. The social engineer is an extremely popular myth; this shows that many are tempted to transfer to the social order mental habits born of our relation to physical nature" (291).

86. Yves R. Simon archives, Box YS 40/01.

87. Simon, "From the Science of Nature to the Science of Society," 117. See also Simon's comments on the tendency of "most of the positive sciences [to] generate a technology." "Each of them," he adds, "sets out to know man in order to act upon him." Yves R. Simon, *Foresight and Knowledge*, ed. Ralph Nelson and Anthony O. Simon (New York: Fordham University Press, 1996), 122.

88. Simon, "From the Science of Nature to the Science of Society," 117.

89. Walter Nicgorski, "Yves R. Simon: A Philosopher's Quest for Science and Prudence," *Review of Politics* 71, no. 1 (Winter 2009): 70, 70n8. Strauss also referenced Simon as a good general account of Aristotle's views on prudence (with some exceptions). Strauss, "Aristotle's Rhetoric," Lecture, Uni-

the condition of society under modern technology as the "normal" situation, it is clear on the basis of the above that Simon does not agree.[90] The new natural science is readily communicable, able to be understood by a larger proportion of society, and it readily delivers material goods. The proper use of techniques now implies the need for a science of proper use that will, in fact, be futile in assisting men's relationship to technology. Simon's response to this situation in *Philosophy of Democratic Government* is to "restrain" evil techniques and "release" beneficent ones.[91]

In a short paper on "Christian Humanism" first published in 1956 (five years after *Philosophy of Democratic Government*) and collected at the end of *Practical Knowledge,* Simon remarks that "In the relation of the human to the technical, we keep our instruments under control insofar as we remain free from attachment to things inferior to man." The fullest sense of that freedom from attachment is "the spirit of poverty," which "preserves the order of human salvation and removes the danger of man's being crushed by the weight of his ideas, his systems, his experiences, his erudition, his constructs, his methods, and his postulations."[92] Only such a "mysticism" could shape "in every particular case" the proper relationship to technical accomplishments. Though the Christian mysticism Simon advises could not be more removed from the rationalism of Strauss, the two do intersect in one respect, the aspect of philosophy most easily grasped by Strauss's readers and the most superficial aspect: its stance. The picture of philosophy that Strauss presents in his "Restatement on Xenophon's *Hiero*" (drawing on Plato's *Theaetetus*) suggests that the philosopher "is as unconcerned as possible with individual and perishable human beings and hence also with his own 'individuality,' or his body."[93] The many qualifications Strauss adds to this statement (not least his emphasis on political philosophy) do not take away from the overall picture of the philosopher's "radical detachment."[94]

---

versity of Chicago, May 18, 1964; transcript in Leo Strauss Center, University of Chicago, https://artflsrv03.uchicago.edu/philologic4/strauss/navigate/9/12/.
    90. Strauss, *What Is Political Philosophy?*, 310–11.
    91. Simon, *Philosophy of Democratic Government*, 288.
    92. Simon, *Practical Knowledge*, 155.
    93. Strauss, *What Is Political Philosophy?*, 118.
    94. Ibid., 122. On this feature of Strauss's presentation, see Pierre Manent, *Le regard politique: Entretiens avec Bénédicte Delorme-Montini* (Paris: Flammarion, 2010): "C'est un point qui me sépare de mes amis straussiens américains.... On est obligé de séparer dans une certaine mesure le savant ou le philosophe de l'homme. Mais cette figure esquissée par Strauss d'un philosophe qui s'accomplirait dans l'abandon de tout intérêt pour les choses humaines, qui laisserait derrière lui tous les

In Strauss's view, "philosophy is now asserted to be essentially subservient to the end which is capable of being actually pursued by all men.... The end of philosophy is now no longer what one may call disinterested contemplation of the eternal, but the relief of man's estate."[95] While arriving at a similar judgment of the character of modern philosophy, Simon thinks that the modern emphasis on technique creates a new situation in which science is asked to guide its own use, which it cannot do effectively. Even if classical philosophy's account of the virtues were correct, the virtues of moderation or prudence do not immediately show which technologies to use, how or when. The new union of society with a "demiurgical" science also goes along with a new separation of common sense (or the world of prescientific opinion) and scientific reasoning. A stance like the philosopher's detachment is in fact necessary for everyone, even if it is only "mysticism" in a way that would be firmly rejected by Strauss. Because ordinary people continue to need a practical science in applying modern techniques (the quasi-metaphysical science of ethics is insufficient to direct their actions), three consequences follow: (1) modern science is not wholly beneficial, because it leaves the proper course of ordinary action unclear (a different objection from Rousseau's); (2) the problems introduced by new technologies frequently exceed the scope of the classical virtues, such as prudence; (3) modern scientific accounts of ethics are either really neutral or in fact damage the possibility of ethical action by downplaying the need for virtue. Because modern science has already proposed a combined effort of philosophy and society, it is unclear how society would be threatened by philosophers' attending to the newly threatened conditions of moral virtue. As the title of Simon's book *The Definition of Moral Virtue* (1986, based on a course transcript of 1957) suggests, Simon was particularly interested in understanding the situation of the virtue of ordinary citizens in modern democracies.[96]

---

intérêts humains, cette figure du philosophe, je n'ai jamais réussi à la comprendre ni à m'en approcher vraiment" (67–68).

95. Leo Strauss, "Liberal Education and Responsibility," in *An Introduction to Political Philosophy: Ten Essays*, ed. Hilail Gildin (Detroit: Wayne State University Press, 1989), 337.

96. Yves R. Simon, *The Definition of Moral Virtue*, ed. Vukan Kuic (New York: Fordham University Press, 1986).

Conclusion

In his introduction to *The City and Man*, Strauss cautions that the study of classical political philosophy will not necessarily lead to a solution to contemporary problems. "For the relative success of modern political philosophy," Strauss says, "has brought into being a kind of society wholly unknown to the classics, a kind of society to which the classical principles as stated and elaborated by the classics are not immediately applicable. Only we living today can possibly find a solution to the problems of today."[97] In offering an alternative to modern historicism, classical political philosophy asserts the possibility of certain knowledge about the political good. Strauss's account of the relationship of the philosopher to the city in classical philosophy thus has a twofold purpose. The separation of the movement of philosophy from the city guarantees that philosophy is not simply a restatement of the opinions of its own day; it is not an expression of the political views of its time. Consequently in the classical view (as, for example, highlighted in Strauss's analysis of Aristotle's presentation of Hippodamus) philosophy does not *through its account of nature* contribute to the amelioration of mankind's condition.[98]

What part of classical philosophy, then, is "not immediately applicable" to the contemporary situation? The simplest answer is, its stance—the distance classical philosophers assumed between philosophy and society. Because of modern science's contribution to the betterment of society, philosophers are now consulted regarding the proper government of human affairs. One might suggest that in this circumstance those who follow classical philosophy—whether in rejecting the fact-value distinction, in affirming the possibility of natural right, or in rejecting the concurrence of purposes between science and society—would do well to conceal their views in the manner of the classical philosophers. But the authentically liberal forms of modern liberalism claim not to be threatened even by the stated rejection of their own principles. The only reason for a philosopher to desire a return to "persecution" would be for the sake of preserving philosophy's true character and avoiding the distortions brought on by aiming at social utility; by instead studying close-

---

97. Strauss, *The City and Man*, 11. Compare Strauss's statement that, "As a matter of fact, there is in the whole work of Machiavelli not a single true observation regarding the nature of man and of human affairs with which the classics were not thoroughly familiar." *What Is Political Philosophy?*, 43.

98. Strauss, *The City and Man*, 17–23.

ly the works of the persecuted authors, he can relive the motion of their thought. Modern students of Strauss learn from him the tension between philosophy and society and the distortions brought on by modern science's aiming at usefulness.[99] But because the ship of esotericism has already sailed, philosophers are expected to say what they think about the diagnosis and cure of contemporary ills.

In the past, however, criticisms of modern virtue have resulted in the further radicalization of modern principles. In Strauss's view, the critiques launched by Rousseau, Kant, and Hegel "led, consciously or unconsciously, to a much more radical form of modernity."[100] Should worry over further radicalization of modernity make contemporary philosophers hesitant to engage in similar criticism? Rousseau's defense of virtue was tied to an account of human nature that posited its original simplicity prior to a historical development toward language and rationality. Today, however, our sense of historical change comes not only from a philosophical doctrine like Rousseau's or Hegel's but from the continually arriving sequence of modern inventions. The history of modern society is the advancing conquest of nature, extending now to human nature itself (in biological manipulation) and potentially to the creation of new intelligent natures (in artificial intelligence). Though Strauss is particularly concerned by the effects of the new relationship between philosophy and society on the conditions of philosophy itself, modern science can also be evaluated for its effects on the practice of ordinary life.

D'Entrèves, McCoy, and Simon highlight the same changed relationship between philosophy and society that Strauss noticed, but with a greater focus on the effects of that change on ordinary citizens of modern politics. They give attention, each in turn, to the difficulties in grounding political obligation, to the corruption of moral virtue by the intellectual art, and to the impossible demands placed on ordinary prudence by the experience of managing modern science. These concerns are less prominent in Strauss's account because he highlights instead the changed circumstances of philosophy. But they follow out the possibility suggested by Strauss's Machiavelli that human beings are more malleable than once thought, even if not so malleable as to become philosophers. As philoso-

99. Leo Strauss, "A Giving of Accounts," in *Jewish Philosophy and the Crisis of Modernity: Essays and Lectures in Modern Jewish Thought*, ed. Kenneth Hart Green (Albany: State University of New York Press, 1997), 463. See also *The City and Man*, 37–38, and many other locations.
100. Strauss, *What Is Political Philosophy?*, 50.

phy adopted the beneficial stance of modern science, it also changed the conditions of moral virtue—the aspect which drew the interest of d'Entrèves, McCoy, and Simon. The benefits brought by modern science had, they concluded, placed moral virtue in a newly difficult position, stripped of its old grounding and context but also unable to provide sure answers in guiding modern science. While the Christian interest in moral virtue may have facilitated their inquiry, I have pointed to the philosophical reasons for that investigation—reasons that happen to be outlined by Strauss's Catholic contemporaries. The question cannot be wished away by confessional or biographical differences. It is a question of philosophy.

7

On the Catholic Audience of Leo Strauss

JOHN P. HITTINGER

In the brief scope of this paper I should like to consider why reading Leo Strauss has been good for Catholics scholars and to indicate some areas of similarity and difference between Strauss and Thomist philosopher Jacques Maritain on the problematic character of modern philosophy and the crisis of our time. One reason that some Catholic scholars have been receptive to the work of Strauss is that he provides an account of the "crisis of modernity"; he makes a serious consideration of premodern philosophers such as Plato and Aristotle, Maimonides and Aquinas; and he makes frequent reference to natural law. But because he speaks about a "quarrel" between ancients and moderns, he also makes a serious consideration of the modern philosophers. The encounter with Leo Strauss provided some Catholic scholars with a unique and more expansive way of engaging the problem of the church in the modern world that was not overly biased or burdened with a somewhat stale debate between a strict Thomistic defense of Catholic truth and the modernist evasion of tradition and affirmation of new methods, rights, and framework. Thinkers such as Charles McCoy, Ernest Fortin, AA, and James Schall, SJ, preeminent among a number of other Catholic readers of Strauss, received the

Straussian project into a Catholic ambience and found it a means of clarification and deepening of the Catholic intellectual tradition. The works of McCoy, Schall, and Fortin are exceedingly deep in breadth and wide in range, so I will make no claim to review or summarize them and their debt to Strauss, although such a project would be very worthwhile.[1] My aim is rather to analyze a very particular set of talks given by Leo Strauss to a Catholic audience on the crisis of our time and then to compare these talks with some talks given by Jacques Maritain on the crisis of our time. Strauss and Maritain were contemporaries, so there is no question here of influence; but rather I shall seek to explain how their respective framings of the question of the crisis of modernity and their projects to recover the wisdom of the ancients share some similarities and yet diverge on some very significant points.

To approach an understanding of Strauss and his Catholic readers one would do well to begin with his two lectures at the University of Detroit (a Jesuit university) in 1963 entitled "the crisis of our time" and "the crisis of political philosophy."[2] As he says in his opening remarks, the subject is more precisely "the crisis of our time as a consequence of the crisis of political philosophy." Although these lectures are more popular in tone, they provide a useful text for our purposes because he is addressing a Catholic audience and he makes a deliberate appeal to their principles and institutions; in addition we can achieve a good overview of his main concerns and concepts.[3] In a way perhaps not unexpected, Strauss himself provides the very principles to the Catholic audience upon which his project ought to be received and used.

Preliminary words about the speeches are in order. The speeches con-

---

1. Charles N. R. McCoy, *On the Intelligibility of Political Philosophy: Essays of Charles N. R. McCoy* (Washington, D.C.: The Catholic University of America Press, 1989); for Ernest L. Fortin, see his *Collected Essays*, ed. J. Brian Benestad. See also Ernest L. Fortin, Michael P. Foley, and Douglas Kries, *Gladly to Learn and Gladly to Teach: Essays on Religion and Political Philosophy in Honor of Ernest L. Fortin, A.A.* (Lanham, Md.: Lexington Books, 2002). For James Schall see his *The Politics of Heaven & Hell: Christian Themes from Classical, Medieval, and Modern Political Philosophy* (Lanham, Md.: University Press of America, 1984); *Reason, Revelation, and the Foundations of Political Philosophy* (Baton Rouge: Louisiana State University Press, 1987); *At the Limits of Political Philosophy: From "Brilliant Errors" to Things of Uncommon Importance* (Washington, D.C.: The Catholic University of America Press, 1996); *Jacques Maritain: The Philosopher in Society* (Lanham, Md.: Rowman and Littlefield, 1998); and with Mark D. Guerra, *Reason, Revelation, and Human Affairs: Selected Writings of James V. Schall* (Lanham, Md.: Lexington Books, 2001).

2. "The Crisis of Our Time" and "The Crisis of Political Philosophy," in *The Predicament of Modern Politics*, ed. Harold J. Spaeth (Detroit: University of Detroit Press, 1964), 41–54 and 91–103.

3. A very similar argument is made, indeed using similar sentences and paragraphs, without the asides to Catholics, in *Liberalism Ancient and Modern* (New York: Basic Books, 1968).

tain some of the most memorable and oft-quoted phrases of Leo Strauss such as "the return to classical political philosophy is both necessary and experimental and tentative," or "the crisis of the West consists in the West having become uncertain of its purpose." There are many others. And yet he says at the outset the lecture is fragmentary; indeed "it is meant to be incomplete." And further he says "I have to argue to a considerable extent *ad hominem*." The fact that it is incomplete allows it to serve as a stimulus to philosophical thinking; a thoughtful reader will want to trace out the incomplete lines of argument and to complete what is missing. A fragmentary lecture will also challenge the reader to consider the whole or wholes in which the fragments belong and from which they receive their meaning. The lectures could be an opportunity for recollection, a gathering of the full meaning of the parts or fragments in a larger whole. As for the *ad hominem* aspect of the lectures, we must understand that such form of argument is not primarily the mode of personal attack, but rather it is a fundamental form of dialectical argument, which proceeds from the premises and admitted truth of the opponent or interlocutor. In a graduate class on the rhetoric at the University of Chicago 1964 Strauss explained it this way:

> The premise from which you start is granted by the opposing member of the conversation. You argue from these premises and it is irrelevant for this argument whether these premises are true or not. But it is sufficient, however, for refuting it, if he grants you something. What he grants you is the premise. And then you will draw inferences from it; and, if the inferences are destructive of his position, then it is refuted. To that extent the argument can be very valuable, but it is not of course a scientific argument proper, because it does not start from premises that are true.[4]

Strauss says that he must argue *ad hominem* so as to get the attention of the citizens and scholars of a modern liberal democratic regime; it is not sufficient to simply state the truth of philosophy concerning the best regime or the alternatives to the present political principles: "In order to carry conviction, I must remain as close as possible to what is generally accepted in the West. I cannot start from premises which today are agreed upon only by a fairly small minority. In other words, I have to

---

4. Leo Strauss, "Aristotle's Rhetoric," Lecture Course, The University of Chicago, Spring 1964, ed. Ronna Burger (2014), https://leostrausscenter.uchicago.edu/sites/default/files/Aristotle,%20Rhetoric.pdf.

argue to a considerable extent *ad hominem*. I hope that this will not create a misunderstanding."[5]

The main tasks of the two talks are (1) a dialectical examination of the goals of liberal society and the presuppositions or assumptions that undergird them; (2) an explanation of the contemporary influences of positivism and historicism and how they contribute to the state of crisis in Western societies; and (3) a comparison and defense of classical political philosophy. It is important to appreciate the audience—he is speaking to Catholics, and more specifically to Thomists. The first two tasks require the *ad hominem* approach in part because the Thomists are already well disposed to the theme of critique of modernity and liberal society; Strauss is teaching them how to proceed with rhetorical effectiveness. The third task he classifies as tentative and experimental, again I believe to engage the Catholic audience in the common task of retrieval of the original sources and meaning of the texts as a rational undertaking.

What Strauss Had to Say to Catholics

Let me say something first about his appeal to the Catholic audience, as I think he provides us with a good set of principles to gauge the Catholic reception of Strauss. Near the end of the first lecture, after articulating various aspects of the crisis of our time, to which we shall return, he speaks about the need to recover the primary understanding of political phenomena. To the audience he says "in a way every one of you knows, it has been done by Aristotle in his politics."[6] He could assume that a Catholic intellectual audience would be familiar with the work of Aristotle and stand in agreement with its essential points: that man is social and political by nature, the importance of the common good, and the limited claims of democracy. And then he goes on to say "when you look around yourself, not at the University of Detroit, not at other Catholic institutions, but at non-Catholic institutions, I think you can say that with very few exceptions political philosophy has disappeared."[7] It has decayed into ideology, or replaced by a history of political philosophies which is nothing more than a survey of errors, and the subject matter has been turned over

---

5. Strauss, "The Crisis of Our Time," 42.
6. Ibid., 51.
7. Ibid.

to social science and the discovery of universal laws of political behavior. This allows Strauss to point out the need to understand the teachings of political philosophers as they themselves meant them and as adversaries understand them. Thus, the crisis of our time has the accidental advantage of enabling us to understand in a nontraditional, or a fresh, manner what was hitherto understood only in a traditional, derivative manner. This challenge to read political philosophers in a fresh, nonderivative manner, may be one of the greatest benefits that Catholics received from Leo Strauss. Although Jacques Maritain, John Courtney Murray, Yves R. Simon, and Heinrich Rommen were accomplishing this task in their work, Strauss provided a deep and prolonged stimulus for it as well. And the return to classical political philosophy, specifically, proves beneficial to modern social science and to Thomism as well. It would bring Thomists to better understand Aristotle as he understood himself, and not simply as interpreted by St. Thomas, however able he might be as a commentator on Aristotle. And further, it would challenge the reader to encounter Plato, a more complex textual challenge than Aristotle. Curiously, Strauss rarely mentions Plato in these talks, which perhaps just underscores their *ad hominem* character and the need to trace out the lines of the argument comparing Thucydides, Aristotle, and Plato.[8]

In his second talk to the University of Detroit audience Strauss mentions Thomism in two very important respects, also indicating the way he was to be received by the Catholic scholars. Strauss admits that "political philosophy is an actuality in the West only in Thomism" (92). This assertion is a very sobering assessment of the crisis in political philosophy: it had all but disappeared from the intellectual scene, save for Catholic universities in their attention to St. Thomas, a commitment in philosophy departments that would very soon be abandoned in favor of the very ideologies of historicism and empiricism so criticized by Strauss. The case of Notre Dame proves very instructive on this point.[9] Strauss points out that Thomism has the support of faith, but does it have the support of reason? "Therefore, it is necessary even for the Thomists to

---

8. *The City and Man* (Chicago: Rand McNally, 1964).
9. See Ralph McInerny, *Thomism in an Age of Renewal* (Notre Dame, Ind.: University of Notre Dame Press, 1968) and *I Alone Have Escaped to Tell You* (Notre Dame, Ind.: University of Notre Dame Press, 2006); Kenneth M. Sayre, *Adventures in Philosophy at Notre Dame* (Notre Dame, Ind.: University of Notre Dame Press, 2014); Michel Florian, *La pensée catholique en Amérique du Nord: Réseaux intellectuels et échanges culturels entre l'Europe, le Canada et les Etats-Unis* (Paris: Desclée de Brouwer, 2010).

show that the Aristotelian conception of political philosophy—Aristotle was not after all a Catholic Christian—has not been refuted by modern thought." Strauss's remarks here are extraordinarily prescient, if not prophetic. Much of the crisis of Catholic theology, particularly in the moral domain, such as regarding Pope Paul VI's *Humanae Vitae* (1968), turned on whether the notion of natural good and natural end/purpose were a viable, defensible standard. Both Aristotle and the Bible were under attack and subjected to radical questioning, and in some way the defense of Aristotle could serve as a defense of the Bible; or the way of reason could serve to defend the way of faith. Now it will be the case that Pope John Paul II would also argue that the way of faith would be a sturdy defender of the way of reason. But both faith and reason, Aristotle and the Bible, need their full defense. John Paul II will state that the "parrhesia of faith" (candid or forthright speech) must be matched with the boldness of reason.[10] Although Strauss has a different account of faith and reason, ultimately denying their compatibility, I think he would agree with the need for both to assert themselves with full vigor. John Paul II, on the other hand, would claim that "each without the other is impoverished and enfeebled. Deprived of what Revelation offers, reason has taken sidetracks, which expose it to the danger of losing sight of its final goal. Deprived of reason, faith has stressed feeling and experience, and so run the risk of no longer being a universal proposition."[11] Nevertheless, the defense of Aristotle, and a form of classical reason, will indeed strengthen and enrich faith, and restore the claim of Thomistic philosophy and theology to attaining "universal propositions" about man, God, and the world. So the lessons of Strauss's visit to the University of Detroit would prove vitally important for the revival of Catholic intelligence.

Strauss proceeds to make a defense of Aristotle against these charges: (1) modern science has destroyed the cosmological basis for Aristotle's philosophy; (2) Aristotle is anti-democratic in that he favors exclusion of the many from rule and defends an inequality among human beings; (3) Aristotle's political philosophy is narrow or provincial because it treats of the *polis*, an association that is no longer a viable social form in the modern world. In making a defense, Strauss opens up a number of deeper, more substantive issues, two in particular: (4) modern conditions that

---

10. *Fides et Ratio*, Encyclical Letter, September 14, 1988, par. 48; available at www.vatican.va.
11. Ibid.

allow a more favorable attitude toward the rule by the many derive in large measure from a new science of nature, a practical science of nature, replacing the speculative science of nature "taught by the schools" as Descartes famously remarked.[12] Strauss does not pursue this issue much beyond the surface question. Bacon and Machiavelli lurk under the surface awaiting further elaboration. A Catholic audience would understand that a world bereft of contemplation is not a fully human world. It is not a world consistent with Catholic life and practice. But what is the philosophical argument for contemplation? It must be recovered from Aristotle and Thomas Aquinas. (5) With respect to the narrowness of the Greek *polis*, we are led to the deeper question pertaining to human happiness. Aristotle assumes that there is a core, publicly available content to human happiness, and this is the great end of political association. Strauss states that Aristotle considers happiness to be the doing of noble deeds and the practice of moral virtue; he also cites the passage in the *Rhetoric* providing a longer list of elements of happiness, a very problematic text, by the way, as Strauss shows in his graduate class at the University of Chicago.[13] But the text from the *Rhetoric* at least lays out what is publicly available common sense to those who would give human life a serious thought. But the modern regime is built upon the thesis that "happiness is entirely subjective." For example, we should be aware of the fact that both Hobbes and Locke (and Kant) deny the very possibility of a true knowledge of the *summum bonum*, highest good for man. The modern account of politics and ethics rides on the shaky rail of total skepticism concerning human happiness. And yet the firmer rail of modern thinking is that we can know for certain the conditions for human happiness—these constitute the natural rights of man. Strauss comments: "So life, liberty, pursuit of happiness are the conditions of happiness, however you understand happiness. They possess the objectivity, that universality, which happiness lacks." No longer then does the political association concern itself with whether the citizens are happy, that is, "doers of noble deeds," or "be men of virtue" but political life functions only to "protect the natural rights of man." Indeed, "under no circumstances may political society impose any notion of happiness upon the citizenry."[14]

12. Rene Descartes, *Discourse on Method*, trans. Richard Kennington (Indianapolis, Ind.: Hackett, 2007), Part VI.
13. Strauss, "Crisis of Political Philosophy," 96.
14. Ibid.

Speaking in the early 1960s, Strauss once again shows his prescience, as the relentless attack on religion or any public avowal of the good and normative gathered its intensity throughout the decades following this speech. The paradoxical skepticism concerning the good had become a near dogma in the West; Pope Benedict XVI rightly referred to the "dictatorship of relativism."[15] I suspect that the Catholic audience at the University of Detroit may have had but a dim awareness of the seismic shifts of ground that were about to be manifest by the end of the decade. And yet even deeper problems emerge out of the quarrel of ancients and moderns on the issue of happiness and public purpose. For the ancients, human happiness had some standing of objectivity in general opinion, as explored in Aristotle's *Rhetoric*, as well as in rational argumentation, as argued in Aristotle's *Nicomachean Ethics*. Thus, it was readily acknowledged that the purpose of the political society is to promote human flourishing, human happiness. As Strauss said: "Happiness means the practice of moral virtue above everything else, the doing of noble deeds. Aristotle assumes something which is today absolutely controversial, especially in scientific circles" (96). But now public purpose must have an air of neutrality precisely because happiness is entirely subjective. Strauss explains (96):

If happiness is entirely subjective, it can no longer be relevant for determining the common good. How then shall we find our bearing politically? The answer given by the founders of modern political philosophy was this: While happiness is radically subjective, the conditions of happiness are not; whatever you may understand by happiness, in order to be happy you must be alive; secondly, you must be able to circulate; thirdly, you must be able to pursue happiness as you understand happiness, and perhaps even as you understand happiness at the moment. So life, liberty, pursuit of happiness are the conditions of happiness, however you understand happiness. They constitute the objective conditions of happiness. They possess that objectivity, that universality, which happiness lacks. Therefore, the function of political society is not to take care that the citizens are happy, that they become doers of noble deeds, as Aristotle called it, but to create the conditions of happiness, to protect them, or to use a technical term, to protect the natural rights of man.

Given that the state is neutral, and human rights are a mere means to happiness variably defined by private interests, to what public goal if any should the state be devoted? Strauss queries how a neutral sphere, such

---

15. Pope Benedict XVI and Peter Seewald, "Dictatorship of Relativism," in *Light of the World: The Pope, the Church and the Signs of the Times* (San Francisco: Ignatius Press, 2010), 50–54.

as must be "the state," could guide collective action. The state is in some way subordinate to society, to citizens, from which the idea of value (or ends) is derived; but if there is no objectivity or public agreement on the questions of ends, purpose must be subjective and private. Strauss simply places a marker—the relative superiorities of state and society "creates a great theoretical difficulty."[16] The state secures the conditions of happiness and proceeds with reason or the sphere of objectivity and universality, but apparently in service to the subjective and particular. The theoretical difficulty easily gives rise to a practical temptation to tyranny and gross injustice (such as by utilitarian appeals to a greater "happiness" or by a passionate political ideology), as well as actual encouragement for the voluntary degradation of human life in the pursuit of base satisfactions.

Strauss makes a third aside to the Thomists saying that the doctrine of natural rights developed in the seventeenth and eighteenth centuries may remind us of "the traditional natural law teaching, the Thomist teaching" (97). And yet "outside of Catholic circles, it is rarely admitted, although it is so obvious, that there is a radical difference between the natural law teaching of the 17th and 18th century, and the medieval and classic ancient teaching." Natural law becomes articulated as the "rights of man." He explains as follows: "rights" replace "law," but law entails primarily a sense of duty and rights only derivatively. And we would thus understand that the modern teaching entails that rights are primary and duties are derivative. As Catholic social teaching was in the process of more fully embracing the language of rights, the Straussian project to reopen the "quarrel" of ancients and moderns could provide a very important perspective as to how coherent and effective this embrace of rights could be. Strauss also reminds the audience that in the modern account of rights, "man" replaces "nature." "In the older notion, natural law is part of a larger [hierarchic] order." In the modern view, "man, taken entirely by himself, is, as it were, the origin of the rights belonging to him" (97–98). The secularist autonomy of reason and will from God or nature is contained in the very idea of "human rights" as a substitute for natural law. Strauss suggests that rights of man are the moral equivalent of the Cartesian *cogito*, and he points out that in *Passions of the Soul*, Descartes never mentions duty but places right in a central passage.[17]

16. Strauss, "Crisis of Political Philosophy," 97.
17. I assume he refers to Part III, §152: free will renders us like God, in a certain measure, in "making us masters of ourselves, provided we do not through remissness [*lâcheté*] lose the rights he

These asides that Strauss makes to his audience could prove very helpful. They suggest that because Catholics have a tradition for authentic political philosophy, they are well positioned to resist the dangers of modern ideology; they are at home in the naturalness of the political or the phenomenon of political life and virtue as such; and they have an affinity for his project of questioning the modern project insofar as they retain a deeper notion of natural law and a respect for the life of virtue and contemplation. Yet they must exercise an effort to recover the original meaning of philosophy, and not rely on tradition alone; that is, they must deepen the exercise of reason and not be pushed into the realm of faith alone. Strauss shows them the task at hand, namely to mount a dialectical defense of their Aristotelianism against the abandonment and ridicule of premodern teleology and the "common sense" view of happiness; they must come to terms with modern natural rights, the doctrine which has wrested away the mantel of "higher law" and yet still trades on ambiguity of the term "natural law."

With these markers and challenges noted, I will briefly review Strauss's account of the crisis of our time and how it relates to the crisis of political philosophy. Then I will compare Strauss's account with the work of Maritain and draw a few conclusions about the Catholic reception of Strauss.

What Is the Crisis of Our Time? Why Political Philosophy?

In this speech Strauss makes it clear that the crisis of our time is that "the West is uncertain of its purpose."[18] Its purpose, he says, is to pro-

---

gives us." *Philosophical Works of Descartes*, trans. Elizabeth Haldane and G. R. T. Ross (Cambridge: Cambridge University Press, 1935), 1:401. See Richard Kennington, *On Modern Origins*, ed. Frank Hunt and Pamela Krauss (Lanham, Md.: Lexington Books, 2004), 198–203.

18. On the issue of the crisis of our time, I have benefitted from reading Nathan Tarcov, "Philosophy & History: Tradition and Interpretation in the Work of Leo Strauss," *Polity* 16, no. 1 (1983): 5–29, and Steven B. Smith, "Leo Strauss: Between Athens and Jerusalem," *Review of Politics* 53, no. 1 (Winter 1991): 75–99, as well as unpublished manuscripts by Richard Kennington, "Leo Strauss and Modernity," and Seth Benardete, untitled, first line "Leo Strauss was a philosopher" (both papers were presented at a memorial for Leo Strauss at the New School for Social Research, New York, October 18, 1974). It is significant that Richard Kennington, a student of Strauss and expert on the work of Descartes, taught for a number of years at The Catholic University of America, pursuing these suggestive leads of Strauss with many Catholic students, including this author. See Richard Kennington, "Blumenberg and the Legitimacy of the Modern Age," in *The Ambiguous Legacy of the Enlightenment*,

mote a society of "free and equal men and women" and "equal nations." He refers to universal statements of purpose, presumably the UN Charter of Rights, but he could also have in mind the Declaration of Independence. The technological breakthroughs in Western science can contribute mightily to this goal or purpose. But positivism and historicism, trends within academic circles that have been popularized in many ways, have made it difficult if not impossible to render a cogent defense or explanation of that Western purpose concerning human dignity, the nobility of human liberty, and the habits of civility and self-restraint. For both positivism and historicism lead to forms of nihilism. Both destroy the possibility of philosophy classically understood as the rational ascent to the right by nature and to eternal forms or ideas. If philosophy has become no more than ideology, or the free construction of the human mind for a political purpose; if there is no truth about human nature and human good; if justice is the irrational imposition of power—then how can the West account for its ideals and its claim to preeminence and leadership in the modern world? The United States, in a speech by its first Catholic president, boldly proclaimed its commitment for the defense of liberty and the call for service to the country. But post-war America, in the heady confidence of its prosperity and hegemony, was on the cusp of its humiliation at the hands of a Soviet-sponsored North Vietnam politburo, racial turmoil and violence, and a cultural revolution that would forever change the moral ecology of society. In his account of the "crisis of our time," Leo Strauss pointed to the abyss lurking under the surface of this facile confidence.

To bring the crisis into better view Strauss articulates three problems or signs of the crisis of our time; these problems have an obvious immediacy and a popular appeal. He then formulates a more specific set of questions indicating the philosophical dimension to the crisis. The three problems facing Americans in 1963 are: (1) the threat of communism, as a form of tyranny implacably hostile to liberal democracy or the challenge to fight for freedom; (2) the emergence of "permissive egalitarianism" or irresponsible lifestyles and the erosion of standards and aspiration to excellence; (3) the invention of atomic weapons and the threat of uncontrolled technology harmful to human beings. As scholars of Strauss

---

ed. William A. Rusher (Lanham, Md.: University Press of America, 1995), 22–37; "Strauss's Natural Right and History," *Review of Metaphysics* 35, no. 1 (September 1981): 57–86; and *On Modern Origins*.

have pointed out, the crisis about which he speaks is not "communism" as such, nor for that matter permissive egalitarianism or atomic weaponry, but rather it is the "certainty of purpose." That is, the teaching of Leo Strauss was not about an ultra-conservative stirring up of Cold War paranoia, or morally righteous indignation at the new permissiveness, or a Luddite attack on technology, but rather a sober and thoughtful questioning of the foundation of modern liberal democracy which would be laid bare through such problems. There is no mistaking the spirited quality of the Straussian inquiry, yet the spirited part of the soul is in service of the philosophic. The spirited as such is itself a reproach to the pure principle of modernity in its Hobbesian and Lockean form and opens a sympathetic ear to the ancient account of the soul and the *polis*. Thus, he says of the threat of communism: "However much the power of the West may have declined, however great the dangers to the West may be, that decline, that danger—nay, the defeat and the destruction of the West—would not necessarily prove that the West is in a crisis. The West could go down in honor, certain of its purpose" (44). But we must grab the philosophical nettle in this spirited display: what precisely is the purpose of the West? What is the ground for noble human purpose? Is there grounding in nature for noble purpose? The search for natural right must commence once again in our day. The quest for natural right has been occluded if not enervated by the very success of the modern project and the facile ideologies of American progressivism and individual autonomy.

So Strauss raises three questions in light of these signs of crisis in order to incline us toward a reconsideration of ancient philosophy. (1) In the face of communist expansion and subversion, is particularism and cultivation of one's own not better than globalism? (2) In the face of permissive egalitarianism, is it true to say that affluence is a sufficient condition for justice and happiness? Is it even necessary? (3) In the face of a threatening new technology of arms, is science really in the service of human power, or does it rather serve domination and degradation? These questions lead back to the central question of Strauss's political philosophy, namely, what exactly is the modern project and what are the arguments for it? That project, of course, is the "mastery of nature for the relief of human estate."[19] It trails back to Francis Bacon and Rene Des-

---

19. Here again I would commend the important work of Richard Kennington, whose work on Rene Descartes and Francis Bacon lays bare the heart, if not the heartlessness, of the modern project; there are deep contradictions coiled at the heart of Baconianism and Cartesianism, and a rhetoric of

cartes; and ultimately Machiavelli fathers the project. Yet Machiavelli is not mentioned in these talks; nor is Plato, I might add. The significance of this silence in front of a Catholic audience is curious, but intelligible, as I shall suggest in the following section of this essay. The crisis of our times is not communism, moral decadence, or technology run amok, but according to Strauss "the consequence of the crisis of political philosophy" because political philosophy (philosophers) initiated the new idea of society, a new deal or arrangement between philosophy and society, and formulated the "modern project." And yet the end result of modern philosophy has been the disintegration of the very idea of political philosophy and political life as such.

Why did this come to be from the origins of modern philosophy? The modern project requires the development of an active science, as opposed to the contemplative science of old. But if science is a means, a technology, which must be brought to serve an end, then the question arises: what end shall that power serve? Strauss formulates the modern proposition as follows: the end shall be "to satisfy in the most perfect manner, the most powerful and natural needs of men" (49). The end needed no argument, in a way, precisely because these ends are powerful and deeply set in human nature. This is no doubt the firmest rail of modern political philosophy because the passions of acquisition and comfortable self-preservation are the strongest and universal. But is the appeal to what is strongest, or supposedly necessary, really an argument in justification of an arrangement that promises to flatter or satisfy them? Perhaps the justification is the goal of peace and the promise of a rational technique and rationale for universal peace. The modern project, according to Strauss, "was successful to a considerable extent" and has "created a new kind of society" (41). But its inadequacy is (now) a matter of "general knowledge and general concern." I suspect he refers to the lack of conscientiousness in the public, the dangerous abuse of power, the permissiveness at large. And in fact, peace is not at hand, despite the dream and promise of modern liberalism. It is peace bought at a price, and a peace that quickly unravels abroad, if not at home. We need, he says, an "animating spirit" other than the one which has "animated it [modern society] from the beginning."

---

philanthropy, coupled with the anti-theological ire of Machiavelli, virtually suppresses the philosophical dialogue concerning the human good and political justice. See Kennington, "Blumenberg and the Legitimacy of the Modern Age," 22–37; "Strauss's Natural Right and History"; and *On Modern Origins*.

But to the public at large the connection between the immediacy of the signs of the crisis and the philosophical root of the crisis is not at all apparent or in anyway compelling. So perhaps the spiritedness in the defense of liberty, virtue, and moderation are salutary after all. But this still leaves undone the importance of philosophical and rational defense of the centrality of "truth, wisdom and virtue," that is, the Socratic philosophy against the Baconian and Cartesian new philosophy. At least the quarrel must be re-engaged. Socrates set off on his quixotic search for "truth, wisdom and the best possible state of the soul" (*Apology* 29d-e) chastising the Athenians for their concern for the wealth, position, and the affairs of the body. Socrates was forced to drink hemlock. Descartes is lionized not only in every department of philosophy and psychology, but also in the very rhetoric of the modern medical establishment. How can we breakthrough to raise again the philosophical question about "the good," if not about truth and being, in modern society, in our day?

Modern political philosophy, by emphasizing the development of power and means for achieving affluence and protecting liberty, has obscured the ends for which such power is to be cultivated and to which such liberty is to be devoted. There is the ever-present danger of abuse of power by the few and voluntary degradation afforded to the many. The intelligentsia gravitates toward a post-Kantian divide of positivism and historicism, both of which have made philosophical questions about nature and the good otiose and irrelevant. The unfolding of modern philosophy along the lines of positivism has led to the very idea of "values" as a subjective preference with no rational standing. Historicism has further intensified this inability and unwillingness to defend purpose or ends, because the good and right are said to be relative to a time or place, a culture, and whatever is celebrated by the majority and the cultured elite is right. Values are a human creation and a product of the spirit of the age. All roads point to Nietzsche and the final conflagration of the strong, or majority (the refashioned *übermensch*) vs. the weaker party, or despised minorities of religion (the refashioned *untermensch*). But we have been there before: Munich, September 30, 1938, capitulate and proclaim "peace is at hand"—and in less than a year Poland is crushed as the West stood helplessly at the margins. Strauss, an émigré from the land of Heidegger and Nietzsche, appears to stand amazed before this humble audience in prosaic and utilitarian Detroit, home of "history is bunk" Henry Ford, that the West is still unable to defend itself in speech or deed as to its superiority to its global rivals, or even to give an account of the beneficence and justice of its project. A few spirited remarks are surely appropriate, and such remarks are designed to rouse reason in the Socratic search.

The return to classical political philosophy and a renewed consideration of the quarrel of the ancient and modern political philosophy promise a way to reinvigorate the role of reason in the search for goodness and justice. The quarrel of the ancients and moderns centers on the proposal for and implementation of the modern project. However tentative and experimental the Straussian project may be, it is vital to the well being of the city and the soul. The Catholic audience could benefit doubly, for the city of man but also for the city of God insofar as the boldness of reason and the blessings of true liberty could come together to protect the treasure of faith and give further impetus for a new evangelization.

Questioning the Modern Project

At the very outset of the speech Strauss says that the crisis of our time is the "doubt" about the "modern project." The doubt pertains to its inadequacy, or the spirit which animates it on the one hand, and its inability to provide or sustain its defense philosophically, on the other. So he recommends that we go back to early modern political philosophy and reengage its quarrel with ancient political philosophy, Socrates and Aristotle. Thus Strauss says that he wishes to "reawaken the quarrel" between ancient and modern philosophy (42). After articulating the three questions about the future of the West—universalism vs. particularism, the relative importance of affluence in development, and the danger of technological power—Strauss makes a final series of three points about the modern project and a provisional comparison with ancient philosophy. First, science is now to become active, no longer contemplative, following the lead of Francis Bacon in his *New Organon*.[20] Mastery of nature is for the sake of the benefit of mankind, that is, the project claims to be justified by an appeal to the many because they are motivated by their

---

20. Strauss mentions this in both lectures; Bacon is mentioned and Descartes is alluded to on page 44, and Bacon, Descartes, and Hobbes are mentioned on page 94.

neediness and they are promised beneficence and charity. As Descartes explained, the new practical science of nature will make human beings as if they were "masters and owners of nature" and make possible a life without pain, a longer life, and an improvement of mental health as well as the connection between body and mind is better comprehended and mastered (so much for Cartesian "dualism" of substance). As science increases human power, there will be progress toward greater prosperity. As Locke formulates it, every human being claims a natural right to comfortable preservation (45). And this results in greater "freedom and justice for all." We must anticipate and expect this progress to embrace all human beings (equally) and all nations. It must be a global project, universal in scope. What has brought the ideal of this project into question? Communism. Marxism, or more properly Stalinism, presents a challenge because communism is an implacable foe of the Western liberal democracies. It forces the West to appreciate its particularity as nation-states.[21] The communist threat forces the West to keep up a military force for its own defense. The sheer ruthlessness of Stalinism raises a question about whether and to what degree the end justifies the means. That is, the West had to affirm some measure of morality upon the means of statecraft. The bold utilitarianism of Stalinism in the name of future equality led Alasdair MacIntyre to reconsider ancient philosophy.[22] Jacques Maritain and Pope John Paul II also drew lessons from the moral or Machiavellian realism of the Soviet bloc leading back to a reconsideration of ancient wisdom.[23] Strauss concludes his first consideration of the project with a ques-

---

21. To appreciate the complexity of the issue of particularity and universality, or nationalism vs. cosmopolitanism, one should read Strauss's essay on Kurt Riezler in *What Is Political Philosophy?*, 233–60.

22. See his "Notes From the Moral Wilderness," in Kelvin Knight, *The MacIntyre Reader* (South Bend, Ind.: University of Notre Dame Press, 1998). MacIntyre wrote to Chris Lutz the following description of Stalinism: "I take it that Stalinism has five salient characteristics. Stalinists (1) believed in the possibility of 'socialism in one country,' rather than in the making of socialism as a world-revolutionary enterprise; (2) made the working class serve the needs of the party and the bureaucracy rather than vice versa; (3) were guilty of 'the cult of personality'; (4) believed that the end of achieving communism justified unlimited terror and unlimited deceit as means; (5) accepted Stalin's crude mechanistic versions of dialectical materialism and historical materialism." This letter was provided to me by Christopher Lutz.

23. Pope John Paul II, in *Centesimus Annus*, Encyclical Letter, May 1, 1991, spoke of the folly of Machiavellian realism and the exaltation of force over reason and law. The downfall of the Soviet Union, he said, "was a struggle born of prayer, and it would have been unthinkable without immense trust in God, the Lord of history, who carries the human heart in his hands. It is by uniting his own sufferings for the sake of truth and freedom to the sufferings of Christ on the Cross that man is able to accomplish the miracle of peace and is in a position to discern the often narrow path between the cowardice which gives in to evil and the violence which, under the illusion of fighting evil, only makes it worse." Maritain charges that the Machiavellian lies are twofold: first, that the just man must be weak and second, that the successful man must practice evil and deceit. Maritain's critique is

tion about the relative role of affluence in the definition of the flourishing of the city and man. It would appear obvious that affluence is certainly not a sufficient condition for human flourishing. What then is needed? We are back to classical political philosophy and the question of virtue.

The second aspect of the quarrel Strauss would have us consider is the question as to whether institutional arrangements, checks and balances, and technical fixes can fully substitute for character and virtue in the ongoing operation, balance, and maintaining of political life. The modern project emphasizes institutions over character, while classical political philosophy emphasized virtue. Strauss explains that the modern project seeks to separate law and morality, whereas the ancients consider law to be in service of morality, however qualified or made suitable to the capacities of the citizens. The result of the modern project reveals a rampant irresponsibility and abuse of power. This problem emerges from both the Hobbesian call for despotism to control the anarchy of individualism and also from the democratic (Lockean) hallowing of the individual. In either case, power needs enlightenment and guidance. Hobbes's sovereign needed the enlightenment of Hobbes.[24] The individual needs formation of conscience, and resolve to follow conscience, conscientiousness, lest it become irresponsible. Once again, the classical teaching makes more sense and promises greater hope. Tocqueville, for example, placed great hope in intermediate groups, and religious association in particular to sustain accountability and the pursuit of human excellence.

The third point for our consideration in this quarrel concerns the unfolding of the meaning of the conquest of nature. The conquest of nature was proposed for the benefit of human beings and it assumed an unchanging or fixed human nature. But we now see that the conquest of nature enfolds the possibility of conquest of human nature. That is, the masters of scientific technology have every reason to consider the plastici-

---

based on an empirical or historical claim. The just man can be strong; and that the doers of evil prosper for the span of life of a man, but not for the extent of a regime. See "The End of Machiavellianism" in his *The Range of Reason* (New York: Scribners, 1968); see also Father James V. Schall, *Jacques Maritain: The Philosopher in Society* (Lanham, Md.: Rowman and Littlefield, 1998), chap. 1.

24. Thomas Prufer would speak about "Hobbes' sovereign teaching" as being the formation of the sovereign for its responsible exercise of power ("Epicurus and Hobbes," Lecture Course, The Catholic University of America, 1975). See also his chapter on Hobbes in *Recapitulations* (Washington, D.C.: The Catholic University of America Press, 1993). Prufer taught that what transforms an avaricious and vainglorious human being into sovereignty "passionless and disinterested in its exercise of power for the sake of the salus populi" is nothing other than "the measuring by the teaching of Hobbes"; thus, "Hobbes's teaching as the specification of sovereignty's exercise of its right is natural public reason" (1975 Lecture Course).

ty and malleability of the human species. Rousseau and Marx overcome nature through progress of human experiment and social will. What is to forestall experimentation and behavioral control? It is reported that Strauss admired the book by C. S. Lewis entitled the *Abolition of Man*, the third chapter of which spells out this danger with great insight, treating the development of the atomic bomb, artificial contraceptives, and modern means of communication in light of their potentially destructive designs upon the human. Strauss asks whether human nature is unchangeable or changeable? Is there a nature at all? Are there natures? And more ominously, we must ask whether the great power unleashed by the modern project and concentrated through technology actually has a wisdom to guide its right use. Does modern philosophy even have a teaching on wisdom? It culminates in a teaching on moral rightness or formal duty (Kant), but that does not constitute a teaching on wisdom as such, but a formality that is all too easily rationalized and manipulated.

With these three aspects of the quarrel of ancients and moderns Strauss sketches for his Catholic audience the importance of the return to classical political philosophy. He speaks about Aristotle, but does not speak about Plato (he mentions him once). Nor does he mention Machiavelli at all; not once. He dwells on Hobbes and Locke, founders of the first wave of modernity to be sure, but not at its deepest root. The problem of faith and reason is also not directly mentioned, although he did explain that Aristotle must be defended. But about the great quarrel of "Athens and Jerusalem" he is silent. Thus, as stated, Strauss's account is incomplete insofar as he suggests elsewhere that Plato is the height of ancient wisdom and Machiavelli is the true founder of modernity. As a reminder, Richard Kennington taught that Descartes derived the goal of mastery and possession of nature from political philosophers, namely Bacon, and ultimately Machiavelli. And Kennington concludes his memorial essay on Strauss with this sentence: "The crisis of the West is reducible to the quarrel of the moderns with Plato."[25] Thus, this Catholic audience would have to go forward to study not only Aristotle, but also his teacher, Plato; and to consider not only Descartes and the epistemological and metaphysical turn of modernity, but also its political turn as taught by Machiavelli. Not many Catholics have done so; James V. Schall and Ernest Fortin

---

25. Kennington, "Leo Strauss and Modernity."

are to be commended for their early study of these sources of modernity, following the lead of Strauss.

For the limited purpose of these lectures, the account of the crisis of our time as hearkening back to Descartes, Hobbes, and Locke is quite profound. And it should sufficiently rouse the audience to recover its Aristotelian roots. The question of faith and reason would be a distraction for this audience; Strauss considered the Bible and ancient philosophy to be allies in their confrontation of the modern myth of progress.[26] But they are in fundamental disagreement as to first principles and ways of life. The problem of Athens and Jerusalem would also be disagreeable for this set of lectures.

Thomism and the Quarrel of the Ancients and Moderns

I would like to conclude with a brief comparison of Strauss and Jacques Maritain on the question of "the crisis of our time." Maritain wrote much about the problem of modernity and its crisis throughout the disasters of the twentieth century.[27] Strauss and Maritain converged upon similar signs or symptoms of the "crisis": the political oppression of tyrannical regimes; the growing permissiveness and lack of personal accountability throughout Western society; and the gathering power and potential for abuse in technological invention and planning. And like Strauss, Maritain found a most disturbing aspect of the crisis was the obliviousness and failure to defend the cause of liberty and human dignity:

The most alarming symptom in the present crisis is that, while engaged in a death struggle for the defense of these values, we have too often lost faith and confidence in the principles on which what we are defending is founded, because

26. See "Progress or Return? The Contemporary Crisis in Modern Civilization," *Modern Judaism* 1 (1981): 17–45.
27. Two essays of note are "Christian Humanism," in his *The Range of Reason* (New York: Charles Scribner's Sons, 1952) and "Integral Humanism and the Crisis of Our Times," in his *Scholasticism and Politics*, trans. Mortimer J. Adler (New York: Image Books, 1960). See also *Integral Humanism*, trans. Joseph W. Evans (Notre Dame, Ind.: University of Notre Dame Press, 1973); *Three Reformers: Luther, Descartes, Rousseau* (New York: Scribners, 1929); *Freedom in the Modern World*, trans. Richard O'Sullivan (New York: Scribners, 1936); *The Rights of Man and Natural Law*, trans. Doris C. Anson (New York: Scribners, 1943); *The Dream of Descartes*, trans. Mabelle L. Andison (London: Editions Poetry London, 1946); *On the Philosophy of History* (New York: Scribners, 1957); and *St. Thomas Aquinas*, trans. Peter O'Reilly (New York: Meridian Books, 1958).

we have more often than not forgotten the true and authentic principles and because, at the same time, we feel more or less consciously the weakness of the insubstantial ideology which has prayed upon them like a parasite.[28]

But the two thinkers diverge in their in their account of the deepest roots of these symptoms and the true source and remedy for the crisis. As we have seen above, Strauss uses the awareness of the symptomatic crisis to challenge the positivism and historicism of contemporary political philosophy. The crisis of our time is a consequence of the crisis of political philosophy, Strauss maintains. So we must reexamine the argument for a new political science once made by Machiavelli, Bacon and Hobbes. Perhaps that would reopen the search for natural right as set forth by Socrates. The full experience of political life is better accounted for by Socrates, Plato, and Aristotle. The tentative and experimental turn to ancient political philosophy could possibly restore a sense of political moderation and a greater aim for human flourishing than acquisition of wealth and comfortable self-preservation.

Maritain, on the other hand, traces the source of the crisis to issues in philosophical anthropology. In his chapter on "The Apostle of Our Time" (in *Thomas Aquinas*), Maritain suggests that "the disease afflicting the modern world is in the first place a disease of the mind: it began in the mind, it has now attacked the roots of the mind."[29] Maritain expounds a set of three diseases affecting the modern mind, exemplified in Descartes, Luther, and Rousseau. The trilogy of (1) agnosticism ("by cultivating a more or less refined doubt which is an outrage both to the perception of the senses and the principles of reason, that is to say the very things on which all our knowledge depends"), (2) naturalism ("The mind at the same time refuses to recognize the rights of primary Truth and repudiates the supernatural order, considering it impossible—and such a

---

28. "Christian Humanism," in *Range of Reason*, 189.

29. *Thomas Aquinas*, 58–59. Here Maritain echoes the warning of Pope Leo XIII in his *Aeterni Patris* on the restoration of Christian philosophy along the lines of Thomas Aquinas. "Whoso turns his attention to the bitter strife of these days and seeks a reason for the troubles that vex public and private life must come to the conclusion that a fruitful cause of the evils which now afflict, as well as those which threaten, us lies in this: that false conclusions concerning divine and human things, which originated in the schools of philosophy, have now crept into all the orders of the State, and have been accepted by the common consent of the masses. For, since it is in the very nature of man to follow the guide of reason in his actions, if his intellect sins at all his will soon follows; and thus it happens that false opinions, whose seat is in the understanding, influence human actions and pervert them. Whereas, on the other hand, if men be of sound mind and take their stand on true and solid principles, there will result a vast amount of benefits for the public and private good." *Aeterni Patris*, Encyclical Letter, August 4, 1879, as cited in Etienne Gilson (ed.), *The Church Speaks to the Modern World: The Social Teachings of Leo XIII* (Garden City, N.Y.: Image Books, 1954).

denial is a blow at all the interior life of grace"), and (3) individualism/angelism ("the mind allows itself to be deceived by the mirage of a mythical conception of human nature, which attributes to that nature conditions peculiar to pure spirit, assumes that nature to be in each of us as perfect and complete as the angelic nature in the angel and therefore claims for us, as being in justice our due, along with complete domination over nature, the superior autonomy, the full self sufficiency, appropriate to pure forms").[30] Maritain says that the Cartesian heritage is the deepest source of the crisis of modernity. It is a crisis of anthropology rather than political philosophy. The heart of Cartesianism is the rupture and rejection of the medieval integration of wisdom: "With Descartes, the interior hierarchies of the virtue of reason were shattered. Philosophy abandoned theology to assert its own claim to be considered the supreme science, and, the mathematical science of the sensible world and its phenomena taking precedence at the same time over metaphysics, the human mind began to profess independence of God and being."[31]

From this fundamental attitude and methodological principle spring the distortions of mind perhaps best identified as (1) idealism, (2) rationalism, and (3) dualism.[32] The rejection of premodern philosophy may have been focused on the Catholic tradition of Thomas Aquinas, but it was both ancient and medieval philosophy that suffered rejection. The turn from contemplative to practical philosophy announced by Descartes, however much influenced by Bacon and Machiavelli, turned on a question of metaphysics and theology, a theology both natural and supernatural. Maritain reminds the reader that Aristotle is ultimately being rejected by Descartes, for it was Aristotle who said that there is "more joy in knowing divine things imperfectly and obscurely than in knowing perfectly the things proportioned to our minds." And thus the nature of our intellect inclines us toward metaphysics ultimately to divine science. Descartes, on the contrary, boasted of devoting only a very few hours a year to the study of metaphysics. In his eyes, it is important "to have thoroughly understood once in one's life the principles of metaphysics," but "it would be very harmful to occupy one's understanding in meditating upon them, because it would then be unable to attend to the function of

---

30. In *Three Reformers* (55) he emphasizes that the root of "angelism" is something that embraces all three in many respects, and this traces back to Descartes primarily.
31. Jacques Maritain, *St. Thomas Aquinas* (New York: Meridian, 1958), 89.
32. This is from his most thorough critique in *Dream of Descartes*, 130–50.

the imagination and the senses as well. Cartesian understanding does not drag itself along toward things divine, it settles comfortably in worldly things."[33]

Strauss acknowledges the importance of the shift from a contemplative science to dominantly practical science, but he seems to pass over the properly metaphysical and theological rationale and dimension of the shift, at least as it is argued in Descartes's *Discourse on Method*. Whereas Strauss will often make reference to Machiavelli's "anti-theological ire," a term often repeated by Strauss's followers, the complex character of such "anti-theological ire" is not fully displayed. Such ire derives from the ecclesiastical meddling with political affairs, particularly in Italy where the Papal States posed an obstacle to the Italian unification. Ecclesiastical appointments, lands, and benefices were bothersome issues throughout Christendom. Machiavelli was concerned about the weakness of the Christian prince who must live morally and aim beyond acquisition and glory. But perhaps the anti-theological ire derived most fundamentally from a *ressentiment* against the high aspirations of Christianity, and so modern philosophers wished to eliminate or disparage the theological and the contemplative orientation of philosophy as such. They turned from any form of transcendence and love of the eternal to a purely this-worldly account of philosophy and human life. The fundamental turn from and refusal of the height of being, namely, God, constitutes the heart of the crisis of modernity according to Maritain. He argued that modern "anthropcentric humanism" is a deformation of true humanism, "theocentric humanism," and its reductions eventually weaken the political strength and cultural confidence of the West. Human liberty now goes without the mastery of self or moral responsibility; the notion of equality without a transcendent justice, or "we could say rights without Right"; technology would deliver a freedom and enjoyment unknown to the ancients; and "happiness is understood without reference to a *summum bonum* or a rational form." Maritain also speaks about the West's lack of confidence in its purpose as a result of the false autonomy of anthropocentric humanism. "Man sought to be self-sufficient and obtain a salvation that is purely and exclusively temporal accomplished without God and against God."[34]

---

33. "Christian Humanism," in *Range of Reason*, 189.
34. *Scholasticism and Politics*, 33.

So why is the West unable to defend itself in word and deed according to Maritain? Because "the modern world was emptied of its own principles and became a universe of words, a dough without leaven. It lost confidence in the impetus from which it was founded. We now feel (more or less consciously) the weakness and insubstantiality of the ideas we stand on." Maritain thus called for the restoration of an integral humanism, a fuller and richer image of human being to sustain and make intelligible the claims of freedom, dignity, and equality.[35] Such an "integral humanism" would integrate the contemplative and practical sciences along the lines of Aristotle, and it would also rediscover a relationship of faith and reason, not in a superficial declaration of harmony, but in the contrapuntal tension so ably set out by Josef Pieper and later by John Paul II. The claims of Jerusalem and Athens stand in tension, but on the basis of a theologically founded worldliness the Thomistic tradition has sought to hold them in mutual regard.

There is much more to understand in the convergences and divergences between Leo Strauss and his followers and a number of Catholic philosophers and theologians who read him and seriously engaged his account of the quarrel of the ancients and moderns. And there is no doubt that the Catholic audience at the University of Detroit could but dimly perceive the prophetic words of Leo Strauss about the challenge of the task facing a tradition that cherished Aristotle and struggled with the meaning of the identity and role of the church in the modern world. But as subsequent Catholic readers of Strauss would learn, the symptoms of the crisis would deepen and the church would be exposed to new assaults on its purpose and would struggle to find the proper intellectual resources to defend its deepest convictions. Some of most astute readers of Strauss, such as James Schall and Ernest Fortin, would rank among the ablest defenders and expositors of the Catholic tradition in the age of renewal. These Catholic readers of Strauss would provide an important philosophical perspective by which to better appreciate the singular theological achievements of Popes John Paul II and Benedict XVI, who saw clearly the depth of the crisis of our times and a way forward to defend human freedom and dignity with both faith and reason.

35. See my *Liberty, Wisdom, and Grace: Thomism and Democratic Political Theory* (Lanham, Md.: Lexington Books, 2002).

8

The Possible Harmony of Reason and Revelation in Politics and Philosophy

A Catholic Reading of Leo Strauss's "Progress or Return?"

CARSON HOLLOWAY

As its title indicates, this essay attempts a Catholic reading of Leo Strauss's "Progress or Return?" At the outset two obstacles appear in the path of such an undertaking. The first is the natural respect—even awe—that any political theorist will feel in the presence of a thinker of Strauss's rank. In what follows I venture to disagree with him on the important issues he raises in his account of the theologico-political problem, but I can only do so with a certain sense of unease. This obstacle can be overcome, however, with the assistance of Strauss himself. He teaches us, after all, that such unease is no excuse for avoiding the most important philosophical issues. He teaches us that we have a duty to struggle with these questions despite the daunting superiority of those who have gone before us.

The second obstacle is the natural sense of embarrassment or impropriety that would accompany seeming to intrude on a private conversation. It might, after all, seem impertinent to offer a Catholic reading of Strauss's "Progress or Return?" because it is a series of lectures given at the Hillel Foundation at the University of Chicago in 1952. Here, then, Strauss appears as a Jew speaking to his fellow Jews. Why should a Catholic intrude on this conversation?

Once again, Strauss himself provides the materials necessary to overcome any scruples on this score. Strauss refers to Catholicism several times in the course of his lectures, thus indicating that the issues with which he deals are not of interest to Jews only. Indeed, the issues with which Strauss deals are nothing less than the greatest political and theoretical issues one can imagine: the fate of Western civilization and the relationship of philosophy to belief in divine revelation. These are obviously not sectarian questions. Moreover, throughout his lectures Strauss seems to be presenting not especially what he takes to be the Jewish view of these questions but rather what he, as a philosopher, takes to be the true view of them. These considerations, I think, justify a Catholic in offering his own understanding of these questions.

Nevertheless, the undertaking remains one of some delicacy. A Catholic cannot argue with Strauss about these questions without, say, taking issue with his reading of the Book of Genesis. This is like telling a Jew—a very intelligent and erudite Jew—that he does not properly understand Judaism, which is ridiculous. This problem exists on both sides, however. As both the Jew and the Catholic accept some of the same texts as being of divine origins, they cannot argue with each other about the meaning of revelation without each implying (at least) that the other has a mistaken understanding of his own religion, because of a mistaken understanding of the materials on which it is based.

This difficulty cannot be avoided, but it can, I think, be borne in a decent and friendly spirit. These are disagreements about the things we care about most deeply. But there is no reason such disagreements cannot be explored with candor and a certain spiritedness in defense of one's own tradition, on the one hand, and, on the other, a genuine affection and admiration for the other tradition and its adherents.

The essay that follows is divided into four main sections. The first briefly sketches the areas where Strauss and Catholicism seem to agree. The second lays out the areas of disagreement. The third and fourth offer a defense of the Catholic position. Throughout the reflections are organized around two themes, which are the two themes of Strauss's lectures—and, indeed, of all of his writings. These themes are political and theoretical. In other words, the argument presented here follows Strauss in trying to understand both what is necessary for a healthy political order and what is true as far as our reasoning can reveal it.

Areas of Agreement

In the first place, the Catholic would find nothing to disagree with in Strauss's critique of the modern idea of progress. On the contrary, the Catholic would find here much with which to agree. Strauss presents modern progressive man as radically denigrating the past. For him, the beginnings of mankind are radically imperfect. He has nothing of positive value to learn from the past. He looks forward to the future as better than the past, as a progressive liberation from the burdens of the past and its poverty of body and mind.[1]

Strauss does not explicitly condemn the mind of progressive man as superficial, but he seems to imply such a criticism by contrasting the progressive man with a sympathetic portrait of the Jew, who venerates the past. Moreover, Strauss suggests that the progressive man's belief in progress rests on an elevation of the importance of technical knowledge, as if such knowledge can tell us how best to live (98). But Strauss casts doubt on this idea and so leaves us thinking that modern progressive man is a somewhat superficial being—very satisfied with himself, but without good reason.

The Catholic will sympathize with much of this critique. Catholics cannot denigrate the past as progressives do. Like Jews, Catholics believe that God provided for man in the beginning and continues to provide for him now. The seeming hostility of nature is the result not of the absence of God, and points not to man's need to rely only on himself. It is instead the result of man's estrangement from God and points to man's need to turn to God. Like the Jew, the Catholic looks back with veneration to a classic past. Catholic belief is organized around a deposit of faith that was given in the past and which it is our duty to preserve and transmit. It is certainly not our duty to "progress" beyond it.

---

1. Leo Strauss, "Progress or Return?," in *Jewish Philosophy and the Crisis of Modernity*, ed. Kenneth Hart Green (Albany: State University of New York Press, 1997), 89–90. Subsequent citations in text.

The Catholic can also agree with Strauss's account of the political flaw in the modern idea of progress—that it leads to an abyss or a moral vacuum. According to Strauss, modern man sought to ensure the realization of the best regime through means considered more realistic than the ancient emphasis on virtue—first through economics and properly designed institutions (that is, through the clever manipulation of self-interest), and later through belief in a progressive history that leads of necessity to the establishment of the best and most just political and social order. This belief in progress requires belief in a kind of moral floor beneath which civilized man cannot sink. The events of the twentieth century, however, have disabused every thinking person of belief in such a floor. Modern man tried to replace the old dichotomy of good vs. bad with a new dichotomy of progressive vs. reactionary. Now that it is no longer possible to believe in progress, modern man is left with no standards at all, no possibility of a rational morality (97–98). This critique of modernity seems to track generally with that offered by some modern popes and by Catholic philosophers and theologians—that modern man, by trying to throw off the old conceptions of good and evil, has not in fact liberated himself, as he intended, but has put himself on the path to destruction.

Turning from the political to the theoretical, the Catholic can agree with Strauss's critique of the idea of progress as incoherent and as ignoring reality, and with much of Strauss's account of the relationship between philosophy and belief in revelation. Strauss suggests that the modern idea of progress is not only morally and politically disastrous but also philosophically bankrupt. It relies on a highly selective appropriation of certain biblical ideas while unaccountably rejecting others. Moreover, while flying under the colors of reason and enlightenment, and thus implicitly claiming to come to grips with reality in a way that the superstitions of the past failed to do, it actually ignores the most important and inescapable reality: eternity. Modern progressive man wants to believe in the possibility, even the necessity, of the infinite improvement of the human condition, while at the same time admitting that the human race will in the end be destroyed—but simply ignoring this rather inconvenient fact (97).

The Catholic can agree with and appreciate much of Strauss's account of the relationship of philosophy to belief in revelation. The Catholic would surely agree with Strauss's claims that belief in revelation is in no way refuted by, and may even be superior to, various modern philosophies that claim to have rendered belief in revelation untenable. According to Strauss, modern, freethinking critiques of revelation claim to have refuted it, but their claims are based on superficial reasoning. Freethinking, he says, is actually based on poor thinking (128). It tries to discredit the Bible by noting apparent problems in the text and by emphasizing its scientific inaccuracies. These critiques, Strauss observes, merely beg the question by excluding the possibility of miracles, the possibility—and indeed the reality—of which the Bible asserts. A successful refutation of revelation would therefore require a proof of the impossibility of miracles. This could be achieved either by disproving the existence of God, or by a natural theology proving the incompatibility of God's nature with the working of miracles. Although these things were attempted by serious thinkers—Spinoza, in the latter case—Strauss contends that they did not and could not succeed. Either alternative would require a completed system—a comprehensive account of the whole that Strauss does not think that human beings can achieve (128–30).

Finally, the Catholic would agree with Strauss that belief in revelation is not even understood by the believer as being capable of rational demonstration. Belief in revelation depends on faith and trust in God. The Catholic claims not to know but to believe the truths revealed by the church.

Areas of Disagreement

Although the Catholic may agree with Strauss's account of the problem of modernity, or of the crisis of the belief in progress, disagreements emerge when we turn to the possible solutions to these problems. Strauss says that the crisis calls for a return to Western civilization in its premodern integrity (104). So far, so good, as far as the Catholic is concerned. But what does Strauss mean by this? The Catholic would probably want to understand it as a return to Christianity: modernity is a kind of rebellion against Christianity which proves disastrous and which calls for, to borrow Strauss's terms, "return" in the sense of "repentance."[2]

Such a solution itself involves problems, however. "Christianity" is

---

2. Pope John Paul II offers a statement of something like this view in his final book, *Memory and Identity* (New York: Rizzoli, 2005).

not a fully unified phenomenon, and therefore it cannot be the basis of a complete civilizational "integrity." A return to Christianity—a return to deep public and private seriousness about Christianity—would entail a return to the conflict between Catholicism and Protestantism. This conflict, however, set the stage for modernity. Modern political philosophy and the belief in progress emerged in part as an attempted solution to this conflict. Thus a return to Christianity seems to be nothing more than a return to an earlier stage of the path that leads right back to the crisis of modernity.

For the Catholic, then, the real answer to the crisis of modernity would be a more complete return or repentance: a return to Catholicism or Christendom. This would, indeed, be a return to Western civilization in its premodern integrity. The sober-minded Catholic will not be under the illusion that such a return is likely. Nor will he be such a partisan of Catholicism as to deny the real and grave abuses that arose within Christendom, and which helped bring on Protestantism and modernity. He will be open to drawing on materials in the Catholic tradition—and on whatever is wholesome and sensible in modern political thought—to prevent such abuses. These prudent qualifications, however, would not dissuade him from thinking that a return to Christendom would be the most desirable thing if it could be achieved. After all, the Catholic must regard Catholicism as true and good, and therefore would welcome a social order in which its truth and goodness is acknowledged. Besides, the alternative seems to be progressive modernity, which, as Strauss says, is heading toward an abyss.

A return to Christendom, however, is not something that seems to interest Strauss, for reasons that are perhaps obvious. One important reason is not obvious but is implied by Strauss. He seems to regard Catholicism as involving a certain intellectual incoherence, at least as it has been traditionally formulated.

This brings us to the theoretical disagreement between Strauss and Catholicism. The return to Western civilization in its premodern integrity is a problem, Strauss contends, because Western civilization is based on an unresolved and unresolvable tension between the Bible and Greek philosophy. This tension is often obscured, he suggests, because "the whole history of the West presents itself at first glance as an attempt to harmonize, or to synthesize, the Bible and Greek philosophy" (104). A "closer study," however, "shows that what happened and has been happening in the West for many centuries, is not a harmonization but an attempt at harmonization." This attempt not only failed but was in fact "doomed to failure," according to Strauss, because these two roots of Western civilization, Greek philosophy and the Bible, present opposed things as the one thing needful. For Greek philosophy it is "the life of autonomous understanding," while for the Bible it is "the life of obedient love" (104). Because Catholicism, and especially Catholic theology, has understood itself as a harmonization of Greek philosophy and the Bible, Strauss is suggesting that Catholicism is theoretically problematic. The synthesis it claims to have achieved it has not achieved and cannot be achieved.

Here it is important to understand what Strauss means by the failure of this synthesis. He does not mean that it is impossible for Catholicism to succeed in incorporating some concepts of Greek philosophy into Catholic theology. Such a thing is surely possible, and it is compatible with treating philosophy as a compartment of life rather than as a way of life, or making it into a handmaiden of theology. Strauss acknowledges that this is possible (104, 122).

Catholicism, however, seeks a more ambitious synthesis of the Bible and Greek philosophy. It wants to understand itself as a synthesis of autonomous understanding and obedient love. It wants to present itself as a reasonable revealed religion in a way that Strauss thinks is impossible.

This is not to say that the Catholic holds that the truth of his religion can be demonstrated by a conclusive chain of reasoning. Catholicism depends on belief in certain historical events, the truth of which cannot be proven in that way. And, again, it is common Catholic understanding that acceptance of these truths depends on faith or trust, which is different from philosophical knowledge.

The Catholic does, however, think that Catholicism is reasonable in the sense of being the most reasonable alternative available to us as human beings. Strauss's defense of the life of philosophy assumes that life presents us with a kind of puzzle or mystery. The Catholic agrees. He thinks, however, that Catholicism is the most reasonable solution to this puzzle. The Catholic thinks, in other words, that the autonomous exercise of reason ought to lead up to acceptance of the Catholic faith. This is not, of course, to impute bad faith or intellectual incompetence to those who reason about things and yet do not become Catholics. The Catholic is aware that many things may impede even the earnest seeker from coming to Catholicism. Nevertheless, the Catholic thinks that the Catholic faith is the most reasonable solution to the problem of life and therefore the solution to which—in principle, in the ideal case—philosophical reason will come in the end.

Strauss pays Catholicism—and all revealed religions—a certain compliment, and the Catholic is no doubt happy to accept it. Modern rationalism claims to have defeated belief in revelation, and that claim has often been trumpeted by the West's intellectual classes. Strauss, however, tells us that this vaunted modern wisdom is not in fact superior to belief in revelation in the decisive respect. Modern rationalism claims to have refuted belief in revelation, but it has not in fact done so. Modern rationalism and the belief in progress have certainly proven to be more influential than belief in revelation, but they have not turned out to be more profound or more reasonable. Moreover, as Strauss suggests by referring to the abyss, their practical results are not better and indeed are much worse than those that seem to come from belief in revelation.

As welcome as it is, however, this compliment is insufficient to the Catholic, who wants to understand Catholicism as reasonable in a more robust and demanding sense. Hence the conflict between Catholicism as it understands itself and the relationship between philosophy and belief in revelation as Strauss understands it.

Moreover, Strauss himself appears to understand and to intend to point to this difference. Again, if his reference to the attempted synthesis of Greek philosophy and the Bible had been intended to refer only to the adoption of certain Greek philosophical concepts in Christian theology, he would not have needed to refer to the enterprise as necessarily doomed. He instead, therefore, seems to refer to some more ambitious synthesis of autonomous reason and obedient love—which he contends is impossible.

Strauss may go even further. He may hint in "Progress or Return?" that philosophy, properly understood, can prove superior to belief in revelation. As his account draws to its close, Strauss famously suggests that philosophy and theology are locked in an unresolvable standoff. Neither can refute the other. Therefore, each must grapple with the other. This conclusion is somewhat supportive of revelation because it suggests that the believer in revelation can hold his head high, as it were, assured that his beliefs are as reasonable as, and cannot be defeated by, the most serious alternative.

If we look more closely, however, we see that Strauss posits this standoff as existing only between revelation and philosophy understood in a certain imperfect sense. Modern philosophy, Strauss indicates, cannot prove superior to belief in revelation. But Strauss elsewhere holds that philosophy in the true sense, the Greek sense, is not any body of propositions and arguments but the way of life in search of autonomous understanding. He thus implicitly opens the door to the possibility that this kind of philosophy might somehow prove superior to belief in revelation (131–32).[3]

There is a second way in which Strauss suggests that the gap between him and the believer might be larger than would at first appear. When Strauss turns to the present-day arguments in favor of revelation, he deals rather dismissively with the argument based on "the needs of present-day civilization, the present-day crisis, which would simply amount to this: that we need today, in order to compete with communism, revelation as a myth." This argument, Strauss says, is "either stupid or blasphemous" (123).

This argument would be stupid, we surmise, because it is ridiculous to suppose that religion can function as a politically invigorating myth if it is openly affirmed as such. It can only perform this function if it is actually believed, but it can hardly be believed if it is openly presented as nothing more than a political expedient.

Alternatively, the argument might be blasphemous because it reduces the God of the Bible to a mere human invention, invented for purely human purposes. Strauss's own account, however, seems to move in the direction of such blasphemy. He presents both the Bible and Greek philosophy as human attempts to solve a—or rather *the*—human problem: the problem of divine law. Strauss suggests that the authors of the Bible devised the idea of an omnipotent God as a way of sustaining and justifying the belief that the divine law of a particular people was in truth the genuine divine law. It is hard to see how it would be blasphemous to make biblical religion serve the political needs of present-day civilization but not blasphemous to claim that it was invented to serve the political needs of an ancient civilization or pre-civilization.

---

3. In *Leo Strauss and the Theologico-Political Problem* (New York: Cambridge University Press, 2006), Heinrich Meier contends that this is in fact Strauss's intention.

Strauss's argument might be understood to imply that this blasphemy is the necessary conclusion of philosophy as he understands it. Strauss notes that the philosopher's disposition is to suspend judgment on revelation, as it cannot be verified or refuted by reason. Strauss then adds, however, that one cannot suspend judgment in matters of ultimate consequence like this. He raises this necessity from the standpoint of revelation: as the stakes are eternal joy or eternal damnation, one is in a way compelled to choose (121–22). The necessity of choosing may be imposed on the philosopher, too, by the nature of his vocation. Perhaps the philosopher cannot simply suspend judgment. He must ask of revelation: what is this phenomenon? This means, according to Strauss, seeking its origins, its causes. And Strauss's account suggests that for him philosophy reveals that the origins of revelation are human and not divine. By asking the questions that it must ask, by reasoning about them to the best of its ability, philosophy is led to this blasphemous conclusion.

A Political Defense of the Catholic Position

Catholicism presents itself as a kind of synthesis of the Bible and Greek philosophy. Strauss, on the other hand, contends that such a synthesis is not finally possible. Can anything be said in defense of the Catholic position? Once again, Strauss's concerns are both political—concerned with what is necessary for a good society—and theoretical—concerned with the truth of the relationship between philosophy and revelation. We may begin, then, with the political side of the issue: is a kind of political synthesis of philosophy and revelation possible?

Strauss's own arguments in "Progress or Return?" point to the possibility of just such a political synthesis. According to Strauss, the Bible and Greek philosophy agree not perfectly but to a considerable extent on the question of morality. They disagree, indeed, on the vital question of what it is that completes morality, or what is "the basis of morality" (105). They agree substantially, however, on the importance of morality and the content of morality. According to Strauss, "Those theologians who identified the second table of the Decalogue, as the Christians call it, with the natural law of Greek philosophy, were well-advised." It is perhaps worth noting at this point that "those theologians" to whom Strauss refers were surely Catholic theologians. Strauss continues, observing that it "is as obvious to Aristotle as it is to Moses that murder, theft, adultery, etc., are unqualifiedly bad" (105). Both the Bible and Greek philosophy emphasize the importance of the monogamous family as the "cell of a society" ruled by "free adult males." Moreover, both the Bible and Greek philosophy agree in making not manliness or courage the highest virtue, but justice or obedience to law. They agree that such justice makes a man happy or blessed. This law is comprehensive, not just civil but religious and moral. Obedience to this kind of law is understood in both traditions to involve humility. For both traditions, Strauss concludes, law and justice "are divine law and divine justice. The rule of life is fundamentally the rule of God, theocracy" (105–6). Finally, both traditions seem to agree in positing active divine support for justice or morality. Both hold that there is divine justice or retribution for injustice or disobedience to law. Both perceive the problem of justice and how to resolve it. That is, both see "the difficulty created by the misery of the just and the prospering of the wicked." Both solve this problem by holding that the divine power will correct this disproportion in the end. Thus the *Republic* ends "with restoring all kinds of property to the just," and "the book of Job ends with the restoration to the just Job of everything that he had temporarily lost" (106).

All of this is also true, of course, of Catholicism. On Strauss's own account of the issues, therefore, it is hard to see why Catholicism could not adequately function as the public religion of a healthy and decent political order—why, in other words, it would not be possible in principle to return to Western civilization in its premodern integrity in the sense of returning to Christendom. This is not so say, of course, that such a return is likely, or that it could be made the aim of some political program. Given the overwhelming power of modernity, however, this is equally true of *any* effort to return to Western civilization in its premodern integrity, however that is conceived. Yet Strauss contends that the crisis of modernity requires us at least to think about such possibilities. The point here, in any case, is not to call for a return to Christendom in practice, but to note that it would seem to be possible in principle, even though it is a kind of synthesis of Greek philosophy and the Bible, and even though Strauss says such a synthesis is not possible.

We may grant—for the present, for the sake of the argument—that Strauss is correct in holding that a philosophically satisfying synthesis of the Bible and Greek philosophy is not possible because when it comes to the highest thing that completes morality, or the fundamental thing that is the basis of morality, they cannot agree. Again, for the Bible it is obedient love and for Greek philosophy it is autonomous understanding. In the pursuit of autonomous understanding, Strauss holds, Greek philosophy ends up transcending belief in divine law in the pursuit of rational knowledge of nature. Finally, then, for Greek philosophy, divine law is "accepted only politically, meaning, for the education of the many, and not as something which stands independently" (114). Nevertheless, this means that Greek philosophy will affirm divine law publicly, seeing it as essential to the well-being of a civilized regime. Such law seems to be essential to the education of the many, and the Greek philosophers always took this education with great seriousness and attended to it with proper public-spiritedness. Even Greek philosophy, it would seem, will publicly honor humble obedience to divine law.

On this view, again, it is hard to see why there cannot be a kind of synthesis on the level of politics between Greek philosophy and belief in biblical revelation. And if this is possible, it would seem that even Greek philosophy could accept, say, Catholicism as the public religion of a satisfactory regime. It is true, as Strauss says, that during the Christian Middle Ages—that is, the high noon of Catholicism as the public religion of the Western regimes—philosophy was "deprived of its character as a way of life, and became just a very important compartment" (122). This is not necessarily an objection to Catholicism, however, or to Catholicism as a kind of synthesis of the Bible and Greek philosophy. The problem, it would appear, is that a Catholic regime would subordinate philosophy to the public religion. But any regime of whatever character that is capable of generating philosophers and is aware of philosophy will try to subordinate philosophy to the official doctrine of the city. This problem, however, is not insuperable. The solution to it can be found in the esotericism which Strauss is famous for having taught. On the basis of such esotericism, it should be possible for the responsible philosopher to pursue the life of autonomous understanding while, at the same time, leaving the public religion undisturbed. At least this will be possible if the public religion fosters a decent public morality and is therefore such that the philosopher will feel no public spirited duty to tamper with it. But, as we have seen, Strauss indicates that biblical morality is such a morality even by Greek philosophical standards.

One can conceive plausible reasons why Strauss might have doubted the political workability of Christendom, or of Catholicism as a public religion. In the first place, it might be that Christendom suffered from disorders that followed from excessive clerical power. In their book *Leo Strauss and the Problem of Political Philosophy*, Michael and Catherine Zuckert suggest that such a line of argument may be implied in Strauss's treatment of Marsilius and Machiavelli.[4] It is not clear, however, that such a problem is unique to Catholicism or that it is insuperable. As Strauss himself notes, the Greek philosophical approach to politics involves the public promotion of beliefs about the divine origins of law and divine support for law. Accordingly, Aristotle lists priestcraft—or superintendence of the city's relationship with the gods—as the "fifth and first" thing that a city requires.[5] Any city, Aristotle seems to suggest, will need a class of people who mediate—or who are believed to mediate—the community's relationship with the divine. Such an arrangement is always open to the danger of abuse. The most decisive way to avoid that possibility is to construct a regime for which the claims of the divine are irrelevant. Such a solution, however, seems to be part of the modern approach to politics that Strauss claims both the Bible and Greek philosophy reject, and that Strauss himself seems to reject as ultimately disastrous. The problem of the abuse of clerical power, in any case, does not appear to be such that it cannot be borne or ameliorated. Certainly it was common during Catholicism's dominance of Western civilization for Catholics to admit that there were limits to the power of the clergy. It is also worth noting that the political influence of the clergy was probably not an unmitigated evil. There may be something to be said for the restraint it may have imposed on rulers from time to time. Moreover, the position of political and social influence that the clergy enjoyed in the Christian Middle Ages is not fundamental to Christianity. The original clergy enjoyed no such position, operating as they did in a non-Christian regime. This is not to say, on the other hand, that such influence is totally incompatible with the vocation of the clergy. All this is to point out that the nature and extent of the social and political influence of the clergy is a prudential question from the standpoint of Catholicism: it is not settled definitively by any fundamental principles. This leaves open the possibility that there can be a regime

---

4. Michael and Catherine Zuckert, *Leo Strauss and the Problem of Political Philosophy* (Chicago: University of Chicago Press, 2014).

5. *Politics* 1328b.

that affirms Catholicism as the public religion but that does not accord the clergy any particular political or social influence, or that accords it but takes care also to limit it.

It might also be the case that Strauss thought Christianity an inadequate remedy for modernity because he thought that Christianity somehow gave rise to modernity. Modernity, after all, arose first in the Christian nations of Europe and has progressed most rapidly in them. Perhaps Christianity unleashes a desire to improve the human condition that leads eventually to modernity. At one point, Strauss indicates that Greek philosophy is "heartless" in comparison to the biblical teaching (108). Greek philosophy looks upon the poor as inadequate material for human virtue and seems uninterested in what might be done to elevate the condition of the poor. The Bible, on the other hand, tends to treat the poor as pious and virtuous. Moreover, we may add, concern for the poor, a desire to ameliorate their condition, is characteristic of biblical morality. Perhaps Christianity intensifies this desire, raising hopes for human improvement that eventually lead peoples shaped by the influence of Christianity to throw it off and to embrace instead a kind of restless conquest of nature with a view to the relief of man's estate. On this view, one cannot hope to return to any form of Christianity as the form of Western civilization in its premodern integrity because Christianity contains the seeds of modernity, the belief in progress, and the abyss to which it leads.

To embrace this critique fully, however, is to surrender a great deal that most people will be unwilling to surrender. To accept it fully would seem to require a return to something like the Greek philosophical solution, or to the pre-Christian biblical solution, both of which seem either not to have been much interested in ameliorating the human material condition, or incapable of ameliorating it. In view of these stark alternatives—life on the material level of the ancient world, with slavery and the rest of it—or an endless, progressive conquest of nature that ends in an abyss, it would seem reasonable to seek some middle ground, if possible. Perhaps traditional Catholicism can provide such a middle ground through its combination of otherworldliness and attention to the needs of the body, its eagerness to exercise charity but its insistence on a natural law that imposes limits on what man may dare to do in this life to improve his condition.

These reflections point to a kind of anthropological advantage that

Catholicism may have over the alternatives with which Strauss deals in "Progress or Return?" On the one hand, Strauss sympathetically portrays the Jewish veneration of the past. On the other hand, he implicitly criticizes as superficial the modern veneration of progress and the future. It may be, however, that this desire for a better future—better than anything that has yet been achieved or even imagined—is rooted more deeply in human nature than Strauss admits. Strauss contends that the disasters of the twentieth century have rendered modernity morally empty by revealing the vacuity of its pretensions to progress. Whatever Strauss may have observed in 1952, it is striking that in 2018 it appears that Western man—or at least the Western elites who set the tone for Western societies—is no less enamored of the idea of progress than were the Western men who lived before the cataclysms of the last one hundred years. Western elites commonly try to settle moral questions by claims to being on "the right side of history," a formulation that indicates a belief in moral progress.

In view of the persistence of the belief in progress, or the human yearning for a perfect future, it might be that a more balanced public philosophy will include something that speaks to that yearning while also keeping it within safe limits. And here is where Catholicism may have an anthropological advantage over the two alternatives sketched by Strauss—Greek philosophy and the pre-Christian Bible. On the one hand, as we noted before, Catholicism is (like Judaism) a conservative religion in the sense that it looks to the past for guidance in the most important questions. It is oriented toward a deposit of faith given in the past, that is not to be modified and that is to guide our steps in the present and into the future. At the same time, Catholicism departs from the Judaism Strauss describes because it does not look to a classic past as the highest thing that human beings can achieve and the restoration of which is all we have to anticipate. It instead looks to an end of history—coming in God's time, and beyond any man's power to impede or hasten—that will result in a state of things better than our origins (the Garden of Eden) and better than any other classic past (such as the age of the apostles), no matter how much we may admire it.

There is something admittedly superficial in looking down on our human origins, as we owe our very existence to those who came before us. Yet there is something admittedly grim in having nothing good to look forward to that is not superior to what we have already had. If human nature somehow longs to live both toward the past and toward the future, perhaps Catholicism answers the needs of human nature better than either of the alternatives than Strauss examines in "Progress or Return?" Perhaps, in other words, it offers a kind of synthesis here that makes it attractive, even from a philosophical point of view.

A Theoretical Defense of the Catholic Position

According to the preceding reflections, it would be possible, even from the standpoint of philosophy as Strauss understands it, to regard Catholicism as the public religion of a decent regime. Therefore, a repentance or return to Christendom is in principle possible as an alternative to modernity (although very unlikely in practice). On this view, Catholicism is viable as a kind of political synthesis of the Bible and Greek philosophy.

Nevertheless, these reflections would be inadequate to the Catholic himself. As I suggested earlier, the Catholic wants to understand Catholicism as a reasonable religion, and even as the religion to which reason points us. Here I should add that by this I mean—obviously—that the Catholic wants to understand Catholicism not only as reasonable but as really true. He wants to view it as not only politically salutary but as actually corresponding to reality. Put another way, the Catholic does not want a politically influential Catholicism only as a kind of noble lie. Nor does he even want to view its supposed reasonableness as a noble lie. That is, he does not want it affirmed as reasonable for political purposes, while behind the veil the philosophically astute Catholic realizes that adherence to Catholicism is possible only on the basis of a pure faith that casts reason aside. It is necessary, then, to consider whether Catholicism can present itself as a kind of synthesis of philosophical reason and belief in revelation, contrary to what Strauss contends.

The first step in making the case for such a synthesis is taking issue with Strauss's presentation of the two alternatives that he contends are radically opposed. Strauss, I would contend, exaggerates the gulf between Greek philosophy and the religion revealed in the Bible. He makes the Bible seem more unreasonable, more hostile to the spirit of philosophy, than it really is; and he makes philosophy seem more rationalistic than it really is, or need be.

Strauss contends that the philosopher as philosopher takes no interest in what is contingent or particular. For him there can never be an absolute sacredness of something contingent or particular. Strauss also presents the Bible, however, as offering a religion the sole purpose of which is to justify the divine code of a particular people. As such, it cannot be of interest to the philosopher. Here, however, Strauss exaggerates the particularism of the Bible. Of course the Catholic will observe that Jesus commanded his apostles to preach his message to all peoples, which shows that Catholicism has a universal character that might at least claim the philosopher's attention. Perhaps Strauss would respond that this universalism of Catholicism is a perversion of biblical revelation in its pure form, evidence of the attempt—doomed to failure—to graft Greek philosophical thinking onto the Bible. The Catholic, however, might well reply that even the oldest portions of the Old Testament contain evidence that the revelation the Bible contains looks beyond the particular to the universal. God promises to raise up a particular people from Abraham, but he also promises that through Abraham's descendants "shall all the nations of the earth bless themselves" (Gn 22:18). Indeed, in "Progress or Return?" Strauss himself characterizes "philosophy and the Bible" as the "alternatives or the antagonists in the drama of the human soul" (123). This formulation, however, necessarily presents the teaching of the Bible as of universal significance and therefore of interest to the philosopher.

Strauss also suggests that revelation is hostile to philosophy inasmuch as revelation does not at all acknowledge the tribunal of human reason (128). The life of obedience to revelation, he says, includes no place for "independent questioning" (114). Nevertheless, the Book of Genesis presents Abraham as questioning God regarding God's resolution to destroy the city of Sodom: "Wilt thou indeed destroy the righteous with the wicked?... Far be it from thee to do such a thing, to slay the righteous with the wicked, so that the righteous fare as the wicked!" (Gn 18:23–25). The point of this story is surely not that God was overcome by wrath and had to be talked out of an unjust act by one of his creatures. It would seem, instead, that it intends to show us that God's justice is not wholly unintelligible to human reason. Abraham's reaction to the fate of Sodom, and the questions that he poses to God, imply that he has some notion of what God is and what actions are consistent with his being.

Finally, Strauss contends that belief in revelation is utterly incompatible with philosophy because the God of the Bible is presented as being omnipotent in the sense of being utterly mysterious, radically free, impenetrable to human reason. The story of Abraham pleading on behalf of Sodom—or on behalf of any righteous men who might inhabit Sodom—already calls this presentation into question. Elsewhere, Strauss claims that the God of the Bible is so radically free, so absolutely inaccessible to man, that there can be no relationship between the two but by way of God's covenant, and that "there is no necessary and therefore intelligible relation" (115). On the other hand, the Bible indicates that God created man in his "image and likeness" (Gn 1:26). This language implies that there is something intelligible about God, and that man shares in it in a way that is intelligible: there is some common ground between God and man. It is worth noting here that Genesis does present man as having some kind of relationship with God prior to the establishment of any covenant. Strauss holds that the proper interpretation of the divine name given in Exodus is "I shall be what I shall be" (114). This is God as, again, radically free: there is no telling what he will be in the future, and this is the opposite of the Greek philosophical understanding of essence, according to which "the being is what is and was and will be." God is presumably the ground of all being. On the view of God that Strauss attributes to the Bible, the ground of all being is absolutely unintelligible to reason because it has no stable essence. If this were true it would indeed be an impediment to philosophy as it was understood by the Greeks. The other passages noted above, however, call into question whether this is really the way the Bible intends to present God.

Strauss does not merely describe how the Bible presents God; he offers an account of why the Bible presents God in the way that it does. There are problems with this account. Strauss argues as if the God of the Bible is an idea that was invented by the authors of the Bible in order to solve the problem of divine law—to justify their claim that a particular divine code is *the* divine code. The authors of the Bible "realized what are the absolutely necessary conditions if one particular law should be *the* divine law" (114). The conditions for such a belief, according to Strauss, are that the giver of that law be a personal God who is omnipotent in the sense of completely uncontrollable and therefore unknowable. There are at least two problems with this argument. First, it is not clear that such a God is really necessary to justify one law as the true divine law. Such a claim does require that this particular people's God be somehow set apart from all other gods. But this could be achieved by holding only that this God is the highest God, superior in insight and power to all other gods. It is not clear that these political and moral needs would even require that this God be conceived as the creator. But even if it required that, it is not at all clear why he would have to be presented as utterly unknowable. To this extent, the Bible actually presents a more robust account of what God is than would be required by the political needs that Strauss says generated belief in this God—which in turn suggests that the political argument Strauss puts forward is not really adequate to explain the God of the Bible.

In any case, there is a second problem, which is that the understanding of God that Strauss puts forward as necessary to the political project of the biblical authors is not only not necessary but actually incompatible with the aims of that project. Strauss contends that the authors of the Bible had to present their God as utterly, radically free, such that there could be no relationship with him except through a covenant. But a covenant with such a God would be worthless. It could guarantee no relationship. If the biblical God is radically free in the sense that Strauss insists, if it is impossible to say at any present moment what he will be in the future, then there is no reason to trust in any covenant he might put forward (119). We would, after all, have no way of knowing whether such a God would continue to be such a God as would remain true to his covenant. It may be that Strauss wants to present belief in revelation in just such terms: it is so irrational that it means trusting where there is absolutely no reason to trust. It is not clear, however, that this is the kind of trust to which the Bible calls men. Nor is it clear why human authors of the Bible—men, as Strauss presents them, reasoning toward a solution to the problem of divine law—would come up with such an unlikely and apparently self-contradictory solution to the problem.

On the other side of the equation, Strauss also widens the gap between philosophy and revelation by presenting philosophy as more rationalistic than it is or need be. Strauss characterizes Greek philosophy as an ascent in understanding that ascends by reasoning from sense perception, sense experience, sense data (114–18). This is not the only possible characterization of Greek philosophy, however, and it does not even appear to be the characterization on which Strauss relies in other contexts. Elsewhere, Strauss famously presents the classical political philosophers as reasoning from common opinion about the important moral and political questions that one encounters in the marketplace. And this is indeed the kind of process we encounter in the works of Plato and Aristotle: beginning from questions about the just vs. the unjust, the good vs. the bad, and the noble vs. the base. The just, the good, and the noble, however, do not appear to be sense data or the objects of sense perception. They instead appear as moral categories that are somehow immediately, if imperfectly, intelligible to the human mind: in need of rational clarification, but rooted in the nature of things as it appears to the human mind and therefore a good beginning point to philosophical inquiry.

We cannot exclude the possibility that the earnest reasoner might think his way from these kinds of questions to a conclusion that affirms the reasonableness of accepting the biblical revelation. This would not be a rational demonstration of the truth of that revelation. Neither would it be a nonrational embrace of revelation, one that disclaims any role for reason in evaluating the claims of revelation. To this extent it would be a kind of synthesis of philosophy and revelation. This inquiry would result, in other words, in something like the Catholic understanding of the reasonableness of the claims of Catholicism.

According to Strauss, the philosopher's activity presupposes the intelligibility of things. He also speaks of the philosopher as being aware of an impersonal necessity that is the framework of all things. On this view, it would seem, the ultimate reality is an intelligible impersonal necessity. This is certainly a plausible understanding of things. I do not think we can exclude the possibility, however, that a real philosopher might reason from the intelligibility of things, including the moral intelligibility of things, to the existence of a *personal* necessity that is the ground of all things: that is, a personal God. Due to the fact that things are intelligible at all, it is reasonable to believe in some ultimate intelligibility. At the same time, the intelligibility of things is only grasped, in our experience, by a conscious mind. On the basis of such considerations a philosopher might conclude that it is reasonable to suppose that the ultimate reality is like a mind and therefore like a person.

This philosopher would also be aware, as all human beings are aware, of the manifold limitations of the world in which we find ourselves, including the persistence of things that we cannot help but regard as evil: injustice and death. And on the basis of such experiences this philosopher might conclude that it is reasonable to suppose that human beings are somehow estranged from this personal God who is the ground of all things. This conclusion would in turn set the stage for belief in the reasonableness of holding that this God—being benevolent, because he is the ground of all goodness—would try to repair this breach by revealing himself to men. This philosopher might then find it reasonable to accept the revelation of the Bible, which is of this character.

This kind of thinking is something like what Strauss presents as the most "impressive" line of argument in favor of revelation, the argument that tries to prove "revelation by the intrinsic quality of revelation. The revealed law is the best of all laws" (126–27). It is not the same argument, exactly, because the considerations sketched above have to do with more than just the quality of the revealed law and reach revelation's presentation of the whole human situation—a presentation that corresponds to and solves the problems as reason alone might view them. In any case, however, Strauss tries to deal with this most "impressive" argument by contending that reason's ability to assent to revelation in fact implicitly denies revelation's character as revelation. That is, if the content of revelation is such as to appear reasonable, then the philosopher will think that it just might be the product of human reason: in other words, a system of belief invented by human beings in order to solve the problem of human life (127).

Strauss's argument puts the person who wants to believe in a reasonable assent to revelation in a kind of bind. As Strauss puts it:

Revelation is either a brute fact, to which nothing in purely human experience corresponds—in that case it is an oddity of no human importance—or it is a meaningful fact, a fact required by human experience to solve the fundamental problems of man—in that case, it may very well be the product of reason, of the human attempt to solve the problem of human life. It would then appear that it is impossible for reason, for philosophy, to assent to revelation as revelation (127).

This is, to be sure, a rationally plausible view of the situation. It is hard to say, however, that it is any more rationally plausible than the alternative view. It would be strange indeed if revelation were to come as a brute fact. Revelation is an attempt to communicate, and it would be pointless if God were to try to communicate himself to men in a manner that is unintelligible to men. On the other hand, if revelation were to occur, one would expect it to be a meaningful fact. The philosopher who is tempted to assent to revelation—or let us say rationally inclined to assent to it—will not, of course, be able to disprove the possibility that it is a mere human invention. He might nevertheless conclude that all the circumstances taken together—including other arguments that Strauss rightly notes are not conclusive on their own, such as fulfillment of prophecy, miracles, and tradition—tip the balance in favor of belief in the genuineness of revelation.

A couple of other considerations might point to the need for some such synthesis of reason and revelation as Catholicism claims to provide. Strauss speaks of the "heartlessness" of Greek philosophy in comparison to the teaching of the Bible. Something, it seems, is missing from Greek philosophy that we want to have. This raises the question whether the thing absent from Greek philosophy is some genuine human reality, and therefore indispensable to a complete account of the human situation, or just some vain hope that we were taught to desire by the cultural influence of the Bible. Strauss's own account, however, implies that the heartlessness of Greek philosophy arises from the absence of something really valuable. At one point, Strauss suggests that in order to fully "understand this conflict between the Bible and Greek philosophy" one would have to "go back to a fundamental dualism in man," a "dualism of deed and speech, of action and thought—a dualism which necessarily poses the question as to the primacy of either—and one can say that Greek philosophy asserts the primacy of thought, of speech, whereas the Bible asserts the primacy of deed" (120). If the dualism is indeed fundamental, as Strauss suggests, then it is rooted in human nature, in the very constitution of man as man. If this is the case, then the Bible's seriousness about morality is a response to a genuine human reality. And if this is the case, then it would seem that Greek philosophy's demotion of morality—its denial that it makes absolute claims, or its suggestion that morality is nothing more than a kind of vulgar reflection of philosophy—involves a failure to do justice to the reality of man. That failure, however, which can be grasped by the philosophizing mind, points to biblical revelation, which grounds the absolute claims of morality, as a more reasonable solution to the human problem than Greek philosophy on its own.

Put another way, the fundamental dualism to which Strauss refers reasonably points to some effort at a synthesis, contrary to Strauss's claims that no such synthesis is possible. Greek philosophy wants to present itself as the perfection of human nature. But the dual nature of man, including the element that is oriented toward deed—man's experience of the insistence of the moral demands he encounters—means that philosophy cannot present itself as an unqualified perfection of human nature. There is a part of human nature to which it does not satisfactorily attend—at least if it is the kind of philosophy that claims to transcend the realm of morality and to treat moral claims as merely instrumental. On the other side, a biblical solution that leaves it at the absolute primacy of deed cannot be adequate, because man is a reasoning being and cannot dedicate himself to deeds that his reason cannot understand to be intelligibly good. In sum, an effort at a synthesis or harmonization of the elements of man's dual nature seems called for to avoid the unacceptable outcomes that arise from the absolutization of either heartless reason or irrational action.

Another version of this argument might be possible based on the following observation in "Progress or Return?": "Humanly speaking, the unity of fear and pity combined with the phenomenon of guilt might seem to be the root of religion. God, the king or judge, is the object of fear; and God, the father of all men, makes all men brothers, and thus hallows pity" (108). Strauss thus suggests that experiences of guilt, fear, and pity are elements of the human condition. They arise from our sense of being somehow in the wrong, and in relation to something—or someone, God—who is all-good and all-powerful. The Greek philosopher, Strauss goes on to say, seeks to transcend this dimension of human existence. Man—at least ordinary man, the man of the multitude who needs tragedy—is in a state of fear and trembling, but philosophers are above fear and trembling. This might be another way of expressing the heartlessness of Greek philosophy as it appears from the perspective of the Bible.

But if these experiences of fear and trembling are genuinely human experiences—as Strauss's own language appears to concede—then it would seem to be open to philosophy to conclude that these experiences point to actual realities, realities that are given the most persuasive presentation available in the Bible. In other words, it may be that our experience of the absoluteness of moral claims, and of the accompanying fear and trembling, is not an illusion that can really be transcended but an ineradicable element of human existence. And it may be that these experiences are most persuasively explained by the conclusion that there is a personal God and that each human being is created in his image and likeness, so that an injustice committed against my neighbor has the character of an offense against something holy. We might illustrate this issue with reference to an example Strauss gives to show the difference between the moral spirit of the Bible and that of Greek philosophy: the difference between the way the prophet Nathan rebukes King David for his crimes against Uriah, on the one hand, and the way Simonides tries to correct the tyrant Hiero in Xenophon's *On Tyranny*, on the other (109–10). There is, as Strauss intimates, no element of fear and trembling in Simonides's effort to get Hiero to see that he would be happier if he acted with more moderation. In view of the events of the last century, however, we might ask ourselves whether Xenophon's approach—as helpful as it is—really does justice to the human situation. Would we think it adequate to write a dialogue in which a rather detached and amused Simonides tries to get Hitler or Stalin to see the error of his ways? If not, we might reasonably conclude that even Xenophon's treatment of the more limited tyranny of which he had knowledge was not adequate, and that its inadequacy points to an account like that provided by the Bible. This sort of thinking about the human situation, and these kinds of conclusions, do not, at any rate, seem evidently less reasonable than that found in Greek philosophy as Strauss presents it, or as evidently less deserving the name philosophy.

The considerations sketched above are all variations on a kind of positive philosophical argument in defense of belief in revelation, the argument that Strauss presents as proceeding from the intrinsic character of revelation. These kinds of arguments, again, try to suggest that belief in revelation really is the best available solution to the problems that confront human reason. Strauss also acknowledges a kind of negative argument in favor of belief in revelation, an argument based on the limitations of or unsatisfactory character of the life of the philosopher. Strauss rejects this negative argument as well. It is stated in a strong form by Pascal, among other theologians or theologically minded thinkers, who claims that "the life of philosophy is fundamentally miserable" (131). Strauss rejects such arguments by saying that they in fact presuppose faith: that is, apparently, they beg the question by assuming some good that faith offers that the philosopher is then assumed to be unable to live without. In contrast, Strauss affirms that it is possible for the philosopher to live untragically even without faith: he can make progress in understanding and enjoy his experience of making such progress.

On the other hand, it seems that it would be possible to conclude even on the basis of Strauss's presentation of the philosophical life that it is, if not miserable, then at least unsatisfactory. Simply put, it is a quest for knowledge that is never fully consummated. Strauss indicates in "Progress or Return?" and in other writings that the life of philosophy is essentially a life of seeking knowledge, not a life of possessing knowledge. The seeking can only be good if the possession is good. But if the possession is good, then failure of complete possession must be experienced as a kind of problem or limitation of the way of life dedicated to the pursuit and achievement of knowledge. This problem would arise even if no one had ever heard of biblical revelation. And being aware of this problem, the philosopher who then learns of biblical revelation might reasonably come to the conclusion that it offers a solution to the problem.

There is another problem, I think, with Strauss's claim that it is possible to live untragically on the basis of philosophical activity. In one sense this is surely true. The activity of the philosopher is pleasant, if not completely adequate, and he can occupy himself pleasantly for a lifetime on the basis of that activity, continually thinking through the alternative answers to the question of the good for man. He can even find some immunity in this activity to the disasters of fortune: he can, for example, overcome the grief of the loss of loved ones by returning to the activity around which he organizes his life, the pleasure of which will drive out other activities of soul, such as grief. On the other hand, as there is pleasure to be had in the continual exercise of our rational faculties, it would be possible to live untragically in other ways than the philosophical life. One might do it as well, for example, by the study and performance of the works of J. S. Bach or by the study of botany. Either of these activities offers an inexhaustible store of pleasant intellectual activity for the person capable of performing them, and hence the possibility of living untragically. Strauss, however, does not view these as serious alternatives to the life of submission to biblical revelation. Philosophy has a superior dignity to these, it seems, not only because it is an exercise of our rational faculties, but because it is an exercise of them with a view to the question of the right way of life. The question of the right way of life, however, would seem to be a moral question. Classical political philosophy uses moral questions as the beginning of its inquiry into things. The genuine seriousness of those moral questions would therefore seem to be essential to philosophy's pretensions to a greater seriousness than other happy intellectual activities. And this in turn seems to mean that the activity of the philosopher is dependent on morality in a way that must tacitly concede its transcendent importance. And on this basis a philosopher might conclude that morality has a kind of absolute importance that is better expressed in the Bible than in Greek philosophy, such that Greek philosophy's efforts to pursue its own activity might lead it to see the reasonableness of biblical revelation. Or, to put it another way, on the basis of these considerations the philosopher might conclude that Greek philosophy's claim to transcend morality is not only heartless but in fact self-undermining, and this problem might point him in the direction of adherence to biblical revelation.

The Possibility of a Synthesis of Reason and Revelation

The Catholic wants to understand Catholicism as a kind of synthesis of reason and revelation—as the solution to the human problem that autonomous reason ought to be able to endorse. Strauss, on the other hand, contends that such a synthesis is not possible. The preceding arguments are not intended as a rational demonstration of the truth of Catholicism, something that is admittedly not possible. They are intended, rather, to defend the Catholic position from the implicit critique of it made by Strauss in "Progress or Return?" Strauss may be correct to hold that neither philosophy nor revelation, in the pure forms in which he presents them, can refute each other. He goes too far, however, he says more than reason can really affirm, in declaring that a synthesis of them is absolutely doomed from the start. This is the case in part because it is not rationally evident that the "pure" forms of reason and revelation that he presents are the true forms, or at any rate the only possible forms of reason and revelation. Strauss is correct when he suggests that reason and revelation cannot refute each other, "considering the enormous difficulty of the problem from any point of view" (131). The nature of the problem is also such, however, that we cannot rule out the possibility of a successful synthesis, such as Catholicism claims to be. Such a synthesis is at least as plausible a solution to the human problem as the other alternatives that Strauss treats, and it deserves to take its place beside them as one of the great fundamental alternatives contending for our allegiance.

 9

What Might a Catholic Reader Learn from Strauss about Catholicism?

On the Supposed Distinction of Natural Right and Natural Law

GARY D. GLENN

Let me begin by observing that Strauss himself appears to regard "Roman Catholic Social Science" as an ally in his attempt to restore to social science the serious study of what justice is. The basis for this observation is in the introduction to *Natural Right and History* (1953) where he explicitly exempts "Roman Catholic Social Science" from his indictment of "present-day American social science" because the latter, but not the former, denies the existence of "natural right."[1] But let me immediately caution that (1) "ally" is my term, not Strauss's, and (2) one can be allies in a common cause and yet be radically opposed in many, even in decisive, ways (e.g., the U.S. and the Soviet Union in World War II). So noting Strauss's commonality with Roman Catholic social science only barely begins to answer the question in the title of this essay.

Strauss has been accused of many things, but never of being a Catholic or even of having a Catholic perspective. On the contrary, a Catho-

---

1. Leo Strauss, *Natural Right and History* (Chicago: University of Chicago Press, 1953), 2.

lic scholar Robert Hunt goes so far as to say that "Strauss's distinction between 'ancients' and 'moderns' in general and between 'classical' and 'modern' political philosophy in particular does tend toward a dichotomizing of intellectual history whereunder even an ostensibly Catholic view of political life is, upon even a favorable reading of Strauss's distinction, more classical than Catholic in its philosophical orientation and political ramifications."[2] On the other hand James Stoner says

> it seems to me that there is in Strauss a certain respect for Catholic teaching and a constant recourse to categories or distinctions that are intelligible to Catholic thought, indeed that Strauss may have helped to save or recover for Catholic thought. That means on the one hand that it would be profitable, maybe even imperative, for contemporary Catholics to study Strauss, not least to understand Catholic intellectual history, to recognize contemporary challenges to Catholic thinking, and perhaps to learn ways to respond. On the other hand, Straussians would do well to reflect on Strauss's rapprochement with Catholic intellectuals in his own time, considering whether this was only a temporary measure of prudence or whether it reflected a deeper, more permanent harmony of principle.[3]

It is even seriously debated whether Strauss's apparent openness to revelation (in particular to Jewish revelation) is genuine or only a cover for atheism.[4]

There is much greater agreement that Strauss understands Catholic natural law to differ, in a decisive way, from classical (Aristotelian and Platonic) "natural right." And I think it worth a Catholic exploring that understanding in order to understand the *great similarity* and yet *purported difference* between them. And this for the sake of clarifying (1) whether it is true that Catholic natural law differs from classical natural right in the manner Strauss says it does, and (2) if that is true, how to defend Catholic natural law against Strauss's implicit criticism of it from the perspective of classical natural right.

Let me begin by restating as best I can Strauss's understanding of classical natural right at the point where he contrasts it with Catholic nat-

---

2. Robert Hunt, "Leo Strauss, and the Ancients/Moderns Distinction," *The Catholic Social Science Review* 14 (2009): 53–63.
3. James R. Stoner Jr., "The Catholic Moment in the Political Philosophy of Leo Strauss," *Voegelin View* (July 29, 2014), http://voegelinview.com/catholic-moment-political-philosophy-leo-strauss/.
4. See the debate between two of Strauss's Jewish students, Hilail Gildin and Werner Dannhauser. Dannhauser argues Strauss's atheism in "Athens and Jerusalem or Jerusalem and Athens" in *Leo Strauss and Judaism: Jerusalem and Athens Critically Revisited*, ed. David Novak (Lanham, Md.: Rowman and Littlefield, 1996), 155–71. Gildin responds in "Deja Jew All Over Again: Dannhauser on Leo Strauss and Atheism," *Interpretation* 25, no. 1 (1997): 125–33.

ural right/law. His understanding is that, for Aristotle but also for Plato, there are no exceptionless principles of action.[5] For them "all natural right is changeable." He understands that to mean "that in extreme situations the normally valid rules of natural right are justly changed, or changed in accordance with natural right; the exceptions are as just as the rules.... there is not a single rule, however basic, which is not subject to exception."[6] In contrast, Strauss understands the Thomistic (i.e., Catholic) doctrine of natural right to teach "the immutable character of the fundamental propositions of natural law; the principles of the moral law, especially as formulated in the Second Table of the Decalogue, suffer no exception, unless possibly by divine intervention."[7] Presumably, "by divine intervention," he has in mind, for example, the case of God commanding Abraham to kill Isaac. Strauss attributes this "profound change" between classical natural right and Christian natural right "to the influence of belief in Biblical Revelation."[8]

This essay began by seeking clarity about what it says about Catholicism if Strauss and Catholicism could be something like allies given this not inconsiderable purported disagreement. At a minimum, a Catholic can become aware of Strauss's criticism that Catholic natural law is importantly different from Aristotelian natural right. So while they might be allies against the regnant relativism, a Catholic has to explain at least to himself why the Catholic understanding of how nature guides us regarding right and wrong ("reason informed by faith") might be (if it is) superior to how natural reason (i.e., reason unassisted by biblical/Christian revelation) does so.[9]

Is Catholic Natural Right Teaching as Exceptionless as Strauss Maintains?

Although there is a question about whether it is clearly true that "all natural right is changeable" for Plato and Aristotle, I would begin by question-

---

5. Strauss, *Natural Right and History*, 157, 162.
6. Ibid., 160.
7. Strauss's explicit thought about Catholic natural law occurs almost entirely in his discussion of Aquinas. So, for present purposes, Strauss's thought about Catholicism equals his thought about Aquinas.
8. Strauss, *Natural Right and History*, 163.
9. "Reason informed by faith" is Strauss's translation of Aquinas. See below for my discussion of this translation.

ing whether Catholic natural right teaching is as exceptionless as Strauss maintains.[10] There is some evidence that it is not.

First, some secondary evidence. John von Heyking argues that Augustine's understanding of political ethics emphasizes practical wisdom and judgment in right-by-nature, and virtue as ordinate loving (*ordo amoris*), rather than either natural law or grace. It examines three cases of moral reasoning in extreme circumstances (lying, adultery, and tyrannicide/rebellion) and shows that Augustine adopts a right-by-nature style of practical reasoning in each case. In extreme circumstances, according to Augustine, the purpose of what appears as a universal rule or commandment can be better fulfilled by breaking the prohibition.[11]

Von Heyking argues that Augustine's emphasis preserves the moral life while maintaining the flexibility necessary for a robust political life and avoiding the pitfalls of a Machiavellian ends-justify-the-means political calculus. Whether or not he is correct about that, von Heyking shows that Augustine provides Catholic thought with the kind of flexibility which Strauss says classical natural right thought necessary (and that Aquinas omits) "to cope with the inventiveness of the wicked."[12] As to whether such flexibility amounts to "exceptions" to universally valid moral teachings, we shall see.

Strauss mentioned Augustine's "flexibility" (this is my word which might alternatively, pending the outcome of the discussion below, be "exceptions") regarding fundamental moral teachings in his lecture course in natural right (fall 1962).[13] Although Strauss does not mention the source in Augustine, I believe it is the following. In chapter 16 of his *Commentary on the Sermon of the Mount*, St. Augustine discusses the commandment against adultery. He asks whether there could be a case in which a wife could, without guilt, have "carnal intercourse" with another man, with her

---

10. After all it is Aristotle who says "Not every action admits of the mean. For the names of some automatically include baseness, e.g.... adultery, theft, murder ... in doing these things we can never be correct, e.g. by committing adultery with the right woman at the right time in the right way." Aristotle, *Nicomachean Ethics*, trans. Terence Irwin (Indianapolis, Ind.: Hackett, 1999), 1106a9–20.

11. Von Heyking, *Augustine and Politics As Longing in the World* (Columbia: University of Missouri Press, 2001), 13. I will question later whether what von Heyking regards as "breaking the prohibition" is a correct understanding of Augustine's thought.

12. Strauss, *Natural Right and History*, 161.

13. In the extant transcript of the course notes this discussion is on page 1 of the tenth lecture. However, this transcript was done in 1962. The Leo Strauss center at the University of Chicago presumably has a new transcript "pending." See https://leostrausscenter.uchicago.edu/courses/page/1/0.

husband's permission.[14] It would seem to be a shocking question from a biblical perspective but his discussion shows it to be an illuminating one.

Augustine considers a case said to have occurred "at Antioch about 50 years ago."[15] One Acyndinus threatened with death a debtor who was unable to repay his debt. However, he proposes to the debtor's "beautiful wife" that "in return for a single night, if she would consent to hold intercourse with him," her husband's life would be spared. She asked her husband's permission and "he thanked her and commanded that it should be done." She follows her husband's command.

Augustine seems to have begun by wondering about the abstract question whether "a wife may seem under obligation to do this [have carnal intercourse with another man] for the sake of that husband himself." But after stating the concrete case, he says "I offer no opinion either way from this story; let each one form his judgment as he pleases .... but yet ... man's instinctive sense does not so revolt against what was done in the case of this woman at her husband's bidding, as we formerly shuddered when the thing itself was set forth without any example."[16]

The course transcript has Strauss reporting Augustine as saying "I would tremble to blame that wife." It is not altogether clear whether Strauss is translating Augustine or merely summarizing his thought. In either case the Latin text does not quite support this translation. The word "tremble" Strauss uses is, in the text, *horruimus* (translated in the previous paragraph as "shuddered"). However the text does not quite say that Augustine "would tremble to blame the wife." Rather, it says "man's instinctive sense [*sensus humanus*] does not so revolt [*respuit*] against what was done in the case of this woman, at her husband's bidding, as we formerly shuddered [*horruimus*] when the thing itself was set forth without any example."[17] Still Augustine suggests the direction toward which Strauss's translation or summary points.

Augustine's "answer" to the abstract question very gently brings to mind the possibility of something like exceptions even to the prohibition against adultery. But it does not say explicitly that it is an exception.

---

14. Augustine, *St. Augustine of Hippo: Our Lord's Sermon on the Mount according to Matthew & the Harmony of the Gospels* (New York: Veritatis Splendor Publications, 2012), Book I, chap. XVI, pars. 49–50. This is a republication of *A Select Library of the Nicene and Post-Nicene Fathers of the Christian Church*, ed. P. Schaff (Buffalo, N.Y.: Christian Literature Company, 1886), vol. 6.
15. Ibid.
16. Ibid., §50 (94–96).
17. This passage occurs at the very end of *Commentary on the Sermon on the Mount*, chap. 16.

Of course, one might doubt that a Christian moralist *could* explicitly acknowledge such an exception. Nevertheless, his "answer" does point to the importance of the question regarding what a responsible Catholic philosopher, and even the church itself, should do in light of the danger of *teaching* anything resembling the idea that sometimes "breaking the prohibition" in "extreme circumstances" might be justified. For saying that explicitly would tend to undermine the prohibition. Perhaps this danger is minimal for the wisest and best readers. But church teaching is not directed only to philosophers, potential philosophers, saints or theologians; it has to be addressed to everyone.[18] So Augustine's delicate "answer" to this delicate question might be a model for teaching this dangerous idea by hint or indirection.

Another possibility is that Augustine might think that there could be extreme circumstances where what *looks like* adultery might not *be* adultery; or at least where it is sufficiently doubtful that it *is* adultery that one might not incur guilt. That possibility would seem to lessen the danger of undermining the rule by acknowledging an exception. But it would still, like acknowledging "exceptions," inject a flexibility into the Christian understanding of the prohibition that is akin to the flexibility the classics achieved (according to Strauss) by acknowledging "exceptions" to all principles of natural right.

There might be an analogy to this possibility in what seems to have happened with the Christian understanding of the commandment in Exodus 20:13. The Hebrew translations say "Thou shalt not commit murder," which preserves a distinction between justified and unjustified killing. The Christian translation, "thou shalt not kill," does not seem to admit such a distinction. Yet the Christian tradition came to accept justified killing in just war doctrine. Thus it *had to* distinguish justified killing from murder; so, for Christianity, as for the original Exodus, not all "killing" is "murder." Today's English however distinguishes "killing" from "murder" in that the latter is not justified but the former might be. But there is some evidence that this distinction did not exist in early English. The O.E.D.'s earliest listing of the Christian translation of Exodus 20:13 (the 1535 Coverdale Bible) treats "Thou shalt not kyll" as equivalent to "Thou shalt not murder."[19]

---

18. See below note 24 and text for Aquinas on this matter.
19. "d absol. To perform the act of killing; to commit murder or slaughter." Oxford English Dictionary, http://www.oed.com/view/Entry/103361?rskey=7Pd9XM&result=5#eid.

If the foregoing speculation is correct, then something that looks like what we would today call "killing" might not be the "murder" which the commandment was originally understood to prohibit. In a similar way, it might be that what Augustine is suggesting is that not quite every instance of carnal intercourse with someone other than a spouse is the "adultery" the commandment was meant to prohibit.

My memory of Strauss's explication of this case from Augustine in the fall 1962 course cited earlier is that he has Augustine suggesting that the case of the debtor's "beautiful wife" is not the kind of case to which the prohibition against adultery was meant to apply. However that suggestion does not appear to exist in the extant transcript of the course.

To summarize: Strauss calls attention to Augustine's seeming countenancing of an apparent exception, in an extreme case, to such a seemingly absolute and immutable moral prohibition as adultery. Yet Augustine does not explicitly call them an "exception," and a prudent Christian moralist can hardly run the risk to the souls of believers of *saying* that sometimes adultery is permitted. It seems safer for him to *suggest* (but only suggest) that what looks like adultery might, as in the extreme case he cites, not be adultery because, as Augustine says, "it was no lust, but great love for her husband, that demanded it, at his own bidding and will."[20] But, as even this "it looks like adultery but isn't" explanation runs some risk, his answer is conveyed in hint and indirection to such an extent that attempting to describe it requires subjunctives at every step.

So what might a Catholic reader learn about Catholicism from Strauss on this matter? Strauss writes: "The Thomistic doctrine of natural right, or, more generally expressed, of natural law" teaches "the immutable character of the fundamental propositions of natural law; the principles of the moral law, especially as formulated in the Second Table of the Decalogue, suffer no exception."[21] However, the case posed by Augustine shows that this does not quite distinguish Catholic natural right from "classical natural right" as it might seem to Strauss. Specifically, this Catholic natural law exceptionlessness does not yield the inflexibility (compared to Aristotle) that it would seem.

Strauss says of Aristotle that "in extreme situations the normally valid rules of natural right are justly changed, or changed in accordance with

---

20. Augustine, *Commentary on the Sermon of the Mount*, par. 50.
21. Strauss, *Natural Right and History*, 163.

natural right; the exceptions are as just as the rules.... there is not a single rule, however basic, which is not subject to exception."[22] In apparent contrast, he says the principles of Catholic natural right are immutable. But this formulation does not account for the case Augustine broaches; this case shows there is still a decisive role for prudence in Christian thought, as there is for Aristotle. At a minimum there is a need for judgment whether a specific act is one to which those principles do or do not apply.

What then might a Catholic reader learn from Strauss about why there is this difference in the manner in which classical and Catholic natural right present themselves? Let me suggest a possible answer from the prologue to Aquinas's *Summa Theologiae*:

Because the teacher of catholic truth ought to teach not only those who have advanced along the road but also to instruct beginners (according to the saying of the Apostle: As unto little ones in Christ, I gave you milk to drink not meat—I Cor. 3.1,2), we purpose in this book to treat of whatever belongs to the Christian religion in a way that is suited to the instruction of beginners.[23]

Might the hypothesis that the classics were writing primarily for philosophers and potential philosophers not for ordinary readers explain why classical natural right *more explicitly* recognizes "exceptions" to its universal principles than does Catholic natural right?[24] For their philosophical audience, the highest goal was to convey the theoretical truth. However, Aquinas and Augustine had to keep in mind the effect of his writing on ordinary priests and believers as well as on philosophers/theologians. For the latter audience, they had to teach the moral precepts with as much philosophical exactitude as possible, but "for beginners" they had to avoid the danger of giving scandal and undermining those principles by bringing up extreme exceptions remote from the troublesome human passions to which the moral precepts were directed.

One might respond that this explanation means that Catholic natural law teaches an untruth, namely, the apparent exceptionless principles of natural law are not quite exceptionless. I would respond that this

---

22. Ibid., 160.
23. Thomas Aquinas, *The Summa Theologica of Saint Thomas Aquinas*, trans. Fathers of the English Dominican Province, revised by Daniel J. Sullivan (London: Encyclopedia Brittanica, 1952), vol. 1.
24. This hypothesis as to the classics' audience is at odds with the thesis of Aristide Tessitore, *Reading Aristotle's Ethics* (Albany: State University of New York Press, 1996). Tessitore argues that Aristotle's *Ethics* and *Politics* were written for both citizens and philosophers. It is a question, however, whether Tessitore sufficiently distinguishes these audiences.

seeming exceptionlessness is not an untruth. The goal of the natural law teaching is to teach the universally true moral principles in such a way as to benefit rather than harm the reader. The goal is not to teach every last thing relevant to those principles or their application to particular cases.

The Zuckerts' 2006 study *The Truth about Leo Strauss* says something like this in defense of Strauss against the charge that he might teach "noble lies." They quote Strauss's 1948 introduction to his commentary on Xenophon's *Hiero*: "I believe that I have not dotted all the i's." The Zuckerts say that "not dotting all the i's is not to tell noble lies. Strauss ... practiced a 'noble reticence' or a 'pedagogical reserve,' rather than noble lying."[25]

One could similarly defend Catholic natural law's apparent exceptionlessness against the charge that it teaches an untruth. It is meant to teach the universal and unchanging moral principles while recognizing that not everything can be spelled out in the principles themselves ("pedagogical reserve"); and that a prudent regard for the well-being of ordinary Catholic readers makes it necessary to be reserved about what might *look like* (but might not *be*) exceptional cases ("noble reticence").

This difference between writing, on the one hand, for philosophers, potential philosophers, and theologians and, on the other hand, for ordinary priests and believers, would also shed light on a related important observation Strauss makes about "the Thomistic doctrine of natural right or, more generally expressed, of natural law." That doctrine

> is free from the hesitations and ambiguities which are characteristic of the teachings, not only of Plato and Cicero, but of Aristotle as well. In definiteness and noble simplicity it even surpasses the mitigated Stoic natural law teaching. No doubt is left, not only regarding the basic harmony between natural right and civil society, but likewise regarding the immutable character of the fundamental propositions of natural law; the principles of the moral law, especially as formulated in the Second Table of the Decalogue, suffer no exception, unless possibly by divine intervention.[26]

It would seem that "definiteness and noble simplicity" are necessary in a moral teaching intended to be taught to society as a whole. Similarly,

---

25. Catherine H. Zuckert and Michael P. Zuckert, *The Truth About Leo Strauss* (Chicago: University of Chicago Press, 2006), 136. The Strauss quotation can be found in Leo Strauss, *On Tyranny: Including the Strauss-Kojève Correspondence*, ed. Victor Gourevitch and Michael S. Roth (New York: Free Press, 1991), 28.

26. Strauss, *Natural Right and History*, 163. "Divine intervention" here may refer, e.g., to God's command to Abraham to sacrifice Isaac.

it would seem that hesitations and ambiguities are apparently unavoidable consequences of a moral teaching addressed to philosophers.

So a Catholic reader might learn from Strauss that the distinction he makes between classical and Christian natural right regarding exceptionlessness is not a distinction between two versions of a true moral teaching that conflict; rather, it is the distinction between the same true teaching addressed to philosophers, on the one hand, and to society as a whole on the other. If this is so, then my suggestion at the beginning of this essay that Strauss "appears to regard 'Roman Catholic Social Science' as an ally in his attempt to restore to social science the serious study of what justice is," can survive the apparent difference between classical natural right and Christian natural law concerning exceptionlessness.

However, this need not mean that the two traditions agree about every important application of the moral principles of natural right. In his 1962 lecture course in natural right, Strauss argued:

Aristotle teaches that exposure of infants and birth control are legitimate, Thomas Aquinas denies that, and the reason is the dignity of man as created in the image of God, and there is, of course, no such creation according to Aristotle. This question of the dignity of man in the Biblical or non-Biblical understanding is of the greatest importance up to the present day. I mean, for example, in penal law. The second massive substantive difference concerns slavery. From Aristotle's point of view legal slavery, i.e., the enslavement of men who are not by nature slaves, is simply unjust. Thomas Aquinas, following the Roman law, asserts that legal slavery is just and has been introduced as a benefit of the so-called *jus gentium*, of the law of nations, and namely it's a benefit because the victor could very well have killed them—the prisoners—and he does them a favor by only enslaving them.[27]

Obviously, these are real and serious disagreements. But what they show is substantive disagreement about what is eternally and immutably right by nature owing to Christianity's belief in biblical revelation, including man's creation by God and the absence of that belief in Aristotle. So the two traditions would not (or might not) be allies on such matters.[28]

---

27. "Natural Right," Lecture Course, Fall 1962, Lecture 11 (8–9). The Leo Strauss Center has the audio available but the transcript is listed as "pending." The audio may be found at https://leostrausscenter.uchicago.edu/course/natural-right-autumn-quarter-1962.

28. On the other hand, perhaps they could become allies even on these matters if one could make a case, purely on the basis of natural reason, that infanticide and birth control are unjust. Classical natural right does not require that there can be no improvement in reasons understanding of what is right by nature.

However, this disagreement would be within the broader agreement that there are eternal and immutable moral principles by nature. This broader agreement could still enable them to be allies against the regnant relativism which denies that there are such principles. But the limit of that alliance would be when belief in biblical revelation was *required* (not merely made easier or more convenient) for knowing the principles.

This returns the argument to where it was at the end of the first section above. However, in the meantime, I have concluded that Catholic natural law includes a flexibility akin to that of classical natural right. So, contrary to Strauss, divine revelation does not make Catholic natural law inflexible and unable "to cope with the inventiveness of the wicked."[29]

How Different Is Classical "Natural Reason" from Christian "Reason Informed by Faith"?

The decisiveness of the difference between belief and nonbelief in man's being created in the image and likeness of God remains to separate the classical and the Christian teachings on natural right. But even here I believe that Catholic readers can learn from Strauss not to overstate the difference between what can be known by reason alone and what can be known only (to use Strauss's phrase) by "reason informed by faith." Even though some things can only be known by reason informed by faith, a person of faith should be able to know what the classics could know by "natural reason simply" (also Strauss's phrase).

Strauss's explicit thought about Catholic natural law occurs almost entirely in his discussion of Aquinas. So, for present purposes, Strauss's thoughts about Catholicism equals his thoughts about Aquinas. Strauss interprets Aquinas's natural right as replacing what can be known by "natural reason simply" with what can be known by "reason informed by faith." The first thing is to understand what Strauss means by that.

"Reason informed by faith" is Strauss's translation occurring in *The City and Man*.[30] "In the words of Thomas Aquinas, reason informed by faith, not natural reason simply, to say nothing of corrupted reason, teaches that God is to be loved and worshipped."[31] The same translation is

---

29. Strauss, *Natural Right and History*, 161.
30. Leo Strauss, *The City and Man* (Chicago: Rand McNally, 1964), 35.
31. He cites the *Summa Theologiae* I-II, q. 104, a. 1, ad 3.

used by Strauss's students Father Ernest Fortin, in *Classical Christianity and the Political Order*, and by Harry Jaffa, in *Thomism and Aristotelianism*.[32] Both cite the same passage in the *Summa* that Strauss cites.

The Catholic scholar Robert Kraynak cites this translation in his essay on Jaffa's thought as presented in the latter's *Crisis of the Strauss Divided*. He says that Jaffa's *Thomism and Aristotelianism* "has shown that 'nature elevated by grace is different from nature simply' and that 'reason informed by faith' is different from reason simply."[33] Charles Kesler also quotes this translation in explicating Jaffa's thought.[34] Kesler merely quotes "reason informed by faith." He does not cite Aquinas. The foregoing would seem to show that "reason informed by faith" is the "Straussian" translation of Aquinas. This is worth noting partly because, as I will try to show, it is not an unproblematic translation and also because it permits the Straussian interpretation that reason so understood is fundamentally distinguished from "natural reason simply."

In contrast, what one might reasonably call the official "Catholic translation" available at the time is different and opens up a potentially different interpretation. *The Complete American Edition of the Summa*, translated by the Fathers of the English Dominican Province, translates the same passage as follows: "Even in those precepts which direct us to God, some are moral precepts, which *the reason itself dictates when it is quickened by faith*; such as that God is to be loved and worshipped."[35] An identical translation is found in Anton Pegis, *The Basic Writings of Thomas Aquinas*.[36] Pegis and the Dominican translations were the two most generally available translations when Strauss published his alternative translation in *The City and Man* in 1964.

Here is why the difference between the Straussian and the Catholic translation might matter. "Quickened" need not quite imply the distinction between "reason ... quickened by faith" and "natural reason simply,"

---

32. See Ernest Fortin, "The Political Thought of Thomas Aquinas," in *Classical Christianity and the Political Order*, ed. J. Brian Benestad (Lanham, Md.: Rowman and Littlefield, 1996), 175n57, and "Augustine, Thomas Aquinas, and the Problem of Natural Law," in *Classical Christianity and the Political Order*, ed. J. Brian Benestad (Lanham, Md.: Rowman and Littlefield, 1996), 221n87. Harry Jaffa, *Thomism and Aristotelianism* (Westport, Conn.: Greenwood Press, 1979), 200n20.

33. Harry V. Jaffa, *Crisis of the Strauss Divided* (Lanham, Md.: Rowman and Littlefield, 2012), 202.

34. Charles Kesler, "A New Birth of Freedom: Harry V. Jaffa and the Study of America," in *Leo Strauss, the Straussians and the American Regime*, ed. Kenneth Deutsch and John Murley (Lanham, Md.: Rowman and Littlefield, 1999), 265.

35. *Summa Theologiae* I-II, q. 104, ad 3; emphasis added.

36. Anton C. Pegis, *The Basic Writings of Thomas Aquinas* (Indianapolis, Ind.: Hackett, 1997).

at least not in the way Strauss understands "reason informed by faith" to do. "Reason informed by faith" would seem to be fundamentally different from "natural reason simply." However, "reason itself ... quickened by faith" need not be. So we need to figure out which translation best reflects Aquinas's thought. Here is the Latin: "Ad tertium dicendum quod etiam in his quae ordinant ad Deum, quaedam sunt moralia, quae ipsa ratio fide informata dictat, sicut Deum esse amandum et colendum."[37] The translation "reason *informed* by faith" implies that revelation adds *content* to the knowledge available to natural reason alone; so that one can know from "reason informed by faith" what cannot be known from "natural reason simply."

Now consider the O.E.D. definition of "quickened" as "made living or lively; animated, revived, stimulated." So "reason quickened by faith" might mean only that, while "natural reason simply" can *know* moral precepts, faith makes that knowledge *lively* to us thus stimulating us to act on the moral precepts that "natural reason simply" discovers. The crux of this difference depends on whether the translation "informed" or "quickened" more faithfully reflects what Aquinas means by "quae ratio fide informata dictat."

Let us begin by noting that Aquinas himself stresses that "natural reason," unaided by revelation, can know moral principles. He writes (objections 1–3, q. 104, a. 1):

As is evident from what we have stated above (Q. 95, A. 2; Q. 99, A. 4), in every law, some precepts derive their binding force from the dictate of reason itself, *because natural reason dictates that something ought to be done or to be avoided. These are called "moral" precepts: since human morals are based on reason*. At the same time there are other precepts which derive their binding force, not from the very dictate of reason (because, considered in themselves, they do not imply an obligation of something due or undue); but from some institution, Divine or human: and such are certain determinations of the moral precepts.

This passage occurs in the *Summa* less than half a page before the passage Strauss quotes to show that for Aquinas "reason informed by faith [is] not natural reason simply." And does this second passage not make explicit that, while Aquinas grants that there are *some* precepts which are based on "some institution human or divine," not all moral precepts are

---

37. *Summa Theologiae* I-II, q. 104, a. 1, ad 3; emphasis added.

so based? Some are based on natural law and can be known from natural reason alone.

So whatever Aquinas might mean by *ratio fide informata* it cannot mean that there is no other kind of reason that provides valid knowledge of moral precepts than that which is "informed by faith." There is also "natural reason" which can know moral precepts merely as a "dictate of reason itself" without the aid of revelation.

This distinction is strengthened by reminding ourselves of the passage quoted by Strauss in which Aquinas refers to *ratio fide informata*: "reason informed by faith, not natural reason simply, to say nothing of corrupted reason, teaches that God is to be loved and worshipped." Even if "that God is to be loved and worshipped" presupposes faith, it does not imply that the existence of "reason informed by faith" suggests that there is not also natural reason simply. And Aquinas makes explicit the existence of "natural reason simply" and its capacity to know some "moral" precepts which exist independently of being known by revelation.

So where does this leave a reader concerning Strauss's interpretation that Catholic (i.e., "Thomistic") natural right replaces what can be known by "natural reason simply" with what can be known by "reason informed by faith"? I think it leaves us with the more accurate understanding that this is not the case. The first reason it is not the case is that *informata* does not have to be understood to add (as Strauss suggests) to what *ratio* ("natural reason simply") can know; rather it can be understood to add in addition to what natural reason simply can know, *motivation to act on that knowledge* (as the "Catholic" translation suggests) in the form of "liveliness, animation, revival or stimulation." The second reason it is not the case is that Strauss seems to think that for Aquinas only "reason informed by faith" and not "natural reason simply" can know the moral precepts of natural law. But Aquinas's explicit statement quoted above shows that this is not his understanding.

It might be a third reason why this is not the case to remind ourselves that Strauss attributes the (allegedly) exceptionless character of Christian natural law "to the influence of belief in Biblical Revelation."[38] It was the burden of the second part of this essay to show that this is not quite the case. But even if it was the case, because we can now say that a Christian could know some of the moral precepts of the natural law from natural

---

38. See above, end of the first section, and Strauss, *Natural Right and History*, 163.

reason simply without the aid of revelation, he could know the exceptions to those precepts that were known to the ancients. Although technically Strauss might not call such knowledge "Christian natural law" (because it is not based on revelation) it would be natural law knowable by and binding on a Christian.

Which Is More Important: The Common Ground or the Distinction between Strauss and Catholic Natural Right?

I hope the foregoing will assist a Catholic reader in figuring out both the very great common ground between classical natural right, as understood by Strauss, and Catholic natural right/natural law as understood by Aquinas and Augustine—as well as the difference between them. They diverge concerning whether human beings are created in the image of God, but that difference does not prevent them from being, to a considerable extent, allies against the relativism of Strauss's time and ours.

I hope it will also assist such a reader in not overstating the distance between these two branches of the natural right tree. It would be understandable if a Catholic reader were to reject Aristotle's ethical teaching as a whole because it sanctions what Strauss gently calls "exposure of infants" (today we would say infanticide) and birth control. And it is well for Catholic readers to be shocked at these things because it reminds us how important it is that we are Christians and that Aristotle is not. Aquinas, it has long been said, "baptized Aristotle." Because Catholics have thereafter largely received Aristotle by way of Aquinas, it is easy for us to forget that the alleged baptism did not do away with these pagan elements in Aristotle's thought itself.

I hope the foregoing study shows that a Catholic reader might learn at least the following three things from this retracing of Strauss's study of Aquinas and of his pointing us to Augustine: (1) that some of the moral precepts of what is right by nature are to some extent knowable by Catholics through "natural reason simply"; (2) that we need to distinguish these from the moral precepts which require revelation (such as that "God is to be loved and worshipped" and that infanticide is contrary to natural right because human nature is made in the image of God); and

(3) that grasping this difference is facilitated by careful study of "classical natural right," which did not have that revelation. I hope that my attempted corrections of Strauss as I proceeded in this study did not distract the reader from what might be learned from him.

Finally, I hope a Catholic reader might learn from studying Strauss's understanding of the history of political philosophy the importance of learning, treasuring, and defending what reason alone can teach us about what is right by nature even if (1) it cannot teach us everything we need to know about that, and even if (2) we find ourselves shocked by what reason alone sometimes teaches without revelation. For it is good for us to learn what should distinguish us morally as believers, as well as what can unite us with those well disposed readers who have only natural reason to guide them.

 10

The Influence of Historicism on Catholic Theology

J. BRIAN BENESTAD

The purpose of this chapter is to show the influence of historicism on the theology of two prominent Catholic theologians, Sister Elizabeth Johnson and Father Charles Curran. Johnson is what the profession calls a systematic or doctrinal theologian, while Curran calls himself a revisionist moral theologian, as do many other moral theologians. After my theological studies it was the remembrance of an essay by Leo Strauss on historicism that alerted me to the overwhelming influence of this philosophical approach on influential strains of contemporary Catholic theology. I chose to examine Johnson and Curran because they are regarded by many Catholic theologians as leaders in their respective fields.

When I was a college student, Father Ernest Fortin introduced me to Strauss's *Natural Right and History* in which is found an insightful chapter on historicism entitled "Natural Right and the Historical Approach."[1] Rereading that chapter after my theological studies led me to see more clearly the role that historicism especially played in the development of revisionist moral theology after the publication of Pope Paul VI's encyclical, *Humanae Vitae*. Historicism denies that anyone can discover uni-

---

1. Leo Strauss, *Natural Right and History* (Chicago: University of Chicago Press, 1953).

versal truths or universal norms that are valid for everyone for all time. Strauss explains: "All human thought is historical and hence unable to grasp anything eternal. Whereas, according to the ancients, philosophizing means to leave the cave, according to our contemporaries all philosophizing essentially belongs to a 'historical world,' 'culture,' civilization, 'Weltanschauung,' that is, to what Plato called the cave. We shall call this view historicism."[2] The study of history teaches us "that a given view has been abandoned in favor of another view by all men, or by all competent men, or perhaps by the most vocal men."[3] The last point means that it may be a vocal minority in a particular age that rejects what was once thought to be a timeless truth, and may or may not persuade the great majority to accept the new view.

Strauss adds: "Since all human thought belongs to a specific historical situation, all human thought is found to perish with the situation to which it belongs and to be superseded by new unpredictable thoughts."[4] An example of what Strauss seems to mean is that marriage required a man and a woman in a great number of historical situations, but is now gradually being superseded by the view that two men or two women can marry. A future age may find that three people may enter into a marriage. With respect to the wisdom of any change on important matters such as marriage, Strauss comments that history "does not teach us whether the change was sound, or whether the rejected view deserved to be rejected.... Strictly speaking, we cannot choose among different views. A single comprehensive view is imposed on us by fate: the horizon within which all our understanding and orientation take place is produced by the fate of the individual or his society."[5]

The Hidden Influence of Historicism on Sister Johnson's Theology

With Strauss's thoughts on the basics of historicism in mind let us first turn to Sister Elizabeth Johnson's *Quest for the Living God: Mapping Frontiers in the Theology of God*. Her book, she argues, aims to express an un-

2. Ibid., 12.
3. Ibid., 19.
4. Ibid.
5. Ibid., 19, 27.

derstanding of God that will more effectively promote justice, peace, and love in the world than traditional theologies of God, which she claims sometimes justified oppression of the poor and women. She is especially interested in the transformation of social structures that will establish justice for women and gradually establish the Kingdom of God on earth.

Johnson further argues that "the practice of justice and peace actually mediates a profound experience of the mystery of God."[6] She seems to mean that the right kind of political and social action gives knowledge of God. In another formulation she says: "Knowing God is impossible unless we enter into a life of love and communion with others."[7] In other words, to come to a deep understanding of the faith, people have to live it in their daily lives. In making this kind of argument she sounds like a disciple of St. Augustine, but a closer look reveals that this is not the case. Other passages in the book seem to indicate that Johnson's theological approach is not based on the faith of the church. That is the contention of the Committee on Doctrine of the United States Conference of Catholic Bishops (USCCB), which issued a statement regarding *Quest for the Living God* on March 24, 2011.

In an open letter (June 6, 2011) to the U.S. bishops' committee Johnson claims that the committee is seriously mistaken to argue that she does not base her book on the faith of the church: "Not only does *Quest for the Living God* begin with the faith of the Church, but it also ends there as well."[8] She is confidently able to make this statement because, in her interpretation, Vatican Council II's *Lumen Gentium* "positions the church as all the people of God.... Such is the understanding of the faith of the church that frames my book. It is the faith of the people of God."[9] The key question is whether or not this is a correct interpretation of Vatican II and an adequate response to the doctrine committee's argument. Does Johnson simply have a theological approach different from that of the bishops' committee, or does she change the faith of the church both by her manner of consulting the people of God and her mode of doing theology? May she properly put more faith in what the people of God say today than in scripture, tradition, and the teaching authority of the church?

---

6. Elizabeth Johnson, *Quest for the Living God: Mapping Frontiers in the Theology of God* (New York: Continuum, 2007), 86.
7. Ibid., 223.
8. Johnson, "Open Letter to the Committee on Doctrine of the United States Conference of Catholic Bishops," *Origins* 41, no. 9 (July 7, 2011): 132, sec. 1, par. 2.
9. Ibid., pars. 8–9.

The first thing to note is that the teaching of Vatican Council II does not allow for the interpretation of the church merely as the "people of God." Vatican II documents use "body of Christ" more often to describe the church. *Lumen Gentium* teaches that the body of Christ is visibly and hierarchically organized.

Secondly, Johnson only makes contact with selected sectors of the people of God by attending to eight theologies emerging from the praxis and thought of eight groups of people. She names these theologies transcendental, political, liberation, feminist/womanist, black, Latino/Latina, interreligious, and ecological. Because Johnson understands them to be "the living Christian tradition in our day" and "deeply concerned with God's relationship to the world," she deems it sufficient to consult these groups alone in order to know the mind and heart of the people of God.[10] What about the views and theologies of other members of the people of God such as pro-life and pro-family organizations, the Knights of Columbus, Opus Dei, Communio e Liberazione, the Neo-Catechumenal Way, etc.?

Johnson ascribes normative character to the view of the faith espoused by her selected groups on the basis of their experience. She does not explicitly measure the praxis of these groups or their theologies against scripture, tradition, or the longstanding teaching of the church's magisterium. She simply assumes that the "people's lived religiosity" is an expression of the *sensus fidelium*, which she defines as "the teaching that the body of the faithful as a whole, baptized, anointed, and moved by the Spirit, has an intuitive grasp of matters of belief that is ultimately reliable."[11] Johnson makes no distinction between those people in her eight groups who adhere to the *sensus fidei* and those who pay no attention to it. She does not acknowledge that people's lived religiosity is only a reliable indicator of the church's teaching if it springs from the *sensus fidei*.

Johnson's mode of theologizing begins with praxis, lived religiosity, lived experience rather than doctrine. The praxis is primary and serves as the norm for judging a religion's vitality. In Sister Johnson's words, "the whole book is written ... to present the knowledge of the living God arising from different insights and practices of the faith in the church, knowledge which I judge to be true."[12] She, of course, is referring to the

10. Johnson, *Quest*, 47, 16.
11. Ibid., 140.
12. Johnson, "Open Letter," 137, sec. 5, par. 4.

contemporary practices of her selected eight groups in the people of God. She does not first look for the knowledge of the living God in the *depositum fidei* preserved by the Catholic church over the centuries. What really matters is what the contemporary people of God say, not the *sensus fidei* and the teaching of the church from the time of Christ.

Still another way to get at the heart of her theological approach based on praxis is to look at what she says in her chapter on the "Liberating God of Life." "Liberation theology has long insisted on the priority of praxis for right thinking. Rather than starting with a correct principle, whether of reason or faith, you have to be walking as a disciple, placing your feet in the footsteps of Jesus and actively seeking to bring about the reign of God, in order for your thought to be true."[13] Without the aid of doctrine, how would people recognize if they were really walking in the footsteps of Marx, and working to realize his vision, rather than the Kingdom of God?

In looking to the views of her selected sector of the people of God as her highest source of knowledge about God, Johnson, not surprisingly, finds scripture and church teaching deficient in significant respects. For example, with respect to scripture she writes that "a profound challenge goes forth to the whole church: stop trivializing the scandalous statements that scripture makes about God."[14] She further slams a New Testament writer for his statement about women in 1 Timothy 2:11–15, claiming that this offensive passage "triggered an appalling tradition" of discrimination against women in the church.[15]

With respect to church teaching Johnson says: "In this wintry season, church statements about God are ordinarily too naive and too superficial to help believers, let alone convince unbelievers."[16] She further adds that traditional teaching and doctrine have been neutral in the face of injustice.[17] In fact, traditional Christian doctrine has encouraged resig-

---

13. Johnson, *Quest*, 83.
14. Ibid., 80–81.
15. Ibid., 92. Translation used by Sister Johnson: "Let a woman learn in silence with full submission. I permit no woman to teach or have authority over a man; she is to keep silent. For Adam was formed first, then Eve; and Adam was not deceived, but the woman was deceived, and became a transgressor. Yet she will be saved through childbearing." A literal translation from the Greek could read: "Let a woman learn in silence with all submissiveness. I permit no woman to teach or to domineer over a man [or her husband]; she is to keep silent. For Adam was formed first, then Eve; and Adam was not deceived, but the woman was deceived and became a transgressor. Yet woman will be saved through bearing children, if she continues in faith and love and holiness, with self control." Johnson omitted the list of virtues necessary for salvation, mentioned in the second part of v. 15.
16. Ibid., 30.
17. Ibid., 80.

nation to the suffering of the poor.[18] The church has also covered up the presence of the Spirit of God in all people because of her long polemic against nonbelievers. She claims that the church is wrong to teach that God is omnipotent or impassible. With Moltmann and Soelle, Johnson believes that God suffers in his divine nature. She further implies that church teaching referring to God as a person is useless. "We don't really understand what it means to attribute personhood to God."[19] In addition, she argues that we "literally don't know what we are saying" when we call God good.[20]

While discussing the experience of African-American women as a *locus theologicus*, she seems to take issue with the doctrine of the redemption in reporting on black women's "experience of surrogacy": "Redemption can have nothing to do with a bloody act of one person being killed in place of another."[21] This way of envisaging the redemption causes the "repugnant slave-master image of God to loom large."[22] She is critical of *Dominus Jesus*, the church document that explains the unique salvific role of Christ while discussing the relation of Christianity to other religions. Believing that the Holy Spirit does unique things in non-Christian religions, she affirms the following statement by Jacques Dupuis: "More divine truth and grace are found operative in the entire course of God's dealings with humankind than are available simply in the Christian religion."[23] For Johnson religious pluralism should be regarded as a "divine gift."[24]

Let us come back to Johnson's skepticism about using words such as person and good to describe God. She also refuses to accept the Father-Son language as revelatory of God's reality. However, without key words the content of faith cannot be intellectually expressed, and then believers cannot express to themselves or others what they really believe. Even more important, the church cannot propose truths to which people can give the assent of faith. How could evangelization be possible if the faith of the church cannot be expressed in intelligible, meaningful words? There has to be unity of faith in the Catholic church, and that faith must

18. Ibid., 73.
19. Ibid., 19.
20. Ibid.
21. Ibid., 129.
22. Ibid., 130.
23. Ibid., 163.
24. Ibid., 178.

be expressible in intelligible words. Otherwise, not only will contrary practices and divergent creeds arise, but also the very intelligibility of the created order is undermined. Faith becomes an irrational leap into darkness.

In her open letter, Johnson denies rejecting the use of all words to talk about God: "Note that the book explicitly states that our words do affirm something of God."[25] Johnson accepts language coming from the people of God to describe their experience of God, but she definitely rejects key words deriving from the greater Catholic tradition.

In order to better understand what stands behind Johnson's historicist approach it is helpful to examine what Pope John Paul II has said about historicism: "The fundamental claim of historicism ... is that the truth of a philosophy is determined on the basis of its appropriateness to a certain period and a certain historical purpose. At least implicitly, therefore, the enduring validity of truth is denied. What was true in one period, historicists claim, may not be true in another."[26] When theologians readily accept this perspective as a philosophical trump card, one can readily see how they can change church doctrine without thinking that they are in any way unfaithful to the ecclesial vocation of the theologian.

Johnson's manner of consulting the people of God reveals that the embrace of historical consciousness or historicism is, wittingly or unwittingly, the ultimate foundation of her theological approach, as it is for many contemporary moral theologians. Her eight groups—not scripture or the magisterium—put us in contact with "the living tradition of the Church" which changes according to the demands of the historical situation. What this means in practice is that there can be no appeal to the longstanding faith of the church to correct or guide the people of God. Church teaching, Johnson argues, has to adjust to "the changing history of human cultures."

When circumstances change, the experience of the divine undergoes a shift. Images, intellectual constructs, and rituals that mediated a sense of God in one age often do not make sense in the next with its change of perceptions, values, and lifestyles. The search must be undertaken anew if religious traditions are to remain vibrant and alive. As her book aims to show, the fact that in our day multiple, rich Christian theologies

---

25. Johnson, "Open Letter," 138, sec. 5, par. 15.
26. Pope John Paul II, *Fides et Ratio*, Encyclical Letter, September 14, 1988, par. 87.

have been seeking and finding the living God in ways coherent with our changing times testifies that this particular way remains a vital, viable option.[27]

These "rich Christian theologies" are, of course, those emerging from the praxis of the eight groups selected by Johnson as most likely to mediate a sense of God. Johnson is actually recommending that teaching about God cohere with the changing times and not vice versa, as the Catholic church has taught from the beginning. She, of course, has faith that her people of God will discern the good from the bad in the changing times.

Johnson believes that her chosen people of God have embraced positions that will bring the kind of *aggiornamento* desired by Vatican Council II. In reading Johnson's account of the emerging theologies of the eight groups, one cannot help but notice that they all are on the same progressive wavelength. Her consultation of the people of God is so selective that there is no doubt as to the outcome: her people of God, tutored by theologians, now embrace the program of the religious and political left and have with their magisterial authority, bestowed by Vatican II, modified the perennial teaching of the church and will continue to do so in the future according to the demands of the times.

As mentioned, Johnson expects the transformation of social structures to "usher in the reign of God" partially and gradually.[28] This position reflects a major tenet of modern political philosophy: change of structures is more effective in bringing about reform than the practice of virtue or holiness. To speak the way Johnson does about the transformation of social structures is to imply, wittingly or unwittingly, that political action is more effective in working for the Kingdom of God than evangelization or the worthy reception of the eucharist. *Quest* does not even mention receiving the sacrament of the eucharist is a special way to know and love God, and to generate love of one's neighbor.

To use Machiavelli's revealing terminology, *Quest for the Living God* is a book that introduces "new modes and orders." By an erroneous interpretation of Vatican II's teaching on the people of God, under the influence of historicism, Johnson removes the traditional foundations of the Catholic faith and places in jeopardy the realization of the love and justice that she ardently desires.

---

27. Johnson, *Quest*, 13, 23.
28. Ibid., 84.

Curran Invokes Historicism to Justify His Moral Theology

Let us now turn to Charles Curran's *The Development of Moral Theology: Five Strands*, published by Georgetown University Press in 2013. Curran's revisionist moral theology, under the strong influence of historical consciousness or historicism, took shape when not a few Catholic theologians dissented from the reaffirmation of Catholic teaching on contraception by Pope Paul VI in his 1968 encyclical, *Humanae Vitae*.

Curran maintains that we can better understand Catholic revisionism, as well as the rest of contemporary Catholic moral theology, if we examine five strands present in the history of the Catholic church: "(1) sin, reconciliation, and the manuals of moral theology; (2) Thomas Aquinas and the Thomistic tradition; (3) natural law; (4) the papal teaching office; and (5) the Second Vatican Council."[29] I will only focus on those aspects of the strands that help clarify the development or shape of Curran's revisionist moral theology.

The purpose of chapter 1, on the first strand, is to explain the understanding of sin and forgiveness that developed over the centuries in the church. Curran especially takes issue with the manuals of moral theology that were written after the Council of Trent in the sixteenth century. With their very limited scope, these manuals could correctly be described as minimalistic. Their only concern was what acts were sinful and the degree of sinfulness. There was no consideration of growth in the Christian life, the call to live out the baptismal commitment, or the virtues perfecting the human person and disposing the person to good actions in this life. Many people familiar with Catholic moral theologians were amazed that Vatican II could insist on the call of all Christians to perfection.[30] Curran sees his revisionist theology as a guide for Christians seeking to answer Vatican II's call to live a life of perfect holiness.

Chapter 2, on "Thomas Aquinas and the Thomistic Tradition," describes the moral theology of Aquinas, the rise of "Second Thomism" in the sixteenth century, and the beginning of "Third Thomism" in the nineteenth century under the leadership of Pope Leo XIII. One conclu-

---

29. Charles Curran, *The Development of Moral Theology: Five Strands* (Washington, D.C.: Georgetown University Press, 2013), ix.
30. Ibid., 24.

sion Curran reaches in this chapter is that "the imposition of Thomistic philosophy and theology had a significant influence in the life of the Catholic Church in the nineteenth and twentieth centuries but never changed or even challenged the approach of the manuals of moral theology that by their very nature were not Thomistic."[31] Curran also believes that Pope Leo XIII and subsequent popes used Aquinas "to prevent any dialogue with contemporary thought in their struggle with modernity."[32] Finally, Curran says that in the twentieth century "a pluralism existed among Thomistic approaches" and that Neo-Scholastic Thomism failed to give "enough importance to historicity and the subject." In other words, Curran is arguing that the prevailing Thomism of the twentieth century did not embrace historical consciousness, the new emphasis on the person, or enter into dialogue with contemporary thought, as he did in his revisionist theology.

Curran believes that revisionist moral theology is a form of natural law (strand three) that is rooted in the teaching of Vatican Council II (strand five) on "historical consciousness," the *"sensus fidelium,"* and the human person. Curran believes that Pope Paul VI endorsed the stress on historical consciousness in his 1971 Apostolic Letter, *Octogesima Adveniens*, which was addressed to Cardinal Maurice Roy. Other revisionist theologians make the same claim. Curran further argues that revisionist theology requires dissent from and disagreement with papal teaching put forth through the ordinary papal magisterium (strand four).

Curran begins his explanation of what he means by historical consciousness in the chapter on natural law. He says that "revisionists agree that a historically conscious approach should replace the classicism of the accepted natural law theory."[33] By classicism Curran is referring to the view that human nature is a given that does not change over time. "The classicist methodology," he says, "tends to be abstract, a priori, and deductive. It begins with the abstract essence that is universal and immutable. Thus, in natural law theory the principle of morality is established and then other universal norms of conduct are deduced from it."[34] The advocates of historical consciousness, on the other hand, use an inductive, *a posteriori*, concrete methodology. They take notice of where people are

31. Ibid., 64.
32. Ibid., 54.
33. Ibid., 99.
34. Ibid., 99–100.

and what they are doing, how "they are performing intentional acts that give meaning and significance to human living."[35] Later in his text Curran gives an example of what his historicist approach means in practice. Because a great number of Catholic married couples practice contraception, he says that the "hierarchical teaching office" should no longer teach that "contraception is a grave moral evil."[36] Otherwise stated, the practice of Catholics should make bishops and pope realize that new truths have developed over time. Curran goes so far as to say that "the discrepancy between hierarchical teaching and the practice of married Catholics raises serious questions about the credibility of the hierarchical teaching office."[37]

The implication of Curran's remarks regarding church teaching on contraception is that truth emerges from the praxis of the Catholic people. He makes clear that he and fellow revisionist theologians believe that a change in Catholic teaching should take place not only in the area of contraception, but also "on such issues as masturbation, sterilization, artificial insemination, in vitro fertilization, homosexuality, divorce, premarital sexuality, and aspects of the abortion issue."[38] Curran's understanding of historicism leads him to draw the conclusion that discrepancies between magisterial teaching and widespread practices among Catholics should necessarily be resolved in favor of the latter.

It is interesting to note that the magisterium said next to nothing about historicism until the appearance in 1998 of *Fides et Ratio*, in which Pope John Paul II briefly mentioned the essence of historicism. It is worth repeating the pope's fundamental insight. "The fundamental claim of historicism ... is that the truth of a philosophy is determined on the basis of its appropriateness to a certain period and a certain historical purpose. At least implicitly, therefore, the enduring validity of a truth is denied. What was true in one period, historicists claim, may not be true in another."[39] So what the Bible said in the past may have been true for its time period, but not for all time. Not surprisingly, historicist theologians claim that the teaching authority of the church can never definitively settle any specific moral issue and some doctrinal matters, such as women's

35. Ibid., 99.
36. Ibid., 132.
37. Ibid.
38. Ibid., 131.
39. John Paul II, *Fides et Ratio*, par. 87.

ordination, with authoritative teaching. This is because reality supposedly does not allow such a thing. For example, not a few theologians and public intellectuals now say that today's historical circumstances call for the legal recognition of same-sex marriage. Some would go so far as to say that the Catholic church should change its teaching on marriage and thus adapt to the concrete historical situation in which different groups are calling upon the church to give moral approval to same-sex unions. The very fact that people in sufficient number or influence object to a particular church teaching is, according to historicist theologians, a *locus theologicus* and should guide the magisterium in its teaching on moral matters.

Curran's claim that Paul VI and Vatican Council II support his acceptance of historicism is without merit. As proof that Paul VI "incorporates a historically conscious methodology" Curran quotes the following paragraph from *Octogesima Adveniens* (par. 4):

> In the face of such widely varying situations, it is difficult for us to have a unified message and to put forward a solution which has universal validity. Such is not our ambition, nor is it our mission. It is up to the Christian communities to analyze with objectivity the situation which is proper to their own country, to shed on it the light of the Gospel's unalterable words, and to draw principles of reflection, norms of judgment and directives for action from the social teaching of the Church.... It is up to these Christian communities, with the help of the Holy Spirit in communion with the bishops who hold responsibility and in dialogue with other Christian brethren and all men of good will, to discern the options and commitments which are called for in order to bring about the social, political, and economic changes seen in many cases to be urgently needed.[40]

Rather than endorsing what Curran means by historical consciousness, Paul VI is describing how Catholics endowed with political prudence apply Catholic teaching to local issues. Take, for example, the introduction of the common core state standards (CCSS) into public and Catholic education. Catholics could not reasonably expect a pope to answer the question whether there is merit to adopting the new educational standards. Rather, it is up to them to study the issue and determine on the basis of perennial Catholic teaching whether CCSS would improve or hurt public or Catholic primary and secondary education.

As for Vatican II, Curran claims that the Council moved from clas-

---

40. Curran, *Development of Moral Theology*, 135.

sicism to an embrace of a historically conscious worldview by the way it discussed *ressourcement* (a return to the sources of Christian teaching, especially biblical and patristic texts) and *aggiornamento* (bringing the Catholic church up-to-date), and by changing the church's teaching on religious liberty. He does concede that *ressourcement* "does not necessarily involve a shift to historical consciousness."[41] He provides no evidence to show that Vatican II's understanding of *aggiornamento* included his view of historical consciousness. Curran does make an unpersuasive argument to show that Vatican II's teaching on religious liberty endorses a view of historical consciousness that would allow theologians to justify dissent from church teaching when it is based on a classicist worldview.

Curran makes much of the fact that the *Declaration on Religious Liberty* begins with these words:

> A sense of the dignity of the human person has been impressing itself more and more deeply on the consciousness of contemporary persons. And the demand is increasingly made that human beings should act on their own judgment, enjoying and making use of a responsible freedom.... This demand for freedom ... regards in the first place, the free exercise of religion in society.... This Vatican Synod takes careful note of these desires.... It proposes to declare them to be greatly in accord with truth and justice.[42]

Curran's comment on this passage is as follows: "The Council fathers thus recognized that they learned the importance of religious freedom from the experience of people."[43] Such experience is of the utmost importance in Curran's approach because it is the experience of persons, which is a *locus theologicus* in his mind. So, if Catholic spouses experience contraception as a good for their marriage, then church authorities should take notice of this experience and declare it to be "in accord with truth and justice." Curran fails to realize that Vatican II does not base its argument for religious liberty on the simple desire of people to have religious liberty. Rather, the Council declares the desire for religious liberty to be "in accord with truth and justice." The implication is that every strong desire of persons and every praxis would have to be submitted to the same criteria.

The reason Curran puts so much stock in the practice of Catholics is

---

41. Ibid., 236.
42. Quoted in ibid., 248.
43. Ibid.

not only his acceptance of historicism, but also his understanding of the people of God and the *sensus fidelium* or the *sensus fidei*. Curran directs attention to Vatican II's *Lumen Gentium*, no. 12, where the Council fathers say that "the totality of the faithful, who have the anointing of the Holy One, cannot err in matters of belief." Because all the faithful participate in the prophetic office of Jesus, it is no longer correct to distinguish between the *ecclesia docens* (teaching church) from the *ecclesia discens* (learning church). Curran further argues that one should no longer refer to the teaching authority of the pope and bishops as the magisterium but as the hierarchical magisterium. He is really saying that the people of God, with their *sensus fidei*, constitute a kind of magisterium because they are guided by the Holy Spirit. Curran then adds that according to Catholic theology, "authoritative Church teaching has to be received by the whole Church."[44] This means that the unwillingness of the laity to receive a particular church teaching calls into question the validity of that teaching. He mistakenly puts forth these points as the teaching of Vatican II.

Lumen Gentium says more about the *sensus fidei* than Curran indicates. Right after its statement about the inability of the totality of the faithful to err in matters of belief, it adds, "[the faithful] manifest this special property by means of the whole people's supernatural sense of faith [*sensu fidei*], when 'from the Bishops down to the last of the lay faithful' they show universal agreement in matters of faith and morals" (no. 12). There's no question of pitting the teaching authority of the lay faithful against the magisterium of the church; it is what the laity and the bishops believe together that is theologically significant. As Avery Dulles noted, "The sense of the faithful should be carefully distinguished from public opinion in the Church, which is not a theological source attributable to the Holy Spirit, but merely a sociological fact. Public opinion ... often reflects the tendencies of our fallen nature, the trends of the times, and the pressures of the public media."[45]

As for the reception of church teaching, Dulles argues that it "is necessary for the efficacy of any teaching," but it may or may not be forthcoming. When it comes to contraception and other areas of sexual morality Curran displays no sense that a majority of Catholics could refuse to accept Catholic teaching for bad reasons. Dulles is again right on the

---

44. Ibid., 265.
45. Avery Cardinal Dulles, *Magisterium: Teacher and Guardian of the Faith* (Naples, Fla.: Sapientia Press, 2007), 45.

mark when he says, "The mere absence of reception does not count as evidence against a teaching unless the opposition is animated by the spirit of Christ and the gospel. Otherwise, the dissent may prove only that the teaching is in conflict with the spirit of the times and what Paul would call the desires of the flesh."[46] Catholic laity may or may not be in tune with the Holy Spirit. When Catholics are deceived by the spirit of the age, some authentic church teaching will appear as a sign of contradiction.

Vatican II's teaching on the person, according to Curran, not only explains the significance of personal experience for the discernment of moral truth, but also requires a "personalistic approach to moral theology."[47] This entails a dismissal of the manuals of moral theology with their emphasis on individual moral actions and their degree of sinfulness. The emphasis must be "on the universal vocation of all Christians to perfection" and on the practice of the virtues as the way to show a grateful response to God's gift of salvation.[48] "The relationship to God is core."[49]

The personalist approach also leads Curran and other revisionist theologians to accuse the popes of embracing physicalism or biologism in their moral teaching. This charge "criticizes the hierarchical approach for identifying the moral and human act with the physical or biological aspect of the act."[50] This is certainly a misplaced criticism of Paul VI and John Paul II. The latter, for example, shows how he approaches moral acts in his interpretation of the conjugal act. Through sexual intercourse spouses say to one another, "I want to be one with you and am willing to have a child with you." This is hardly physicalism. Ironically, the revisionists are the real physicalists, as they downplay the object of an act in favor of the intention, so that human acts remain merely physical until you ascertain the intention of the acting agent. Following the revisionist understanding, for example, an umpire should not penalize a pitcher for throwing at a batter until he ascertains the pitcher's intention. The mere throwing at a batter is the physical act; the intention of the pitcher reveals the real nature of the act, as if there is not an intention built into the act of throwing at the batter.

Curran's emphasis on our relationship with God, seeking perfection

46. Ibid., 107.
47. Curran, *Development of Moral Theology*, 246.
48. Ibid., 246, 258.
49. Ibid., 258.
50. Ibid., 98.

and the practice of the virtues is, of course, right on target as a teaching of Vatican II. Curran, however, effectively undermines the Vatican II teaching by his interpretation of historical consciousness, which in many cases reduces the moral demands on the acting agent.

Curran's revisionist theology also calls for overcoming what he calls the papalization of the church, by which Curran means that popes have arrogated too much authority for themselves. Popes must admit, Curran argues, that their non-infallible, authoritative, and official teaching has been wrong in the past and can be wrong in the future. They must also be willing to recognize a greater teaching role for bishops, theologians, and the *sensus fidelium* which, Curran believes, existed in the past. One way to enhance the authority of the bishops would be to change the way the Synod of Bishops operates. Pope Paul VI established the Synod in 1965 to counsel the pope. "But if the synod were truly an exercise of collegiality in the Church," argues Curran, "it should have the power to share in the governing of the Church and not just give advice to the pope."[51] The reason Curran calls for more sharing of authority is his interpretation of the operation of the Spirit in the church. "As a consequence of recognizing the work of the Spirit in all the baptized, it follows that the teaching role in the Church is broader than just that of the hierarchical magisterium."[52] The total magisterium should not only include the *sensus fidelium* of the Catholic laity, but also the magisterium of the theologians. "Recall," Curran writes, "that in the Middle Ages everyone recognized that theologians had a magisterial role, but now that role is not authoritative."[53] Curran does not address the issue of coordinating the various organs of the all-encompassing magisterium in the church, though he does say, as previously mentioned, that the beliefs and praxis of the laity as well as the consensus of revisionist theologians can trump authoritative papal teaching.

Eternal Truth and History

When all is said and done, the key issue in the revisionist theology of Curran and the systematic theology of Johnson is their deference to a particular view of historical consciousness. Elizabeth Johnson and Charles

---
51. Ibid., 271.
52. Ibid., 249.
53. Ibid., 193.

Curran are the kind of historicist s described in Pope John Paul II's *Fides et Ratio*, no. 87, and in Strauss's *Natural Right and History*. Why should we all bow down before the historicist understanding of historical consciousness? Why should Catholic moral theology and systematic theology now take their bearings by historicism? Neither Curran nor Johnson ever adequately answers these two questions.

Curran and Johnson owe their readers answers because there is a lot at stake in the acceptance of historical consciousness by revisionist moral theology and systematic theology. Writing way back in 1940, Strauss captured the high drama of the situation using almost the same words as John Paul II's *Fides et Ratio*: "The view that truth is eternal and that there are eternal standards, was contradicted by historical consciousness, i.e. by the opinion that all 'truths' and standards are relative to a given historical situation, and that, consequently a mature philosophy can raise no higher claim than to express the spirit of the period to which it belongs." Strauss went on to say that historical consciousness came into being at a certain point and will again pass out of existence, to be replaced by something else, most likely a "new barbarism."[54] One could, at least, argue that the acceptance of historical consciousness by Catholic theologians is self-complacent because it blithely accepts that truths are relative to a given historical period and gives up the quest to transcend the limitations of the culture in which one lives. In my mind, such self-complacency may pave the way to an even greater eclipse of Catholic moral and doctrinal teaching among large numbers of Catholics.

Catholics owe a debt of gratitude to Strauss for revealing the elements and implications of historicism. Unfortunately, most Catholic theologians have no familiarity with Strauss's descriptions of historicism. Even if revisionist moral theologians became familiar with Strauss, their thought would most likely not change because they are convinced that historicism is a philosophical truth trumping many church teachings. Historicism, I would note, is the perfect tool to bring about changes in church teaching based on the reigning opinions in the culture (or in Plato's cave) without having any misgivings about overturning the deposit of faith. No truth from the past can stand up to the contemporary truths dictated by historicism.

---

54. Leo Strauss, "Living Issues of German Postwar Philosophy," in Heinrich Meier, *Leo Strauss and the Theologico-Political Problem* (New York: Cambridge University Press, 2006), 132–33.

PART 3

Leo Strauss on Christianity, Politics, and Philosophy

 11

The City and the Whole

Remarks on the Limits and the Seriousness of
the Political in Strauss's Thought

GIULIO DE LIGIO

> Insight into the limits of the moral-political sphere as a whole can be
> expounded fully only by answering the question of the nature of political
> things. The political ... owes its legitimation to the seriousness of the
> question of what is right.
>
> —Leo Strauss

Leo Strauss's project was not *political* but, in the classical sense of the term, *theoretical*. At the center of his work was the understanding, and in the first instance the recovery, of the fundamental problems and alternatives of human life. He invited his reader to consider attentively the conflicting "solutions" to these problems, without having recourse to the "miracle" of synthesis.[1] The Catholic perspective certainly shares Strauss's concern for the abiding vitality of the Western tradition and, more broadly or more precisely, for the good life, for the problem of jus-

---

1. Strauss, "Restatement" (1950), presented in a critical edition in *Interpretation* 36, no. 1 (2008): 49.

tice or for what *completes* morality. However, as we know, the common ground between them does not reveal the whole picture.

It may be argued that Catholicism, if one reads carefully between the lines of Strauss's work, appears somewhat in the latter as part of the problem, perhaps not because philosophy can disprove the claims of faith, but because Catholicism seems to contribute to the questionable belief in such a synthesis, or in such miracles. Catholicism could have played a role in that "attempt at harmonization" that raised modernity's unwarranted hopes and its eventual crisis: in order to preserve the substance and the articulations of the human world, it tries to *mediate*, if without *confusing* them, Athens and Jerusalem, philosophy and the moral-political sphere. Strauss's rigorous rendering of the essential *differences* between the possible ways of life then implies by itself a discreet but radical criticism: the Catholic mediation could eventually bring about a corruption of the specific elements of the human world—philosophy, the law, politics itself.

Now, our situation, the metamorphoses of what Strauss called the crisis of our time, might show at a closer look the enduring relevance of Strauss's approach, of Strauss's warning, and the plausibility of Catholicism's mediating efforts. One may think that I too believe in the miracle of synthesis, but what Strauss himself helps us understand about our time makes my inchoate reflection at least legitimate.

Western societies found themselves, as it were, in the grip of a compromise, or of an oscillation. On one hand, they affirm the *identity* of democracy and philosophy, the satisfaction of man, the achieved movement from government of men to the administration of things. On the other hand, they orient themselves by the claim of the full *separation* between democratic life (understood as the condition of the plurality of "values" guided by a "value-free" science) and the question of the good. The result of such a compromise, or oscillation, appears to Strauss as the public action of a dogmatic skepticism, which may be questioned in its claim to be practically sound and theoretically true. In other words, what appears to be a synthesis could turn out to be the source of a Napoleonic momentum conveying tyrannical temptations or leading eventually to a loss of confidence in Western societies' common project. The "liberal lesson" we draw from the totalitarian experience reminds us then of something of the ambivalence of the foundations of modern democracy: in order to escape from any form of absolutism, modern man runs the risk of abandoning the most important questions *and to lose insight into the nature of the political.*

I could then conclude these introductory remarks with a daring but perhaps plausible reformulation of the problem: Strauss seems to warn us against both the synthesis *and the separation* of the elements of the human world, that is, in a way, against the two prevailing public dispositions of our time. Whatever one thinks of the final word of his interpretations, his warning conveys at least a compelling invitation insofar as it inclines us to question the orientation of our thoughts regarding principles—to begin with, of our way of thinking about politics.[2] Some remarks on the latter could shed some light on the primary questions that define the common ground shared by Strauss and Catholicism and which are indeed fundamental for us.

Politics and Truth: The Double Lesson of the Twentieth Century

Strauss maintained that the political experience of his century, and in particular the ambivalent relationship between the modern project and its communist offshoot, had given the Western movement a "twofold lesson": a "political lesson" and "a lesson regarding the principles of politics."[3] In an era when blind hope was being placed in the supposedly necessary construction of the city of reason, while at the same time reason itself began so to speak to desert humanity and transform itself into history, Strauss returned to the wisdom of the ancients in order to understand the "things themselves." For Strauss, the "unprecedented" experience of modern tyranny confirmed the permanence and necessity of the political, or the impossibility (at least for the foreseeable future) of the construction of a universal society. In other words, human society is destined to remain, Strauss wrote, what it has always been: that is *political,* a collection of particular societies, separated by frontiers, plagued by internal contradictions, and "concerned with self-improvement."[4] The aim of political society, if it is understood in this way, is not the planetary

---

2. Strauss, "The Crisis of Our Time," in *Predicament of Modern Politics,* ed. Harold J. Spaeth (Detroit: University of Detroit Press, 1964), 43.
3. Ibid., 46.
4. Ibid., 42.

realization of the good of humanity, as the ends of politics are local and particular. But such a "return" to the particular does not signify an abandonment of the universal, a surrender to necessity, a narrowing of the mind or a "closing" of the soul, because political societies are concerned not simply with "what is their own," but with "their own *betterment*." The political life of a society, Strauss explains, must always manifest itself in the tension between two fundamental tasks: "self-preservation" and "self-improvement."[5] The "political lesson" of communism, therefore, is not that the question of justice or of human perfection is meaningless, or that it no longer has any meaning in our time. Perhaps, indeed, this question can be truly posed only once we have understood the vacuity of the simplified or perverted ways in which we have learned to ask it. Perhaps the true "condition" of this question is political. On one point, at least, Strauss is quite clear: the highest human possibilities have not been condemned as destructive illusions by the experience of modern tyranny, and they will not be exhausted for as long as the greatest "human tasks" remain possible, as long as the great questions of human existence remain unanswered and the "fundamental riddles" have not been solved.[6]

In opposing the historicist claim, which the unprecedented brutality of modern tyrannies might seem to confirm, Strauss's insistence on the permanence of the fundamental human problems was in the first place meant to show that the *search* for truth is still necessary, that philosophy is still *possible*. Philosophy, in Strauss's work, recovers its original meaning: consciousness of and meditation upon the fundamental alternatives of human experience, consideration of the transhistorical criteria for the best regime, the quest for knowledge of the best way of living, of true virtue, and thus of the whole.[7] If the validity of Strauss's *response* to that fundamental search remains to be proven, the *problem* he recovers remains then both unresolved and crucial. In occupying himself more

---

5. Ibid., 47.
6. Ibid., 43.
7. Among the several formulations of this point, see Strauss, *Persecution and the Art of Writing* (Chicago: University of Chicago Press, 1952), 7; "Restatement," 56; *Natural Right and History* (Chicago: University of Chicago Press, 1965), 29–32. It seems useful to recall how Strauss outlines the "content" of the problem of the whole: "The Whole is not a pure ether or an unrelieved darkness in which one cannot distinguish one part from the other, or in which one cannot discern anything. Quest for knowledge of 'all things' means quest for knowledge of God, the world, and man—or rather quest for knowledge of the natures of all things: the natures in their totality are 'the whole.'" Strauss, "What Is Political Philosophy?," in *An Introduction to Political Philosophy: Ten Essays by Leo Strauss*, ed. Hilail Gildin (Detroit: Wayne State University Press, 1989), 4.

with questions than "solutions," Strauss chose eventually the life of the philosopher, as he understood such a life. By that movement of thought, he was also led to rediscover in the ancient antagonism between Athens and Jerusalem, between philosophy and revelation, the insoluble but fruitful tension that determines the destiny of Western civilization and represents the "nerve" of human life.[8] From the crisis of his time Strauss seems indeed to have drawn a *double* lesson: the affirmation of the permanence of the walls of the city—of the political—is accompanied by the rediscovery of the heavens of thought.

This double rehabilitation is at once profoundly meaningful and enigmatic. Strauss himself does not hesitate to discuss the importance and the complications to which it leads. Although he wrote in a time when both philosophy and politics were rejected as relics of a past of oppression and necessity, Strauss did not simply seek to render plausible the persistence of the essential characters of political life and of the search for truth. He sought just as much to remind his reader of the problematic character of the relation between philosophy, or revelation, and the city, or the irreducible *tension* which characterizes it. By so doing, Strauss recovers a situation that would seem quite unfortunate for the rational and "naturally political" man, and which he sometimes presents as his "central interest," or the "highest theme of *political* philosophy."[9] To him, the character of the philosopher is fundamentally different from that of his fellow citizens; the alterity of motives, or ends, between philosophy and the city can easily lead the philosopher to live "privately," "apart from the city," almost as a "hermit."[10] Strauss explores this tension by discussing the different forms that it assumed, first in pagan antiquity and then in the context of Judaism, Christianity, and Islam. He also occasionally presents it in general terms by contrasting the questionable universalism of the city with the true universalism of philosophy. "The 'synthesis' of

---

8. Cf. Strauss, "Progress or Return?," in *The Rebirth of Classical Political Rationalism*, ed. Thomas L. Pangle (Chicago: University of Chicago Press, 1989), 270; *Natural Right and History*, 74–75; "Thucydides: the Meaning of Political History," in his *The Rebirth of Classical Political Rationalism*, 72–73; and "Jerusalem and Athens: Some Preliminary Reflections," in *Studies in Platonic Political Philosophy*, ed. Thomas L. Pangle (Chicago: University of Chicago Press, 1983), 147–73.

9. Strauss, "A Giving of Accounts: Jacob Klein and Leo Strauss," in *Jewish Philosophy and the Crisis of Modernity*, ed. Kenneth H. Green (Albany: State University of New York Press, 1997), 464; cf. also *Persecution and the Art of Writing*, preface.

10. Cf. Strauss, "Liberal Education and Responsibility," in *An introduction to Political Philosophy*, 329–30; *On Tyranny*, introduction; *Natural Right and History*, 156–57; *Persecution and the Art of Writing*, 7, 16–21; "A Giving of Accounts," 463–64; and "Restatement," 66–67.

the two universalisms is indeed impossible. It is of the utmost importance that this impossibility be understood. Only by understanding it can one understand the grandeur of the attempt to overcome it and sensibly admire it."[11] Strauss's way of posing the terms of the problem leads us to the exact and crucial reformulation of the double lesson of the twentieth century: the comprehension of the relation between political life and truth is a permanent and difficult task, one "of the utmost importance."

It is worthwhile to underline this preliminary, if decisive, point, precisely because we tend not to recognize the difficulty, the terms, or even the fact itself of the abiding problem that Strauss poses. The modern liberal order, and the liberal political science that accompanies it, often seems to forget the problematic status of truth in the city or history: as I said at the beginning, it either affirms with confidence the essential harmony between thought and the city, or ignores the problem of their relation in the name of the seemingly inoffensive principle of the plurality of opinions.[12] The prevailing liberal perspective either asserts that the old questions Strauss sought to revive were answered long ago or it affirms that they are simply "private things." To put it differently, it seems to have changed not only the answers but also and first of all the *questions* that orient political thought and reveal the stakes of political conflict. Their disputations—our debates—seem to have nothing to do with the search for the best regime, or for perfect justice, for the good citizen, or the best man—that is, with what Strauss shows to be the *political* questions *par excellence*.[13] It should not be surprising, then, that Strauss seeks, in the first place, to draw the attention to the fundamental, permanent problem of ruling human beings and of the conflictual relation between this problem and the inexhaustible question of the whole.[14] Strauss indicates in this way the "first" situation of the understanding, an "epistemological" relationship that obliges us to begin by exploring the opinions of common sense, but at the same time he seems to emphasize the "latitude" of a problem, the amplitude of which he works to understand and illustrate.[15] In order to address properly the issue, one could then say that Strauss en-

---

11. Strauss, *The City and Man* (Chicago: University of Chicago Press, 1978), 230.
12. At least in the sense that such a principle seems to rely on the faith in a society in which "no one would suffer any harm from hearing any truth." *Persecution and the Art of Writing*, 34.
13. Strauss, "On Classical Political Philosophy," in *An Introduction to Political Philosophy*, 59–62, 73.
14. Strauss, "Restatement," 34, 56, 76.
15. Strauss, *Natural Right and History*, 164.

courages us to recognize both the *limits* and the *seriousness* of the political.

That such a dialectic is both decisive and troublesome was confirmed by a paradox that some of Strauss's best readers underlined during the recent debate on the political implications of his work, when the latter could not for once shun the limelight. If one reads his work carefully, Strauss, who has contributed more than any other thinker to the contemporary rediscovery of *political* philosophy, who sought to restore to politics the architectonic position which the ancients had given to it, would have been the teacher of a "transpolitical" or a "impolitic" lesson.[16] Far from being the secret inspiration of a political movement, Strauss—as one of his best interpreters has written while recalling his choice for the solitary life of the philosopher—might instead be reproached for "his constant effort to lure the best minds away from political life," for "his philosophical detachment from politics," for a defense of the philosophical life that inevitably implied "a constant devalorization of political and moral life."[17] The dialectic or tension that Strauss saved from the dangerous obscurity into which it had fallen would thus be characterized by a "substantial" disequilibrium, something that might lead a careful reader to doubt if the "tension" between the political and the philosophical ways of life is in fact as fundamental and serious as Strauss at first lets on. Only when the reader keeps this ambiguity in mind can the full subtlety and importance of Strauss's teaching regarding the limits and the seriousness of politics be appreciated. This teaching, important in itself, has a special relevance for us: as a result of the oscillation I mentioned at the outset, it seems that the question of the ultimate aim of foreign policy and the very meaning of the political community is today as essentially controversial as ever before.

The Whole of Politics, or Politics and the Whole: A Fundamental and Insoluble Problem

To distance oneself from a perspective that aspires to grasp the whole of human life, and hence to understand its parts both in their heteroge-

---

16. D. Janssens, "A Change of Orientation: Leo Strauss's 'Comments' on Carl Schmitt Revisited," *Interpretation* 33, no. 1 (2005): 102.

17. Daniel Tanguay, "Néoconservatisme et religion démocratique: Leo Strauss et l'Amérique," *Commentaire* 114 (2006): 316, 322–24. For the premises of this reading, see by the same author the remarkable *Leo Strauss: une biographie intellectuelle* (Paris: Grasset, 2003).

neous essences and as parts of the whole, is perhaps a "methodologically" arbitrary and fatal option, one that fails to capture the phenomenon under investigation. This is a point that Strauss often repeats. The whole seems to elude us, we never know it completely, but "to articulate the situation of man means to articulate man's openness to the Whole."[18] The fact that we do not know the whole, and that our knowledge of each part, or sphere, is affected by this basic uncertainty, does not mean that we should abandon either the question of the whole or *the reflection of the relation between the whole and the different parts* of which we have some knowledge. We must remain open to the question of what is common to all human beings (even in different degrees), and to the innate final ends of human life. There is nothing politically or scientifically "absolutist" in this attitude. We never fully understand the articulation between homogeneity and heterogeneity, but it is impossible to truly understand the unity, the truth, of the phenomena we study unless we renounce the temptation to explore only the one or the other. We must not "force the issue" of the human questions in *either* direction.[19] The discussion of some major elements of the Straussian reading of the question under discussion will help us to understand the well-founded character of the ideas that have just been presented.

Strauss begins his investigation with a specific part of the whole: the political. As I have already remarked, he did not understand the phenomenon of politics as a "province of culture," a separate "domain" among others as modern social sciences do. Following classical Greek political science, Strauss recognized the superior rank, the architectonic character, of the political. Politics is more revealing, and therefore more important, than economics, art, or "culture," because it determines the "form" taken by the human material of a society and thus its ends; therefore, the political cannot be derived from the subpolitical.[20] It is by virtue of this architectonic character (which one has to consider as the key to Strauss's whole position), that the political takes on such a special significance, both for human experience and for our comprehension of the vaster whole in which human experience takes place. By such statements, I have

---

18. Strauss, "What Is Political Philosophy?," 38. On this elusion, see among others Strauss, *Progress or Return?*, 260, 262; "What Is Political Philosophy?," 38; and *The City and Man*, 20–21.
19. Strauss, "What Is Political Philosophy?," 39.
20. Strauss, "An Epilogue," in his *Liberalism Ancient and Modern* (Ithaca, N.Y.: Cornell University Press, 1989), 207.

in a sense anticipated Strauss's main argument—that politics, rightly understood, is a whole that leads us to the question of the whole—because we are first of all concerned with establishing the nature and the importance of the political. Strauss indeed maintains that, if one wishes to be truly scientific, it is necessary to begin with the question: "what is the political?" Thereby one studies the element that most characterizes a given society, and therefore the *end*, or the *purpose*, toward which the society is formed. Failure to do this leads almost inevitably to contradiction, omission, or interpretive partiality.[21] In a sense, Strauss's revival of the concept "regime" is an effort both to rediscover a satisfactory understanding of "action" in the political context, and to avoid that "begging of all important questions" characteristic of contemporary social science.[22] This constitutes an effort "to understand things as they are."[23] Strauss gets to the core of our subject when he writes: "The ultimate political goal ... urgently calls for coherent reflection.... The ambiguity of the political goal is due to its comprehensive character. Thus the temptation arises to deny, or to evade, the comprehensive character of politics and to treat politics as one compartment among many. But this temptation must be resisted if it is necessary to face out situation as human beings, i.e., the whole situation."[24] This classic formulation of the problem of the political is a challenge to the self-understanding, and to the social science, of contemporary European societies. It is exactly because the political goal is related to the totality of human existence that it will always be contested and ambiguous. One cannot then refuse to consider the opaque question of the ends of politics without at the same time refusing to engage with the question of human life in its totality. It is doubtless this intrinsic link that makes the political the eternal and fundamental problem whose permanence Strauss identified, as we have seen, as one of the great lessons of his century.

"The Jewish Question"—a problem of which Strauss had personal experience in his youth, and which preoccupied him more than any other—seemed to Strauss to offer the clearest example of this lesson. In contradiction to the opinion of a century which shared Marx's belief that

21. Strauss, "What Is Political Philosophy?," 18.
22. Strauss, "An Epilogue," 215.
23. Strauss, "What Is Political Philosophy?," 21; and "On Classical Political Philosophy," in *An Introduction to Political Philosophy*, 79.
24. Strauss, "What Is Political Philosophy?," 11–12.

humanity only sets itself problems that it is capable of solving, Strauss affirmed that the political problem *has no solution*.[25] We understand today this proposition as it were a "weak" statement, the expression of a postmodern consciousness, but it reflects important presuppositions and leads to fundamental developments. In a justly famous passage from the fundamentally "autobiographical" preface Strauss wrote to the English translation of his early book on Spinoza (Strauss's *Seventh Letter*), Strauss expresses this point, with his implications, laconically: "Human beings will never create a society which is free from contradictions."[26] Even the most perfectly designed political regime will be imperfect in certain regards. This brings us back to the double lesson evoked at the beginning of this essay. No man can escape from the political condition of mankind: it is impossible to avoid the permanent problems, although of course they can be ignored. For the same reason, one cannot try to make man absolutely at home on earth without denying man's humanity, without finally making him absolutely "homeless."[27] Strauss's argument leads the reader to a crossroads. If his line of reasoning is an accurate description of the human condition, we are forced either to accept the "uneasy solutions with which sensible people will always be satisfied," characteristic of political life, or to devote ourselves to the philosophical quest for absolute truth, i.e. to live as "citizens of the whole."[28] The two alternatives do not appear to be equally satisfying. Yet one can also wonder to what extent one can set them "in tension" with one another.

In any case, it would be hasty to object that this interpretation only concerns the Jewish problem, a unique and "religious" problem, and therefore that it does not apply to the political problem in its entirety. Strauss was among those who saw the Jewish problem as "the most simple and available exemplification of the human problem," or "the most manifest symbol of the human problem *insofar as it is a social or political problem*."[29] One can therefore assume that, as a problem consubstantial with the human condition as political, the insoluble problem I outlined above also confronts the citizens of liberal democracies, even if they of-

---

25. Strauss, "Restatement," 34–35, 56, 76.
26. Strauss, "Preface to *Spinoza's Critique of Religion*," in *Jewish Philosophy and the Crisis of Modernity*, 143.
27. Strauss, *Natural Right and History*, 18.
28. Strauss, "Why We Remain Jews: Can Jewish Faith and History Still Speak to Us?," in *Jewish Philosophy and the Crisis of Modernity*, 340; and Strauss, "Restatement," 78.
29. Strauss, "Why We Remain Jews," 340; Strauss, preface to *Spinoza's Critique of Religion*, 143 (emphasis added).

ten seem unaware of its importance and permanence—for example, by refusing to see that it is the essence of political things not to be neutral, but to raise a claim to men's decisions and judgment.[30] Strauss's perspective is somewhat disturbing for the authoritative opinion of our time; as I mentioned, the double conclusions he draws from the experience of his century are not weak claims: the modern liberal order is no more capable of providing a satisfactory "solution" to the political problem than any other political construction, although it is far superior in dignity to the other regimes it has confronted in the past century.[31] In other words, in spite of what is commonly believed, the ultimate lesson to be drawn from the understanding of the insolubility of the political problem would not be represented necessarily by the "liberal solution," or the "individualist solution."[32] Rather, it would be represented by the very insight that one cannot avoid facing the political problem and its consequences—the political problem to which liberal democracy offers an uneasy or fragile "solution," doubtlessly reasonable but neither exhaustive nor complete, that is *not* a *solution*. The true lesson to be drawn would then concern the permanence of the tension between political life and philosophy—or revelation. Whatever may be the case, we seem still to be led to think about the political, to consider its importance for the entirety of human life—and its shadows.

Beyond the Twin Dangers: On Political Action and Theory

Sometimes this lesson is explicit in Strauss's work; generally it is presented indirectly, through the arguments by which he illustrates the problem of the nature and limits of political life; in both cases, it appears to be the other side, so to speak, of his protreptic speech. One could go so far as to say that the entirety of Strauss's work conveys or represents such an invitation. He sought to avoid, and to guard against, the sort of "grandiose failure" into which Marx, Nietzsche, and their intellectual progeny fell; against the *double* error illustrated by the "biggest event of 1933" and by the experience of communism. Strauss sought to put again philosophy

---

30. Strauss, "What Is Political Philosophy?," 5.
31. Strauss, preface to *Spinoza's Critique of Religion*, 141–44.
32. Strauss, "Why We Remain Jews," 338–39.

in direct relation to the primary questions and basic distinctions of political life.[33] He also hoped to remove it from the catastrophic, misleading choice between "irresponsible indifference to politics and irresponsible political options," or from the "twin dangers of visionary expectations from politics and unmanly contempt for politics."[34] Even a philosopher who seeks only to meditate upon Being must first understand tyranny and its consequences, otherwise he will fail to understand the question of Being itself. It must be said that Strauss regards attentiveness to politics as a fundamental "responsibility" of man, but also as something peculiar to *man*, because "man cannot abandon the question of the good society."[35] To fail to respond to this question is to put man's humanity in danger. This is why the perspective of classical philosophy is to Strauss still pertinent when it argues that wisdom cannot be separated from moderation, or philosophy from prudence.[36] The tension between truth and the life of the city could have many significations, many different articulations, which must be fully understood or lived "in action."[37] We need to follow Strauss's reflection closely.

When discussing the relation between philosophy and political life, Strauss returns first to the Aristotelian distinction between theoretical science and practical wisdom. He affirms the specificity of the realm of action, and restores prudence to its rightful place as queen of the practical world. The virtue of prudence must deal with circumstances that, although they are encountered in ordinary human experience (and not in theoretical investigation), reveal in fact the most important of questions, those questions which demand to be formulated in theoretical terms.[38] Strauss thus implicitly illustrates the character of political action and argument, or the "latitude" of political deliberation: "political controversy has a natural tendency to express itself in universal terms."[39] Beginning from its own, "limited" questions, action would seem to lead to the highest subjects of inquiry. It is important to make more explicit the possible

33. Strauss, "On Classical Political Philosophy," 59–62.
34. Strauss, "What Is Political Philosophy?" 57; and "Liberal Education and Responsibility," in *Liberalism Ancient and Modern*, 24.
35. Strauss, "What Is Political Philosophy?" 24. Such a reference expresses in Strauss's speech a certain ambiguity, see Strauss, "Liberal Education and Responsibility," 10–11; and *Persecution and the Art of Writing*, 36.
36. Strauss, *Natural Right and History*, 156–64.
37. Strauss, "Progress or Return?," 270.
38. Strauss, "What Is Political Philosophy?" 3–4.
39. Strauss, "On Classical Political Philosophy," 67.

implication for the subject of this essay: political action, and the kind of knowledge that determines it, is not philosophy, but it finds itself in an essential relationship with philosophy. This relationship is many-sided. Political action and its issues show themselves to be the "entering wedge" for the questions peculiar to philosophy, they *contain* or *nourish* something that will later be considered philosophical.[40] The workings of prudence bring this situation about.

Strauss points to this fact when he writes: "The sphere governed by prudence is then in principle self-sufficient or closed. Yet prudence is always endangered by false doctrines about the whole of which man is a part, by false theoretical opinions; prudence is therefore always in need of defense against such opinions, and that defense is necessarily theoretical. The theory defending prudence is, however, misunderstood if it is taken to be the basis of prudence."[41] What is most characteristic of politics—action—is not founded in theory, but it is possible to act well only if one is not corrupted by "false doctrines about the whole of which man is a part." Political action and the search for truth thus cannot, or at least should not, be completely separated. It would seem that to act well, to be prudent, it is necessary to have a good conception of the whole, or at least not a false one, hence of the limits of human projects.[42] It would also seem that the realm of action retains a degree of significance that the partisans of a "theoretical" perspective do not always assign to it. Political philosophy rightly understood defends practical knowledge while developing all of the implications of such knowledge, because politics is a part of the whole and must remain as such: *a part of the whole,* "limited" in its possibilities but constructively related to the "whole" of human life.[43]

The "Political" Responsibility of the Philosopher and the "Questionable" Character of the City

When, like Strauss, one does not ask questions with the simple intention of "guiding action" one adopts a perspective that is, at least in part, exte-

---

40. Ibid., 79.
41. Strauss, "An Epilogue," 206. On the decisive question of the relation between theory and practice, see also *Natural Right and History*, 320–21; "What Can We Learn From Political Theory?," *Review of Politics* 69 (2007): 520; and Strauss's important letter to Voegelin of March 14, 1950.
42. Strauss, "What Can We Learn From Political Theory?," 520, 527.
43. Strauss, "On Classical Political Philosophy," 69.

rior and superior to the imperatives of politics. From such a perspective one can remind the city of its limits and highest ends, or its relation to the whole, but one also runs the risk of misunderstanding the specificity of politics, of devalorizing its true meaning. In warning us of those twin dangers, contempt for politics and the absolutization of politics, Strauss revives the understanding of such a risk. He sometimes maintains, as I have said, that philosophy has a "practical implication," in that it defends the form of reason which governs political action, for example by reminding the city of the limits of human hopes, the risks of any expectation, the fragility of every accomplishment.[44] This lesson in political moderation—the importance and urgency of which Strauss often underlines in his polemic against modern utopianism—is not the only "humanizing and civilizing" service that philosophy can "indirectly" render to the city.[45] The defense of moderation is not philosophy's only duty. In spite of the alluring image Strauss presents of the detached life of the wise man, his work sometimes presents the *political* importance of philosophy in such a manner that one is tempted to see in his teaching not simply a defense of philosophy before the tribunal of the city, but a real—if intrinsic—concern for the city itself.[46] At least, one can read Strauss's arguments in both directions.

One might suggest, for example, that by their "actualization," philosophical questions keep political life open to *all* human possibilities: they remind it of a nobility that surpasses it, but also of the question of justice, which the city cannot avoid. This "presence" offers the city the mediating judge which it needs to be a "political whole."[47] At the same time it prevents the city from "identifying *any actual* order, however satisfying in many respects, with the *perfect* order": political philosophy shows itself in this sense to be "the eternal challenge to the philistine," or the antidote to forgetfulness of the question of true justice, and it is difficult to imagine a point in the human adventure when the medicine of philosophy will no longer be necessary.[48] In the twentieth century, as I mentioned, Strauss filled this salutary role by emphasizing the limits of any political order, thus showing the inhuman character of modern tyrannies. He

---

44. Strauss, "What Can We Learn From Political Theory?," 520, 527.
45. Strauss, "Liberal Education and Responsibility," 15.
46. Strauss's mention of the life of the philosopher in Farabi's *Plato* is in this regard quite revealing, see Strauss, *Persecution and the Art of Writing*, 17.
47. Strauss, "On Classical Political Philosophy," 62–63.
48. Strauss, "What Can We Learn From Political Theory?," 521.

also insisted, from the same perspective, that what *limits* the domain of politics is what is *superior* to politics: for Strauss, "man transcends the city only by what is best in him."[49] If Greek philosophy is both the source of all political wisdom and the horizon of Strauss's second navigation, there is maybe no better way to understand the validity and implications of Strauss's interpretation of the political than by seriously studying *The City and Man*, Strauss's overall presentation of the problems and way of thinking which are peculiar to classical Greek political philosophy. I will limit myself here to recall the "conclusions." The book presents Strauss's lectures on the most magnificent cure ever devised for every form of political ambition supplied by Plato's *Republic*, on the "apparent contradiction" in Aristotle's teaching about the difference between the good man and the good citizen, and on the hidden teaching of Thucydides's *Peloponnesian War*. In other words, Strauss engaged there a deep dialogue with the three thinkers who were the first to attempt to fully understand the *nature* and the importance of political life also in order to discover its *limits*.

At this point it might be useful to recall the principal characteristics of Strauss's teaching I have discussed so far. The political problem has no "solution" because the possibilities of political life are limited, and subjected to chance and necessity. The question of ends, or the hierarchy of priorities, is nevertheless not as exterior to political life, because it is this question that gives character and determination, both to each specific regime and to politics as a whole.[50] But if the wise man, as Strauss sometimes seems to imply, does not owe to the city his gift, if a gulf separates the wise man from his fellows, he would not be obliged to discuss the ends of his regime, to participate in political life the "unmanly contempt" of which he should avoid.[51] The discovery of the fact that the most excellent of men do not owe their excellence to the city, that their gifts have no political *origins*, seems to put the importance of the political *actualization* of this excellence into question.

Here again we encounter the tension or ambivalence characteristic of the Straussian perspective. We can go back to the broadest formulation

---

49. Strauss, *The City and Man*, 49; "The Crisis of Political Philosophy," in *Predicament of Modern Politics*, 103.

50. On the hierarchy of priorities, cf. Strauss, *Natural Right and History*, 162–63, 309.

51. On the "gulf," see Strauss, *Persecution and the Art of Writing*, 34. On the ends of the regime, see Strauss, "Liberal Education and Responsibility," 14–15.

I mentioned before. The city is both closed to the whole and open to the whole.[52] It is the necessary starting point, or the original "condition," for all fundamental reflection on human life, but it is not the true "cause" of human life and cannot be the "whole": the universalism of the city is "questionable."[53] To say that an experience is "questionable" does not necessarily imply that its ways and ends are illusory, but for example difficult, opaque, or true but partial. Such a claim may by contrast go so far as to devalorize the pretensions of the city, and not just to moderate them. Strauss judges the "questionable" character of the city by comparison with the "possibilities" of thought. He does not forget that the city lodges and educates the philosophers, but he also leads the reader to see it as the domain fatally dominated by opinion, incessant action, and convention.[54] He implicitly leads us to draw a lesson from the fact that "the city as city is more closed to philosophy than opened to it."[55] The most important problems, the greatest happiness, are beyond the city's reach. Again, while on the one hand Strauss thinks that political life cannot avoid the questions of the best regime, the good life, or true justice (that is, the most important questions), on the other hand these questions nevertheless "substantially" transcend in his view the limits of the city.

One can at least admit a perplexity about the relation of the *fundamental questions*—what I can name Strauss's criterion—to philosophy and political life. In Strauss's reflection, these questions are first and foremost the very essence of philosophy, but they also seem to be unalterably tied to the actions and the judgments of the city, albeit with different degrees of clarity in different cases, because there are different men of action, with a different understanding of the whole latitude of the political problem, as there are different men of thought, actual philosophers or "intellectuals." Moreover, we know that the essential difference between the practical-political and the philosophical approach to the permanent problems, between these two possible ways of living, cannot be derived from the fact that one or the other is able to offer a final response to the ultimate questions of human life. For Strauss, to repeat, there is no solution to the political problem and a philosopher ceases to be a philosopher when, instead of endlessly interrogating the permanent problems—that

52. Strauss, *The City and Man*, 29.
53. Ibid., 226–36.
54. Strauss, "A Giving of Accounts," 465–66.
55. Strauss, "Liberal Education and Responsibility," 15.

is, of being zetetic—he succumbs to the "attraction of solutions."[56] This is a point, or a puzzle, of decisive importance, one which deserves to be further developed beyond the limits of this essay.

Jerusalem and Athens: On the True Lesson of Political Life

I have discussed in broad terms the relation between political life and philosophical investigation as it concerns the response to the fundamental problems of human life. Strauss formulates again this relationship in a rather explicit passage from his essay "On Classical Political Philosophy," in which one can grasp the overall meaning of his work while being nonetheless somewhat astonished. He sums up what he presents as a "finding of crucial importance" in the following terms: "Philosophy—not as a teaching or as a body of knowledge, but as a way of life—offers, as it were, *the solution to the problem that keeps political life in motion.*"[57] "As it were," philosophy—which must never surrender to the "attraction of solutions" and which does not know the whole—is here credited with the capacity to "offer the solution" to political life, which the absence of solutions keeps in motion. This paradoxical affirmation is probably made simply to indicate that the contemplation and investigation of the permanent problems is the highest of human possibilities, the highest achievement available to the human soul, one that is inaccessible to political life. But we should not be too quick to dismiss the puzzlement to which Strauss's chain of arguments gives rise.

If philosophy and politics *share* the same problem, which keeps the one in movement, and to which the other knows the solution, then it would seem that the *end* of the city, both of the gentleman and of the simple citizen, is eventually the same as the *end* of philosophy, in spite

---

56. Strauss, "Restatement," 56; and "What Can We Learn From Political Theory?," 517.

57. Strauss, "On Classical Political Philosophy," 74–75 (emphasis added). Elsewhere, Strauss wrote in the same spirit: "Education, they felt, is the only answer to the always pressing question, to the political question par excellence, of how to reconcile order which is not oppression with freedom which is not license." *Persecution and the Art of Writing*, 37. But one could argue that education is what the city and philosophy *share* the most—as the city educates, for better or worse, all the citizens—or that education is the human task in which the tension/collaboration between the former and the latter reveals itself inevitable. It is probably this "double" condition of education which makes the political question "always pressing."

of what Strauss occasionally suggests.[58] If, moreover, philosophy cannot speak with certainty about the whole, because philosophy gets its character, and the happiness that is specific to it, from endless *questioning*, then philosophy cannot devalorize the political and moral sphere because this sphere is limited and incomplete. Philosophical life is also, as it were, limited and incomplete. What Strauss, in his commentary on Thucydides, calls the "fantastic political universalism" would then not, because of its essential flaw, necessarily point toward the "true universalism" of thought, but instead toward a sort of articulation of the two universalisms, toward the awareness of the imperfection of all forms of human universalism, or perhaps to the "solution" (which presents itself as such) of Revelation—if the latter, of course, deserves man's allegiance.[59] In any case, a conclusion comes to the fore: the rigorous examination of the political, or so to speak the impossibility to shy away from it, really leads us to consider the fundamental alternatives of human existence, the question of the best life or of *quid sit deus*. This "capacity" would suffice to show the seriousness of the political phenomenon.

It is important to mention a further clarification of it by Strauss's analysis of the "eminent case" I mentioned before. Strauss does not confine himself to "normatively" declaring the existence of man's fundamental alternatives and their political point of departure. In his commentaries on the great thinkers of the past and his analysis of the opinions and phenomena peculiar to his century, he shows them to be *interior* to political life and in political thought, even when the questions that define them are not immediately clear, or when they are dismissed as obsolete or arbitrary. He makes use of his characteristic theses in several different contexts. From experience one learns, or at least those who are gifted learn that "the ultimate aim of political life cannot be reached by political life, but only by a life devoted to contemplation, to philosophy," or that a "tangible comfort—a man-made eternal peace and happiness—*non datur*. We have to choose between philosophy and the Bible."[60]

But if, so to speak, this alternative "leaves" political life, as it emerges from the *contemplation* of political life, in another sense it remains interior to political life, it belongs to the choices and the thoughts that are char-

---

58. Strauss, "Liberal Education and Responsibility," 14.
59. "True univeralism" taken from Strauss, *The City and Man*, 230.
60. Strauss, "On Classical Political Philosophy," 74; and "What Can We Learn from Political Theory?," 529.

acteristic of political life as the element in which man searches for his humanity. Strauss himself seems to confirm this way of thinking when he discusses "the most manifest symbol of the human problem insofar as it is a social or political problem," in particular, when he powerfully describes the implacable cycle of "solutions" to the Jewish question that the Zionist movement allowed to be unveiled. Political Zionism, if it understands itself well, inevitably leads to cultural Zionism, but the contradictions of cultural Zionism eventually point toward religious Zionism, which serious people understand as the clearer and more rigorous position: the Zionist is then forced to confront the "content" that the political or cultural form of Zionism was created to protect or express, with the possibility of an unqualified "return" to the Jewish Law, of a religious solution to the Jewish problem in light of which all human "solutions" may reveal themselves to be blasphemous.[61] Political action or the life of a people entails, and sometimes imposes, the highest of questions which are at the center of the philosopher's questioning life.

The Gentleman and the Philosopher

These two figures—the practical man and the theoretical man—embody in more than one sense the principal elements of the problem of the seriousness and limits of the political that concerns us. Strauss discusses explicitly—in a surprisingly explicit way, one could add—the conflicting relationship and the hierarchy of virtues illustrated by these two types of man. He makes sure to indicate the importance of reasonable civic action, and in particular of "gentlemen," those members of the governing class who are responsible for the well-being of all the citizens and who set the tone of society "by ruling it in broad daylight." They are "earnest people" because "they are concerned with the most weighty matters, with the only things which deserve to be taken *seriously* for their own sake, with the good order of the soul and of the city."[62] Certainly, Strauss does not despise politics.

Yet he does not stop at affirming the "seriousness" of gentlemen and the gravity of their business, the good regime for the city and for the soul,

---

61. Strauss, preface to *Spinoza's Critique of Religion*, 142–43; and "Why We Remain Jews," 319–20.
62. Strauss, "Liberal Education and Responsibility," 11 (emphasis added).

that is, of those matters which, as I have observed, seem to reflect the questions which occupy the philosopher. It seems that to him the concerns of the gentleman are just a "reflection," or an "imitation," of the concerns of the philosopher, that the former occupies himself with an earthly and perishable equivalent of the lofty and eternal matters that occupy the latter.[63] Political men must presuppose, in acting, the knowledge after which philosophers seek: in this sense their motives, their virtues and their goals are not the same. Political life embraces all of the aspects of the city, from the most tragic to the vulgar and trivial. This is also why wise men—who seek to lead a life that is neither vulgar nor tragic—seem to have no inner *desire* to participate in politics, a way of living that seems to them characterized by a limited and ambiguous horizon. Politics could then appear "serious" only to those who prefer, among the things "of decisive importance," the salvation of their city to the salvation of their soul.[64] Those who are animated by a desire to understand the whole are always inclined to "look down" on the hustle and bustle of political life, on the actions of political men and perhaps on political men themselves.[65] Looked at in this light, political life would only be important because of the defense of the philosophical life that can represent its specific concern.[66] The "tension" between the two poles, at a closer look, would therefore prove to be nothing else than a hierarchical relationship, one in which the "condition" that politics represents, as well as its agents, are always at risk of being "looked down upon." Strauss's final teaching, if this were true, would in fact be nonpolitical, not to say impolitic.

One could then read Strauss's most profound and instructive suggestion regarding the vitality of Western civilization, or the secret of human existence, in this light: every one of us can and ought to be either a philosopher open to the challenge of theology or a theologian open to the challenge of philosophy, and so not necessarily *a citizen* opened to the question of the whole.[67] Yet this very injunction leads the reader to con-

---

63. Ibid., 14; see also *Natural Right and History*, 142: "The gentleman is not identical with the wise man. He is the political reflection, or imitation, of the wise man." Is the philosopher not himself a reflection of the truly wise man?

64. Strauss, "Thucydides: The Meaning of Political History," 74.

65. Ibid.

66. Strauss, "On Classical Political Philosophy," 77–79.

67. Strauss, "Progress or Return?," 270. On the central significance of the confrontation between philosophy and revelation, and the relation between the latter fundamental alternative and political life in Strauss's oeuvre, see Daniel Tanguay, *Leo Strauss*, and H. Meier, *Leo Strauss and the Theologico-Political Problem* (Cambridge: Cambridge University Press, 2006).

sider and to experience this fundamental antagonism "in action," and we have seen that for Strauss the question of the good life, which is the core of the conflict between philosophy and the Bible, first manifests itself in the context of the political whole, in the question of the best regime. Similarly, as I mentioned above, Strauss's critique of the concerns of the gentleman can also be formulated as a reminder of the true ends and limits of political action, and so as a service of the philosopher to the city, to the determination of its most complete justice.

Without discussing at length the virtues and specific desires of these two types of man, one aspect of the character of the political deliberation, which seems to bring them closer and to complicate the hierarchy of their "natures," should at least be noted. Strauss often presented Churchill at once as the summit of political excellence in his century, and as a symbol of the grandeur and seeming tragedy, of the noble tasks and perishable achievements that define the political.[68] In his lecture on "What Can We Learn From Political Theory?," Strauss describes the political wisdom of the great Englishman in these terms: "We do not need lessons from that tradition [of political philosophy] in order to discern the soundness of Churchill's approach, e.g., but the *cause* which Churchill's policy is meant to defend would not exist but for the influence of the tradition in question."[69] One could of course interpret this passage as a confirmation that, for Strauss, it is the role of politics to defend the philosophical life, or its tradition. It is also true that we owe the most just or elevated causes to the dialogue between philosophy and theology. But if one brings to light the importance of the "cause" for which a statesman acts, and if what is at stake in the political finds its source in philosophy or is nourished by philosophy, then the statesman's actions must be in a way intrinsically "philosophical": in some sense, that is, political life can, by its specific virtues, express another form of the "desire for truth" that is the essence of philosophical inquiry. Political life just as well as philosophy can be "inspired by love," or by a noble fear of seeing lies triumph in the city and in the souls of its citizens. In this case, one could not look down from on high upon "Churchill's cause"—nor Churchill's virtues—without fall-

---

68. Cf. Strauss, "La mort de Churchill," in *Commentaire* 75 (1996): 568; letter to Karl Löwith, August 20, 1946, in "Correspondence Concerning Modernity," *Independent Journal of Philosophy* 4 (1983): 111.

69. Strauss, "What Can We Learn from Political Theory?," 527 (emphasis added). On the "cause" in whose service the statesman acts, see also "On Classical Political Philosophy," 65.

ing into a form of that ignoble contempt for politics which is to Strauss "unmanly."

The Common Question of Justice: Taking the Limits of Politics Seriously

The fact that Strauss's well-known "change of orientation" found its first expression in the penetrating commentary that he wrote on Carl Schmitt's *Concept of the Political* in 1932 was indeed, for many reasons, "not entirely by accident." As Strauss himself would have affirmed, an orientation based on the political preserves the most fundamental things, and perhaps "the one thing needful," from oblivion.[70] In his dialogue with the German jurist, Strauss illustrates in his own way—by rightly formulating the question—how the political reveals the human situation, or how even in modern times it maintains its *real* seriousness:

> Agreement at all costs is possible only as agreement at the cost of the meaning of human life; for agreement at all costs is possible only if man has relinquished asking the question of what is right; and if man relinquishes that question, he relinquishes being a man. But if he seriously asks the question of what is right, the quarrel will be ignited (in view of "the inextricable set of problems" this question entails), the life-and-death quarrel: *the political*—the grouping of humanity into friends and enemies—*owes its legitimation to the seriousness of the question of what is right*.[71]

In this revealing dialogue one has a foreboding of the successive movements of Strauss's thought, his search for a "horizon beyond liberalism," his return to the ancients and eventually his understanding of the nature of *political* philosophy. As the density of the passage I have just cited makes manifest, Strauss's commentary on Schmitt is also a text that powerfully, if indirectly, illuminates the nature of the political problem in its relation with the mysterious or elusive whole of human life. The ambivalence of Strauss's understanding of the political, which would need more searching discussions, perhaps reflects a certain ambivalence in the very nature of the political phenomenon. One can probably describe

---

70. Strauss, "Thucydides: the Meaning of Political History," 102.
71. Strauss, "Notes on Carl Schmitt's *The Concept of the Political*," in *Carl Schmitt and Leo Strauss: The Hidden Dialogue*, ed. Heinrich Meier (Chicago: University of Chicago Press, 1995), 114–15 (emphasis added).

Strauss's intellectual evolution in the terms that Strauss himself uses to describe Lessing: for the "political problem" and the understanding of the essential imperfection which belongs to political life is what moved both authors toward an "intransigent classicism" or toward "the way leading to absolute truth," which Strauss distinguished sharply from political life.[72] "Ultimately," the understanding of politics would then prefigure nothing else than the "deeper meaning" of political philosophy. *Political philosophy refers not so much to a subject matter—political life—but to a manner of treatment* that culminates in the praise of the philosophical life, or in the examination of the alternatives which lead to absolute truth and which are the only things truly worth of study: "we have to choose between philosophy and the Bible."[73]

Nevertheless, this implicit reference to the city as a danger or as a "passage" that is merely instrumental to true human excellence, or to the completion of morality, seems only to illustrate a part of the road that one follows in interpreting Strauss's movement of thought. Even the philosopher does not transcend his political situation *from the beginning* (otherwise he risks being misled in his premises), or *completely*, he does not know the whole. Human life is living together, or "more exactly, is political life," and the *dialectical* task of transcending the partiality or the falsity of the city's opinions is never ending.[74] The understanding of the nature and the manifestations of the political does therefore reveal its limits, but also the virtues that belong to it and the enduring relevance of the question that it raises. In a sense, Strauss went so far and deep in showing the importance of the political that he illustrated at the same time the *difficulty* of removing oneself, in act or thought, from the horizon of political issues and alternatives, even when one's eyes and soul are turned on the fundamental questions.

At any rate, Strauss would have perhaps approved a conclusion like the following: the true limits of the political are a permanent task to be accomplished in the human soul just as in the city—"man transcends the city only by what is best in him." The "dissatisfaction" that weakens contemporary dogmatic skepticism and the crisis of the project of a universal society seem indeed to confirm that it is true *in more than one sense* that

---

72. Strauss, "Exoteric Teaching," in *The Rebirth of Classical Political Rationalism*, 70–71.
73. Strauss, "On Classical Political Philosophy," 77–78; see "What Can We Learn from Political Theory?," 529.
74. Ibid., 76.

"man cannot abandon the question of the good society," that he cannot free himself from the responsibility to understand and to live the "wholes" of which he is a part. One could then say again that philosophy and political life can remain faithful to their vocations—irreducible to a synthesis—only by aiming at their *mediation*, only by sharing those "objectives which are capable of lifting all men beyond their poor selves."[75]

75. Strauss, "What Is Political Philosophy?" 4.

12

Aristotelian Metaphysics and Modern Science

Leo Strauss on What Nature Is

JAMES R. STONER JR.

> The slenderest knowledge that may be obtained of the highest things is more desirable than the most certain knowledge obtained of lesser things, as is said in *de Animalibus* xi.
>
> —Aquinas

"Tell a lie and learn the truth." This is not a recipe for esoteric writing, but an old proverb, meant for amateur detectives and practiced interrogators. It also describes the way of thinking that lies behind the modern scientific method, with its formula of testing a proffered hypothesis: not that a hypothesis is necessarily a lie, but it is a statement whose truth is not known, and the point of asserting it boldly is to call forth the evidence for and against. In this spirit, then, I shall state a hypothesis, which I think is a bold one and perhaps not a true one. After acknowledging its irregularity, I will give my reasons why I think it might be true.

My hypothesis is that Leo Strauss accepted classical metaphysics as true. To clarify: I am using the term "metaphysics" to include the principles of nature as Aristotle understood them, thus including his physics and the various concepts and categories by which they are articulated. Among these would be the real existence of things, the distinction between actuality and potentiality, the distinction between substance and accident, the categories of accident—quantity, quality, relation, action, reception, place, orientation, environment, and time—and the causes: material, formal, efficient, and final.[1] I use the term "metaphysics" rather than "physics," which literally means the things of nature, so as not to create the mistaken impression that I (much less Strauss) would endorse those parts of Aristotle's physics that have been refuted by, for example, the principles of inertia and heliocentricity. Any reader of Strauss, after all, will recognize that his essays often enough include reference to actuality and potentiality, to the distinction between substance and accident, to final causes, and the like.

Still I realize that this is not the usual interpretation. For one thing, Strauss never endorsed classical metaphysics in his own name, at least to my knowledge, although it is obvious from his many commentaries on medieval and modern works that he was familiar with the classical teaching. On the contrary, he comes very close to rejecting classical metaphysics, or at the very least classical physics, in this well-known passage from the introduction to *Natural Right and History*:

Natural right in its classic form is connected with a teleological view of the universe. All natural beings have a natural end, a natural destiny, which determines what kind of operation is good for them. In the case of man, reason is required for discerning these operations: reason determines what is by nature right with ultimate regard to man's natural end. The teleological view of the universe, of which the teleological view of man forms a part, would seem to have been destroyed by modern natural science. From the point of view of Aristotle—and who could dare to claim to be a better judge in this matter than Aristotle?—the issue between the mechanical and teleological conception of the universe is decided by the manner in which the problem of the heavens, the heavenly bodies, and their motion is solved. Now in this respect, which from Aristotle's own point of view was the decisive one, the issue seems to have been decided in favor of the nonteleological conception of the universe.[2]

---

1. For my terminology here, see note 20.
2. Leo Strauss, *Natural Right and History* (Chicago: University of Chicago Press, 1953), 7–8.

Leaving aside the significance of the two "seems," commentators have generally solved Strauss's difficulty here by suggesting his affinity to Plato rather than Aristotle. Daniel Tanguay calls this Strauss's "Farabian turn," suggesting that from reflection on Farabi Strauss learned that classic natural right could be based on Platonic/Socratic skepticism or the zetetic philosophy.[3] Catherine and Michael Zuckert seem to have arrived independently at the same conclusion: Strauss learned from Farabi that "it was possible ... to revive Platonic political philosophy without insisting on or even affirming the truth of Aristotelian cosmology in the face of modern physics."[4] These readings of Strauss make sense of some of his strikingly skeptical sentences: his description of Platonic ideas as fundamental problems rather than as eternal forms, or his comment that "the evidence of all solutions is necessarily smaller than the evidence of the problems."[5] And they also make sense of why Strauss concentrates on *political* philosophy rather than philosophy simply: if one cannot know the whole of nature, but only the longing in the soul of man for wisdom, then it is the ordering of souls that commands our attention.

Straussian Metaphysics

But this solution does not seem to me to do justice either to all that Strauss says about the philosophical life nor to the experience of philosophy as he presents it. Unless something can be grasped that is beyond the human soul, the defense of philosophy only in terms of its activity of seeking wisdom (not in terms of the kind of knowledge sought) is a fundamentally humanistic defense, and Strauss makes clear enough that he thinks this inadequate:

Man, while being at least potentially a whole, is only part of a larger whole. While forming a kind of world and even being a kind of world, man is only a little world, a microcosm. The macrocosm, the whole to which man belongs, is not human. That whole, or its origin, is either subhuman or superhuman. Man cannot be

---

3. Daniel Tanguay, *Leo Strauss: An Intellectual Biography*, trans. Christopher Nadon (New Haven, Conn.: Yale University Press, 2007), 80.

4. Catherine and Michael Zuckert, *The Truth about Leo Strauss: Political Philosophy and American Democracy* (Chicago: University of Chicago Press, 2006), 41.

5. Leo Strauss, *On Tyranny: Including the Strauss-Kojève Correspondence*, ed. Victor Gourevitch and Michael S. Roth (New York: Free Press, 1991), 196.

understood in his own light but only in the light of either the subhuman or the superhuman. Either man is an accidental product of blind evolution or else the process leading to man, culminating in man, is directed toward man. Mere humanism avoids this ultimate issue. The human meaning of what we have come to call "Science" consists precisely in this—that the human or the higher is understood in the light of the subhuman or the lower. Mere humanism is powerless to withstand the onslaught of modern science. It is from this point that we can begin to understand again the original meaning of science, of which the contemporary meaning is only a modification: science as man's attempt to understand the whole to which he belongs.[6]

This passage seems to me not to contradict but to reinforce Strauss's discussion of the elusive character of knowledge of the whole in his essay "What Is Political Philosophy?," where he speaks of the need for knowledge of the whole to combine knowledge of heterogeneity and homogeneity, a combination which he says "is not at our disposal."[7] To be sure, philosophy here is described in human terms, as "the gentle, if firm, refusal to succumb to either charm," that is, "the charm of competence which is engendered by mathematics and everything akin to mathematics, and the charm of humble awe, which is engendered by meditation on the human soul and its experiences." Still, the philosophical attitude requires moving beyond meditation on the soul toward thought about intelligible things, or toward a balance between thought about the soul and thought about the things. Strauss concludes the essay with a discussion of Nietzsche's "oblivion of eternity, or in other words, estrangement from man's deepest desire and therewith from the primary issues."[8] Philosophy, by implication in this passage and more explicitly in other contexts, appears in Strauss as concerned with the nature of things and so with the eternal things. To be sure, Strauss makes clear that longing for eternity does not make it so: "Philosophy, we have learned, must be on its guard against the wish to be edifying—philosophy can only be intrinsically edifying."[9] Yet even in this passage Strauss points toward something

---

6. Leo Strauss, "Social Science and Humanism," in *The State of the Social Sciences*, ed. Leonard D. White (Chicago: University of Chicago Press, 1956), 420, reprinted in *The Rebirth of Classical Political Rationalism: An Introduction to the Thought of Leo Strauss*, ed. Thomas L. Pangle (Chicago: University of Chicago Press, 1989), 7–8.

7. Strauss, "What Is Political Philosophy?," 39–40.

8. Strauss, "What Is Political Philosophy?," 55. Strauss repeats his point that philosophy "of necessity" edifies in the last sentence of *Thoughts on Machiavelli* (Glencoe, Ill.: Free Press, 1958), 299.

9. Leo Strauss, "What Is Liberal Education?," in *Liberalism Ancient and Modern* (Chicago: University of Chicago Press, 1995), 8.

transcendent, precisely "the understanding of understanding, ... *noesis noeseos*, and this is so high, so pure, so noble an experience that Aristotle could ascribe it to his God."[10]

If my first argument in favor of an implicit Straussian metaphysics concerns Strauss's description of philosophy, my second concerns his description of political philosophy, which seems to me to require serious attention to metaphysics. While there is no doubt that Strauss made his signal contribution to political philosophy, not philosophy simply, and that he interpreted many philosophical texts in their political context under the light supplied by his discovery of esoteric writing, Strauss writes, "According to the classics, political life as such is essentially inferior in dignity to the philosophic life."[11] This is not precisely the same as saying, as Aristotle does, that political science is not the best science because man is not the best being, but Strauss does acknowledge that political philosophy is a branch of philosophy—special in being "that branch of philosophy which is closest to political life, to non-philosophical life, to human life," but not in itself knowledge of the whole. "Quest for knowledge of 'all things' means quest for knowledge of God, the world, and man—or rather quest for knowledge of the natures of all things: the natures in their totality are 'the whole.'"[12] Political philosophy remains close to man and so to man's primary experience both in its object of study and its mode of presentation, in Strauss; political philosophy, in being politic as well as concerned with politics, indicates a philosopher who remembers himself and his predicament even as he looks outside himself. Still, Strauss never to my knowledge describes political philosophy as though it is only about the political situation of the philosopher, or more to the point, the political situation of that philosopher whose sole concern is with his political situation. Precisely because he leaves the cave, to borrow Plato's image, he needs to show caution when he returns to the cave; political philosophy, in this account, is not possible for one who never leaves, maybe not even for one who, without prompting, much less coercion, is eager to return.

Thirdly, I think that Strauss's acceptance of the outlines of classical

---

10. Richard L. Velkley, *Heidegger, Strauss, and the Premises of Philosophy: On Original Forgetting* (Chicago: University of Chicago Press, 2011), 6, stresses the importance for Strauss's thought of Heidegger's rediscovery of the question of Being through his radical reinterpretation of Aristotle's *Metaphysics*, quoting many of the same passages just quoted, though he concludes that "Strauss undertakes a return to classical thought without a return to metaphysics as the tradition conceives it" (69).
11. Strauss, *Natural Right and History*, 145.
12. Aristotle, *Nicomachean Ethics* VI.1141a20; Strauss, "What Is Political Philosophy?," 10–11.

metaphysics appears in his interpretation of the great texts of the tradition. For all that can be said in favor of the Farabian turn in Strauss, I do not believe he ever repudiated his reading of Maimonides or interpreted the latter solely in the light of the former. More to the point, although Strauss seems in the instructions he left for his last book to have described his own political philosophizing as Platonic, the genius of his work throughout most of his intellectual life was to assimilate Plato and Aristotle to one another, not repudiate the latter in favor of the former. As in Raphael's famous painting, the numerous disputes between Plato and Aristotle in the context of shared questions might seem to be, for Strauss, the very paradigm at the heart of the philosophical life; on the one hand, Strauss's characterization of the Platonic ideas as fundamental problems perhaps adopts Aristotle's critique of the forms, but on the other hand, in writing that "No one has ever succeeded in giving a satisfactory or clear account of this doctrine of ideas," Strauss surely remembers that Aristotle gives an account of what he critiques.[13] Even after the Farabian turn, Strauss wrote about medieval and Renaissance Aristotelians, especially Marsilius of Padua. His interest may well have been especially in their politics, particularly their incipient republicanism that expressed itself in opposition to papal monarchism. But he also praised the understanding of Plato by a great defender of papal authority, Thomas More.[14] To assimilate Plato and Aristotle shows that for Strauss, the differences between them are less significant than the similarities. I do not think that this necessarily means that for Strauss their political similarities cancel their metaphysical differences, both because there are significant political differences between Plato and Aristotle and because some of the concepts they use to describe the natural world are the same. Nor do I think that their agreement about the value of the philosophical life—what Allan Bloom nicely describes as the friendship they exhibit "at the very moment they were disagreeing about the nature of the good"—allows us to dispense with the observation that both appear to suppose that the question of the nature of the good requires an account of the nature of the whole.[15]

Moreover, despite Strauss's adage to understand thinkers as they understood themselves and his recognition that modern political philoso-

---

13. Leo Strauss, "Plato," in *History of Political Philosophy*, ed. Leo Strauss and Joseph Cropsey, 3rd ed. (Chicago: University of Chicago Press, 1987), 53.

14. Leo Strauss, *The City and Man* (Chicago: University of Chicago Press, 1977), 61.

15. Allan Bloom, *The Closing of the American Mind* (New York: Simon and Schuster, 1987), 381.

phers understood themselves as seeking to change the plane of philosophical argument—to found a new way of thinking that emphasizes human making and the conquest of nature, not contemplation of what is—Strauss nevertheless makes an extraordinary effort to show how the arguments of, for example, Hobbes and Locke contradict biblical religion and therewith the traditional metaphysical understanding of the order of things.[16] Likewise, the most peculiar and thereby the most distinctive section of Strauss's book on Machiavelli is the discussion of his views on nature and fortune, addressing not only his undermining of biblical Christianity but his break with Aristotelian metaphysics as well.[17] To be sure, the political implications of the metaphysical revisions are readily and vibrantly drawn; and it might be that, in reference to the moderns, the metaphysical question needs to be raised defensively. But the defense only works if the metaphysics are sound and defensible, or at least if they are thought to be such; it seems clearer that Strauss thinks they are than that he thinks the world agrees.

As these last remarks suggest, the ubiquitous question in reading Strauss—is he writing what he thinks, or esoterically?—has to be addressed in relation to his treatment of classical metaphysics. Here, as always, the point of departure is an assessment of the rhetorical situation in which he writes. What are the dominant opinions of the audience he is appealing to, what can be safely or effectively said, what must be conveyed only to those with the motivation and the patience to go behind the veil?[18] As he writes in a slightly different context in the beginning of *Natural Right and History*, outside of the circle of Catholic Neo-Thomists (i.e., "as far as it is not Roman Catholic"), classical metaphysics was not accorded intellectual respectability.[19] What Kant had not flattened or Hegel buried, scientific progress obliterated, or seemed to. To be sure, Nietzsche and then Heidegger called the authority of Kant and Hegel and science into question; though in some ways Strauss seems to suppose their critiques, their gesture on the question of metaphysics was not to restore the classical view but to accuse the Enlightenment critics of retaining the metaphysical outlook they themselves pretended to refute. In short, to be tak-

16. Cf. Strauss, *Natural Right and History*, chap. 5, with "On the Basis of Hobbes's Political Philosophy" and "Locke's Doctrine of Natural Law" in *What Is Political Philosophy?*
17. Strauss, *Thoughts on Machiavelli*, 207.
18. See Arthur M. Melzer, *Philosophy Between the Lines: The Lost History of Esoteric Writing* (Chicago: University of Chicago Press, 2014).
19. Strauss, *Natural Right and History*, 2.

en seriously in Strauss's generation—indeed, maybe still today ("as far as it is not Roman Catholic")—one would have had to keep any affinity for classical metaphysics hidden in the background; the situation now is the reverse of what it was for the early moderns. Indeed, no small part of the ridicule Strauss himself suffered from established scholars in his time came from what he did say about the legitimacy of reviving, not classical politics (as Machiavelli and Rousseau claimed to do) or classical poetry (as in Nietzsche and Heidegger), but classical philosophy, even when he stressed merely the political part.

Now at this point in the essay, I should recommend that I suspend the argument and that my political scientist readers and I all put aside our plans for the next six months and delve into the study of classical physics and metaphysics, and then perhaps plan to spend the remainder of the year studying their critics, philosophical and scientific. But because that would be the equivalent of expelling from the academy everyone over the age of ten, and because it would not address the problem of whether we could find an adequate teacher, I will pass over the suggestion as impractical—noting only that, to recognize and understand what Strauss is doing with them, we would have to know what he is talking about at least as well as he did.[20] To the best of my knowledge, he did not claim any extraordinary knowledge of natural science, nor dismiss it as irrelevant or, in Nietzsche's formulation, as just another interpretation of the world. As for classical metaphysics, he seems to speak of it with ease and respect, if not full and obvious conviction. While he admitted inevitable limitations on what one could know—one cannot know all languages, he wrote, though apparently one could know that what one gets in translation is always imperfect—he does seem to suppose familiarity with philosophical questions widely speaking in his books. That he rejects doctrinal philosophy seems clear enough; that he supposes classical metaphysics ought to be understood as doctrinal seems again, to me, unclear.

20. But see the work of Anthony Rizzi: *The Science Before Science: A Guide to Thinking in the 21st Century* (Baton Rouge, La.: IAP Press, 2004); "The Science before Science: The Grounding and Integration of the Modern Mind and its Science," in *Reading the Cosmos: Nature, Science, and Wisdom*, ed. Guiseppi Butera (Washington, D.C.: The Catholic University of America Press, 2011); and *Physics for Realists* (Baton Rouge, La.: IAP Press, 2008 and 2011), vol. 1 (*Mechanics*), vol. 2 (*Electricity and Magnetism*). See also his *A Kid's Introduction to Physics (and Beyond)* (Baton Rouge, La.: IAP Press, 2012). I offer a preliminary introduction to Rizzi's work and reflect on its implications for political science in "Categories and Causes: Physics and Politics for Aristotle and for Us," in *Concepts of Nature: Ancient and Modern*, ed. R. J. Snell and Steven F. McGuire (Lanham, Md.: Lexington Books, 2016), 101–15.

The Theological Question

But is not all this worry (about the metaphysical question that Strauss may or may not have seriously raised) a distraction from a distinction Strauss clearly does draw between philosophy and theology? Is this not the context in which Strauss pronounces more clearly on the existence of God and on that which is higher and nobler than man? One has begun to understand what I am saying Strauss is teaching when one realizes this is not necessarily the case. The theological question itself is not only about God; it is about what he commands, and thus about how we are obliged to live. Philosophy offers a competing way of life—but also a competing vision of the divine. The issue of Jerusalem and Athens, that is, the issue of religious law and philosophy, is posed by Strauss as fundamental and insoluble: either theology is prior and philosophy inferior, or the reverse. Strauss makes this plain in multiple writings, and it has been the source of much comment in recent years, varying from the thesis of Heinrich Meier that the Jerusalem/Athens dichotomy is an exoteric device that covers Strauss's atheism, to Daniel Tanguay's carefully wrought thesis that the dichotomy exemplifies Strauss's intellectual biography and the ultimate limits of his project—for if the philosophical way of life rests on no more than a blind decision, then Strauss has not escaped from the value relativism that he critiques, the humanism he finds inadequate.[21] Strauss himself attributes to this dichotomy nothing less than the continued vitality of the West—by which I think he means, not what keeps it advancing technologically or economically, but what keeps philosophy itself alive.

From the point of view of metaphysical philosophy, what seems important to note is what classical metaphysics and biblical religion have in common, as well as how they differ. This is, of course, a well-rehearsed theme, not least in Strauss, but it bears summary. Both acknowledge the existence of something divine above man; both think that there is unity in the divine; both think that man's life is affected by the divine and that

---

21. Heinrich Meier, *Leo Strauss and the Theologico-Political Problem* (Cambridge: Cambridge University Press, 2006); Tanguay, *Leo Strauss*. See Leo Strauss, "Jerusalem and Athens: Some Preliminary Reflections" and "The Mutual Influence of Theology and Philosophy" in *Faith and Political Philosophy: The Correspondence Between Leo Strauss and Eric Voegelin, 1934–1964*, ed. Peter Emberley and Barry Cooper (Columbia: University of Missouri Press, 2004); and "Progress or Return?," in *The Rebirth of Classical Political Rationalism*.

man's happiness depends upon partaking in the divine, to which he has imperfect access; both find in God eternity and the source of good and truth. Philosophy and biblical religion differ, to be sure, on whether God created the world out of nothing, whether he knows men personally and watches over them providentially, and maybe on whether their souls can be said to be made in his image and destined for his presence. They differ on whether the relation of God to man is described by *eros* or *caritas*, but both agree that it is described by *love*. They agree that God cannot be known perfectly in this life: in biblical religion this is a matter of text and doctrine, while in philosophy it is the experience that leads to the conclusion that philosophy is not wisdom but always the quest for wisdom, an adage Strauss repeats.

For all his insistence upon the distinction between Jerusalem and Athens, then, I think that Strauss would agree with the synopsis just made. It applies most clearly to the relation of Aristotelianism and Catholic Christianity; if the philosophy is more Platonic and the religion more Hebraic, as of course they were for Strauss, the differences are probably greater. The closer ties might be better for politics; the more distant, better for philosophy, all things being equal, for Strauss. My point is simply that all of this makes sense—and the harmony between philosophy and orthodox religion, too—if Strauss accepts classical metaphysics, even on the rather latitudinarian model I have sketched. That leaves one admitting, with Meier, that Strauss at times exaggerates the gap between religion and philosophy—though not in the title of a critical essay, which speaks of "mutual influence," not mutual incompatibility.

Morality and Politics

In all that I have written thus far, I have abstracted from the moral and political questions of natural right and natural law. Both in his *International Encyclopedia of the Social Sciences* essay on natural law and in the fourth chapter of *Natural Right and History*, Strauss distinguishes between natural law and natural right, tying the latter to the philosophical tradition and the former to the Catholic faith. The natural right of the wise to rule, and of the philosopher to claim the mantle of human wisdom, is the moral conclusion of classical philosophy; its precise relation to the question of what the philosopher knows is hard to grasp, for classical philosophy seems to be concerned especially with the eternal things and only incidentally with the ordering of human affairs. How are the two related? That is the question. To us who live in a technological age, who suppose that wise theory leads to sound practice, the claim of the ancients seems obscure: why cannot science be tapped by whoever rules? But for the ancients, theory was its own reward and practice reflected it, though was not dictated by it; the model, at least in Aristotle, was magnanimity, the virtue of men who can see further or deeper than they may ever be able to act and who act in the light of their large-mindedness. Aristotle writes of such men that they are a law to themselves. They have, in short, no need for natural law, and they can be supposed to act in a crisis with imagination, calm, and grace.

In developing a doctrine of natural law which takes precedence over natural right, Strauss charges, Aquinas seeks to synthesize what cannot be synthesized; his faith, it seems, colors his philosophical judgment, and he (Thomas) claims for nature what cannot be known by nature and claims for law what can only be settled by right. Does this charge violate the spirit of understanding a man as he understood himself? I think it does if one insists on the claim of synthesis: Thomas presumes and often finds a harmony between nature and grace, and so between reason and revelation, and his presumption makes sense if the author of nature is the same as the giver of grace, if "grace perfects nature" or if nature is a "first grace," as the Catholic adages have it—but there is nothing synthetic here, for Thomas, just the natural effect of an order that is harmonious. Thomas even allows that magnanimity is a virtue—Strauss writes as though for Christianity it is a vice, pride, while the corresponding virtue is humility—though he (Thomas, again) allows that magnanimity without justice is not even a virtue, just haughty highmindedness.[22] That justice is central for Thomas makes sense in the context of natural law; whether its commands are such as to be too inflexible to rule wisely is another matter, though my own reading of Thomas is that natural law is supple and flexible on most points, though there are certain moral absolutes. Although Strauss's emphasis on political flexibility might seem to eschew these—there is, it seems for Strauss and for Plato and Aristotle as

22. *Summa Theologiae* II-II, q. 129; cf. q. 58, a. 12.

he explains them, no law that in some imaginable circumstance must not rightly be broken—the political world he describes is no perpetual Machiavellian moment where necessity can always stake its claim. Whatever has been said by his admirers, Strauss himself makes clear that there are moments when noble defeat, even death, is to be preferred to success or even survival—for instance, when talking about the fate of the West in the context of the Cold War with communism.[23] Consider also his critique of Machiavelli, who, he writes, "is silent about the soul because he has forgotten about the soul, just as he has forgotten tragedy and Socrates."[24] If man must be understood only in terms of what is lower, even if he is to be understood only in terms of himself, I do not see how sacrifice can be noble, logically or psychologically. If it is, then it does not seem to me that Strauss sees the good only as an Epicurean. Rather, I think, he must hold that classical metaphysics is, in some essential way, an account of reality that can still with moral certainty be known.

In the opening chapter of *Natural Right and History*, in which he critiques radical historicism, Strauss twice couples "theoretical metaphysics and ... philosophic ethics or natural right," both of which historicism holds to be impossible.[25] Between these parallel passages he writes: "There cannot be natural right if all that man could know about right were the problem of right, or if the question of the principles of justice would admit of a variety of mutually exclusive answers, none of which could be proved to be superior to the others."[26] He does not say the same about theoretical metaphysics, which as I have noted throughout he presents not as a dogma—dogmatism, he writes in the same chapter, quoting Lessing, is "the inclination 'to identify the goal of our thinking with the point at which we have become tired of thinking'"—but as an understanding of fundamental problems.[27] Natural right can be known only insofar as the quest to understand these problems, which necessarily entails the quest for their solution, remains vital. If then my hypothesis, "that Leo Strauss accepted classical metaphysics as true," is understood to mean, not that he accepted Aristotle's metaphysics as dogma, but that

23. Strauss, *The City and Man*, 3.
24. Strauss, *Thoughts on Machiavelli*, 294.
25. Strauss, *Natural Right and History*, 19, 29.
26. Ibid., 24.
27. Ibid., 22.

he held the contemplation of its problems as essential to a truly philosophical life, then I think it stands unrefuted by the arguments I have considered and addressed. At least it is necessary to hold this hypothesis if Strauss's case for classical political philosophy and for classic natural right is thought sound.

 13

Strauss and Pascal

Is Discussion Possible?

PHILIPPE BÉNÉTON

Pascal and Strauss confront us with a radical choice. But the terms of the choice differ and the arguments lead in opposite directions. Is the door open to dialogue? According to Strauss, the answer is no. He quotes, he paraphrases, he refers to Pascal several times. He never really discusses his thought as a whole.[1] The reason is that philosophy and revelation are mutually exclusive and cannot refute each other:

> It seems to me that all these attempts (made, for example, by Pascal and by others) to prove that the life of philosophy is fundamentally miserable presuppose faith; these arguments are not acceptable and possible as a refutation of philosophy. Generally stated, I would say that all alleged refutations of revelation presuppose unbelief in revelation, and all alleged refutations of philosophy presuppose faith in revelation. There seems to be no ground common to both and therefore superior to both.[2]

---

1. See in particular Leo Strauss, *Natural Right and History* (Chicago: University of Chicago Press, 1953), 83n3; Leo Strauss, *What Is Political Philosophy?* (Chicago: University of Chicago Press, 1959), 114–15; Leo Strauss, *The Rebirth of Classical Political Rationalism*, ed. Thomas L. Pangle (Chicago: University of Chicago Press, 1989), 3, 269.

2. Strauss, *The Rebirth of Classical Political Rationalism*, 269. What follows is based on ibid., 241–70.

So, there is an abyss between reason and revelation. In both cases, the choice is a question of faith. A discussion is useless and hopeless. Is this true?

Two Radical Choices

There is at least one piece of common ground between Pascal and Strauss. The starting point is the same: the limits of human reason or the natural uncertainty concerning the first things. Philosophical reason is unable to fully understand the nature of the whole and, in particular, it is unable to settle the question of the existence or of the nonexistence of God.

The natural condition of man is uncertainty, says Pascal. Without God, man is lost in "this remote corner of nature," he is lost between the abyss of the infinite and the abyss of nothingness. He lives in an "eternal despair of knowing" either the beginning or the end of things.[3] Philosophy cannot help. The so-called philosophical demonstrations of the existence of God are powerless or ineffective. Pascal dismisses them in short and categorical sentences.[4] First, these demonstrations are too "impliquées" (complicated or confused), they do not fit in with the natural life of the mind; secondly, insofar as they prove anything, it is only the existence of a supreme principle which is called God. But what is really at stake is the truth of the God of Abraham, Isaac, and Jacob, the God of Jesus Christ. On this point, philosophy is silent. The life according to a self-sufficient reason is made up of uncertainties; it is also made up of errors or illusions.

For Strauss, the first thing that the philosopher knows is that he does not know the most important things. He should also know that philosophy cannot demonstrate or refute revelation and that revelation cannot refute philosophy. Strauss does not attach more importance than Pascal to the philosophical demonstrations of the existence of God or gods. He does not discuss them and, concerning the demonstrations of the Greek philosophers, he presents them only as a step in their inquiry. On the other side, the choice of the philosophical life cannot be fully justified by philosophy. Life according to reason is based on uncertainty.

But what follows, follows different paths. According to Strauss, the

---

3. Blaise Pascal, *Pensées de Pascal*, texte de l'édition Brunschvicg (Paris: Librairie Garnier frères, 1925), §72.
4. Ibid., §543, §547.

crucial choice is the choice between reason and revelation or between Athens and Jerusalem, that is to say the choice between two ways of life: the life according to Greek philosophy and the life according to the Bible. The first is a life of autonomous understanding, the second a life of obedient love. The disagreement or the conflict is a radical one. Any attempt at harmonization is doomed to failure. Greek philosophy can use obedient love in a subservient way, the Bible can use philosophy as a servant but what is so used in each case rebels against such use. The philosopher is meant to be a theoretical, knowing, contemplative being. He lives in a state above fear and trembling as well as above hope. The man of biblical faith is meant to live in childlike obedience. He lives in fear and trembling as well as in hope. For the philosopher, the beginning of wisdom is the sense of wonder; in the Bible, it is the fear of God. Strauss speaks as a professor, he takes a moderate tone. He explains, he distinguishes, he reasons. Nevertheless, he argues discreetly but clearly in favor of the philosophical life.

For Pascal, the vital choice has to be made between the life according to revelation (more precisely, the Christian revelation) and the life of the man without God, whether he is a philosopher or not. Insofar as we can know, the "partner" of Pascal is the *libertin*, that is to say an *esprit fort* (a man who has a great esteem of himself and does not want to be fooled by common beliefs), a man who has no interest in religion and who lives as if the problem of the truth of revelation does not exist. This choice is even more radical than Strauss's choice. The natural human condition is miserable (uncertainty, restlessness, boredom) and man fusses over not thinking about that. He flees the true vision of his condition and takes refuge in *divertissement* (diversion). Once more, philosophy cannot help. "One [philosopher] says that the sovereign good consists in virtue, another in pleasure, another in the knowledge of nature, another in truth ..., another in total ignorance, another in indolence, another in disregarding appearances, another at wondering at nothing.... We are well-paid."[5] Generally, they "put forward as the good the good which is in ourselves."[6] But the true good is in God. Following Augustine, Pascal says that the deepest longing in the human heart is to love and to be loved, and that only God can fill the human heart.

5. Ibid., §73.
6. Ibid., §430.

Pascal of course does not speak as a professor. He writes an apology for Christianity, his *parti pris* is explicit. He takes his reader by the hand and follows his path with him. He is appealing to his heart but also to his reason. So reason is not on one side only. Let us add that Pascal has an extraordinary way of writing—nothing esoteric but a powerful voice, a dense style, many brilliant and vibrant formulations and images.

On the Life According to Revelation

For Strauss, the man of faith is *par excellence* the Jewish believer. Christianity is an attempt to harmonize the Bible and Greek philosophy. In such an attempt, the purity of both reason and revelation is fated to be lost. The Jewish people needs only their scripture which is their law. They embody Jerusalem's position. A true man of faith lives in childlike obedience.

But is it true? Should the believer surrender his reason? It is certain that the call to reason is less necessary for the Jews and the Muslims than for the Christians—in the first case, religion is primarily conceived as a law, in the second a large field is left to the guidance of reason. Does this mean that the faith is impure in the second case and pure in the first? Pascal is a good counter-example. There is no doubt that he was a man of great faith. Indeed he belonged to the camp of the enemies of philosophy (more precisely, of metaphysics and moral philosophy) but he was not at all an enemy of reason in any field. His rules were: "Two extremes: to exclude reason, to admit only reason," "Submission and the use of reason in which consists true Christianity," and "We need to doubt where necessary, to be sure where necessary, to submit where necessary."[7] Pascal was a great scientist, and as a scientist he lived a life of autonomous understanding. In his debate with Father Noël on the existence or not of the vacuum, he dismissed any argument of authority and based his interpretation on experimental reason. And it turns out he was right and Aristotle was wrong. Furthermore, in any revealed religion, there is a problem with the reading of scripture. If there is no way of discriminating between individual interpretations, the result will be the multiplication of sects or the belief in false messiahs.

Let me add a marginal remark on this topic. The stumbling-block between Jews and Christians is linked to the reading of the Bible. The

7. Ibid., §253, §269, §268.

prophets foresaw Jesus Christ, say the Christians—they did not, say the Jews. Strauss interpreted the Bible as a Jew, Pascal as a Christian. The irony of the story is this: it is Pascal who, following Christian tradition, said that the Bible has a double meaning or that God spoke in an esoteric manner. The prophets must be understood spiritually and not literally. But it is true that it is not the kind of esoteric meaning Strauss discovered in the ancient philosophers. Here, according to the Christians, it is the heart that commands, not the mind.

On the Philosophical Life

For Strauss, philosophy rightly understood (i.e., Greek philosophy) is not a set of propositions, a teaching, or even a system. It is a way of life—and it is the right one. Obviously, philosophy needs some propositions to establish the primacy of the philosophical life. There are as follows:

> Philosophy is the quest for knowledge regarding the whole. Because it is essentially a quest, because it is not able ever to become wisdom (as distinguished from philosophy), philosophy finds that that the problems are always more evident than the solutions. All solutions are questionable. Now the right way of life cannot be established except by an understanding of the nature of man, and the nature of man cannot be fully clarified except by an understanding of the nature of the whole. Therefore, the right way of life cannot be established metaphysically except by a complete metaphysics, and therefore, the right way of life remains questionable. But the very uncertainty of all solutions, the very ignorance regarding the most important things, makes quest for knowledge the most important thing, and therefore makes a life devoted to it the right way of life.[8]

Let us summarize the argument: the uncertainty about the right way of life makes the quest for the right way of life the right way of life even though the quest for the right way of life cannot make certain that the quest for the right way of life is the right way of life. The philosophical life is the right one or it is not. But Strauss adds that the philosopher finds his happiness in philosophizing. Is this not the best reason in favor of the philosophical life?

In any case, the philosopher strives to discover, as much as possible, the first things on the basis of inquiry. As a theoretical, contemplative being, he attempts to grasp the eternal things, so he is "chiefly concerned

8. Strauss, *Rebirth*, 260.

with eternal beings, or the 'ideas,' and hence with the 'idea' of man. Consequently, he is as unconcerned as possible with individual and perishable human beings and hence also with his own individuality, or his body, as well as with the sum total of all individuals beings and their 'historical' procession."[9] So the life of the philosopher is asocial and apolitical—he has the greatest self-sufficiency that is humanly possible. His spirit is serenity on the basis of resignation, he is above fear and hope, he lives untragically.

The picture is impressive but sometimes the reader needs some explanation: (1) Strauss refers to Greek philosophy but the philosophical life is not exactly the same according to Socrates, Plato, Aristotle, Epictetus, Epicurus, etc. Are these differences meaningless? (2) Wisdom is detachment, say the Greeks, but to what extent? Is the Straussian philosopher a radically selfish man? Strauss grants this: the philosopher is radically detached from human beings as human beings, but he cannot help living as a human being who as such cannot be dead to human concerns, although his soul will not be in these concerns. On the scope of these concerns, his explanations seem slightly hesitant, especially regarding the natural affections.[10] In any event, the fact is that human love plays a very weak role in the life of the philosopher. (3) What is the result of the philosophical inquiry? Strauss seems to give two answers. The first is that wisdom is out of reach and that all solutions will remain questionable. The second is that the philosopher has a glimpse of the eternal order, that the Greeks have brought to light the existence of an impersonal necessity, or in other words, of a natural order.

Pascal of course gives a very different picture. The philosopher shares the human condition; without God, he is as miserable as the common man. This natural human condition has two features: it is strange, it is tragic. The beginning of the philosopher's wisdom is the sense of wonder, says Strauss. The philosophers are not surprised enough, answers Pascal. They are not surprised enough about the strange state of man in the universe: his extraordinary smallness in front of the infinite space, his extraordinary grandeur which lies in his thought. "Man is but a reed but he is a thinking reed."[11] They are not surprised enough about the strange state of human knowledge: man is incapable of knowing with

---

9. Strauss, *What Is Political Philosophy?*, 118.
10. See Strauss, *What Is Political Philosophy?*, 119–22; and Strauss, *Natural Right and History*, 122.
11. Pascal, *Pensées*, §347.

certainty but he is also incapable of totally ignoring. His condition is contrary to his inclination.[12] They are not surprised enough about the fact that we are all condemned to death. Death is so horrible, so terrible that men have decided not to think about it. Without God, life is tragic. The one who considers his own natural condition is "like a man who would be carried to a dreadful desert island and would awake without knowing where he is and without means of escape. And therefore, I wonder how people in a condition which is so miserable do not fall into despair."[13]

As we have seen, Strauss disagrees. The philosopher lives untragically. Pascal would say that it is the effect of an illusion, that this philosophy is a *divertissement*, a way of escaping a true vision of the human condition. Perhaps it is possible to add another argument. Pascal and Strauss have in common the fact that they lower the importance of human love. Let us assume that death is a leap into nothingness: it is, no doubt, less unnatural to think of his own death untragically than to think the same way about the death of his kin. If there is nothing after death, to give life is also to give an eternal death. If there is nothing after death, the loss of a child is an eternal loss. For a believer such a loss is a terrible drama, for a nonbeliever, it is a tragedy. In any case, to love is to put oneself at risk. The serenity of the philosopher supposes that he does not love anybody. Is it the right way to live?

On the Choice Itself

It is a matter of faith, says Strauss. The word *faith* does not seem appropriate here as it does not have the same meaning in the case of a believer and in the case of the philosopher. What is the philosopher's faith? If one understands well, it is not a belief but an unbelief. In any case, reason is out of play.

Pascal is again on the opposite side. According to reason, the only possibility of revelation involves the obligation to go in quest of God. "There are only three kinds of persons: some who serve God, having found him; others who are occupied in seeking him, not having found him; others who live without seeking him and without having found him. The first are reasonable and happy, the last are foolish and unhappy; those be-

---

12. Ibid., §72.
13. Ibid., §697.

tween are unhappy and reasonable."[14] The philosophical way advocated by Strauss is foolish and leads to unhappiness. The critical distinction is not between reason and revelation but between the attitudes of men toward God. On this theme, Pascal puts forward a specific argument and, on the other hand, a long series of arguments.

The first takes the form of a wager.[15] It is famous, it is a mathematician's argument. It is extremely complicated and has been differently interpreted. Here is a simplified version. The question is: either God exists or he does not. Reason cannot answer. But given that you cannot not choose—*vous êtes embarqués* (you are embarked)—there is a rational choice. The calculation of gains and losses combined with the calculation of chances (the mathematical hope) lead to this conclusion: wager without hesitation that he exists. Did Pascal think that his reasoning was convincing? It is too complicated, it does not fit in with real life. At the end of the dialogue, the *libertin* says: "I am so made that I cannot believe. What then would you have me do?" He is not convinced by the argument despite his rational strength. If this interpretation is right, it follows that the true *apologia* should take another way.

This way is that of the *Pensées* as a whole. Pascal strives to show that there are good reasons to go in quest of God: (1) "The last proceeding of reason is to recognize that there is an infinity of things which are beyond it."[16] (2) The Christian religion is mysterious but it is enlightening as it gives an account of the strange condition of man and of his double nature. (3) The Christian religion cannot be proved philosophically but history is on its side (this part is largely out of date but one finds in it many insightful things). Ultimately, faith that is a gift of God is received in the heart. "It is the heart which experiences God, and not reason. This, then, is faith: God felt by the heart, not by reason."[17] According to Pascal the heart is both the place of the evidence of first principles, the place of love and the place of meeting with God. It is the highest faculty of man which feels God.

---

14. Ibid., §257.
15. Ibid., §233.
16. Ibid., §267.
17. Ibid., §278.

The Few and the Many

The last differences are not the least. Strauss's good choice concerns the few, Pascal's choice concerns everyone. It is surprising that Strauss presents his alternative as the drama of the human soul. True philosophers, he says, are extremely rare. What then about mankind in general? The difference between Strauss and Pascal is related to the fact that the first gives primacy to the mind and the second to the heart. For Strauss the well-ordered soul is that of the philosophers. For Pascal, we should distinguish three orders: the order of the bodies, the order of the minds, and the order of charity. "All bodies, the firmament, the stars, the earth and its kingdoms are not worth the lowest mind.... All bodies together and all minds together, and all their products, are not worth the least feeling of charity. This is of an order which is infinitely more elevated."[18] The young Pascal had the strong feeling that he belonged to the camp of the strongest minds. But he abandoned his pride. He strived to give to love the primacy that the mind claims for itself, to bow to the pride of the mind before the nobility and the greatness of certain lives which are humble and pure.

On the other hand, we cannot deny the nobility of Strauss's undertaking. He tried to save the meaning of life in the absence of God. He tried also to preserve the old morality. For Nietzsche, it is impossible to preserve biblical morality while abandoning biblical faith. Yes, it is possible to preserve a morality of the same kind, answers Strauss, if we go back to Greek philosophy. The question is open but the present state of the West seems to show that Nietzsche was right.

---

18. Ibid., §793.

 14

Leo Strauss's Profound and Fragile Critique of Christianity

RALPH C. HANCOCK

> The quarrel between the ancients and the moderns concerns eventually, and perhaps even from the beginning, the status of "individuality."
>
> —Leo Strauss

This is the next to last sentence in Leo Strauss's *Natural Right and History*. In the last sentence, Strauss takes the side of virtue and "sound antiquity" against individuality. He does not advertise the connection he clearly sees between modern individualism and the Christian break with sound antiquity concerning the eternal status of the individual human being. Brief reviews of three celebratory versions (Larry Siedentop, Alain Badiou, Alexandre Kojève) of the derivation of modern secular individualism or rationalism from Christianity will serve to frame Leo Strauss's discreetly anti-Christian defense of "sound antiquity."

Siedentop: The Christian Origins of Western Liberalism

Larry Siedentop certainly agrees with Strauss's suggestion concerning the centrality of the notion of the individual to the development of the

West. He has recently argued, in *Inventing the Individual: The Origins of Western Liberalism*—a work of impressive scope and erudition, and at the same time of charming liberal simplicity—that Christian belief is the wellspring of the moral ideal of a community of equal and free individuals that we associate with modern "secularism." And for Siedentop (unlike Strauss) this religious genealogy of liberalism is clearly good news; he calls on Christians and secular liberals to embrace the Western heritage of equal freedom they share.

Siedentop argues that modern individualism sprang from the Christian revolution (especially St. Paul's revolution) against the hierarchical political, spiritual, and intellectual framework of pagan civilization. This framework, a certain conception of reason as ruling in the soul and in the city, was bound up with a hierarchical view of the cosmos. According to Siedentop, St. Paul blasted this aristocratic framework, igniting a transformation with revolutionary social and intellectual consequences that are still unfolding in our times. The new view of reason prepares modern rationalism because it abandons the hierarchical claims of reason's rule and instead bases reason on an egalitarian and universalist faith. The effectual truth of Jesus Christ for Siedentop's Paul is the imperative of universal freedom and equality.

Siedentop sees that the ancient city, the ancient cosmos, and therefore the ancient understanding of reason were profoundly and inherently hierarchical. The analogy in Plato's *Republic* between a stratified soul and a stratified society is just the clearest example of the "aristocratic" moral and intellectual framework that pervasively structured the thinking and the sensibility of the ancient world.[1]

The moral revolution that Christianity would bring about was prepared, on the one hand, Siedentop argues, by the Jewish law, and on the other by developments within Platonic philosophy. On the philosophical side, the "ancient sense of rationality" had been deeply conditioned by the experience of "public discussion and decision making in the polis," and thus by the belief "that reason could govern." The decline of the *polis* compromised the very meaning of classical reason. Philosophers began to look beyond "the model of a rational ascent up the great chain of being by a few—that ascent which tied thought and being so closely

---

1. Larry Siedentop, *Inventing the Individual: The Origins of Western Liberalism* (Cambridge, Mass.: Belknap Press of Harvard University Press, 2014), 36.

together," and they "began to worry about the source of all being," considered as "the Absolute, a first cause that was beyond all comprehension." The emergence of the this idea of the absolute "begins to reshape ethical thinking ... for it led to moral rules being considered, not so much as rational conclusions from the nature of things, but as commands issuing from an agency that was 'beyond' reason."[2]

This philosophical reorientation away from the rule of reason in accordance with nature merged with the influence of Jewish monotheism, the belief in a God not beholden to the rule of reason, a God who "refused to be pinned down: 'I will be who I will be.'" With the waning of the *polis*'s ethic of rational deliberation in an ordered community, "conforming to an external will was becoming the dominant social experience. And the voice of Judaism spoke to that experience, as no other did. The message of the Jewish scriptures was radical. Virtue consisted in obedience to God's will."

The confession of human dependence on an absolute beyond reason would seem clearly to mark the end of reason's career: "All that could be said about the Absolute was negative: that it was not limited, not necessitated, not the subject of knowledge."[3] But the miracle of Christianity consists precisely in transforming this negation of humanity's alleged natural capacity for rational self-government into a liberation. Already within philosophy there had emerged the idea that the "act of submission" is "the precondition of knowledge."[4] But it is the apostle Paul's "vision of a mystical union with Christ" that "introduces a revised notion of rationality—what he sometimes describes as the 'foolishness of God.'"[5] This new understanding of rationality "overturns the assumption on which ancient thinking had hitherto rested, the assumption of natural inequality. Instead, Paul wagers on human equality," a wager that "turns on transparency" between the self and others.[6]

"In his conception of the Christ, Paul brings together basic features of Jewish and Greek thought to create something new."[7] Judaism's favoring of law and command over *logos* or reason, its preoccupation with "conformity to a higher or divine will" is miraculously combined with the

2. Ibid., 53.
3. Ibid., 55.
4. Ibid.
5. Ibid., 59.
6. Ibid.
7. Ibid., 60.

maximal extension of reason's empire, with "the abstracting potential of later Hellenistic philosophy."[8] Greek reason had for centuries been extending its scope: "For the discourse of citizenship in the polis had initiated a distancing of persons from mere family and tribal identities, while later Hellenistic philosophy had introduced an even more wide-ranging, speculative 'universalist' idiom. That intellectual breadth had, in turn, been reinforced by the subjection of so much of the Mediterranean world to a single power, Rome."[9] One is reminded here of Pierre Manent's tracing of Western history as that of the ascendency of the Roman and then Christian figure of the One/all over the classical tension between the few and the many. In Manent's narrative, the aristocratic tension between the few and the many gives way over the course of Western history to the power of the One as guarantor of the all: "In the eyes of the One, all became the people, all were equal."[10] But the cost of the rout at the hands of the One/all of the unjust partisan claims of the few has been not the simple victory of equality—the ascendancy, let us say, of the simple dignity of the common man. Instead, equality and inequality, now uncoupled and unconditioned by each other, enjoy a joint and unlimited reign: modern society embodies extremes of equality and inequality, and we aspire at once to universal compassion and to unbridled competitiveness. "In brief, all are equal and everyone has his price."[11] Thus, for Manent, the extremes of glory (the perspective of universal empire) and of the reduction of meaning to individual consciousness tend to meet: the One and the all, radical transcendence and reductive equality, are two sides of the same spiritual coin.

Larry Siedentop sees the same convergence, but seems to regard the joint reign of the absolute One and the formless all as unproblematic, and so he embraces this dynamic with an enthusiasm that Pierre Manent cannot share. Manent is concerned about the evacuation of human and political content under the sway of the One that is also all; Siedentop is very satisfied that the Christian synthesis of divine law and abstract, universal reason can ground a new morality, a new freedom and moral agency, radically individual and radically universal, that is "utterly different

---

8. Ibid., 53, 61.
9. Ibid., 61.
10. Pierre Manent, *The Metamorphoses of the City* (Cambridge, Mass.: Harvard University Press, 2016), 99.
11. Ibid., 100.

from the freedom enjoyed by the privileged class of citizens in the polis," a freedom that is bound up with a new understanding of "community as the free association of the wills of morally equal agents, what Paul describes through metaphor as the 'body of Christ.'"[12]

The individual is liberated from family, tribe, and *polis* with the help of the idea of the One absolute divine will, but now this will is no longer understood in the Jewish way as "an external, coercive agency."[13] Rather, Paul's doctrine of Christ "overturns the assumption of natural inequality by creating an inner link between the divine will and human agency," a kind of fusion that justifies "the assumption of the moral equality of humans."[14] "The Christ provides a foundation in the nature of things for a pre-social or individual will. Individual agency acquires roots in divine agency. The Christ stands for the presence of God in the world, the ultimate support for individual identity."[15] This new universal standard overcomes the externality of the Jewish law on the one hand and the hierarchical presuppositions of Greek reason on the other. We see "the advent of the new freedom, freedom of conscience." Thus "the Greek mind and the Jewish will are joined." Rationality is now extracted radically from concrete social and political existence and therefore from "language as a social institution." "For Paul, the gift of love in the Christ offers a pre-linguistic solution, through a leap of faith—that is, a wager on the moral equality of humans."[16] Thus the believer's submission "to the mind and will of God as revealed in Christ" is at the same time the "beginning of a 'new creation,'" the revelation of human equality and autonomy. This liberation of the individual from law and reason and for his consecration to the moral equality of humanity is the object of Paul's "almost ferocious moral universalism."[17] Siedentop appears to see no practical tension between Pauline "Christian liberty" as, on the one hand, the liberation of the individual from all given social bonds and, on the other, the individual's submission to the Christ, a submission "in which charity overcomes all other motives." There is no problem in reconciling the liberal liberation of the individual with Christian submission to the demands of charity, as long as charity is interpreted liberally as implying "moral equali-

12. Siedentop, *Inventing the Individual*, 60.
13. Ibid., 61.
14. Ibid.
15. Ibid., 64.
16. Ibid., 65.
17. Ibid., 64.

ty and reciprocity."[18] Thus Siedentop believes that he has dispelled the illusion of an essential tension between Christian ideals and "Godless secularism."[19] The liberal idea of reciprocity based on moral equality is virtually identical with the New Testament injunction "to love thy neighbor as thyself"; and the Christian doctrine of the incarnation cashes out as liberal commitment to "equal liberty." The "moral equality of humans implies that there is a sphere in which each should be free to make his or her own decisions, a sphere of conscience and free action."[20]

Badiou: St. Paul's Universalism

The appropriation of St. Paul as the forerunner or even founder of one or another version of modern secular idealism is of course nothing new.[21] Another recent and prominent such appropriation is that of Alain Badiou's *Saint Paul: The Foundation of Universalism*. Badiou's version of Christian secularism has more of a radical edge than Siedentop's and does not culminate in liberalism, but rather in an extremely vague but unmistakable invocation of collective, indeed "communist" revolutionary action.

Like Siedentop, Badiou sees St. Paul's teaching as the overcoming of Jewish exceptionalism or particularism on the one hand and of Greek resignation to cosmic order on the other hand. But where Siedentop understands Christianity as preserving essential moments of these two alternatives (divine law and abstracting reason), Badiou breaks radically with both in the name of the "event."

For Badiou, the event of the resurrection (which has nothing essential to do with some miracle of immortality) signifies absolute innovation beyond all claims of conceptual ordering; the submission of reason to the "folly of our preaching" thus liberates human action from all "rational" limits.[22] The pure form of universality exhausts the meaning of this event of liberation. Philosophy is not transformed but is simply abolished, and the pure event of "the son" dispenses with all Trinitarian nonsense concerning the Father: "Jesus" is simply the name of this absolute and

18. Ibid., 65.
19. Ibid., 360.
20. Ibid., 361.
21. See Mark Lilla, "A New, Political Saint Paul?," *New York Review of Books*, October 23, 2008.
22. Alain Badiou, *Saint Paul: The Foundation of Universalism* (Palo Alto, Calif.: Stanford University Press, 2003), 49.

therefore purely formal and revolutionary "event."[23] Human subjectivity is constituted by the "evental" rupture; event evokes a process without end, a negation of law and reason without any stable content. The event has no assignable content but only the form of revolutionary subjectivity and universality, radical individuality opening up upon radical collectivity. There is no truth to guide action; the only truth is the active response to the pure event. Love is under the authority of the event, and love converts thought into sheer power, "the real materiality of militant universalism."[24] Badiou's revolutionary "event" is as formal and empty as possible in order to be as radical as possible. But in the end the event must "inscribe" itself in the world in some way, and we can assume that Badiou would not regard all inscriptions as equally faithful to St. Paul's universalistic revolution. Revolutionary "univeralism" must imply some content, some stable features of the reality to be inscribed, or else any gesture of radical rupture with the given—say, throwing in one's lot with a violent *völkisch* movement, or waiting upon gods poetically—might be considered as authentically "evental" as another. We know the tenor of Badiou's "event" from his undefended allusions to communism, and we can discern the content of his "rebirth" in the phrase, "the real materiality of militant universalism." As a good communist, Badiou projects mankind's universal material redemption—the overcoming by and for humanity of the realm of material necessity—as the horizon and implicit *telos* of his passion for the radical destruction of all given horizons.

In its content Badiou's interpretation of the ethical meaning of Christianity is not that far from Siedentop's reduction of charity to "reciprocity." But, in contrast to Siedentop's very complacent liberalism, which is content to progress within a revolutionary ethical frame inherited from the distant past, Badiou's intransigent radicalism must perpetually reenact the exemption of grace from nature and defer the content of reciprocity to a new world beyond the natural economy of liberalism. To state this comparison in terms of the figure of transcendence of the One/all: Siedentop is content that the absolute One has done its revolutionary work at the Christian or Pauline origins of Western civilization; for us today, he thinks, the prosaic work of universal equality, freedom, and reciprocity can proceed in the now familiar world that the One produced long ago by

23. Ibid., 67.
24. Ibid., 92.

blasting the aristocratic paradigm of reason, which presupposed an eternal tension between the few and the many.

Kojève's Post-Christian Universalism

Leo Strauss considers Alexandre Kojève's philosophy to be an exemplar of the interpretation of secular rationalism as the real fulfillment of Christian universalism.[25] Following Hegel, Kojève understands modern secular rationalism as a transformation, but also as a fulfillment, of Christian universalism and subjectivity. His Hegelian version displays a firmer grasp than Siedentop's of the philosophical stakes of such an interpretation, and in a way combines Siedentop's prosaic liberal and democratic sympathies with Badiou's revolutionary resolution.

Kojève agrees with Siedentop in cashing out the meaning of universalism in the rather prosaic democratic morality of reciprocity. For Kojève, the great political, military, and religious actors who drove the march of history understood themselves as serving some god or some understanding of truth and right, but the only real and abiding motive in the historical process proves to be the desire to be recognized in one's humanity by other human beings. The medium or currency of this recognition can be nothing other than effective attention to the simple material needs and interests of our common, bodily humanity. The Christian leveling of aristocratic pride released the energy of human labor for the service of common human needs; thus the effectual truth of a God who transcends social differences is an ethic of formal universality, and this can have no concrete meaning except a universal society of equal recognition. Kojève's advantage in sobriety over Badiou's enthusiasm for the revolutionary "event" lies in his acceptance of the prosaic and democratic and therefore humble or low substance of the revolutionary *telos*: there is no meaning of life except the satisfaction of the most ordinary desires of the most ordinary human beings. Kojève's advantage in realism over Siedentop lies in his awareness that the fulfillment of the idea of a universal society of equally freedom and reciprocity will require a coercive apparatus—the universal and homogenous state. Thus, Kojève acknowledges, the final and abso-

---

25. The brief summary of Kojève's view that follows is drawn from his engagement with Leo Strauss in *On Tyranny*, ed. Victor Gourevitch and Michael S. Roth (Chicago: University of Chicago Press, 2013).

lute ascendancy of the plainest democratic satisfaction is the only real truth of the ecstatic religion of grace: a collective life supported by total technological mastery, the absolute victory of a final, rational tyranny, a prosaic life in which all poetic projections have been banished along with the cruelty of history—this, Kojeve sees, is the final and irrefragable meaning of the transcendent Christian event that first laid the axe to the root of all aristocratic pretensions.

For Kojève, one might say that history has a rational meaning, but that meaning is finally meaningless—this is the shadow of nothingness that Heidegger casts over Kojève's Hegelian story of rational completion. And here we see the culmination and exhaustion of the dynamic polarity between the One and the all that, as Pierre Manent has shown, has driven Western and therefore world history. The complicity between absolute transcendence and formal universality has progressively dissolved the human tension between the few and the many; neither the ambitions of nobility nor the simple duty of common decency seem able to resist the allied force of the notions of absolute freedom and universal necessity.

Resistance to this pincer movement of the One and the all against the natural and limited space of human existence was, I propose, the central purpose of Strauss's philosophical career. The great debates he engaged in or staged, notably the questions of ancients vs. moderns and of Athens vs. Jerusalem can only be adequately grasped as responses to this dehumanizing dynamic of Western history.

Strauss's Response to the Victory of Universalism: *On Tyranny*

Despite impressions that Leo Strauss willingly conveyed, his thought agrees fundamentally with Siedentop's diagnosis of the Christian roots of modern liberal democracy. The important difference, of course, is that Siedentop celebrates this development, whereas Strauss deplores it.

In his "Restatement" to Kojève, Strauss does not really contest the Hegelian thesis (whether in Kojève's or Voegelin's version) of the Christian root of modernity. In fact he explicitly leaves open the question "how far the epoch-making change that was effected by Machiavelli is due to the indirect influence of the Biblical tradition," but insists only that first "that change" must be "fully understood in itself."[26] In other words, once the Machiavellian effectual truth of modern rationalism is understood, then Christians and others inclined to give the modern revolution a Christian baptism, to cover this very this-worldly project with a veil of vaguely Christian humanitarian "spirituality," can judge for themselves whether they want to be responsible for this interpretation. Let us not sugarcoat modernity, he is saying, by evoking its "spiritual roots" before we ask the question in all sobriety: what *is* the modern project? Thus, although Strauss emphatically prioritizes the question of the character of modernity over that of its "indirect" biblical origins, he quite clearly does not either refute or even dismiss the proposition that such religious influences were a significant factor in the rise of modern rationalism.

Strauss is thus less immediately interested in the historical question of "influences" than in the essential character of modernity, and nowhere does Strauss make clearer than in this text his fundamental assessment of the modern project, understood in its full implications—that is, as Kojève understands and embraces it. He makes clear, that is, that he abominates this project and considers it antithetical to any adequate understanding of genuine nobility or of plain human decency. The identification of philosophy and tyranny, the liquidation of philosophical transcendence in total devotion to the cause of an utterly unphilosophical humanity, the extreme separation and fusion of the high and the low, the One and the all, represents for Strauss the collapse of all human meaning, the end of humanity. Kojève is of course resigned, with more than a touch of irony, no doubt, to this inhuman or posthuman culmination of secular humanism. But Strauss bends every effort to resist this culmination, even allowing himself (no doubt with a touch of his own irony) a militant call to resistance: "Warriors and workers of all countries, unite, while there is still time, to prevent the coming of 'the realm of freedom.' Defend with might and main, if it needs to be defended, 'the realm of necessity.'"[27] Freedom as an all-too-human project has necessarily degenerated into a rational and technological tyranny; the compulsion to make mankind completely at home in this world, a world of his own making, has left him utterly homeless. To turn to the "realm of necessity" would be to recover an appreciation of the permanent contours and therefore the

26. Ibid., 185.
27. Ibid., 210.

permanent limits of the human condition. But how can "necessity" provide a home for human existence, for meaningful action and reflection? Leo Strauss is perfectly aware of the irony in this militant call to action on behalf of a supposed realm beyond the reach of all human action. The irony lies precisely in the fact that the "realm of necessity" does indeed need to be defended. The idea of an eternal realm of pure, impersonal necessity untouched by human concerns is the projection of a very human claim to rule, the mostly implicit horizon of an essentially aristocratic assertion of human meaning.

Strauss here tips his hand more than once to reveal the human and political springs of the philosophical idea of a "realm of necessity," but he also provides plenty of encouragement to the pride of philosophers who would not wish to be reminded of their dependence on moral and political sources of meaning. He appeals to the pride of philosophers even as he defines philosophy as beyond human pride.

Strauss tips his aristocratic hand, at least for those who are paying close attention, when he more than once resorts shamelessly to argument by highminded assumption or by peremptory definition: we must *assume* that philosophers do not desire to rule (they do not care what other people—at least common people—think); and a "philosopher" who is concerned with recognition is, by definition, not a philosopher. Moreover, Strauss explicitly concedes to Kojève that his pure, transhistorical idea of philosophy depends upon the thesis of eternal, immutable being—but then he explicitly acknowledges (in a critical concluding paragraph that was withheld from the original English edition) that this thesis is altogether questionable.[28]

Strauss most extravagantly indulges the pride of the self-styled philosopher when he proclaims that "the philosopher's dominating passion is the desire for truth, i.e., for knowledge of the eternal order, or the eternal cause or causes of the whole. As he looks up in search for the eternal order, all human things and all human concerns reveal themselves to him in all clarity as paltry and ephemeral, and no one can find solid happiness in what he knows to be paltry and ephemeral."[29] Any would-be "philosopher" who has not already heard the resounding tone of hyperbole in this celebration of philosophy will likely not pause to reflect on the

28. Ibid., 213.
29. Ibid., 198.

implication of the sentence that immediately follows: "He has then the same experience regarding all human things, nay, regarding man himself, which the man of high ambition has regarding the low and narrow goals, or the cheap happiness, of the general run of men."[30] That is: the philosopher is to the political man, "the man of high ambition," as the political man is to the common man. The philosopher's ambition is to be beyond ambition. Strauss's philosopher defends the realm of necessity, without recognizing the irony implicit in the need to defend it, in the very human and personal assertion of an eternal, impersonal necessity.

For Strauss the possibility of satisfaction in serene contemplation grounds wisdom's moderation. But it would be at least as true to say that a moderate practical wisdom, the noble reserve represented by Jane Austen (as opposed to Dostoyevsky), the aspiration to resignation concerning common human hopes, is the very human ground of the idea of the contemplation of an inhuman eternity.[31]

Strauss's most decisive concession to Kojève is his acknowledgement that "subjective certainty" is impossible, that all knowledge is embedded in social-political context. He does not disagree that the "classics were fully aware of the essential weakness of the mind of the individual," but affirms the superiority of an aristocratic over a democratic-universalist context.[32] The Straussian philosopher takes his bearings from the admiration of the few; his orientation is determined originally and fundamentally by a concern for *honor*, whereas the modern philosopher is conditioned by an original motive of "love" for human beings, or concern for the "love" of other human beings, irrespective of their humanly esteemed qualities.[33] This critical examination of "love" makes it clear that Kojève's universal recognition is indeed for Strauss a descendent—a perversion, to be sure, but still in a very significant sense a descendent—of the Christian idea of universal charity.

Strauss recognizes that friendship (as opposed to *caritas* or universal love) is fundamental to the classical idea of philosophy, and that such friendship always arises from and depends upon some prephilosophical understanding of the meaning of the noble. Thus the risk of or tendency toward "sectarianism" is inherent in philosophy. This tendency of course

30. Ibid.
31. Ibid.
32. Ibid., 195.
33. Ibid., 156–58.

should be resisted, but with the understanding that the only alternatives to the "noble" conception of philosophy, the linking of philosophy with an aristocratic understanding of "things beautiful," are (1) the reduction of philosophy to its impact on the many and thus on history, that is, to ideology and propaganda, or (2) the dilution of philosophy to a superficial and unserious academic exercise, a "Republic of Letters" detached from vital human concerns.[34]

Of course I am aware of another move that Strauss makes, which almost all readers take to be his most adequate and therefore final move, namely, his proposal that philosophy be understood as Socratic "knowledge of ignorance," or knowledge of the permanent questions or fundamental problems.[35] Certainly there is truth and indeed beauty or nobility in this characterization of the philosophical life. I am convinced, however, that this "zetetic" teaching finally has a certain exoteric bearing for Strauss; it is addressed precisely to the pride of philosophers who aspire to transcend pride. The "fundamental alternatives" share a common core that now has a moral and political bearing because now, at the end of history, this core is threatened with extinction precisely by a perverse but powerful synthesis of the radicalized alternatives, aristocratic and democratic, Greek and biblical, the absolute and the universal, the One and the all. To retreat from the modern synthesis is necessarily, for Strauss, to distrust the Christian impulse toward synthesis and to wish to restore the original tension between the few and the many. But such a restoration is inseparable from a moderate partisanship on behalf of the few, it is bound up with that "noble reserve" that characterizes the man of classical prudence, and that implies an aristocratic metaphysics and cosmology associated with resignation to the limitations of human action and therefore with serene detachment from human concerns. Thus Strauss's proposal of the zetetic option is here embedded in an account that seems to culminate in the metaphysical idea of an "eternal order." But this finally acknowledges, for the attentive reader, that the taste for such an order is rooted in a practical hierarchy, in "the immediate pleasure which we observe when we observe signs of human nobility."[36] The fundamental alternatives are certainly real, but they are also presented as it were as a package to the modern or postmodern classical philosopher (the Strauss-

34. Ibid., 196.
35. Ibid.
36. Ibid., 202.

ian philosopher) as divine ideas anchoring his aristocratic pride, as an eternal horizon worthy of defending "with might and main" against the "realm of freedom."

I do not mean to say that Strauss reduces philosophy to narrowly "political" motives. My view is that Strauss recognizes that the truth of "philosophy," classically understood, is in a very deep sense a partisan truth, or a truth inherently tinged with a certain pride and a certain partisanship on behalf of excellence, on behalf of "the noble." The intrinsic satisfactions of understanding come to light only by positioning themselves "above" common necessities. In the absence of this vertical orientation, the work of reason must be drawn into the horizontal field of universalization and technology.

Grace and Nature in the Spinoza Preface

The fundamentally moral-political bearing of Strauss's defense of classical philosophy indeed lies deeper than his formal openness to the perennial questions of the Western tradition. The recovery of the primordial unity of Athens and Jerusalem, a unity that he often leaves all but unspoken, now depends upon respecting their difference, even their incommensurability.

Strauss's preface to his *Spinoza's Critique of Religion* is an extremely dense and sinuous text, a rare venture of Strauss's into autobiography, and therefore a potential holy grail for seekers of the deepest intention underlying Strauss's sometimes gnomic utterances. What has not been appreciated is that his critique of the "New Thinking" leads him to provide glimpses of a deep unity or convergence between Jerusalem and Athens.

Strauss argues in this preface that the crisis of Judaism is embedded in the crisis of liberal rationalism; Judaism has hitched its wagon to a train that is heading for a major wreck, in fact a conflagration. The honorable pretensions of Judaism to rationalism have led it to throw in its lot with modern rationalism, which turns out to be fundamentally irrational because it has tried to provide its own ground and thus has flouted the limits of human nature. Modern rationalism is thus fundamentally constructivist, and has seduced Jews into thinking of God as product of the human mind. But an anti-rationalist "New Thinking" (e.g., Franz Rosenzweig) has opened up the possibility of moving beyond metaphysical rationalism in order to ground Judaism in an "immediate experience" of God, man, and the world. This Jewish embrace of the New Thinking is very ill-advised, however, because, first, this Jewish version is hard to distinguish from the Christian version, but more fundamentally because this thinking in its Jewish form has not yet hit bottom. It is Heidegger, instead, who reveals the dark depths of the rejection of the philosophical tradition, the fall into an abyss of death and nothingness.

How can we respond to Heidegger's critique of rationalism and his abyssal thinking? It is at this point that Strauss directs us, as he did in *Natural Right and History*, to a ground common to the Bible and to classical philosophy. And this statement brings us to the heart of Strauss's project of a "return" to classical political philosophy, and indeed in a deeper way to the alternative of Athens or Jerusalem. Against the New Thinking, Strauss affirms that the biblical experience is not contrary to nature; indeed, he writes, strikingly adopting the most recognizable Thomistic motto: "Grace perfects nature, it does not destroy nature."[37] The Bible and the classics agree, he says, on the natural authority of nobility and justice: every noble man is concerned with finding transcendent support for justice. "The Biblical God forms light and creates darkness." A truly "empirical" reading of human experience would reveal, not the radical otherness of some absolute, but rather the ground common to Aristotle and to Judaism expressed in the traditional Jewish belief in "the Torah as prior to world."[38] Our openness to grace must not tempt us to forget the authoritative character of Law: against the Jewish New Thinking that reinterprets the law as "liberation, granting transformation" (that is, along the lines of Heideggerian "possibility"), Strauss insists on the primordial meaning of Jewish Law as prohibition, which recognizes the power of evil and thus the "necessity of coercion."[39] Further on he refers to "the law of reason or the natural law as the right mean between hard-heartedness and soft-heartedness."[40]

Spinoza, on the contrary, anticipates Nietzsche and Heidegger, Strauss

---

37. Leo Strauss, *Spinoza's Critique of Religion* (Chicago: University of Chicago Press, 1997), 10.
38. Ibid., 13.
39. Ibid., 14.
40. Ibid., 33. The reference to this mean is a very striking echo of Strauss's lecture on "German Nihilism," an argument that finally turns as well on the necessity of coercion.

argues, in that his God is beyond good and evil; this God's absolute transcendence implies an absolute freedom to be what he will be. Thus Spinoza "lifts Machiavellianism to theological heights."[41] Just as Siedentop would wish, the absolute transcendence of the One clears the space of this world of all given norms and hierarchy and makes way for a universal religion of humanity. This religion of humanity appears first in its realist or Machiavellian-Spinozist version, in which the necessity of the cruel substitution of human coercion for divine authority is embraced, and then in Hermann Cohen's idealist or Kantian version, which radically differentiates morality from nature and thus obfuscates the necessity of coercion by dreaming of infinite progress.

Strauss here thus implicitly traces the self-destruction of modern reason through what he has elsewhere named "the three waves of modernity": Machiavellian-Spinozist, Kantian (which includes Cohen), and Nietzschean-Heideggerian (which includes the Jewish New Thinking).[42] This much is familiar to students of Strauss. But the additional element that is clearly if delicately present here is the fundamental complicity of Christianity in this collapse of reason. The New Thinking centered on the notion of the experience of a "call" from an "absolute" radically removed from all human meaning is described as "a secularized version of the biblical faith as interpreted by Christian theology."[43] Rosenzweig, who tried to redeem the New Thinking for Judaism, is blamed for displacing the Law in favor of a "sociological" notion of the Jewish nation in a way that emulates the doctrine of Christ. Christianity seeks to replace the *Law* with a more "spiritual" *teaching* that turns away from the reality of Law as prohibition, from a sober awareness of the power of evil and the necessity of coercion, and redefines the law as "liberation, granting, transformation," that is, as openness to some vague possibilities beyond the world as we know it. Thus Strauss associates "the law of reason or the natural law" with the right mean between hard-heartedness and soft-heartedness, the moderate acceptance of the necessity of coercion.[44] The Christian attempt to place both reason and biblical faith under the notion of some "absolute," and thus to transcend the authority of a law

---

41. Ibid., 18.
42. Leo Strauss, "The Three Waves of Modernity," in his *Political Philosophy: Six Essays by Leo Strauss*, ed. Hilail Gildin (New York: Pegasus-Bobbs-Merrill, 1975).
43. Strauss, *Spinoza's Critique of Religion*, 12.
44. Ibid., 22.

understood to be inscribed more or less clearly in an eternal order (the first wave of modernity), tends ultimately to liberate the individual from the natural limits of the human condition and to subject him to the authority of history (second wave) and finally to the abyss of nothingness (third wave).[45] The promise of a transcendent home for the individual spirit alienates man from the primordial experience of the law and finally leaves him radically homeless.

This reading of course goes against the grain of many interpretations of Strauss by uncovering Strauss's awareness that, at the deepest level, the idea of absolute transcendence is the ground of a noxious synthesis between reason and revelation. In other, more accessible texts, Strauss proposes the "brute fact of revelation" as an obstacle to the completion or the sealing of this synthesis. My suggestion is that it is Strauss's *esoteric* teaching that biblical law and classical reason spring from a common root in the orientation toward an eternity that limits and defines humanity; he sees this natural, finite horizon as opposed to the Christian and modern destruction of a finite moral order in favor of the "spiritual" teaching of a "transcendent" or fully open possibility, whether Christian or "rationalist." Strauss's *exoteric* teaching presents biblical Law as pure command and thus as reason's other, a check on the modern instrumental rationalization of law. Thus the familiar Straussian opposition between a life based on revelation and the life of autonomous reason, a choice that he sometimes presents as fundamentally arbitrary, is a staged showdown, a stopgap measure that attempts to use modernity against itself, one facet of modern willfulness against another.

A further consequence of this interpretation is a reversal of priority between Strauss's two famous polarities: ancient/modern and Jerusalem/Athens. Contrary to a common reading, the ancient/modern distinction, or, more precisely, the "progress or return" alternative, proves to be the more fundamental once we see why Christianity belongs for Strauss clearly on the "modern" side. Classical nobility and Jewish Law, while by no means equivalent or even compatible in their full ramifications, are both "ancient" in the decisive sense they represent two rival versions of "return" to a finite horizon; the absolutizing of the Jerusalem/Athens distinction, which Strauss blames on a Christian radicalization of Platonic transcendence, in fact lies at the root of modernity. The rejection of con-

---

45. Ibid., 11 (for "absolute").

crete form and limits (whether these limits are articulated as divine law or as natural virtue) is the common root of Christian transcendence and of modern immanence.

The primordial unity, the common root, of Jerusalem and Athens consists in a tension between broadly aristocratic and democratic motives or sensibilities that is inherent in the moral phenomenon. As we read in *Natural Right and History*, the prephilosophical origins of natural right, are also, or are at least bound up with, "the most elementary premises" of the Bible.[46] The Bible and the classics agree on the primacy, the givenness, of nobility and justice, but the articulation of nobility and justice requires favoring one over the other of the primordial norms. Classical political philosophy favors nobility, and wants to believe that justice can be subsumed without remainder under nobility. Jewish piety distrusts prideful claims to nobility, and tends to subordinate nobility to justice, to the duty of obedience to the divine law to which we are all equally subject. Leo Strauss is respectful of both of these developments, because each in its own way honors the natural or primordial human phenomenon. On the other hand, the Christian project of producing a universal synthesis of nobility and justice, of overcoming the tension between the self-assertion of virtue and openness to the needs of the other, undertakes too much. It makes a promise it cannot keep, at least "in this world," and thus prepares humanity for the modern project, which associates the pretension of transcendence, the adoption of a standpoint outside nature, with devotion to the needs of our most common humanity. The tension between the few and the many is overcome in the conflation of the One and the all.

The Fragility of the Straussian Project

It is now clear, then, why Strauss employs Thomistic language (natural law as the right mean; grace perfects nature) while blaming Christianity for the modern collapse of reason. Is Thomism part of the problem or part of the solution? The answer is elusive because it is "both": though Strauss might prefer Aristotelian Christianity to, say, Pascal or Kierkegaard, he is convinced that the Christian promise of the individual's salva-

---

46. Strauss, *Natural Right and History*, 80.

tion beyond the *polis* and beyond the law necessarily contains the germ of modern irrational rationalism.

There is of course a truth in the figure of universality, as Strauss clearly recognizes. This is another aspect of the biblical side of natural or primordial condition of humanity that precedes and grounds the very idea of "nature." It is also reflected in the egalitarian, apolitical understanding of natural right that Strauss acknowledges as among its primordial meanings.[47] But Strauss's project requires his favoring of the political and aristocratic tradition of natural right. Noble contemplation, the aristocratic configuration of philosophy, provides, he thinks, a very necessary shelter for the natural and ordinary power of "sacred restraints," the rudimentary distinction between good and bad that "we learn as children." Without the shelter of this horizon of eternity, and its inherent recognition of the limits of human action, tyranny can claim the excuse of the highest ideals for the lowest deeds; humans can be tempted to do obviously bad things in the name of universal, transformative ends.

The great Catholic novelist Flannery O'Connor, in her introduction to *Memoir of Mary Ann*, saw this danger as clearly as anyone: "In the absence of this faith now, we govern by tenderness. It is a tenderness which, long since cut off from the person of Christ, is wrapped in theory. When tenderness is detached from the source of tenderness, its logical outcome is terror. It ends in forced labor camps and in the fumes of the gas chamber."[48] The universalization of Jewish righteousness in Christianity and then modernity, the transformation of simple justice or decency, produces the project of universal recognition as understood by Hegel and Kojève. For Strauss, the only alternatives to this universalization are (1) a return to orthodoxy, to the Jewish law; or (2) a return in some form to classical, political (that is, aristocratic) natural right. This is not the place to develop the practical implications of such a postmodern "return" to the classics, except perhaps to signal the two key elements of the practical side of Strauss's project: (1) liberal education, the promotion of a corps of academic gentlemen led and defended by the spirited warriors of serene contemplation or transerotic solitude; and (2) liberal democratic constitutionalism as the best possible approximation of a classical mixed regime.

47. Ibid., 118–19.
48. Flannery O'Connor, introduction to Dominican Nuns of Our Lady of Help Home, *A Memoir of Mary Ann* (New York: Farrar, Straus and Cudahy, 1961), 19.

These two elements translate essentially into what are called the "East coast" and "West coast" Straussian projects.

We will not attempt here to assess the current prospects for these academic and political visions. It is important to emphasize, though, that Strauss is very aware of the one-sidedness of his grounding of morality and politics. He is aware that his aristocratic strategy gives short shrift to another dimension of morality and indeed of the meaning of human existence. This is the dimension he refers to, as it were in passing, when he asserts quite flatly that humanity is unthinkable without reference to "sacred restraints." We are subject to mysteriously grounded limits, divine commands that cannot be accounted for from the perspective of the nobility of aristocratic self-sufficiency. These commands issuing from a divinity beyond the reach of natural, political reason suggest to the mind the universality of humanity and tend to elevate common human hopes for the redemption of what is dearest to us as simple human beings. This is to say that the idea of sacred restraints suggests a divine, universal lawgiver who humbles the proud and commands love for our fellow human beings regardless of claims to excellence.

Strauss, however, judges it best to preserve philosophy from getting mixed up in the articulation of personal love or with the hopes of universal salvation associated with love; instead he prefers to keep sacred law separate from the nobility of philosophy, Jerusalem (i.e., Judaism) separate from Athens: proud reason on the one hand, and divine law on the other—and never the twain must meet. But the decisive point that has not been appreciated in interpretations of Strauss is that his insistence on the separation between Athens and Jerusalem is intended as a means of preserving the sense of eternal order and natural limits that they share. It is precisely this sense of a limiting order that Strauss believes is undermined by Christian spirituality, which craves a synthesis of Greek philosophical transcendence with the mysterious God who gave the Law to the Jews. The modern, progressive synthesis of reason's pride with the claims of universal justice was directed against but also prepared by the Christian project of integrating Athens and Jerusalem.

Strauss's praise of the nobility of philosophy as contemplation of the permanent questions is a fragile strategy tailored to a post-Christian age. It requires the downplaying of the demands of simple justice, or their relegation to the biblical Law as observed by a particular people, because these demands soften up the soul and make it vulnerable to Christian and modern universalism. The strategy is fragile because the cementing of the alliance between the aristocrat and the philosopher requires the suppression of the gentleman-philosopher's very natural and also biblical doubts about his own righteousness, the suppression of the humbling claims of conscience, the dismissal of the claims of "purity of heart" as meaningless apart from the allegedly gratuitous assumption of a God who searches hearts, the subsumption of justice under virtue, and the promotion of a kind of mutual admiration society between gentlemen and philosophers.

A Thomistic Alternative?

But what of Catholic and in particular Thomistic Christianity? Does not Thomas's Christian appropriation of Aristotle, or Aristotelian interpretation of Christianity, provide an alternative to the inevitably levelling tendency of Christian universalism, the alliance between the One and the all against the claims of the few and the proud? Much like Siedentop, Leo Strauss sees Thomas as an exception, a detour, an outlier in relation to the necessary and dominant path that leads from Christianity to modernity. But the difference is that Siedentop disapproves of the Thomistic pause in the progress of Christian universalism-individualism, whereas Strauss conditionally approves of Thomas's efforts, which he regards as well-meaning but inevitably flawed.

From Strauss's point of view, the Thomistic synthesis of Christianity with an Aristotelian philosophical elevation must finally fail; it is inherently vulnerable to the more consistent modern synthesis of extreme elevation and extreme generalization. The problem with the modern synthesis is not that it is incoherent. Rather, it is an all-too-coherent conflation of the One and the all, the attainment of a transmundane absolute purified of all content but the open process of universalization itself.

This modern fusion of the One and the all can in fact be understood as the perfect synthesis of the two ways of life Strauss posits as representing the essence, respectively, of Athens and Jerusalem. Free understanding understood classically as the aristocratic ascent from opinion necessarily retains an aristocratic cast. But absolutely free understanding would have no end, no content but the production from itself of the universal.

Obedient love, on the other hand, as understood traditionally, would necessarily involve understanding of the kind of being one is called to love, and thus of the good proper to such a being. But such a good must be of at least one of the two following kinds: (1) the good of the soul or virtue, which necessarily draws upon a hierarchical frame of reference; or (2) plain bodily needs, to be served as directed and within limits set by the commandments of the Law. Noble contemplation, the aristocratic configuration of philosophy, had provided, most notably in the form of Thomist philosophy, a very necessary shelter for the natural and ordinary power of "sacred restraints," the rudimentary distinction between good and bad "we all learn as children."[49] However, if purified of all reference to Greek virtue as well as Jewish Law, obedient love as Christian charity becomes reducible in practice to Kojève's "recognition" (or Siedentop's "reciprocity"—the Golden Rule), and thus open to the instrumentalities of rational tyranny called for by universal technological reason. As Badiou exemplifies, devotion to the cause of the universal homogeneous state is the effectual truth of Christian love purified of proud virtue and of particularist Law.

Thomas would of course be shocked and appalled by this reduction of charity to its effectual truth, as any serious Christian ought to be. But Strauss would say that, by subordinating natural, aristocratic reason to faith, natural virtue and its extension, the virtue of contemplation, become ministerial to charity, which is then left without any definite "higher" content; the notion of a good above bodily necessities depends for its content upon some minimal political and social hierarchy transposed in the very notion of "elevation." But pure charity humbles the pride implicit in all such hierarchical virtue and thus fatally opens the horizon and undermines the implicit teleology of natural right. The effectual truth of the evacuation of any worldly finalities (in the name of the absolute transcendence of the One) in favor of an end projected by faith but understood to be beyond all human comprehension is the eventual filling of that horizon with the All, the plain and universal needs of humanity and the self-defined and sovereign "dignity" of every individual.

49. Strauss, On Tyranny, 192, 191.

Leo Strauss for Believers

Strauss does not publicize the affinities or parallels between the Christian and modern syntheses, because he values a practical alliance with Christian natural law, and because he prefers to hold the founders of modernity rationally accountable. Only if we consider the rise of modern universalistic hopes as a rational project can we hold modernity rationally responsible, and thus hold open the possibility of a more responsible view of reason. It is thus on eminently practical grounds that Strauss resists portraying modernity as the "secularization" of Christianity (as in Voegelin's "immanentization of the eschaton," for example).

Whatever one thinks of Strauss's disposition on the question of biblical religion (and he certainly seems not to have been a believer in any familiar sense), he remains an indispensable thinker for believers because of his unrivaled deconstruction of the faith of modernity. The modern rationalist critique of religion is itself based, he shows, on an unexamined faith in the mastery of nature as the end of knowledge. This critique is invaluable to all who would resist the blind colossus of modern rationalism, whatever we think of the alternative Strauss proposed—that is, the alleged self-sufficient goodness of philosophical inquiry itself. And this proposed Straussian solution appears much more nuanced and deliberately political, I believe, on close examination.

Leo Strauss offers the most perspicacious critique of modern rationalism because he never loses sight of the question of the good of thinking, and therefore of the problem of the relation between theory and practice. The moderns deny the linchpin of classical thought, the intrinsic good of philosophizing, and thus make knowing instrumental to power. Power in turn can only be interpreted according to the most "natural," that is, universal, human needs and appetites, at least until Nietzsche's attempt to liberate the will to power from this democratic conception of nature.

Even—or especially—serious Christians can appreciate the force of Strauss's very discreet argument that Christianity is vulnerable to co-optation by "social justice," as its Jewish humility undermines aristocratic pretensions, and its Hellenism undermines the particularity of Jewish commandments. To be sure, some Christians will appeal to scripture as a check on progressive interpretations of "spirituality," others mostly to "conscience," and others mostly to the mediating authority of the church. But the very pertinent question with which Strauss confronts us Christians is this: can any of these alternatives to the progressive synthesis of divine otherness and human "progress" stand without relying on content derived from Jerusalem and from Athens in their original, pre-Christian forms, that is, from sacred commands and from the pride of human nature?

This is Leo Strauss's advice to Christians: the only brakes on the secular appropriation of Christian humility and universalism are Jewish Law and pagan honor. A very sober and pious Christian Straussian would hold on to the promise of a salvation beyond worldly limits while acknowledging the inescapability in this world of both pagan pride and coercive law. "Il faut avoir l'esprit dur et le coeur doux" (Jacques Maritain). How to welcome the grace of a soft and open heart without sacrificing the natural virtue of a clear and firm mind—how to be lucidly in the world (a world that I believe Strauss has understood as clearly as any human being) yet not finally of the world—this is a problem without a definite, conceptual solution, and we have to believe that dealing with this problem, both in theory and in practice, is not only a mortal necessity but somehow an apprenticeship in our eternal freedom.

BIBLIOGRAPHY

Anscombe, Elizabeth. "Mr. Truman's Degree." In her *Ethics, Religion and Politics*, vol. 3 of *Collected Philosophical Papers of G. E. M. Anscombe*, 62–71. Oxford: Blackwell, 1981.

———. "War and Murder." In *Ethics, Religion and Politics*, vol. 3 of *Collected Philosophical Papers of G. E. M. Anscombe*, 51–61. Oxford: Blackwell, 1981.

Aristotle. *Nicomachean Ethics*. Translated by Terence Irwin. Indianapolis, Ind.: Hackett, 1999.

Aquinas, Thomas. *The Summa Theologica of Saint Thomas Aquinas*. Translated by Fathers of the English Dominican Province. Revised by Daniel J. Sullivan. London: Encyclopedia Brittanica, 1952.

———. *The Basic Writings of Thomas Aquinas*. Edited by Anton C. Pegis. Indianapolis, Ind.: Hackett, 1997.

Arkes, Hadley. *First Things: An Inquiry into the First Principles of Morals and Justice*. Princeton, N.J.: Princeton University Press, 1986.

Aron, Raymond. "Sur le machiavélisme. Dialogue avec Jacques Maritain (1982)" [On Machiavellianism: A Dialogue with Jacques Maritain]. *Commentaire* 8, nos. 28–29 (Winter 1985): 511–16.

———. "French Thought in Exile: Jacques Maritain and the Quarrel over Machiavellianism." In *In Defense of Political Reason: Essays*, edited by Daniel J. Mahoney, 53–66. Lanham, Md.: Rowman and Littlefield, 1994.

Augustine. *Of True Religion*. In *Augustine: Earlier Writings*, edited and translated by J. H. S. Burleigh. The Library of Christian Classics 6. Philadelphia: Westminster, 1953.

———. *St. Augustine of Hippo: Our Lord's Sermon on the Mount according to Matthew & the Harmony of the Gospels*. Edited by Paul A. Boer. N.p.: Veritatis Splendor Publications, 2012.

Badiou, Alain. *Saint Paul: The Foundation of Universalism*. Palo Alto, Calif.: Stanford University Press, 2003.

Batnitzky, Leora. "Leo Strauss and the 'Theologico-Political Predicament.'" In *The Cambridge Companion to Leo Strauss*, edited by Steven B. Smith, 41–62. Cambridge: Cambridge University Press, 2009.

Beitzinger, A. J. "Retrospect on Charles N. R. McCoy," *Review of Politics* 53, no. 2 (1991): 416–18.

Benedict XVI, Pope. *Deus Caritas Est.* Encyclical Letter. December 25, 2005. Available at www.vatican.va.

———. "Europe's Crisis of Culture." In *The Essential Pope Benedict XVI: His Central Writings & Speeches,* edited by John F. Thornton and Susan B. Varenne, 325–36. New York: HarperOne, 2007.

———. "Address at the Reichstag Building, Berlin." In *Liberating Logos: Pope Benedict XVI's September Speeches,* edited by Marc D. Guerra, 39–48. South Bend, Ind.: St. Augustine's Press, 2014.

———. "Faith, Reason and the University: Memories and Reflections." In *Liberating Logos: Pope Benedict XVI's September Speeches,* edited by Marc D. Guerra, 23–38. South Bend, Ind.: St. Augustine's Press, 2014.

Benestad, J. Brian, ed. *Classical Christianity and the Political Order.* Lanham, Md.: Rowman and Littlefield, 1996.

Bernstein, Jeffrey A. *Leo Strauss on the Borders of Judaism, Philosophy, and History.* Albany: State University of New York Press, 2015.

Bireley, Robert. *The Counter-Reformation Prince: Anti-Machiavellianism or Catholic Statecraft in Early Modern Europe.* Chapel Hill: University of North Carolina Press, 1990.

Bloom, Allan. *The Closing of the American Mind.* New York: Simon and Schuster, 1987.

Blythe, James M. "The Mixed Constitution and the Distinction between Regal and Political Power in the Work of Thomas Aquinas." *Journal of the History of Ideas* 47, no. 4 (1986): 547–65.

Bruell, Christopher. "A Return to Classical Political Philosophy and the Understanding of the American Founding." In *Leo Strauss: Political Philosopher and Jewish Thinker,* edited by Kenneth L. Deutsch and Walter Nicgorski, 335–38. Lanham, Md.: Rowman and Littlefield, 1994.

Burns, Timothy W. "Strauss, Leo." In *Encyclopedia of Modern Political Thought,* edited by Gregory Claeys, 779–84. Thousand Oaks, Calif.: SAGE Publications, 2013.

———. "Strauss on the Religious and Intellectual Situation of the Present." In *Reorientation: Leo Strauss in the 1930s,* edited by Martin D. Yaffe and Richard S. Ruderman, 131–56. New York: Palgrave Macmillan, 2014.

Chroust, Anton-Hermann. "The Philosophy of Law of St. Thomas Aquinas." *American Journal of Jurisprudence* 19 (1973): 1–38.

Clarke, Arthur C. "Clarke's Third Law on UFO's." *Science* 159, no. 3812 (January 19, 1968): 255.

Curran, Charles. *The Development of Moral Theology: Five Strands.* Washington, D.C.: Georgetown University Press, 2013.

d'Entrèves, Alexandre Passerin. "The Case for Natural Law Re-Examined." *Natural Law Forum* 1, no. 5 (1956): 5–52.

———. *The Medieval Contribution to Political Thought: Thomas Aquinas, Marsilius of Padua, Richard Hooker.* New York: Humanities Press, 1959.

———. *The Notion of the State: An Introduction to Political Theory.* Oxford: Clarendon, 1967.

———. *Natural Law: An Introduction to Legal Philosophy.* Revised edition. London: Hutchinson, 1970.

Dannhauser, Werner. "Athens and Jerusalem or Jerusalem and Athens." In *Leo Strauss and Judaism: Jerusalem and Athens Critically Revisited*, edited by David Novak, 1–24. Lanham, Md.: Rowman and Littlefield, 1996.
De Koninck, Charles. "In Defense of St. Thomas." In *The Writings of Charles De Koninck*, vol. 2, edited and translated by Ralph McInerny. Notre Dame, Ind.: University of Notre Dame Press, 2009.
———. "The Primacy of the Common Good against the Personalists: The Principle of the New Order." In *The Writings of Charles De Koninck*, vol. 2, edited and translated by Ralph McInerny. Notre Dame, Ind.: University of Notre Dame Press, 2009.
———. *De la primauté du bien commun contre les personalistes* [The Primacy of the Common Good against the Personalists]. In *Œvres de Charles de Koninck*, 2:107–52. Québec: Les Presses de l'Université Laval, 2010.
———. "La Conféderation, rempart contre le Grand État" [Confederation: Rampart against the great state]. In *Œuvres de Charles De Koninck*, 3:65–98. Québec: Les Presses de l'Université Laval, 2010.
Dechert, Charles. "In Memoriam Charles N.R. McCoy (1911–1984)." *Laval théologique et philosophique* 41 (1985): 109.
Descartes, Rene. *Philosophical Works of Descartes*. Translated by Elizabeth Haldane and G. R. T. Ross. Cambridge: Cambridge University Press, 1935.
———. *Discourse on Method*. Revised edition. Translated and edited by Richard Kennington. Indianapolis, Ind.: Hackett, 2007.
Dulles, Avery. *Magisterium: Teacher and Guardian of the Faith*. Naples, Fla.: Sapientia Press, 2007.
Eschmann, Ignatius. "In Defense of Jacques Maritain." In *The Writings of Charles De Koninck*, edited and translated by Ralph McInerny, 2:173–204. Notre Dame: University of Notre Dame Press, 2009.
Eusebius. *The Life of the Blessed Emperor Constantine*. In *Nicene and Post-Nicene Fathers*, Second Series, vol. I, edited by P. Schaff and H. Wace. Grand Rapids, Mich.: Eerdmans, 1955.
Finnis, John. *Natural Law and Natural Rights*. Oxford: Clarendon Press, 1980.
———. "Aristotle, Aquinas, and Moral Absolutes." *Catholica: International Quarterly Selection* 12 (1990): 7–15.
———. *Aquinas: Moral, Political, and Legal Theory*. New York: Oxford University Press, 1998.
———. "Law and What I Truly Should Decide." *American Journal of Jurisprudence* 48, no. 1 (2003): 107–29.
———. "Hart as a Political Philosopher." In *Philosophy of Law: Collected Essays*, edited by John Finnis, 4:257–79. New York: Oxford University Press, 2011.
———. *Human Rights & Common Good, Collected Essays*, vol. 3. Oxford: Oxford University Press, 2011.
———. *Reason in Action, Collected Essays*, vol. 1. Oxford: Oxford University Press, 2011.
Finnis, John, Joseph M. Boyle, Jr., and Germain Grisez. *Nuclear Deterrence: Morality and Realism*. Oxford: Clarendon Press, 1987.
Florian, Michel. *La pensée catholique en Amérique du Nord: Réseaux intellectuels et

échanges culturels entre l'Europe, le Canada et les Etats-Unis [Catholic thought in North America: recent intellectual and cultural exchanges between Europe, Canada, and the United States]. Paris: Desclée de Brouwer, 2010.

Fortin, Ernest L. "Augustine and the Hermeneutics of Love." In *The Birth of Philosophic Christianity: Studies in Early Christian and Medieval Thought*, edited by J. Brian Benestad, 1–19. Lanham, Md.: Roman and Littlefield, 1996.

———. "Augustine, Thomas Aquinas, and the Problem of Natural Law." In *Classical Christianity and the Political Order*, edited by J. Brian Benestad, 199–222. Lanham, Md.: Roman and Littlefield, 1996.

———. "Natural Law and Social Justice." In *Classical Christianity and the Political Order*, edited by J. Brian Benestad, 233–34.

———. "The New Natural Rights Theory and the Natural Law." In *Classical Christianity and the Political Order*, edited by J. Brian Benestad, 265–86.

———. "The Political Thought of St. Thomas Aquinas." In *Classical Christianity and the Political Order*, edited by J. Brian Benestad, 151–76.

———. "Rational Theologians and Irrational Philosophers: A Straussian Perspective." In *Classical Christianity and the Political Order*, edited by J. Brian Benestad, 287–96.

———. *Dissent and Philosophy in the Middle Ages: Dante and His Precursors*. Translated by Marc LePain. Lanham, Md.: Rowman and Littlefield, 2002.

———. "Why I Am Not a Thomist." In *Ever Ancient, Ever New: Ruminations on the City, the Soul, and the Church*, edited by Michael P. Foley, 175–82. Lanham, Md.: Rowman and Littlefield, 2007.

Fradkin, Hillel. "Philosophy and Law: Leo Strauss as a Student of Medieval Jewish Thought." *Review of Politics* 53, no. 1 (1991): 40–52.

Fuller, Lon L. "Positivism and Fidelity to Law—A Reply to Professor Hart." *Harvard Law Review* 71, no. 4 (1958): 630–72.

———. *The Morality of Law*. New Haven, Conn.: Yale University Press, 1964.

George, Robert P. "Kelsen and Aquinas on the Natural Law Doctrine." In *Thomas Aquinas and the Natural Law Tradition: Contemporary Essays*, edited by John Goyette, Mark S. Latkovic, and Richard S. Myers, 237–60. Washington, D.C.: The Catholic University of America Press, 2004.

Gildin, Hilail, ed. *An Introduction to Political Philosophy: Ten Essays by Leo Strauss*. Detroit: Wayne State University Press, 1989.

———. "Deja Jew All Over Again: Dannhauser on Leo Strauss and Atheism." *Interpretation* 25, no. 1 (1997): 125–33.

Glendon, Mary Ann. *Rights Talk: The Impoverishment of Political Discourse*. New York: Free Press, 1970.

Green, Kenneth Hart. *Leo Strauss and the Recovery of Maimonides*. Chicago: University of Chicago Press, 2012.

Grisez, Germain. "The First Principle of Practical Reason: A Commentary on the *Summa Theologiae*, 1–2 Question 94, Article 2." *Natural Law Forum* 10 (1965): 168–201.

———. *Way of the Lord Jesus, Vol. 1: Christian Moral Principles*. Quincy, Ill.: Franciscan Press, 1983.

Haggerty, William P. "Beyond the Letter of his Master's Thought: C.N.R. McCoy on Medieval Political Theory." *Laval théologique et philosophique* 64 (2008): 467–83.
Hart, H. L. A. "Positivism and the Separation of Law and Morals." *Harvard Law Review* 71, no. 4 (1958): 593–629.
Hittinger, John P. "Jacques Maritain and Yves Simon's Use of Thomas Aquinas in Their Defense of Liberal Democracy." In *Thomas Aquinas and His Legacy*, edited by David M. Gallagher, 119–72. Washington, D.C.: The Catholic University of America Press, 1994.
———. *Liberty, Wisdom, and Grace: Thomism and Democratic Political Theory*. Lanham, Md.: Lexington Books, 2002.
Hittinger, Russell. *A Critique of the New Natural Law Theory*. Notre Dame, Ind.: University of Notre Dame Press, 1987.
Humphrey, John. *On the Edge of Greatness: The Diaries of John Humphrey, First Director of the United Nations Division of Human Rights*. Edited by Allan John Hobbins. Kingston: McGill-Queens University Press, 2000.
Hunt, Robert. "Leo Strauss, and the Ancients/Moderns Distinction." *The Catholic Social Science Review* 14 (2009): 53–63.
International Theological Commission. "Communion and Stewardship: Human Persons Created in the Image of God." 2000–2002 Plenary Session.
Jaffa, Harry V. *Thomism and Aristotelianism*. Chicago: University of Chicago Press, 1952.
———. *Crisis of the Strauss Divided*. Lanham, Md.: Rowman and Littlefield, 2012.
Janet, Paul. *Histoire de la science politique dans ses rapports avec la morale* [History of political science in its relation with morals]. 2 vols. Paris: Ancienne Libraire Germer Ballière et Compagnie, 1887.
Janssens, David. "A Change of Orientation: Leo Strauss's 'Comments' on Carl Schmitt Revisited." *Interpretation* 33, no. 1 (2005): 93–104.
———. *Between Athens and Jerusalem: Philosophy, Prophecy, and Politics in Leo Strauss's Early Thought*. Albany: State University of New York Press, 2008.
John Paul II, Pope. *Fides et Ratio*. Encyclical Letter. September 14, 1988. Available at www.vatican.va.
———. *Centesimus Annus*. Encyclical Letter. May 1, 1991. Available at www.vatican.va.
———. *Memory and Identity: Conversations at the Dawn of a Millennium*. New York: Rizzoli, 2005.
Johnson, Elizabeth. *Quest for the Living God: Mapping Frontiers in the Theology of God*. New York: Continuum, 2007.
———. "Open Letter to the Committee on Doctrine of the United States Conference of Catholic Bishops." *Origins* 41, no. 9 (2011): 29–47.
Kennington, Richard. "Strauss's Natural Right and History." *Review of Metaphysics* 35, no. 1 (1981): 57–86.
———. "Blumenberg and the Legitimacy of the Modern Age." In *The Ambiguous Legacy of the Enlightenment*, edited by William A. Rusher, 22–37. Lanham, Md.: University Press of America, 1995.
———. *Modern Origins*. Edited by Frank Hunt and Pamela Krauss. Lanham, Md.: Lexington Books, 2004.

Kesler, Charles. "A New Birth of Freedom: Harry V. Jaffa and the Study of America." In *Leo Strauss, the Straussians and the American Regime*, edited by Kenneth Deutsch and John Murley. Lanham, Md.: Rowman and Littlefield, 1999.

The Koran. Translated by N. J. Dawood. London: Penguin, 1995.

Kries, Douglas. "Thomas Aquinas and the Politics of Moses." *Review of Politics* 52, no. 1 (1990): 84–104.

———. "Strauss's Understanding of the Natural Law Theory of Thomas Aquinas." *The Thomist* 57, no. 2 (1993): 215–32.

———. "Augustine as Defender and Critic of Leo Strauss's Esotericism Thesis." *Proceedings of the American Catholic Philosophical Association* 83 (2010): 241–52.

Kuic, Vukan. *Yves Simon: Real Democracy*. Lanham, Md.: Rowman and Littlefield, 1999.

Lampert, Laurence. *The Enduring Importance of Leo Strauss*. Chicago: University of Chicago Press, 2013.

Lewis, Bradley V. "Personalism and Common Good: Thomistic Political Philosophy and the Turn to Subjectivity." In *Subjectivity Ancient and Modern*, edited by R. J. Snell and Steven McGuire, 175–96. Lanham, Md.: Lexington Books, 2016.

Lewis, Clive Staples. *The Abolition of Man*. New York: Harper Collins, 2000.

Lilla, Mark. "A New, Political Saint Paul?" *New York Review of Books* 55, no. 6 (October 23, 2008): 1–9.

Lisska, Anthony J. *Aquinas's Theory of Natural Law*. New York: Oxford University Press, 1996.

Locke, John. *The Works of John Locke in Nine Volumes*, vol. 6: *The Reasonableness of Christianity*. London: Rivington, [1695] 1824.

Macedo, Stephen. "Against the Old Sexual Morality of the New Natural Law." In *Natural Law, Liberalism, and Morality*, edited by Robert P. George, 27–48. Oxford: Clarendon Press, 1996.

Machiavelli, Niccolò. *The Discourses of Niccolò Machiavelli*. Translated by Leslie J. Walker. 2 vols. London: Routledge and Kegan Paul, 1950.

MacIntyre, Alasdair. *Whose Justice? Which Rationality?* Notre Dame, Ind.: University of Notre Dame Press, 1988.

———. *Three Rival Versions of Moral Enquiry: Encyclopaedia, Genealogy, and Tradition*. Notre Dame, Ind.: University of Notre Dame Press, 1990.

———. "Notes From the Moral Wilderness." In *The MacIntyre Reader*, edited by Kelvin Knight, 31–51. South Bend, Ind.: University of Notre Dame Press, 1998.

Mahoney, Daniel J. Foreword to *Classical Christianity and the Political Order*, edited by J. Brian Benestad, vii–x. Lanham, Md.: Rowman and Littlefield, 1996.

Manent, Pierre. *An Intellectual History of Liberalism*. Translated by Rebecca Balinski. Princeton, N.J.: Princeton University Press, 1994.

———. *Le regard politique: Entretiens avec Bénédicte Delorme-Montini* [Seeing things politically: interviews with Bénédicte Delorme-Montini]. Paris: Flammarion, 2010.

———. *The Metamorphoses of the City*. Translated by Marc LePain. Cambridge, Mass.: Harvard University Press, 2013.

———. *Seeing Things Politically: Interviews with Bénédicte Delorme-Montini*. Translated by Ralph C. Hancock. South Bend, Ind.: St. Augustine's Press, 2015.

Mansfield, Harvey C. *Machiavelli's New Modes and Orders: A Study of the "Discourses on Livy."* Chicago: University of Chicago Press, 1979.
———. *Machiavelli's Virtue*. Chicago: University of Chicago Press, 1996.
———. "Strauss on *The Prince*." *Review of Politics* 75 (2013): 641–65.
Maritain, Jacques. *Three Reformers: Luther, Descartes, Rousseau*. New York: Scribners, 1929.
———. *Freedom in the Modern World*. Translated by Richard O'Sullivan. New York: Scribners, 1936.
———. "Integral Humanism and the Crisis of Modern Times." *Review of Politics* 1, no. 1 (1939): 1–17.
———. "The End of Machiavellianism." *Review of Politics* 4, no. 1 (1942): 1–33.
———. *The Rights of Man and Natural Law*. Translated by Doris C. Anson. New York: Scribners, 1943.
———. *The Dream of Descartes*. Translated by Mabelle L. Andison. London: Editions Poetry London, 1946.
———. Introduction to *Human Rights: Comments and Interpretations: A Symposium*. Edited by UNESCO. New York: Allan Wingate, 1949.
———. "Christian Humanism." In his *The Range of Reason*. New York: Charles Scribner's Sons, 1952.
———. *On the Philosophy of History*. New York: Scribners, 1957.
———. *St. Thomas Aquinas*. Translated by Peter O'Reilly. New York: Meridian Books, 1958.
———. "The Crisis and Integral Humanism." In his *Scholasticism and Politics*, translated by Mortimer J. Adler. New York: Image Books, 1960.
———. *Integral Humanism*. Translated by Joseph W. Evans. Notre Dame, Ind.: University of Notre Dame Press, 1973.
———. *Man and the State*. Washington, D.C.: The Catholic University of America Press, 1998.
Marx, Karl. *Capital*. Translated by Samuel Moore and Edward Aveling. New York: Modern Library, 1936.
McCoy, Charles N. R. "The Place of Machiavelli in the History of Political Thought." *American Political Science Review* 37, no. 4 (August 1943): 626–41.
———. "The Logical and the Real in Political Theory: Plato, Aristotle, and Marx." *American Political Science Review* 48 (1954): 1058–66.
———. "On the Revival of Classical Political Philosophy." *Review of Politics* 35 (1963): 161–79.
———. "St. Augustine." In *History of Political Philosophy*, edited by Leo Strauss and Joseph Cropsey, 151–59. Chicago: Rand McNally, 1963.
———. "St. Thomas Aquinas." In *History of Political Philosophy*, edited by Leo Strauss and Joseph Cropsey, 201–26. Chicago: Rand McNally, 1963.
———. *The Structure of Political Thought: A Study in the History of Political Ideas*. New York: McGraw-Hill, 1963. Reprinted with a new introduction by Thomas M. Neumayr and Richard J. Dougherty. New Brunswick, N.J.: Transaction, 2016.
———. "On the Revival of Classical Political Philosophy." In *On the Intelligibility of Political Philosophy: Essays of Charles N. R. McCoy*, edited by James V. Schall and

John J. Schrems, 131–49. Washington, D.C.: The Catholic University of America Press, 1989.

———. "St. Thomas and Political Science." In *On the Intelligibility of Political Philosophy: Essays of Charles N. R. McCoy*, edited by James V. Schall and John J. Schrems, 24–38. Washington, D.C.: The Catholic University of America Press, 1989.

———. "Contemplation Passes into Practice: Religion and Reality." *Catholic Social Science Review* 11 (2006): 303–8.

McInerny, Ralph. "Charles De Koninck: A Philosopher of Order." *New Scholasticism* 39 (1965): 491–516.

———. *Thomism in an Age of Renewal*. Notre Dame, Ind.: University of Notre Dame Press, 1968.

———. "The Principles of Natural Law." *American Journal of Jurisprudence* 25 (1980): 1–15.

———. *Ethica Thomistica: The Moral Philosophy of Thomas Aquinas*. Washington, D.C.: The Catholic University of America Press, 1982.

———. *Aquinas on Human Action*. Washington, D.C.: The Catholic University of America Press, 1992.

———. *I Alone Have Escaped to Tell You*. Notre Dame, Ind.: University of Notre Dame Press, 2006.

McInerny, William P. "Book review of Charles N. R. McCoy, *Structure of Political Thought*." *New Scholasticism* 39 (1965): 405–7.

Meier, Heinrich. *Leo Strauss and the Theologico-Political Problem*. Cambridge: Cambridge University Press, 2006.

———. "How Strauss Became Strauss." In *Reorientation: Leo Strauss in the 1930s*, edited by Martin D. Yaffe and Richard S. Ruderman, 13–32. New York: Palgrave Macmillan, 2014.

Melzer, Arthur M. *Philosophy Between the Lines: The Lost History of Esoteric Writing*. Chicago: University of Chicago Press, 2014.

Merrill, Clark A. "Leo Strauss's Indictment of Christian Philosophy." *Review of Politics* 62, no. 1 (2000): 85.

Michel, Florian. *La pensée catholique en Amérique du Nord* [Catholic thought in North America]. Paris: Desclée de Brouwer, 2010.

Murphy, Mark C. "The Common Good." *Review of Metaphysics* 59, no. 1 (2005): 133–64.

Nederman, Cary J. Introduction to A. P. d'Entrèves, *Natural Law: An Introduction to Legal Philosophy*. New Brunswick, N.J.: Transaction, 1994.

———. *Lineages of European Political Thought: Explorations along the Medieval/Modern Divide from John of Salisbury to Hegel*. Washington, D.C.: The Catholic University of America Press, 2009.

Nicgorski, Walter. "Yves R. Simon: A Philosopher's Quest for Science and Prudence." *Review of Politics* 71, no. 1 (2009): 68–84.

O'Connor, Flannery. Introduction to *A Memoir for Mary Ann*. New York: Farrar, Straus and Cudahy, 1961.

Orr, Susan. *Jerusalem and Athens*. Lanham, Md.: Rowman and Littlefield, 1995.

Pakaluk, Michael. "Is the Common Good of Political Society Limited and Instrumental?" *Review of Metaphysics* 55, no. 1 (2001): 57–94.

Pascal, Blaise. *Pensées de Pascal.* Paris: Librairie Garnier frères, 1925.
———. *Pensees.* Translated by A. J. Krailsheimer. London: Penguin, 1995.
Petrina, Allessandra. *Machiavelli in the British Isles: Two Early Modern Translations of "The Prince."* Farnham: Ashgate, 2009.
Pieper, Josef. "The Rights of Others." In his *Problems of Modern Faith: Essays and Addresses,* translated by Jan van Heurck, 203–18. Chicago, Ill.: Franciscan Herald Press, 1985.
Prufer, Thomas. *Recapitulations.* Washington, D.C.: The Catholic University of America Press, 1993.
Rahner, Karl, and Joseph Ratzinger. *Revelation and Tradition.* Translated by W. J. O'Hara. New York: Herder and Herder, 1966.
Ratzinger, Joseph. "The Church and Scientific Theology." *Communio: International Catholic Review* 7, no. 4 (1980): 332–42.
———. *Principles of Catholic Theology: Building Stones for a Fundamental Theology.* Translated by Sister Mary Frances McCarthy, SND. San Francisco: Ignatius Press, 1987.
———. *In the Beginning ... A Catholic Understanding of the Story of Creation and the Fall.* Translated by Boniface Ramsey, OP. Grand Rapids, Mich.: Eerdmans, 1995.
———. *The Spirit of the Liturgy.* Translated by John Saward. San Francisco: Ignatius Press, 2000.
———. *Introduction to Christianity.* Translated by J. R. Foster and Michael J. Miller. San Francisco: Ignatius Press, 2004.
———. *Truth and Tolerance: Christian Belief and World Religions.* Translated by Henry Taylor. San Francisco: Ignatius Press, 2004.
Rizzi, Anthony. *The Science Before Science: A Guide to Thinking in the 21st Century.* Baton Rouge, La.: IAP Press, 2004.
———. *Physics for Realists.* 2 vols. Baton Rouge, La.: IAP Press, 2008 and 2011.
———. "The Science before Science: The Grounding and Integration of the Modern Mind and its Science." In *Reading the Cosmos: Nature, Science, and Wisdom,* edited by Guiseppi Butera, 60–79. Washington, D.C.: The Catholic University of America Press, 2011.
———. *Kid's Introduction to Physics (and Beyond)* Baton Rouge, La.: IAP Press, 2012.
Rommen, Heinrich A. *The Natural Law: A Study in Legal and Social History and Philosophy.* Indianapolis, Ind.: Liberty Fund, 1998.
Schall, James V. "Aquinas and the Proper Life of Man." In *Reason, Revelation, and the Foundations of Political Philosophy,* edited by Schall, 93–128. Baton Rouge: Louisiana State University Press, 1978.
———. *The Politics of Heaven & Hell: Christian Themes from Classical, Medieval, and Modern Political Philosophy.* Lanham, Md.: University Press of America, 1984.
———. "'Man for Himself': On the Ironic Unities of Political Philosophy." *Political Science Reviewer* 15 (1985): 67–108.
———. *Reason, Revelation, and the Foundations of Political Philosophy.* Baton Rouge: Louisiana State University Press, 1987.
———. "A Latitude for Statesmanship? Strauss on St. Thomas." *Review of Politics* 53, no. 1 (1991): 126–45.

———. "Transcendent Man in the Limited City: The Political Philosophy of Charles N.R. McCoy." *The Thomist* 57 (1993): 63–95.

———. *At the Limits of Political Philosophy: From "Brilliant Errors" to Things of Uncommon Importance*. Washington, D.C.: The Catholic University of America Press, 1996.

———. *Jacques Maritain: The Philosopher in Society*. Lanham, Md.: Rowland and Littlefield, 1998.

———. "Transcendent Man in the Limited City: The Political Philosophy of Charles N. R. McCoy." In *Reason, Revelation, and Human Affairs: Selected Writings of James V. Schall*, edited by Marc D. Guerra, 143–61. Lanham, Md.: Lexington Books, 2001.

———. "On the 'Right' to be Born." In *Political Philosophy and Revelation: A Catholic Reading*, edited by James V. Schall, 217–26. Washington, D.C: The Catholic University of America Press, 2013.

Sayre, Kenneth M. *Adventures in Philosophy at Notre Dame*. Notre Dame, Ind.: University of Notre Dame Press, 2014.

Schlueter, Nathan. "Leo Strauss and Benedict XVI on the Crisis of the West." *Modern Age* 55, nos. 1–2 (Spring 2013): 22–33.

Schrems, John J. "A New Annotated Bibliography of Charles N.R. McCoy." *Catholic Social Science Review* 11 (2006): 275–92.

Shils, Edward. "Robert Maynard Hutchins, 1899–1977." In *Remembering the University of Chicago: Teachers, Scientists, and Scholars*, edited by Edward Shils, 185–96. Chicago: University of Chicago Press, 1991.

Siedentop, Larry. *Inventing the Individual: The Origins of Western Liberalism*. Cambridge, Mass.: Belknap Press of Harvard University Press, 2014.

Sigmund, Paul E. "Law and Politics." In *The Cambridge Companion to Aquinas*, edited by Norman Kretzmann and Eleonore Stump, 217–31. New York: Cambridge University Press, 1993.

Simon, Anthony O. "Presentation of the Book: Yves Simon, *La tradizione del diritto naturale: le riflessioni di un filosofo*." Conference paper presented at The Ethical Traditions of Europe and the USA: Common Roots and Possibilities for Dialogue, July 18–23, 2004. http://www.thomasinternational.org/conferences/20040718 palermo/simon_paper.htm.

Simon, Yves R. *Nature and Functions of Authority*. Milwaukee, Wis.: Marquette University Press, 1940.

———. *Philosophy of Democratic Government*. Chicago: University of Chicago Press, 1951.

———. *A General Theory of Authority*. Notre Dame, Ind.: University of Notre Dame Press, 1962.

———. *Freedom of Choice*. Edited by Peter Wolff. New York: Fordham University Press, 1969.

———. *The Definition of Moral Virtue*. Edited by Vukan Kuic. New York: Fordham University Press, 1986.

———. *Practical Knowledge*. Edited by Robert J. Mulvaney. New York: Fordham University Press, 1991.

---. *Foresight and Knowledge*. Edited by Ralph Nelson and Anthony O. Simon. New York: Fordham University Press, 1996.
Smith, Steven B. "Leo Strauss: Between Athens and Jerusalem." *Review of Politics* 53, no. 1 (1991): 75–99.
---, ed. *The Cambridge Companion to Leo Strauss*. New York: Cambridge University Press, 2009.
---. "Leo Strauss: The Outlines of a Life." In *The Cambridge Companion to Leo Strauss*, ed. Smith, 13–40.
Stoner, James R., Jr. "The Catholic Moment in the Political Philosophy of Leo Strauss." *Voegelin View* (July 29, 2014). http://voegelinview.com/catholic-moment-political-philosophy-leo-strauss/
---. "Categories and Causes: Physics and Politics for Aristotle and for Us." In *Concepts of Nature: Ancient and Modern*, edited by R. J. Snell and Steven F. McGuire, 101–15. Lanham, Md.: Lexington Books, 2016.
Strauss, Leo. "On Locke's Doctrine of Natural Right." *Philosophical Review* 61, no. 4 (1952): 475–502.
---. *Persecution and the Art of Writing*. New York: Free Press, 1952; reprinted in Chicago: University of Chicago Press, 1988.
---. *Natural Right and History*. Chicago: University of Chicago Press, 1953.
---. "Social Science and Humanism." In *The State of the Social Science*, edited by Leonard D. White, 415–25. Chicago: University of Chicago Press, 1956. Reprinted in *The Rebirth of Classical Political Rationalism: An Introduction to the Thought of Leo Strauss*, edited by Thomas L. Pangle, 3–12. Chicago: University of Chicago Press, 1989.
---. *Thoughts on Machiavelli*. Chicago: University of Chicago Press, 1958; reprinted in Chicago: University of Chicago Press, 1984.
---. *What Is Political Philosophy?* Glencoe, Ill.: Free Press, 1959.
---. "How to Begin to Study *The Guide of the Perplexed*." Introduction to Moses Maimonides, *The Guide of the Perplexed*. Translated by Shlomo Pines, 1:xi–xiii. Chicago: University of Chicago Press, 1963.
---. *The City and Man*. Chicago: Rand McNally, 1964; reprinted in Chicago: University of Chicago Press, 1978.
---. "Aristotle's *Rhetoric*." Lecture, University of Chicago, May 18, 1964. Transcript in Leo Strauss Center, University of Chicago. http://leostrausstranscripts.uchicago.edu/navigate/5/12/.
---. "The Crisis of Our Time." In *The Predicament of Modern Politics*, edited by Harold Spaeth, 41–54. Detroit: University of Detroit Press, 1964.
---. "The Crisis of Political Philosophy." In *The Predicament of Modern Politics*, edited by Harold Spaeth, 91–103. Detroit: University of Detroit Press, 1964.
---. *Spinoza's Critique of Religion*. Translated by E. M. Sinclair. New York: Schocken Books, 1965; reprinted in Chicago: University of Chicago Press, 1997.
---. "The Three Waves of Modernity." In his *Political Philosophy: Six Essays by Leo Strauss*, edited by Hilail Gildin, 81–98. New York: Pegasus-Bobbs-Merrill, 1975.
---. "The Mutual Influence of Theology and Philosophy." *Independent Journal of Philosophy* 3 (1979): 111–18.

---. "On the Interpretation of Genesis." *L'Homme: Revue Francaise d'Anthropolgie* 21, no. 1 (1981): 5–20.

---. "Correspondence Concerning Modernity: Karl Löwith and Leo Strauss." *Independent Journal of Philosophy* 4 (1983): 105–19.

---. "Jerusalem and Athens. Some Preliminary Reflections." In *Studies in Platonic Political Philosophy*, edited by Thomas L. Pangle, 147–73. Chicago: University of Chicago Press, 1983.

---. "Note on the Plan of Nietzsche's *Beyond Good and Evil*." In *Studies in Platonic Political Philosophy*, edited by Thomas L. Pangle, 174–91. Chicago: University of Chicago Press, 1983.

---. "On Natural Law." In *Studies in Platonic Political Philosophy*, edited by Thomas L. Pangle, 137–46. Chicago: University of Chicago Press, 1983.

---. "Locke's Doctrine of Natural Law." In *What Is Political Philosophy? and Other Studies*. Chicago: University of Chicago Press, 1988.

---. "On the Basis of Hobbes's Political Philosophy." In *What Is Political Philosophy? and Other Studies*. Chicago: University of Chicago Press, 1988.

---. "What Is Political Philosophy?" In *What Is Political Philosophy? and Other Studies*. Chicago: University of Chicago Press, 1988.

---. "Liberal Education and Responsibility." In *An Introduction to Political Philosophy: Ten Essays*, edited by Hilail Gildin, 321–48. Detroit: Wayne State University Press, 1989.

---. "Marsilius of Padua." In his *Liberalism Ancient and Modern*. Ithaca, N.Y.: Cornell University Press, 1989.

---. "Plato." In *History of Political Philosophy*, edited by Leo Strauss and Joseph Cropsey, 33–89. Third edition. Chicago: University of Chicago Press, 1989.

---. "Progress or Return?" In *The Rebirth of Classical Political Rationalism: An Introduction to the Thought of Leo Strauss*, edited by Thomas L. Pangle, 227–70. Chicago: University of Chicago Press, 1989.

---. "The Three Waves of Modernity." In *An Introduction to Political Philosophy: Ten Essays by Leo Strauss*, edited by Hilail Gildin, 81–98. Detroit: Wayne State University Press, 1989.

---. "What Is Liberal Education?" In his *Liberalism Ancient and Modern*. Ithaca, N.Y.: Cornell University Press, 1989.

---. "Some Remarks on the Political Science of Maimonides and Farabi." *Interpretation* 18, no. 1 (1990): 3–30.

---. *On Tyranny: Including the Strauss-Kojeve Correspondence*. Edited by Victor Gourevitch and Michael S. Roth. New York: Free Press, 1991.

---. "Notes On Carl Schmitt's *The Concept of the Political*." In Heinrich Meier, *Carl Schmitt and Leo Strauss: the Hidden Dialogue*, translated by Harvey Lomax, 91–119. Chicago: University of Chicago Press, 1995.

---. *Philosophy and Law: Contributions to the Understanding of Maimonides and His Predecessors*. Translated by Eve Adler, edited by Kenneth Hart Green. Albany: State University of New York Press, 1995.

---. "La mort de Churchill." *Commentaire* 75 (1996): 568.

---. "A Giving of Accounts." In *Jewish Philosophy and the Crisis of Modernity: Essays and Lectures in Modern Jewish Thought*, edited by Kenneth Hart Green, 457–65. Albany: State University of New York Press, 1997.

———. "Preface to *Spinoza's Critique of Religion*." In *Jewish Philosophy and the Crisis of Modernity: Essays and Lectures in Modern Jewish Thought*, edited by Kenneth Hart Green, 137–79. Albany: State University of New York Press, 1997.

———. "Progress or Return?" In *Jewish Philosophy and the Crisis of Modernity: Essays and Lectures in Modern Jewish Thought*, edited by Kenneth Hart Green, 87–136. Albany: State University of New York Press, 1997.

———. "Why We Remain Jews. Can Jewish Faith and History Still Speak to Us?" In *Jewish Philosophy and the Crisis of Modernity*, edited by Kenneth H. Green, 311–57. Albany: State University of New York Press, 1997.

———. *Leo Strauss on Plato's Symposium*. Edited by Seth Benardete. Chicago: University of Chicago Press, 2003.

———. "Living Issues of German Postwar Philosophy." In *Leo Strauss and the Theologico-Political Problem*, edited by Heinrich Meier, 115–40. New York: Cambridge University Press, 2006.

———. "Reason and Revelation." In *Leo Strauss and the Theologico-Political Problem*, edited by Heinrich Meier, 141–80. New York: Cambridge University Press, 2006.

———. "What Can We Learn From Political Theory?" *Review of Politics* 69, no. 4 (2007): 515–29.

———. "Restatement." *Interpretation* 36, no. 1 (2008): 29–78.

———. *Hobbes's Critique of Religion: A Contribution to Understanding the Enlightenment*. Edited and translated by Gabriel Bartlett and Svetozar Minkov. Chicago: University of Chicago Press, 2011.

Strauss, Leo, and Eric Voegelin. *Faith and Political Philosophy: The Correspondence between Leo Strauss and Eric Voegelin, 1934–1964*. Translated and edited by Peter Emberley and Barry Cooper. University Park: Pennsylvania State University Press, 1993.

Syse, Henrik. *Natural Law, Religion and Right*. South Bend, Ind.: St. Augustine Press, 2004.

Tanguay, Daniel. *Leo Strauss: une biographie intellectuelle* [Leo Strauss: An intellectual biography]. Paris: Grasset, 2003.

———. "Néoconservatisme et religion démocratique. Leo Strauss et l'Amérique" [Neoconservatism and democratic religion: Leo Strauss and America]. *Commentaire* 114 (2006): 315–24.

———. *Leo Strauss: An Intellectual Biography*. Translated by Christopher Nadon. New Haven, Conn.: Yale University Press, 2007.

Tarcov, Nathan. "Philosophy & History: Tradition and Interpretation in the Work of Leo Strauss." *Polity* 16, no. 1 (1983): 5–29.

Tessitore, Aristide. *Reading Aristotle's Ethics*. Albany: State University of New York Press, 1996.

Tierney, Brian. "Author's Rejoinder." *Review of Politics* 64, no. 3 (2002): 416–20.

———. "Natural Law and Natural Rights: Old Problems and Recent Approaches." *Review of Politics* 64, no. 3 (2002): 389–406.

Tollefsen, Christopher. "Pure Perfectionism and the Limits of Paternalism." In *Reason, *Morality, and the Law: The Jurisprudence of John Finnis*, edited by John Keown and Robert P. George, 204–18. New York: Oxford University Press, 2012.

Vaughan, Fredrick. *The Tradition of Political Hedonism: From Hobbes to J. S. Mill.* New York: Fordham University Press, 1982.

Veatch, Henry B. *For an Ontology of Morals.* Chicago: Northwestern University Press, 1971.

———. *Swimming Against the Current in Contemporary Philosophy.* Washington, D.C.: The Catholic University of America Press, 1981.

Veatch, Henry, and Joseph Rautenberg. "Does the Grisez-Finnis-Boyle Moral Philosophy Rest on a Mistake?" *Review of Metaphysics* 44, no. 4 (1991): 807–30.

Velkley, Richard L. *Heidegger, Strauss, and the Premises of Philosophy: On Original Forgetting.* Chicago: University of Chicago Press, 2011.

Voegelin, Eric. "The Oxford Political Philosophers." *Philosophical Quarterly* 3, no. 11 (April 1953): 97–114.

———. *Plato.* Columbia: University of Missouri Press, 2000.

Von Heyking. *Augustine and Politics as Longing in the World.* Columbia: University of Missouri Press, 2001.

Ward, Leo R. "The 'Natural Law' Rebound." *Review of Politics* 21, no. 1 (January 1959): 114–30.

Weinreb, Lloyd L. "Natural Law and Rights." In *Natural Law Theory*, edited by Robert P. George, 278–305. New York: Oxford University Press, 1992.

Wolfe, Christopher. *Natural Law Liberalism.* New York: Cambridge University Press, 2009.

Yaffe, Martin D., and Richard S. Ruderman, eds. *Reorientation: Leo Strauss in the 1930s.* New York: Palgrave Macmillan, 2014.

Zuckert, Catherine, and Michael P. Zuckert. *The Truth about Leo Strauss.* Chicago: University of Chicago Press, 2006.

Zuckert, Michael P., and Catherine Zuckert. *Leo Strauss and the Problem of Political Philosophy.* Chicago: University of Chicago Press, 2014.

CONTRIBUTORS

J. BRIAN BENESTAD is D'Amour Professor of Catholic Thought at Assumption College. His first book was *The Pursuit of a Just Social Order: Policy Statements of the United States Catholic Bishops, 1966–1980* (1982). His most recent book is *Church, State, and Society: An Introduction to Catholic Social Doctrine* (2011).

PHILIPPE BÉNÉTON is professor emeritus at l'université de Rennes I and l'Institut Catholique d'Etudes Supérieures. His recent books include *Equality by Default: An Essay on Modernity as Confinement* (2004) and *The Kingdom Suffereth Violence: The Machiavelli / Erasmus / More Correspondence and Other Unpublished Documents* (2012).

GIULIO DE LIGIO is associate researcher at the Ecole des hautes études en sciences sociales of Paris and at the Catholic University of Paris. His most recent book is *Le problème Machiavel: Science de l'homme, conscience de l'Europe* (2014). He is co-founder and member of the editorial board of the Italian journal *Rivista di Politica*. He was awarded the Prix Raymond Aron in 2007.

GARY D. GLENN is distinguished teaching professor emeritus of political science at the University of Northern Illinois. He has published widely on the history of political philosophy, American political thought, and religion. He has also published, with Thomas K. Lindsay, *Investigating American Democracy: Readings on Core Questions* (2012).

MARC D. GUERRA is associate professor and chair of the Department of Theology at Assumption College. Among his books are *Pope Benedict XVI and the Politics of Modernity* (2013) and *Christians as Political Animals: Taking the Measure of Modernity and Modern Democracy* (2010).

RALPH C. HANCOCK is professor of political science at Brigham Young University. He has published widely in the area of political philosophy and has translated many works from French. His most recent book is *The Responsibility of Reason: Theory and Practice in a Liberal-Democratic Age* (2011).

JOHN P. HITTINGER is professor of philosophy at the Center for Thomistic Studies, University of St. Thomas, Houston. Recent books include *The Vocation of the Catholic Philosopher: From Maritain to Wojtyła* (2011) and *Liberty, Wisdom and Grace: Thomism and Modern Democratic Theory* (2002).

CARSON HOLLOWAY is associate professor of political science at the University of Nebraska at Omaha. His books include *The Way of Life: John Paul II and the Challenge of Liberal Modernity* (2008) and *Hamilton versus Jefferson in the Washington Administration: Completing the Founding or Betraying the Founding?* (2016).

ROBERT P. KRAYNAK is professor of political science and director of the Center for Freedom and Western Civilization at Colgate University. Among his publications are *Christian Faith and Modern Democracy* (2001) and *Reason, Faith, and Politics*, edited with Arthur M. Melzer (2008).

DOUGLAS KRIES is the Bernard J. Coughlin, S.J., Professor of Christian Philosophy at Gonzaga University. He has published many essays on virtue, the history of political philosophy and, in 2007, *The Problem of Natural Law*.

V. BRADLEY LEWIS is associate professor of philosophy at the Catholic University of America. He has published extensively on Platonic political philosophy.

GLADDEN J. PAPPIN is assistant professor in the Department of Politics at the University of Dallas, permanent research fellow of the Notre Dame Center for Ethics and Culture, and deputy editor of *American Affairs*.

JAMES R. STONER JR. is Hermann Moyse Jr. Professor of Political Science and director of the Eric Voegelin Institute for American Renaissance Studies at Louisiana State University. His books include *Common Law and Liberal Theory: Coke, Hobbes, and the Origins of American Constitutionalism* (1992) and *Common-Law Liberty: Rethinking American Constitutionalism* (2003).

GEOFFREY M. VAUGHAN is associate professor of political science at Assumption College. He has published on major figures in the history of political philosophy from Hobbes to Habermas and Catholic authors from Newman to Tolkien. His book is entitled *Behemoth Teaches Leviathan: Hobbes on Political Education* (2002).

INDEX

abortion, 89–90
Abraham, 35–37, 114, 206, 225, 291
Adler, Mortimer J., 40–41, 185
Aeterni Patris, 186
aggiornamento, 240, 245
Al-Farabi, 99, 279
ancient philosophy, 49, 178, 181–82, 185
ancients, 45, 49, 95, 99, 110, 127, 143, 167, 174–75, 181, 183–85, 189, 218, 299, 307
angelism, 187
angels, 91, 187
apostles, 5, 204, 206
Aquinas, 1–2, 5, 33, 42–43, 49, 54, 65, 69, 80, 91, 187, 226, 229–30, 241–42; and Aristotle, 41–42, 52–53, 55–58, 63–64, 66, 69, 71, 75, 84, 171, 226, 231, 319; and Augustine, 7, 224; and natural law, 38, 40, 56, 58–59, 74–75, 78, 81, 89, 91, 127–28, 167, 230–31, 287; and Strauss, 5, 20, 28, 41, 57, 84, 88, 92, 219, 227, 229, 231, 287, 319–20; and synthesis of faith and reason, 29, 56
aristocrats, 158, 306, 312, 319
Aristotle, 57, 60–63, 70, 86, 130, 151, 153, 172–73, 187, 189, 202, 223–24, 278, 287, 313; and Aquinas, 41–42, 52–53, 55–58, 63–64, 66, 69, 71, 75, 84, 171, 226, 231, 319; baptized, 231; *Metaphysics*, 60, 281, 283, 289; *Nicomachean Ethics*, 58, 61–62, 70, 86–87, 174, 224; and Plato, 67–72, 74, 76, 79, 119, 167, 209, 219, 279, 282, 288, 295; *Politics*, 40, 55, 66; *Rhetoric*, 174
Assumption College, ix, 3
atheism, 2, 24–25, 218
Athens, 5, 32, 318, 322
Athens and Jerusalem, 4–5, 10, 32, 84, 184–85, 189, 254, 257, 285–86, 292, 307, 312–13, 315–16, 318–19, 322
Augsburg Confession, 38
Augustine, 1, 6–7, 10, 48, 54, 94, 96, 117, 147, 220–24, 231, 235, 292
Austen, Jane, 310
authority
    magisterial, 240
    papal, 282
    political, 91, 123
Averroes, 34

Bach, J. S., 214
Bacon, Francis, 178, 181, 184, 186–87
Badiou, Alain, 13, 299, 304–5, 320
Bellarmine, Robert, 1–2, 9, 42, 54
Benedict XVI, 1–2, 8, 80, 94–95, 101–10, 112–14, 174, 189
best regime, 7–8, 40–41, 57, 77–78, 80, 82–84, 90–93, 154, 169, 193, 256, 258, 268, 273
Bible, 12–13, 22–24, 29, 35, 95, 111, 172, 194, 196, 205–8, 211, 213, 243, 292–94, 316; and Greek philosophy, 22–23, 95, 103, 110, 185, 195–96, 198–201, 203, 205–6, 211–13, 215, 273, 275, 292–93, 313
biblical revelation, 20, 31, 41, 59, 68, 74, 201, 206, 209, 211, 214–15, 226–27
Blaise Pascal, 12
Bloom, Allan, 124–25, 282
Born Alive Infant Protection Act, 90
Boyle, Joseph M., 89
Bruell, Christopher, 118
Bruno, Giordano, 104, 107
Buber, Martin, 30

339

340 Index

Burke, Edmund, 65, 73, 131
Burns, Timothy W., 120
Burnyeat, Miles, 13

Caesar, Julius, 39–40
Cajetan, Thomas, 42, 50
caritas, 286, 310
Cassirer, Ernest, 118, 152
Catechism of the Catholic Church, 12
Catholic church, 5, 12, 94, 117, 132, 237–38, 240–42, 244–45
Catholic faith, 20, 112–13, 145, 196–97, 240, 287
Catholicism, 191, 195–96, 204, 219, 227; as political religion, 205; and Protestantism, 195; public religion, 200–203, 205; synthesis, 3, 100, 102, 104, 196–97, 199, 201, 205, 215, 219, 254–55, 286
Catholic social teaching, 44, 241, 243–44, 246
Catholic theology, 11, 20, 38, 94, 172, 196, 233, 246
Ceaser, James, 3
Centesimus Annus, 8, 117, 130, 132, 182
Christ, 38, 94, 104, 106–7, 113, 182, 224, 238, 247, 301, 303, 314, 317; promises of, 10; second coming of, 26
Christendom, 188, 195, 200, 202, 205
Christian faith, 103, 106, 109, 114
Christianity, 13, 33–38, 45, 76, 106–7, 112, 141; and belief, 103, 300; and charity, 6, 38, 40, 182, 203, 298, 303, 305, 310, 320; and Greek philosophy, 293, 319; and humility, 200, 287, 322; and modernity, 194–95, 203, 300, 307, 314–15, 317, 319, 321
Churchill, Winston S., 273
Cicero, 225
Circe, 90
citizens, 9, 52, 57, 61, 82, 85, 114, 169, 173–75, 183, 224, 262, 269, 271–73, 303; good, 68, 143, 258, 267; ordinary, 9–10, 138, 144, 146, 163, 165
citizenship, 67, 302
classical natural right, 67–68, 77–80, 82–84, 87, 89–90, 92–93, 153, 218–20, 223–24, 226–27, 231–32, 288–89
classical philosophy, 12, 31, 82, 95–96, 98, 146, 159, 164, 175, 264, 281, 284, 287, 312–13, 321
classical political philosophy, 12, 32, 67, 142, 164, 170, 183, 215, 289, 316
classical virtues, 43, 149, 163
Cohen, Herman, 118, 314
Cold War, 130, 177–78, 288, 305
common good, 62, 71, 75
communism, 132, 178–79, 182, 198, 256, 263, 288, 305
conscience, 15, 25, 43, 183, 303–4, 319, 321
consent, 77–78, 122–23, 143
contemplation, 66, 163, 173, 176, 269–70, 283, 289, 310, 317–18, 320
contraception, 41, 80–81, 89, 226, 231, 241, 243–246
cosmology, 8, 22, 30, 32, 42, 45, 111, 311
Council fathers, 245–46
Council of Trent, 241
crisis of political philosophy, 9, 168, 176, 179, 186
Crito, 146
Cropsey, Joseph, 48
Curran, Charles, 233, 241–49

Dante Alighieri, 117
death, 13, 24, 32, 37, 122, 210, 288, 296, 313
Declaration of Independence, 177
Declaration on Religious Liberty, 245
dehellenization, 2, 106–7
De Koninck, Charles, 50–52, 55, 63, 66, 69
democracy, 42–44, 85–86, 155–56, 161–62, 170, 254
D'Entrèves, A. P., 9, 138–39, 141–47, 165–66
Derrida, Jacques, 14
Descartes, Rene, 109, 173, 175–76, 178, 180–82, 184–88
detachment, 162–63, 295, 311
Deuteronomy, 29
dignity, 52, 75, 111, 115, 189, 226, 245, 263, 281, 302, 320
  human, 110, 177, 185, 188
dissent, 242, 245, 247
divine commands, 34, 87, 318
divine governance, 56, 96
divine intervention, 219, 225
divine law, 20, 29–30, 33–40, 43, 99, 198, 200–201, 207–8, 302, 304, 316, 318

divine lawgiver, 81
divine omnipotence, 23, 111
divorce, 37, 89, 243
Dostoyevsky, Fyodor, 310
Dulles, Avery, 246
Dunn, John, 14
Duns Scotus, 8, 106, 112
Dupuis, Jacques, 238
duties, 43–44, 120, 126–27, 129, 131, 133, 175

economics, 14, 193, 260
Eden, 204
education, 50, 122, 157–58, 201, 269
effectual truth, 143–44, 300, 306, 320
enlightenment, 3, 24–25, 42, 123; modern, 20, 42, 118, 133; premodern, 133; project, 118–19, 123; universal, 101
Epictetus, 295
Epicurus, 183, 288, 295
equality, 143, 182, 188–89, 302; human, 110, 301–3; moral, 303–4; universal, 300, 305
eros, 6, 31, 286
esotericism, 25, 31, 165, 201, 277, 281
Eusebius, 1
Euthyphro, 113
evangelization, 181, 238, 240
Eve, 91, 237
Exodus, 207, 222
exoteric, 10, 285, 311

faith, 20, 33–36, 38, 72, 102–3, 106, 112, 181, 196, 213, 227, 229–30, 235–40, 293, 317; articles of, 36, 38; deposit of, 192, 204, 249; in God, 24, 26, 103, 194, 297; irrational, 25, 27; and law, 20, 33, 36–38, 45; leap of, 27, 303; philosopher's, 23, 31, 72, 213–14, 291, 296; and reason, 12, 20–23, 26–27, 29–30, 35–36, 45, 106–7, 171–72, 184–85, 189, 219, 227–30, 237, 254, 320; religions of, 20, 33, 35–36, 38
Feuerbach, Ludwig, 50, 65–66
Fides et Ratio, 11, 249
Finnis, John, 44, 47, 59, 87, 90–91, 128–29
Ford, Henry, 181
Fortin, Ernest, 6, 8, 20, 43–44, 49–50, 54–58, 68, 116–17, 122, 124–33, 167–68, 184, 189, 233
freedom, 61, 114, 162, 177, 182, 188–89, 245, 269, 303, 305–6, 308; absolute, 307, 314; and duty, 44, 62; and love, 105, 114–15
Fuller, Lon L., 86–87

Galileo, 104
Genesis, 22, 29, 191, 206–7
God, 29, 35, 46, 69, 103, 113, 192, 207–8, 211–12, 314, 319; and Abraham, 36, 206, 219; belief in, 24, 30, 37, 39, 194, 228, 297, 301; commands of, 29, 35–36, 38, 82, 112, 285, 301; existence of, 26, 29, 57, 84, 194, 285, 291, 297; incarnation of, 37–38, 113–14, 182; knowledge of, 104, 235, 256, 281; and love, 39, 108, 114–15, 230–31, 235, 286, 292; personal, 29, 99, 103–4, 114, 238, 286, 291, 296; and reason, 29, 103, 108, 112–13, 175, 206–7, 227, 297, 301
good life, 98, 253, 268, 270, 273
Gospels, 7, 38, 40, 76, 101, 110, 115, 244
grace, 105, 187, 220, 238, 287, 305, 307, 313, 322; nature perfected by, 4, 30, 228; and reason, 103, 287
Greek philosophy, 195; and God, 23; heartlessness of, 211–12; synthesis with revelation, 103–4, 196–97, 199–201, 205, 293; in tension with the Bible, 110–11, 195–96, 200–201, 205, 211, 213, 215
Grisez, Germain, 2, 87, 128
Grotius, Hugo, 65
Guttmann, Julius, 28, 30, 118

happiness, 127, 156, 173–76, 178, 188, 286 philosopher's, 32, 45, 111, 268, 270, 294
Hebrew prophets, 26, 30
Hegel, Georg Wilhelm Friedrich, 2, 4, 24, 97, 108, 141, 144, 165, 283, 317
Heidegger, Martin, 180, 283–84, 307, 313
historical consciousness, 239, 241–42, 244–45, 248–49
historicism, 2, 4, 164, 288; and Catholic theology, 11, 233–34, 239, 241, 243, 249; and philosophy, 157, 171, 177, 186, 239, 249, 288; and relativism, 20, 40, 180
Hobbes, Thomas, 2, 121, 183–84; and natural rights, 8, 96, 117, 119–21, 123, 126–27, 142, 173; and religion, 118, 132, 283
Humanae Vitae, 81, 172, 233, 241

humanism, 65, 148, 280, 285
human reason, 45, 110; limits of, 28, 106, 113, 206–7, 291; and revelation, 206, 210, 213
human rights, 44, 46, 91–92, 126–27, 132, 174–75
Humphrey, John, 92

idealism, 187, 304
incarnation, 4–5, 7, 12, 29, 37, 113
individualism, 183, 187, 299
integral humanism, 148, 189
Isaac, 114, 219, 291
Isaiah, 26
Islam, 3, 20, 33–40, 43, 45, 99, 257

Jacob, 114, 291
Jesus, 5, 37, 101, 206, 237, 246, 304
Jewish Law, 38, 271, 300, 303, 313, 315, 317, 320, 322
Jewish Philosophy, 121, 165, 192, 257, 262
Jewish Thomism, 28–30
John Paul II, 8, 11, 44, 93, 117, 130, 132, 172, 182, 189, 239, 243, 247, 249
John XXIII, 93
Judaism, 3; and law, 30, 33, 35–37, 45, 301, 313–14; and philosophy, 30, 118, 257, 312, 318
Judaism and Islam, 33–35, 38–40, 43

Kant, Immanuel, 97, 165, 173, 184, 283
Kennington, Richard, 184
Kerwin, Jerome, 49
Kesler, Charles, 228
Kierkegaard, Soren, 27
Kingdom of God, 235, 237, 240
Kojève, Alexandre, 85, 306–10, 317, 320
Koran, 34–38, 99

Laslett, Peter, 14
law, 144–45, 151, 182–83, 200, 226, 254, 293, 315; biblical, 315, 318; civil, 37–38, 43, 67, 99; divine, 29, 33, 35, 37–38, 87, 201–2, 207, 210, 293, 301, 313–14, 318, 320; human, 38–39, 41, 54, 79–80, 84–85, 89–91, 119; moral, 38, 40, 99, 219, 223, 225; religions of, 3, 20, 33, 35–36, 38
lawgiver, 31, 38, 81–82, 84

Leo XIII, 44, 129, 186, 241–42
Lessing, Gotthold Ephraim, 275, 288
liberal democracy, 19, 46, 86, 91, 93, 132, 177–78, 262–63, 307
liberalism, 145, 152, 300, 304–5
Locke, John: and Christianity, 81, 120, 283; and natural rights, 2, 109, 120, 123, 127, 131, 182
love, 188, 235; as charity, 6, 38, 40, 105, 114, 240, 310, 318; as *eros*, 286, 296; of God, 39, 108, 114–15, 292, 297
Luther, Martin, 104, 106
Lutz, Christopher, 182

Machiavelli, Nicolo, 5, 48, 89, 140, 144, 149–50, 155–56, 179, 187, 284, 288; and Christianity, 101, 146, 188, 202, 283; and modernity, 8, 64, 96, 100, 109, 120, 123, 130, 139, 147, 154–55, 157, 161, 184, 307
MacIntyre, Alasdair, 49, 182
Madison, James, 91–92
magisterium, 11, 239, 243–44, 246, 248
Maimonides, Moses, 28, 30, 34, 167, 282
Manent, Pierre, 15, 47, 93, 302, 307
Mansfield, Harvey C., 116–17
Maritain, Jacques, 7, 40–43, 51, 86, 92, 128, 139, 147–48, 160, 168, 171, 176, 182, 185–89, 322
Marsilius of Padua, 100, 141, 282
Marx, Karl, 65, 71, 108, 144, 151, 157, 237, 263; and historicism, 2, 4, 97, 184
marxism, 50–52, 64–65, 85, 151, 182
Masters, Roger, 64
McCoy, Charles N. R., 7, 9, 47–56, 58–75, 138–39, 141, 146–53, 155–56, 159, 165–68
McInerny, Ralph, 66, 88
McKeon, Richard, 50
Meier, Heinrich, 27, 285–86
Mendelssohn, Moses, 118
Merriam, Charles, 49
metaphysics, 12, 31, 42, 47, 50, 68, 70, 107, 111, 158–59, 187, 278, 281, 283–84, 293
miracles, 22–24, 194, 211, 254, 304; impossibility of, 24, 194
modern democracy, 8, 20, 39, 158, 161, 163, 254
modernity, 95, 97–98, 130, 141, 150, 165, 178, 200, 242; and Catholicism, 110, 114,

194; and Christianity, 203, 205, 307–8, 315, 317, 319; crisis of, 10, 95, 167–68, 185, 187–88, 193–95, 200, 204; founding of, 39, 95, 99, 102, 109, 184, 321; and philosophy, 9, 138–39, 141, 159; secular, 25, 107; three waves of, 64–65, 97, 184, 314–15
modern liberalism, 123–24, 132, 143, 164, 179
modern natural rights, 44, 117, 120–21, 125, 127, 129, 176
modern science, 9, 24, 88, 105–6, 137–39, 144, 146–48, 150, 153–57, 159–61, 163, 165–66, 172, 280
modern tyrannies, 255–56, 266
modern utopianism, 266
Mohammad, 37
Moltmann, Jurgen, 238
monotheism, 26, 35–37, 39; corruptions of, 37
morality, 107, 128, 131, 151, 182, 199–201, 211, 242, 254, 275, 314, 318; and the Bible, 201, 203, 211, 215, 298; and reason, 81, 160, 193, 201, 212
moral theology, 233, 241–42, 247, 249
moral virtue, 57, 139, 156, 159, 163, 165–66
More, Thomas, 282
Mosaic law, 36, 38
Moses, 7, 28, 32, 84, 200
Murray, John Courtney, 128, 171
Muslims, 1, 33, 99, 293
mutakallimûn, 83

natural law, 10, 56–59, 64, 67, 74, 77, 79–80, 92–93, 223–27, 230–31, 241–42, 286–87, 313–14, 316, 321; fundamental propositions of, 219, 223, 225; new, 2, 7, 44, 87–91, 128
natural reason, 50, 219, 226–27, 229–30, 232
natural rights, 44, 119–24, 127, 173–75, 219; and Catholic social thought, 20; and natural law, 8, 43, 117, 127–29, 131
natural science, 88, 96, 147, 149–50, 156, 159, 161, 284; modern, 40, 96, 115, 148, 161, 278; new, 161–62
natural virtue, 316, 320, 322
nature, 7, 23–26, 32, 36, 60, 65, 67, 105, 111, 153; as authority, 69–72, 74, 78, 80, 150, 152–53, 175, 226–27, 278; fallen, 246;

grace perfects, 4, 30, 228, 287, 313, 316; knowledge of, 23, 292; laws of, 3, 23–24, 121, 148, 151–52, 154; mastery of, 13, 96, 98, 107, 151, 156, 165, 178, 181, 183–84, 187, 203, 283, 321; philosophy of, 50; and reason, 1, 69, 81, 231
Neo-Thomism, 7, 20, 40–42, 50, 92
Nicene Creed, 38, 147, 221
Nicgorski, Walter, ix, 118, 161
Nietzsche, Friedrich, 97–98, 180, 188, 263, 280, 283–84, 298, 313, 321
nihilism, 98, 177
noble lies, 10, 225
nuclear weapons, 59, 88–89

obedience, 22, 144, 146, 200, 206, 301, 316
obedient love, 196–97, 201, 292, 320
obligations, 114, 119, 121, 133, 141, 221, 229, 296; moral, 87, 122; political, 165
O'Connor, Flannery, 317
Octogesima Adveniens, 242, 244
orthodoxy, 3, 35–36, 317
orthopraxy, 3, 34, 36

Pascal, Blaise, 12–13, 26, 213, 290–98, 316
Passerin, Alexandre, 138, 141
Paul, 5, 247, 300–301, 303–5
Paul IV, 5, 140
Paul VI, 233, 241–42, 244, 247–48
philosophical life, 62, 153, 214, 259, 270, 272–73, 275, 279, 282, 289, 291–92, 294–95, 311
philosophizing, 234, 294, 321
philosophy, 4, 22, 34, 100, 150, 154, 177, 264, 270, 286, 309, 312; and theology, 20, 22, 27, 34, 45, 75, 98, 111, 187, 197, 199, 207, 209, 272–73, 285; as a way of life, 7, 32, 83, 100, 196, 198, 201, 214, 256, 269–70, 279, 285, 291, 294, 309; zetetic, 94, 279
physics, 149, 278; modern, 64, 152, 279
Pieper, Josef, 133, 189
Plato, 66–69, 71–72, 74–75, 79, 81, 96, 153–54, 184, 186, 219, 225, 234, 279, 282, 295; Aristotle, 4, 67–72, 74, 76, 79, 119, 167, 209, 219, 279, 282, 288, 295; Plato's cave, 249; *Laws*, 21, 124; philosopher-king, 31, 81; *Republic*, 40, 66, 267, 300; *Symposium*, 78; *Theaetetus*, 162

Pocock, J. G. A., 5, 14
political wisdom, 77, 133, 267, 273
polytheism, 26, 35–36
practical reason, 87, 102, 107, 149, 220, 264, 310
pride, 121, 287, 298, 309, 312, 320, 322; human, 309; pagan, 322; reason's, 318
progress, 2, 21, 25, 32, 161, 182, 184–85, 192–93, 204, 214, 260, 305, 319, 322; belief in, 192–95, 197, 203–4; idea of, 193, 204; modern idea of, 10, 99, 192–93
prophecy, 5, 211
prophets, 30–31, 35, 37–38, 294; unarmed, 101

Ratzinger, Joseph, 102
Rawls, John, 90
reason and revelation, 3, 54, 211, 215, 287, 291–93, 297, 315
reason informed by faith, 219, 227–30
redemption, 104, 238, 318
Reformation, 2, 99, 106, 185, 187
Regensburg Address, 2, 5
relativism, 20, 40–41, 90, 146, 174, 219, 227, 231, 285; dictatorship of, 174; historical, 146
Renaissance, 64, 104
Rerum Novarum, 8, 11, 117, 129–32
revelation, 191, 210; belief in, 29, 193–94, 197–98, 205, 207, 213; and philosophy, 22, 32, 39, 45, 208, 291; possibility of, 3–4, 23, 26, 34–35, 118, 296; and reason, 3, 32, 39, 45, 50, 54, 172, 197, 199, 206, 208–9, 211, 215, 232, 287, 291–93, 297, 315
Roman law, 39, 55, 226
Rome, 5, 93, 102, 115, 132, 302
Rommen, Heinrich A., 20, 40, 43, 146, 171
Rosenzweig, Franz, 313–14
Rousseau, Jean-Jacques, 4, 48, 65, 73, 97, 105, 107, 127–28, 143, 163, 165, 184, 284
Roy, Cardinal Maurice, 242

salvation, 6, 13, 162, 189, 237, 247, 272, 316, 322
Schall, James V., 5, 20, 43–44, 71, 167–68, 184, 189
Scholem, Gershom, 28

sensus fidei, 236–37, 242, 246, 248
Shari'a law, 34, 37
Siedentop, Larry, 13, 299–300, 302–6, 314, 319–20
Simon, Yves R., 9, 20, 40, 42, 86, 91, 138–39, 142, 156
Skinner, Quentin, 14
Socrates, 7, 11, 28, 31–32, 70, 72–73, 160, 180–81, 186, 288, 295
Socratic ignorance, 31, 42, 45
Socratic philosopher, 31, 98, 111, 115
Socratic philosophy, 28, 32, 45, 180
Spinoza, Baruch, 24, 109, 118, 123, 127, 161, 194, 262, 312–14
statesmanship, 5, 41, 46, 59, 64, 68, 70, 79, 83, 92, 153
Stoics, 78, 81
Strauss, Leo and Athens and Jerusalem, 4–5, 10, 32, 84, 184–85, 189, 254, 257, 285–86, 292, 307, 312–13, 315–16, 318–19, 322; and the crisis of philosophy, 9, 168, 176, 179, 186; and esotericism, 25, 31, 165, 201, 277, 281; and historicism, 2, 4, 164, 288; and natural law, 10, 39–40, 42–43, 46, 58–59, 75, 77–78, 81–84, 86, 88–89, 93, 175–76, 223, 225, 313–14; and natural right, 2, 40, 67–68, 77–80, 82–84, 87, 89–90, 92–93, 217–20, 223, 226, 232, 279, 287–89, 316–17; and philosophy as a way of life, 7, 32, 83, 100, 196, 198, 201, 214, 256, 269–70, 279, 285, 291, 294, 309; and recovery of classical natural right, 6, 8, 40, 77, 279, 317; and recovery of classical political philosophy, 2, 77, 118, 164, 169, 171, 181, 184, 313; and revelation, 3, 32, 39, 45, 197–99, 206, 208–11, 215, 232, 287, 291–93, 297, 315; and zetetic philosophy, 31, 269, 311
Straussians, 14, 19, 140, 145, 218, 228, 260, 311
Suarez, Francisco, 9, 42–43, 54, 126
Summa Theologiae, 33, 38, 80, 228–29
summum bonum, 107, 173, 188

Tanguay, Daniel, 27, 285
Taylor, Charles, 47
teleology, 71, 87–88, 97, 122, 130, 278
Ten Commandments, 34, 36, 38, 199, 219–20, 222–23, 225, 320

Tertullian, 4
Thornton, John F., 95
Thucydides, 171, 257, 270, 272, 274
Tierney, Brian, 129
Torah, 29, 34, 36, 38
totalitarianism, 62, 72, 145
Trinity, 6, 29, 38–39
tyranny, 77, 79–81, 84–85, 92, 175, 177, 213, 225, 257, 264, 279, 306–8, 317, 320

Vatican Council II, 235–36, 240–42, 244–47
Vico, Giambattista, 121

Voegelin, Eric, 31, 40–42, 145, 265, 307, 321
voluntarism, 8, 105–6, 112

Weimar Germany, 118, 123
Western civilization, 4, 22, 27, 110, 191, 194–96, 200, 202–3, 257, 272, 305
World War II, 59, 217

Xenophon, 85, 213, 225

Zionism, 27, 118, 271

Leo Strauss and His Catholic Readers was designed in Scala and
Scala Sans and composed by Kachergis Book Design of Pittsboro,
North Carolina.

www.ingramcontent.com/pod-product-compliance
Lightning Source LLC
Chambersburg PA
CBHW020912020526
44107CB00075B/1666